COMPREHENSION
ACROSS THE CURRICULUM

D1496093

Solving Problems in the Teaching of Literacy

Cathy Collins Block, *Series Editor*

RECENT VOLUMES

Comprehension Across the Curriculum
Perspectives and Practices K–12

Edited by

KATHY GANSKE
DOUGLAS FISHER

THE GUILFORD PRESS
New York   London

© 2010 The Guilford Press
A Division of Guilford Publications, Inc.
72 Spring Street, New York, NY 10012
www.guilford.com

Printed in the United States of America

This book is printed on acid-free paper.

Last digit is print number: 9 8 7 6 5 4 3 2 1

Library of Congress Cataloging-in-Publication data is available
from the Publisher.
ISBN 978-1-60623-511-9 (paperback)
ISBN 978-1-60623-512-6 (hardcover)

About the Editors

Kathy Ganske, PhD, is Associate Professor of Literacy in the Graduate Teacher Education Program at Oberlin College. She is the author of numerous articles and books on literacy, including *Supporting Struggling Readers and Writers: Strategies for Classroom Intervention 3–6* (with Dorothy Strickland and Joanne Monroe); *Word Journeys: Assessment-Guided Phonics, Spelling, and Vocabulary Instruction; Word Sorts and More: Sound, Pattern, and Meaning Explorations K–3;* and *Mindful of Words: Spelling and Vocabulary Explorations 4–8.* Prior to her move to Ohio, she was a professor at Rowan University in Glassboro, New Jersey. Dr. Ganske is a former classroom teacher of primary through upper-elementary grades and has taught in many regions of the country.

Douglas Fisher, PhD, is Professor of Language and Literacy Education in the College of Education at San Diego State University and a classroom teacher at Health Sciences High and Middle College in San Diego. He is a recipient of the Celebrate Literacy Award from the International Reading Association, the Paul and Kate Farmer *English Journal* Writing Award from the National Council of Teachers of English, as well as a Christa McAuliffe Excellence in Teacher Education Award from the American Association of State Colleges and Universities. Dr. Fisher has published numerous articles on reading and literacy, differentiated instruction, and curriculum design, and many books, including *Creating Literacy-Rich Schools for Adolescents* (with Gay Ivey); *Checking for Understanding: Formative Assessments for Your Classroom* (with Nancy Frey); *Better Learning through Structured Teaching* (with Nancy Frey); and *Content-Area Conversations: How to Plan Discussion-Based Lessons for Diverse Learners* (with Carol Rothenberg).

Contributors

Heather Anderson, MA, teaches English at Health Sciences High and Middle College in San Diego. She has taught K–12 students at both public and charter schools and has worked as a math specialist and staff developer in the areas of literacy, math, and English learners at the elementary level.

Diane August, PhD, is a consultant and a Senior Research Scientist at the Center for Applied Linguistics in Washington, DC. She is the Principal Investigator or Co-investigator for a number of large, federally funded studies that investigate the development of literacy in language-minority students and has written numerous journal articles and books.

Diane Barone, EdD, is Foundation Professor of Literacy at the University of Nevada, Reno. Her research has always focused on young children's literacy development and instruction in high-poverty schools. She has published in such journals as *Reading Research Quarterly, Journal of Literacy Research, Elementary School Journal*, and *The Reading Teacher.* Among her books are *Resilient Children, Research-Based Practices in Early Literacy, Writing without Boundaries*, and *Your Core Reading Program and Children's Literature (K–3 and 4–6).*

Xiufang Chen, PhD, is Assistant Professor of Reading at Rowan University in Glassboro, New Jersey. Before joining the Rowan faculty, she worked as a part-time instructor and field supervisor at Texas Tech University, and was a faculty member at Beijing Normal University. Dr. Chen has presented at the National Reading Conference, the International Reading Association, and the National Council of Teachers of English, and has authored several articles on English language learners and literacy, and Internet reading.

Nell K. Duke, EdD, is Professor of Teacher Education and Educational Psychology and Co-director of the Literacy Achievement Research Center at Michigan State University in East Lansing. Dr. Duke's work focuses on early literacy development, particularly among children living in poverty. She has won a number of awards for her research, including the Early Career Award from the American Educational Research Association. Among her books is *Reading and Writing Informational Text in the Primary Grades: Research-Based Practices.*

Douglas Fisher, PhD (see "About the Editors").

Nancy Frey, PhD, is Professor of Literacy in the School of Teacher Education at San Diego State University. She is the recipient of the 2008 Early Career Achievement Award from the National Reading Conference. Dr. Frey has published in *The Reading Teacher, Journal of Adolescent and Adult Literacy, English Journal, Voices in the Middle, Middle School Journal, Remedial and Special Education,* and *Educational Leadership.* She also learns alongside students and teachers at Health Sciences High and Middle College in San Diego.

Jesse Gainer, PhD, is Assistant Professor of Education in the Department of Curriculum and Instruction at Texas State University in San Marco. He teaches undergraduate and graduate classes in both university-based and field-based settings. Dr. Gainer has been a bilingual elementary school teacher and has done educational research in elementary, middle, and high school settings. His major areas of research and instruction include critical literacy and the intersections of literacy with linguistic diversity, culture, and media.

Kathy Ganske, PhD (see "About the Editors").

Maria Grant, EdD, is Associate Professor in the Department of Secondary Education at California State University in Fullerton and a classroom teacher at Health Sciences High and Middle College in San Diego. She works with both preservice and veteran teachers in the credential and graduate programs. Her work includes research and publications in the area of literacy integration into content areas, with a central focus on science education. Additionally, Dr. Grant is involved in professional development centered on formative assessment.

Jennifer Letcher Gray, MA, is a research assistant at the Center for Applied Linguistics in Washington, DC. She is pursuing her doctorate in Reading Education at the University of Maryland, College Park, where she teaches undergraduate and graduate courses in reading methods and children's literature. Ms. Gray has worked as a classroom teacher, a reading specialist, an ESL instructor, an adult literacy program coordinator, and a literacy specialist with the Office of Reading of the Massachusetts Department of Education.

Ellin Keene, MA, consults with schools and districts throughout the country and abroad on issues related to literacy teaching and learning and leadership. She is the coauthor of *Mosaic of Thought: Teaching Reading Comprehension in a Reader's Workshop* and the author of *To Understand.*

Donna L. Knoell, PhD, is an educational consultant and author. She has spoken at and consulted with schools worldwide in reading and language arts, social studies, science, and mathematics. She has special expertise in the effective use of trade books for instruction but also consults on various other literacy-related topics, including content-area reading, reading comprehension, and vocabulary development. Dr. Knoell is a former classroom teacher, program developer, and instructional specialist, and has taught at the university level.

Diane Lapp, EdD, is Distinguished Professor of Education at San Diego State University, where she directs and teaches school-based preservice and graduate programs in literacy education. She has taught in elementary and middle school, and is currently teaching 11th and 12th grade English at an urban high school. Her major areas of research and instruction focus on issues related to struggling learners and their families who live and learn in low socioeconomic status urban communities.

Valarie G. Lee, EdD, is Assistant Professor in the Department of Reading at Rowan University, in Glassboro, New Jersey. After teaching high school English for 10 years in New Mexico and Colorado, she finished her doctorate degree in reading and research methods and completed her dissertation on adolescent boys and reading attitudes. Her research interests include adolescent and content-area literacy, especially concerning motivating readers.

Elizabeth Birr Moje, PhD, is Arthur F. Thurnau Professor of Literacy, Language, and Culture in Educational Studies at the University of Michigan, Ann Arbor, and Faculty Associate in Latino/a Studies at the Institute for Social Research. Dr. Moje's research focuses on academic and youth literacy skills, practices, cultures, and texts.

Donna Ogle, EdD, is Professor of Reading and Language at National-Louis University in Skokie, Illinois. Her current funded research is focused on supporting English language learners in content literacy, Project ALL (Advancing Literacy for Learning). She is Senior Advisor to the Chicago Striving Readers Project, now in 16 schools and expanding to 32 next year. Dr. Ogle's current publications include: *Building Literacy in Social Studies*, *All Children Read*, and *Coming Together as Readers*.

P. David Pearson, PhD, is Dean of the Graduate School of Education at the University of California, Berkeley. He has written and coedited several books about research and practice, most notably the *Handbook of Reading Research*, now in its fourth volume. Dr. Pearson has received numerous honors, including the William S. Gray Citation of Merit from the International Reading Association, the Oscar Causey Award from the National Reading Conference, and the Alan Purves Award from the National Council of Teachers of English.

Kathryn L. Roberts, MS, is a doctoral candidate in the Teacher Education Program at Michigan State University in East Lansing and is pursuing a specialization in language and literacy. She also teaches in the Teacher Education Department at Michigan State University and has worked as a teacher in various public schools.

Contents

PART III. HISTORICAL PERSPECTIVES

COMPREHENSION
ACROSS THE CURRICULUM

Introduction

Kathy Ganske
Douglas Fisher

As many readers know, the International Reading Association's annual convention is a wonderful place to garner fresh ideas, meet new people, and imagine possibilities. The seed for this book germinated from an International Reading Association institute on reading comprehension in which we, along with several of the contributors, participated. As with this text, the institute encompassed a broad view of reading comprehension instruction, because comprehension doesn't just happen during the Language Arts block. Students from kindergarten through grade 12 need to understand text and visual images throughout the school day, whether the focus is on math, social studies, science, or language arts, and whether the students are native English speakers or English language learners. In order to help learners develop their ability to think deeply and critically as they read and view for pleasure or to gain information, in school or out, teachers need to understand what we currently know about comprehension and how to teach our students to comprehend.

Because *Comprehension Across the Curriculum: Perspectives and Practices K–12* addresses comprehension from many points of view, the book is one that could easily be used for a study group or book club to stimulate school- or districtwide conversation about how to improve comprehension instruction across the grades for all students. Individuals seeking to increase the breadth and depth of their knowledge of comprehension will also find it valuable. We hope that ideas from the text will take root and enable you to advance your students' understanding of text and visual images and their engagement with both.

This book is structured in three parts: Theoretical Perspectives (Chapters 1–3), Classroom and School Applications (Chapters 4–12), and Historical Perspectives (Chapter 13). Chapter contributors consider comprehension from varied perspectives, each with a different lens, as you'll see in the brief descriptions that follow. Because lenses are for seeing, authors have made a strong effort to *show* readers information and ideas, not just talk about them. As a result, examples abound across the chapters, providing seasoned as well as novice or preservice teacher readers with a clear direction for implementing the ideas presented.

- *Chapter 1. To Understand: The Small Changes That Make a Big Difference.* Ellin Keene sets the stage for later chapters by challenging readers to rethink what it means "to understand." She urges teachers, in the excitement of teaching a strategy, not to neglect what she believes may well be the most important component of strategy instruction: making explicit to students just how the strategy helps them to better comprehend what they read.

- *Chapter 2. Comprehension in the Elementary Grades: The Research Base.* Kathryn L. Roberts and Nell K. Duke bring readers up to date on what research has to say about reading comprehension in the primary grades (i.e., kindergarten through grade 3). The authors note that this grade range has been the hardest for researchers to make a case on behalf of comprehension instruction and one in which comprehension instruction has been the most limited. They highlight classroom-ready instructional strategies and describe primary classrooms in which attention to comprehension thrives.

- *Chapter 3. Comprehending in the Subject Areas: The Challenges of Comprehension, Grades 7–12, and What to Do about Them.* Elizabeth Birr Moje explores the demands of comprehending text at the secondary level, where students are confronted with longer and more complex texts involving increasingly abstract and complex concepts and high expectations for background knowledge. Not surprisingly, comprehension instruction at this level also demands a lot of teachers. The author describes teaching implications related to text selection and teaching practices that support students' work with those texts.

- *Chapter 4. Comprehension in the Primary Grades.* Diane Barone examines the crucial role of books in young children's comprehension and the profound impact that teachers can have on young children's literacy through the ways in which they engage them with literature. She explores means for developing content and vocabulary background knowledge and strategies to encourage meaningful understanding as well as ways to heighten students' understanding of text and illustrations through listening and talking, reading and writing, and viewing.

- *Chapter 5. Active Thinking and Engagement: Comprehension in the Intermediate Grades*. Kathy Ganske emphasizes the importance of motivation and active learning in teaching students in grades 3–5 to comprehend deeply and thoughtfully. Writing and reading, talking and questioning, imagining and drawing, and performing are avenues that can help students monitor for meaning and deepen their understanding of texts, whether fiction or nonfiction. The author presents numerous before, during, and after reading strategies.

- *Chapter 6. Promoting Comprehension in Middle School and High School: Tapping into Out-of-School Literacies of Our Adolescents*. Xiufang Chen and Valarie G. Lee share ideas for revitalizing strategy instruction in middle school and high school, using technology to bridge students' in-school and out-of-school literacies. They focus on moviemaking as means for setting a motivating purpose, rewriting texts on social network websites, wikis as a note-taking tool, critical examination of websites using an Internet Reading Guide, and the integration of contemporary texts in the language arts classroom.

- *Chapter 7. Thinking and Comprehending in the Mathematics Classroom*. Douglas Fisher, Nancy Frey, and Heather Anderson focus on the role of reading and writing in mathematics. Following a discussion of experiences they have had in math classrooms, the authors focus on three areas known to be effective for engaging students in thinking about mathematics: modeling, vocabulary development, and productive group work.

- *Chapter 8. Comprehension in Social Studies*. Donna Ogle makes a case for why teachers should use social studies content and materials as the basis for comprehension instruction. The author argues that combining social studies with literature creates a purpose, provides sufficient context for comprehension, and increases motivation. She describes ways in which teachers can further students' comprehension through social studies, including working with various types of texts (primary sources among them), understanding different text structures, and learning to question authorship.

- *Chapter 9. Comprehension Connections to Science*. Maria Grant highlights the importance of wide reading to motivate learners and make content more accessible, in an area such as science where students may have limited background knowledge. She also describes the use of shared reading experiences to deepen older students' background knowledge and explains instructional routines that develop students' competence in strategy use through the teacher's gradual release of responsibility.

- *Chapter 10. Comprehension Instruction: Using Remix as a Tool for Meaning Making.* Diane Lapp and Jesse Gainer take readers into the world of multiliteracies. They describe the changing demands of literacies and explain comprehension as "remix," a creative process of creating something new out of used parts. The authors clearly detail remix lessons for use in upper-grade classrooms; the four lessons include sampling, fan fiction, mash-ups, and bubbling—activities that draw on popular culture and a variety of media.

- *Chapter 11. Developing Comprehension in English Language Learners: Research and Promising Practices.* Diane August and Jennifer Letcher Gray present a brief overview of the research base related to comprehension instruction for English language learners. The remainder of the chapter focuses on methods that have been successful with English language learners, both for building English proficiency and for developing comprehension of text.

- *Chapter 12. Selecting and Using Nonfiction in Grades K–12: Social Studies and Science.* Donna L. Knoell advocates for the use of nonfiction texts, including various types of trade books and periodical literature, in the teaching of social studies and science. She also describes criteria and sources for selecting books, periodicals, and electronic resources. An appendix includes a selected but extensive listing of nonfiction books and periodicals for children and youth, arranged by subject area and grade range of interest.

- *Chapter 13. The Roots of Reading Comprehension Instruction.* P. David Pearson takes us on a historical journey documenting the trends in practice in reading comprehension instruction as well as the underlying theories that are implied by the practices dominant in each era. He ends with a set of predictions about the next steps we could and should take as a field to ensure that students are as facile in constructing models of meaning for the texts we ask them to read as they are in grappling with the orthographic, phonological, and graphophonemic aspects of reading.

Part I

THEORETICAL PERSPECTIVES

1

To Understand

The Small Changes
That Make a Big Difference

Ellin Keene

I find myself standing, late in the day in a school parking lot some-where outside Chicago, trying to remember which car is mine. When one travels nearly every week and drives every conceivable make and model of rental car, the dilemma isn't quite as crazy as it sounds (don't they all look alike to you?). The key fob has no emergency siren button; too bad because I've gotten very good at pushing the alarm button, locating the car (really, don't they all look alike to you?) and deactivating it before the screeching car disturbs too many of the locals. Now I'm relegated to wandering through the parking lot, peering into cars searching for some of my stuff. I realize that this kind of behavior could raise suspicions with law enforcement, but the alternative is to wait until all the teach-ers have come out of the building, claimed their cars and driven away, leaving only my white sedan. Not only is this likely to lead to a long wait (teachers work way too late), but as they emerge from the building, I'll have to make up something to explain why I'm lurking around the park-ing lot peering into cars I don't own.

As I begin my systematic search up and down the rows of parked cars, I think back on the day. Days like this make all the lost rental cars, airport security lines, lousy hotel beds, and missed flights worth it. I spent the day, computer on my lap, watching kids and teachers in an elementary school. I recorded their interactions—teacher to child, child to child—and tonight, if I ever locate the car, I'll pour through the notes. They'll help me relive the scenes I observed throughout the day; I'll "listen" again to the hundreds of interactions and marvel at how teachers manage to respond to all of the queries and demands from children, let alone the other adults in the building.

For the better part of 8 years, I've set aside time each month to observe in schools around the country. I've had to make it a priority; it would be all too easy to fall into the rhythm of running around the country conducting workshops, demonstration lessons, and planning with teachers only to rush back to the airport, go on to the next city and do it all again the next day. These days of watching and listening have allowed me the chance to uncover and reflect upon some of the ideas that interest me the most. When I finally locate my car (a white Ford Taurus), I'm wishing that all educators had the opportunity to stand back and watch, but mostly *listen* to, the interactions in their own and colleagues' classrooms.

I'm interested in comprehension, in the nature of understanding; I'm fascinated by what we humans do when we understand deeply and can retain and reuse what we've understood. I've found that the way teachers and students talk about what they understand is extremely revealing with respect to what children can remember and reapply. My observations have led to more questions than answers—I can't be surprised by that at this point in my career—but the questions have been genuinely helpful when I do find myself teaching a demonstration lesson or coaching a teacher as he or she works with children. Reflecting on my notes has caused me to rethink how I talk with children—what I say, how much I say, the pace and volume I use, and what I listen for in their responses. Perhaps more important, these observations have led to the realization that our expectations of how much and how deeply children can comprehend are enhanced (or limited) by the way we define and describe what it means to comprehend.

In this chapter, I:

- Describe two common current practices in comprehension teaching and suggest ways in which I, and other teachers with whom I work, have modified those practices to raise expectations for students when they are working to understand.
- Discuss some of the most common ways in which we use language to define and describe comprehension to students and suggest ways in which we might elevate that language in order to help students comprehend at higher levels far more consistently.

The proposals I make in this chapter need to be examined by researchers who share my interest before we can confidently describe implications for the classroom. However, I am encouraged and optimistic about how much difference I have seen in students' comprehension with relatively small alterations in practice.

AN OUTSIDER LOOKS IN

The day I lost my car in a suburban Chicago school parking lot was warmer than it should have been—it was only mid-March, but the windows were thrown open in a fifth-grade classroom where I spent the morning. I followed Jeff, the teacher, as he conferred with individual students, typing as quickly as I could, trying to record as much of his interactions as possible. The students were reading nonfiction books of their own choosing, and I was impressed with how well they'd chosen, given their interests and present performance as readers. Clearly, a great deal of time had been invested in teaching them to make wise choices and to navigate the hurdles in nonfiction text. They were reading intently, very independently for a long period of time, and many turned to each other, rather than to Jeff, to solve problems. The classroom was humming—there was a strong sense of productivity and engagement, and Jeff had somehow carved out a long period of time for the students to read independently, during which he was able to confer with individual students. I propped my laptop on my knees and started to record his conferences. The first was with Derrick.

"Hey, Derrick, what's up? What is this piece mostly about?" Jeff asked Derrick, who was immersed in a text about the space shuttle.

"Mostly about how they build them and how they get launched into space," Derrick replied.

"Do you like it; are you enjoying reading this article?" Jeff queried.

"Yep," was all the response he got.

Derrick's monosyllabic response seemed to push Jeff into asking more specific questions about the text. "When did they first start launching space shuttles?" he asks.

"1981."

"Wow—so long ago. How many launches have there been?"

"I don't know, but two crashes."

"What happened in the crashes?" Jeff asked.

"I haven't read that part yet," Derrick replied, thumbing ahead in the book.

"Well, let me know when you get there, okay?"

"Okay."

"Anything I can help you with," Jeff asked, standing up.

"Nope," was the predictable reply.

Jeff moved on to another student and another conference and another litany of questions that sounded very much like the conference with Derrick.

As I reviewed my notes that evening, I was left wondering: What did Derrick (and many of the others) gain from the interaction, and what did Jeff teach the children about improving their comprehension? When we spoke during lunch, Jeff had acknowledged real frustration with the conferences that day.

"I just don't feel like I'm getting anywhere with them. I know it's good to have this time to confer, and I think I kind of keep them going, but it doesn't feel very effective. I'm just asking a bunch of questions, and they respond either in one or two words *or* they tell me absolutely everything they can remember about what they're reading. Either way, I'm just not sure where to go with them." I asked him what he hoped to gain through the conferences, why he was making the time to confer in the first place. He paused a moment and said, "I guess in nonfiction, I want them to remember more of what they've read and use what they're learning in new ways. I know for many of these kids, it's tougher to comprehend nonfiction, and I want to help, but I'm not sure how to do it. You can't just *tell* them to 'remember more and use it later!'"

Jeff had a very clear sense of what he wanted the kids to be able to do when reading nonfiction. The conference setting provided an all-too-rare and potent opportunity to assess an individual's needs in an authentic reading context and to provide immediate instruction pertinent to that student's needs. What form of instruction could be timelier and potentially effective than a one-on-one conference in which the teacher's full and immediate attention is directed to the needs of just one child? Yet Jeff's impact on Derrick would have to be considered minimal. Perhaps he satisfied himself that Derrick was, in fact, reading nonfiction, but he didn't accomplish what he told me he'd hoped to: He didn't really teach Derrick anything new, and he didn't discover whether Derrick comprehended the text more effectively because of the conference. Jeff said that he wanted Derrick to retain and reapply what he learned from the article on the space shuttle, but how could he increase the likelihood that Derrick will, in fact, retain and reapply that new knowledge?

As I looked back over my notes, I wondered, what might have made this a more effective conference? Among other factors, Jeff needed a clearer sense of what it really means to comprehend—what it looks and sounds like when someone comprehends, what readers can expect in their mind and in their life when they comprehend—if he wanted to push Derrick forward. He needed a much better sense of what to say to Derrick to describe how good readers ensure that they comprehend effectively and lastingly. He needed to be able to say to Derrick, "This is what you should experience when you comprehend."

Unfortunately, most of us operate with an antiquated view of what it means to comprehend—a view that we developed when we were students and one that has changed little since. When we were in school, teachers "taught" comprehension mainly through posing questions about text content and asking us to retell or summarize the text in some way. In many U.S. classrooms, the same approach is common today. Whether in large- or small-group settings or in conferences, we ask students an almost endless stream of comprehension questions ("What did character X do in Chapter 3?"); we "chat" about a book ("Did you like it … do you like this author … what else have you read of hers?") and when students are done reading, we ask them to retell what they read in one form or another ("Write in your literature log … write a book report … make a diorama or some other project"). What bothered Jeff that day in March is what has bothered many teachers: the feeling that we aren't *teaching* children to comprehend more effectively. In fact, at the very moment when we know that our teaching could be most potent, we find ourselves not teaching; instead, we *assess* their comprehension through questions, not about them as readers, but about the text. We find ourselves *assessing* short-term memory for details in the text and/or students' ability to summarize effectively. Jeff's goal was to teach Derrick something as a reader that would matter to him later, but what he accomplished was, at best, a rough assessment of whether Derrick was reading and able to recall details. *Assessing* students' comprehension isn't the same thing as teaching students to comprehend *better*.

MOVING FROM TESTING TO TEACHING

Observing in classrooms throughout the grade spectrum and in a wide range of schools has convinced me that there are two predominant forms of comprehension instruction: the ask-them-to-answer-questions/ ask-them-to-retell (which is really assessment) approach and the teach-them-comprehension-strategies approach. The former frequently leads to the kind of interaction documented above; the latter, studied now for over two decades, has a far better track record, but is still problematic because we haven't yet fully defined and described what we hope the *outcome* of comprehension strategy use is likely to be.

I've noticed that the way we talk about comprehension to students has everything to do with the outcomes we can expect from them. If we believe, even subconsciously, that comprehension means getting kids to answer questions and summarize, then that is exactly what we can expect them to do. Any insight a child has that goes beyond answering questions and retelling is merely a "happy accident," not a result of teaching intention. Similarly, if we spend time teaching children to generate questions, synthesize, determine importance, use relevant background knowledge, and infer (some of the comprehension strategies many of us teach) and don't go to the next step to discuss what the *outcome* of their strategy use is likely to be, we may well be teaching strategies for the sake of teaching strategies.

In our debriefing, we realized that Jeff had a leftover concept of what it means to comprehend that stemmed back to his own K–12 learning experiences. This isn't his fault—when we were preservice teachers or even in graduate school, most of us did not have the opportunity to engage in long conversations about the nature of understanding and how we could help children understand more deeply, more consistently. When it came to conferring or working with students in small groups, Jeff realized that his effectiveness was limited by his old ideas about what it means to understand. His interactions with students revealed what he valued: that they could answer questions and retell. He was thrilled when students found themselves deeply engaged in their reading or spoke about ideas enthusiastically, but he wasn't doing anything to help them do those things more consistently.

If Jeff wants to move from testing comprehension to teaching children to comprehend more deeply and lastingly, he may well need to rethink what it means to understand. If he wants to dramatically improve the quality and consistency of children's thinking, if he wants to move students from the occasional "happy accidents" in which they trip upon a probing insight or apply their learning to a new challenge inadvertently, he's going to have to be explicit with children about what he wants them to do in the name of comprehension. If he values deeper engagement—conversations with kids that go beyond "yep" and "nope" and "okay"—he may well want to be more purposeful in his instruction, thinking aloud and modeling to show kids what it looks and sounds like when someone understands something deeply.

A STUDY IN CONTRASTS: RETHINKING WHAT WE WANT KIDS TO DO WHEN THEY COMPREHEND

After dozens of observations similar to the one in Jeff's classroom— where the teacher's way of thinking about comprehension may actually *limit* children's comprehension—I began to think about a new way to conceive of comprehension instruction. Changes in instructional practice would be based on a new way of thinking about what it really means to comprehend. I realized that there are subtle but important changes we might make in our everyday interactions with students. I experimented with practices we might decrease or eliminate altogether in favor of new ways of teaching kids what we experience when we comprehend well and what they can expect to experience. Table 1.1 shows some proposed changes in the way we approach common instructional (and assessment) practices in comprehension.

In my experience, when teachers begin to reshape their interactions with students using these "what would happen ifs," the change in children's responses can be dramatic. When children begin to anticipate that they're going to be asked to describe their thinking about a book, rather than merely recalling details, as they're reading they begin to think about their thinking; they become more metacognitive as they read. When children know that they won't be asked to write in the same old reading log every day, but instead will be asked to explore ideas they may not understand through writing and speaking to others, they begin to focus on the pieces that are unclear, jotting notes they need to clarify later. When they know that if they say "I don't know" in a class discussion, their teacher may well say, "I know you don't know, but if you did know, what would you say?" they are far more willing to think publicly because they have the time to consider an idea and don't feel rushed to say something quickly so the teacher can move on. And when students know that conferences consist of more than a friendly chat about a book, they begin to prepare for a more rigorous discussion that includes sharing their thinking about the book long before their teacher pulls up a chair next to them.

These small changes in our interactions—changes that occur when we move away from a "retell and answer my questions" definition of comprehension in our own minds—can help us move from the frustration of few and unpredictable "happy accident" moments to the much greater likelihood that all kids can engage in inspired thinking.

A STUDY IN CONTRASTS: RETHINKING THE OUTCOMES OF COMPREHENSION STRATEGY USE

On another of my school observations (this time in Denver, where I live, so all I had to do was find my own car!), I observed Delia, who is probably young enough to be my daughter. Fresh out of preservice training, she was bright, articulate, and related beautifully to her second graders

TABLE 1.1. Proposed Changes in the Way We Approach Common Instructional (and Assessment) Practices in Comprehension

Instead of ...	What would happen if ...
Asking students to answer endless comprehension questions that focus on the details of the text they're reading ...	We spoke with students about how it feels when a reader loses him- or herself in books or ideas, reads intently, with the most fervent concentration, and gains intellectual gratification from those moments of intense learning?
Asking children to retell what they have read or learned from a text ...	We talked with them about times when our comprehension was enriched because we made emotional connections to what we read; about times in our own lives when we discovered that we understood better because the writing was compelling or beautiful; when we found ourselves reveling in passages that are luminously written and times when we began to imagine how these passages mattered in our lives?
Rushing to get everything taught, everything jammed into a day, teaching a little bit of this and a little bit of that before rushing the students off to another class, telling them to turn this in before Friday and study that before the test ...	We encouraged students to pause in their reading, dwell in an idea, taking time to reread in order to rethink, and then write or speak about how they revised their existing knowledge, beliefs, feelings, or values?
Orienting our conferences and small groups toward trying to find out if students are doing the assigned reading and if they "get" it ...	We talked with students about situations in which we have struggled to learn something difficult or complex, when we had to fight our own doubts in order to finally gain some insight; about the realization that those struggles often provide us with the deepest sense of gratification and that we have learned to savor and learn from the struggle itself?
Asking children to write endless journal entries about their reading or create projects that have little to do with their insights from the text ...	We provided a wide range of ways in which children could share their thinking about books; showed them how readers sometimes engage in conversation with other readers in order to understand more, sometimes write to explore areas of confusion or insight, or even use art or drama to explore their thinking about a book, rather than reporting directly about the details in the book?
Implying through our instruction that there is a main idea or limited ways to interpret a text ...	We modeled ways in which readers discuss texts and consider the perspectives of others, even arguing with or challenging others until they better understand their own (and others') opinions, emotions, and principles;

(continued)

TABLE 1.1. (*continued*)

Instead of ...	What would happen if ...
	demonstrated how readers *revise* their thinking by incorporating new knowledge, beliefs, and opinions; showed how readers can describe how their thinking has changed over time, how books and other learning experiences change them?
Hurrying to let everyone have a chance to speak in each group discussion every day ...	We showed kids how to slow down the conversation and spend time with some students' ideas, knowing that, in the course of a year, everyone will have ample opportunity to explore an idea in a group setting?
Cutting students off when they've shared a bit of their thinking or accepting that some children just don't want to speak in a group setting ...	We gently coached more reluctant students to trust that their ideas will be relevant and important to the group? If a child says "I don't know," might we buy him some time to explore his thinking by saying, "I know you don't know, but if you did know, what would you say?" When a child shares an insight, instead of saying, "Great, anybody else?", we pause to restate her idea and encourage her to probe it further by saying, "What else?" and publicly valuing the time she takes to think by saying, "I love it when kids don't feel rushed to say the first thing they think—it's amazing to watch someone like Jennifer think like she is thinking right now."
Quizzing students to determine if they recall details from the text ...	We reframed our conferences and small-group meetings to ask students to describe their thinking about text (using the language of comprehension strategies as a guide)? For example, we might ask, "What questions did you have about that section ... can you describe the image you had in your mind as you read this piece ... or how did you decide what was important on that page?" By querying children about their thinking rather than about the details in the text, we'll soon discover if they've read the text and if they recall details, *and* we're giving them an opportunity to go much deeper in their response to the text.

Note. Adapted from Keene (2008). Copyright 2008 by Heinemann. Adapted by permission.

in an urban school so large she told me she hadn't yet met all the teachers. She was eager to tell me that her reading methods professor had assigned *Mosaic of Thought* (Keene & Zimmermann, 2007) in her class and that she was excited for me to see how her second graders made connections, referring to their use of one of the well-researched comprehension strategies we described in the book.

Delia gathered the students on the rug in front of her and began to read *An Angel for Solomon Singer* (Rylant, 1996), Cynthia Rylant's extraordinary book about a desperately lonely, nearly homeless man living in New York City. In the story Solomon Singer befriends a waiter and begins to reimagine a life he had nearly forsaken. Delia reminded the students that they would be making text-to-text, text-to-self, and text-to-world connections as she read.

A few pages into the book, Delia paused to think aloud.

"When I read this part about Solomon wandering the streets at night in search of the feelings he'd had as a child in the Midwest, it reminded me of the times I'm driving home from school after dark, and I see a homeless person on the street corner, asking for money." At this moment, 20 hands shot up in the air and, to her credit, Delia motioned for them to put their hands down. She knew that the connections she was likely to hear would be exact replicas of her own and wouldn't push the children's thinking forward. "I know you have lots of connections, too, but I want to tell you what else I was thinking. In a moment you'll have a chance to turn and talk to a partner about your connections, and they'll probably be different from mine. Right now I want to tell you that my heart always breaks when I see someone who is homeless, and I can't help but think that Solomon Singer may soon be someone who has no place to live. Thinking about the homeless people I see made me understand what Solomon Singer may be facing."

Delia's think-aloud not only emphasized a personal connection to the book, but importantly, she went one step further to describe how her *connection helped her better understand the book.* Too often, we are so eager to share our use of a particular strategy that we neglect what may well be the most important part of a think aloud: helping the children see how using the strategy helps us understand the text more deeply.

Delia paused to think aloud several more times before asking the children to turn to a partner and discuss the connections they'd made. I eavesdropped on a pair of students. The tiny girl seated closest to me began. "I had a connection. I saw a guy who was asking for money when cars went by." Her partner responded, "I saw him too." They turned to Delia to see what they should do next.

Delia pulled the children's attention back in her direction and finished reading the book. When she closed it, she shared a final think-aloud.

"You know, as I close the cover on this book, I think about how much difference Angel made in Solomon Singer's life, how his presence, every night at the West Way Café, made Solomon feel that he had a real friend in the world. I connected that to my own life. My grandmother has to be in a nursing home for a while to help build her strength after she broke her hip. When she first went to the nursing home, she was so lonely, she didn't know anyone, she didn't have anyone to talk to, and her room didn't look and feel like her home and that made her even lonelier. When I thought of my grandmother, I realized that Solomon's feelings aren't just the feelings of a man who is living in a place he doesn't love. People we love can experience those feelings too. My grandmother and Solomon are two very different people, but knowing how my grandmother feels helps me understand how Solomon must have felt before he met Angel."

Sitting in the back of the group taking notes, I wanted to stand up and shout, "*Halleluiah!!*" Delia again shared her connection, but then went the next step to say how the connection actually helped her understand the book better. Still, I was concerned, based on the pair I had overheard, that the children weren't fully aware of that crucial additional insight Delia had added to her connection.

"Today in your reading," she said, "I'd like for you to pay attention to your thinking to see if you have any connections. I'll be around to confer with you, and I may pull together one Invitational Group" (a small group that meets to work through a common need Delia identifies in conferences). I noticed that she didn't say anything about attending to the *outcome* the children might expect—specific ways in which they might understand the book they're reading better when they are aware of their connections.

Delia conferred with several children and, not surprisingly, they shared connections—some original, some extensions of those Delia had made in the lesson—but none shared (nor were they asked) how their connections enhanced their overall understanding.

Observing Delia that day made me aware of how difficult it is to remember everything we want to emphasize when we're in the heart of a lesson or conference, so I suggested that we pull together an Invitational Group together and see if we might get the children to take the next step that Delia had modeled so beautifully. She named five children with whom she had conferred and who had actually made some interesting and original connections. We gathered at a small table lit by a lamp with a bright red lampshade, and I took the lead.

"Ladies and gentlemen, while you've been reading, Ms. Gardiner and I talked for a moment about your amazing connections to *An Angel for Solomon Singer*. I think you're ready to hear about what can happen in your mind when you make connections. In our Invitational Group today, I want to tell you about something amazing that can happen in your mind when you make connections." I try to repeat my objective a couple of times. "Remember in the book when Ms. Gardiner made a connection right at the end? She talked about how her grandmother may have felt similar to the way Solomon Singer felt? Do you remember her telling us that she understood Solomon's feelings better because she connected to her grandmother's feelings? It's an amazing thing that happens sometimes when you make connections—you can actually *feel exactly what the character may have felt*—in your own heart!! And today, I want to tell you exactly what it's called when you do." I adopted a bit of a conspiratorial voice and stance. "Now, you'll be the first kids in the room to know this, so it will be up to you to think about ways to share what you know with the others."

I turned to an easel and wrote the words CHARACTER EMPA-THY on the chart paper. I pronounced the phrase slowly, pointing out each phoneme in the word *empathy* (they knew the word *character*). I pronounced it and invited them to do the same. I asked them to close their eyes until they could see a mental picture of the word *empathy* and told them again, "*Character empathy* means that, in your own heart, you can feel just what the character in a book feels!"

We talked about other read-aloud favorites they had read and how they felt empathic toward the characters in those books. I left them with a challenge. "Okay, you guys, I want you to go back to independent reading and pay attention to the connections you make—maybe, just maybe, when you make a connection, you'll start to feel empathy with the characters in your own books, and if you do, put a sticky note in the book so that when Ms. Gardiner comes to confer with you, you can share it with her."

The response was almost immediate. Every one of the Invitational Group members had an example (some were a bit of a stretch!) of a connection that led to character empathy. I find that children often respond this way—if we teach them the language associated with the cognitive and emotional experiences we often have as we read (I call these *outcomes*), they become more aware of where comprehension strategies lead them and more articulate in describing the outcomes because we've actually *taught* them! In Table 1.2 I describe some of the other outcomes I've observed when teachers or children are asked to describe how their use of a comprehension strategy helped them understand a text more deeply. Though the outcomes are divided into fiction and nonfiction categories, you'll find that there is a great deal of overlap; in many cases, you'll observe nonfiction outcomes in fiction reading, and vice versa.

In my experience, if teachers want to enhance strategy instruction, they can begin in a think-aloud lesson, as Delia did. First share how you use any one of the comprehension strategies. During the think-aloud, take an additional moment to talk about how your use of the strategy enhanced your comprehension. As you send the children back to independent reading, don't forget to remind them that they should attend to their use of the strategy *and* to the *outcomes* of comprehension. Per-

TABLE 1.2. The Outcomes of Understanding

In fiction/narrative/poetry, the use of one or more comprehension strategy may lead us to ...	In nonfiction, the use of one or more comprehension strategy may lead us to ...
Experience general empathy—a belief that one is a part of the setting, knows the characters, stands alongside them in their trials, brings something of oneself to the events and resolution; emotions are aroused	*Make connections*—the realization that newly learned concepts "fit" into existing background knowledge, make sense in relation to what is already known; affirms one's existing knowledge
Experience character empathy—a sense that one feels what the character feels	*Understand leadership*—explore and understand the lives of those who have made significant contributions to a field
Experience setting empathy—a sense that one is actually there, in the setting feeling the conditions, experiencing the time and place	*Understand the context and conditions* that lead to important discoveries in the scientific, technological, or social scientific world
Experience conflict empathy—a sense that one has been there, experienced a conflict similar enough that one can feel the internal sensations of dealing with the conflict or the external struggle the characters will go through as they deal with the conflict	*Understand the problems that lead to discoveries and new solutions*—a sense of the elements that make a situation problematic and some sense of the steps to be taken to solve the problem
Experience author empathy—understand why/how one's interpretations have been shaped in the way they have; what literary tools (diction, foreshadowing, imagery, voice, plot structures) did the author use to shape one's interpretation?	*Understand the author's intent*—a sense that one understands what the author thinks is important
Predict—the ability to predict and anticipate the events; the propensity to "lean into" the series of events that may be forthcoming with a sense of anticipation	*Understand chronology*—a sense of the general order of development or the progression of a series of events; the ability to predict with some accuracy what is likely to occur or be described next; a sense of the importance of chronology in a given context
Show confidence—the ability to discuss and contribute to others' ideas about the book	*Show confidence*—the ability to discuss and contribute to others' knowledge about a concept
Act—an urge to *do* something or act in some way to mitigate or resolve related conflicts in the world	*Act*—an urge to *do* something or act in some way to mitigate or resolve related conflicts in the world
Experience the aesthetic—a desire to linger with or reread portions of the text or the events that one finds beautiful or moving; the desire to experience it again	*Experience the aesthetic*—a sense of wonder about the complexities and inherent subtleties or nuances related to the concept

(*continued*)

TABLE 1.2. (*continued*)

In fiction/narrative/poetry, the use of one or more comprehension strategy may lead us to ...	In nonfiction, the use of one or more comprehension strategy may lead us to ...
Ponder—the desire to pause and consider new facets and twists in the text; the desire to discuss or share ideas in some way	*Revisit*—choosing to reread or explore other texts in order to learn more about a concept; a sense that one wants to review and rethink a concept
Advocate —the feeling of being "behind" the character(s) or narrator; wanting events to evolve in a particular way, believing that it is right that the plot moves in a certain way	*Understand important ideas*—a sense of what matters most, what is worth remembering, the confidence to focus on important ideas rather than details that are unimportant to the larger text ·
Establish believability—a sense that the characters/setting/events are real and believable; a sense of satisfaction with the way the events evolved	*Experience fascination*—a growing sense of wanting to know more, a developing passionate interest
Recognize patterns and symbols—the ability to use literary tools to recognize motifs, themes, and patterns as well as symbols and metaphors	*Recognize cause–effect*—knowledge of how events relate to each other
	Recognize comparisons and contrasts—developing a sense of how concepts are alike or different
Revise knowledge—changing one's mind, rethinking and reshaping understanding	*Revise knowledge*—forgoing previously held knowledge/beliefs in favor of updated factual information
Recognize the influence of beliefs/ values/opinions—affirmation of existing beliefs/values/opinions and/ or newly developing beliefs/values/ opinions because of what is read	*Recognize the influence of beliefs/values/ opinions*—affirmation of existing beliefs/ values/opinions and/or newly developing beliefs/values/opinions because of what is read
Sustain—the willingness to maintain interest and attention to the exclusion of competing or distracting interests	*Sustain*—the willingness to maintain interest and attention to the exclusion of competing or distracting interests
Gain insights for writing—the ability to learn from great expository writers, to "serve as apprentice" to them; the ability to read their work with a writer's eye and to incorporate writer's tools into one's own writing	*Gain insights for writing*—the ability to learn from great narrative writers, to "serve as apprentice" to them; the ability to read their work with a writer's eye and to incorporate writer's tools into one's own writing
Remember—the sense of permanence that comes with deeply understanding something; the ability to use something one understands in a new situation	*Remember*—the sense of permanence that comes with deeply understanding something; the ability to use something one understands in a new situation

Note. Adapted from Keene (2008). Copyright 2008 by Heinemann. Adapted by permission.

haps they'll experience a sense of empathy or a desire to advocate, for example. When you confer with children, be sure to discuss not only how they've used the strategy you're teaching, but how it enhanced their understanding.

By defining some of the outcomes I've noticed, I'm suggesting merely that, when we're teaching comprehension strategies, we are careful to articulate how the use of the strategy helps us better understand the text and that we say *exactly how* we experienced a new level of understanding (the outcomes). You and your students may well find new outcomes and/or change the language of these outcomes to better suit your needs. Whatever outcomes are identified, when everyone is using the same language to describe the same outcome and when that language is posted in the classroom, I have noticed that the likelihood that the children will use the language to describe their thinking goes way up.

WHY REVISE OUR APPROACHES
TO COMPREHENSION INSTRUCTION?

I described Jeff's and Delia's (both fine teachers) experiences in this chapter because I find that they are representative of many, many other teachers I've observed. We work so hard to teach children to select appropriate texts (as Jeff had), and we perfect our think-alouds (as Delia had), and then we're frustrated with the relatively low-level responses we sometimes hear from children. We relish the occasional happy accidents but aren't certain how to make them more habitual. I am suggesting here that some of the changes we need to make may be relatively minor and that the results of those changes can be extraordinary.

What happens when we rethink the language we use to define and describe understanding? What happens when we take the next step in articulating the outcomes children can expect when they use comprehension strategies? We will find that children rise to the occasion; that they begin to relish the intensity of their own minds at work; that they become far more deeply engaged in learning and come to believe in the potency of their own intellect. That engaged learning leads them to crave more intellectually challenging experiences, which, in turn, challenges us to attend to more outcomes in our own minds, more new ways of defining what we can expect when we understand deeply—which reignites the entire cycle again. In the end, no matter how we modify our language to express a different definition of comprehension, and no matter how we define and describe the outcomes of understanding, it's tough to dodge the conclusion that we are largely responsible for children's intellectual lives. Wouldn't we prefer that those lives were spent pursuing topics about which children are passionately interested? Don't we hope that they will be able interact with others from whom they'll learn even more deeply? And, don't we want them to remember and reuse the learning experiences of their lives—even if they can't find their own car in the parking lot?

REFERENCES

Rylant, C. (1996). *An angel for Solomon Singer.* New York: Scholastic.

Keene, E. O. (2008). *To understand: New horizons in comprehension.* Portsmouth, NH: Heinemann.

Keene, E. O., & Zimmermann, S. (2007). *Mosaic of thought: The power of comprehension strategy instruction* (2nd ed.). Portsmouth, NH: Heinemann.

2

Comprehension in the Elementary Grades

The Research Base

Kathryn L. Roberts
Nell K. Duke

During self-selected reading time, a teacher observes a student quietly reading a book aloud to himself in a corner of the room. She approaches the student and comments, "Wow! That's a very hard book, and you were reading it with almost no mistakes!" The child, clearly pleased with himself, beams. The teacher then attempts to engage the child in a conversation about the book by asking him if he can tell her a little about the story. The child thinks for a moment or two, and then responds by shaking his head no. "Sure you can," she persists, "tell me what's happening so far in the story." "I can't," the child replies, "I wasn't listening."

Imagine this vignette with the student at different grade levels. If the student were a seventh grader, all would agree that there is a concern. But what if the student were in first grade? For much of the history of U.S. education, there would be no concern. In fact, in many classrooms the student would not have been asked to talk about the meaning of the story in the first place. The primary focus of reading education in the elementary grades, particularly the primary years, has been to develop the ability to decode words. The ability to comprehend is often viewed as either coming naturally, given good decoding and normal oral language comprehension (Gough, Hoover, & Peterson, 1996), or viewed largely as a later concern (e.g., Chall, 1983).

It is now widely agreed that comprehension needs to be a strong focus throughout the elementary years, even in the primary grades (e.g., National Reading Panel, 2000; New Standards Primary Literacy Committee, 1999; Pressley, 2005; Snow, Burns, & Griffin, 1998). Supporters of early comprehension instruction point to evidence that children are able to engage in higher-level thought about the books they read or are read and that comprehension instruction does not necessarily detract from, and can even enhance, the learning of decoding skills (e.g., Pearson & Duke, 2002).

The purpose of this chapter is to provide a synopsis of what research has to say about increasing comprehension in the primary grades, which we define as kindergarten through third grade. Although our original charge was to address the entire elementary grades, we have chosen to focus on the primary grades for several reasons. First, the case for strong attention to comprehension has been hardest to make, and comprehension instruction is least often seen, in the primary grades. Second, reviews of research on comprehension instruction across all of the elementary grades already exist, including, notably, in the National Reading Panel (NRP) Report (2000; see also Duke & Pearson, 2002 for a general review; and Gersten, Fuchs, Williams, & Baker, 2001, for reviews of research on comprehension instruction for students with learning disabilities). Although the NRP report has had its greatest influence on K–3, many of the studies on comprehension reviewed were actually conducted exclusively with older students. Yet we cannot assume that what is effective in the upper elementary grades will always be effective in the primary grades.

Clearly, there has been much less research on effective comprehension instruction conducted in the primary grades. However, we do have a small, but growing, body of research on promising comprehension instructional practices at these grade levels. In fact, the rapid accumulation of research in this area is the third reason we focus the chapter on the primary grades. In 2004 Katherine Stahl published an excellent review of the literature on comprehension instruction in the primary grades (which she operationalized as kindergarten through second grade), but even in the few intervening years the field has gathered momentum, producing a number of new studies in this area. Our intention is to bring together the extant research that is ripe for classroom implementation. We first discuss research-tested instructional strategies, followed by a description of common characteristics of classrooms in which comprehension flourishes. Although they often have participants in other grades as well, all of the studies presented below include, as part of their sample, students in kindergarten through third grade.

WHAT IS INCLUDED IN THIS CHAPTER?

Although there are many approaches to instruction that impact comprehension in one way or another, this review is focused on instructional approaches that improve comprehension by focusing on it specifically. Research and common sense tell us that improving skills such as decoding, fluency, and vocabulary in young children can improve comprehension of independently read texts (e.g., National Reading Panel, 2000). We, of course, agree that being able to read the words and know what they mean help children understand text. However, instructional approaches designed to improve other aspects of reading do not directly improve comprehension; rather they are one step removed—they impact skills other than comprehension, which in turn impact comprehension (Figure 2.1). In this chapter, we focus on instructional strategies that aim to influence comprehension directly.

Moreover, we focus on instructional approaches that have been shown to positively impact comprehension of uninstructed texts. That is, if an instructional approach improved students' comprehension of the text with which it was used during instruction, but did not appear to improve comprehension skills in general or independent comprehension of text, it is not included in this review. This difference may seem subtle, but it has profound implications for literacy learning. Each text that

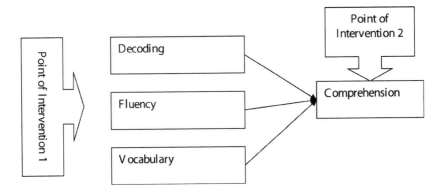

FIGURE 2.1. Two points of intervention in reading comprehension. In this chapter, we focus on Point of Intervention 2.

teachers use with children in the classroom presents at least two opportunities: learning/comprehending the text at hand and learning how to comprehend in general. To illustrate this point, imagine a first-grade teacher reading her class a book about the life cycle of a frog that contains a flowchart depicting the cycle. One goal of the lesson is for children to learn the life cycle of the frog. For this purpose, if the children don't seem to understand the book's explanation, the teacher can explain it in her own words and probably clarify the concept for most students. Although potentially very effective at conveying the desired content and even improving comprehension of the text at hand, this approach does not necessarily teach children how to comprehend similar texts or move them toward being able to derive information from text independently. In contrast, if the teacher models how to interpret the flowchart and understand the prose, the children may come away from the lesson both understanding the content *and* with a better idea of how to interpret similar texts in the future. Because we believe that the ultimate goal of instruction is to develop independent learners, we focus this review on instructional practices that are designed to teach comprehension skills that can eventually carry over into independent reading.

Finally, in this chapter we focus primarily on two kinds of studies: experimental and correlational. We believe that many kinds of studies are valuable to the field. However, in making recommendations to teachers about instructional practice, we often rely on these kinds of studies, each of which affords different kinds of claims. The first kind of studies we discuss in this chapter is experimental (and quasi-experimental). In these studies an instructional practice is implemented with one group of students and not implemented with an otherwise comparable group of students. If students' growth or achievement at the end of the study differs in the two groups, we infer that it is likely because of the instructional practice implemented. All of the instructional practices we discuss in the following section have been shown to improve children's reading comprehension skills statistically significantly more than in otherwise comparable classrooms that did not use the instructional practices. Of course, this doesn't mean we can be sure that these practices will work better than other practices in all situations—for example, if a practice was studied only with first-grade struggling readers, we don't know that it would work equally well (or better, or not as well) with third-grade high-achieving readers. Moreover, unless we conduct another experiment to find out, we don't know whether there is something out there that would have worked even better than the approach that proved to be more effective. So we do have to be cautious with this kind of research. Still, it provides us with valuable information for use in decision making in this all-important area.

In the second half of the chapter we rely largely on correlational studies. In these studies we look for relationships among things we observe. For example, we might investigate whether there are relationships between particular classroom characteristics and children's reading comprehension growth by asking questions such as, "What are the characteristics of classrooms in which students have relatively strong comprehension growth as compared to characteristics of classrooms in which students have relatively weak comprehension growth?" These kinds of studies allow us to identify important patterns, but they do not easily allow us to make causal claims (although see Stanovich & Cunningham, 2004, and Schneider, Carnoy, Kilpatrick, Schmidt, & Shavelson, 2007, for ways to do so). It is hard to know, for example, which of the classroom characteristics are the ones really *causing* children's reading comprehension growth and which often go hand in hand with the other characteristics but are not actually affecting comprehension. For example, classrooms that produce relatively strong comprehension growth may also often produce relatively strong mathematics learning, but the practices that teachers are using to develop strong mathematics learning (e.g., using a spiral curriculum or using a wide variety of manipulatives) may not be the practices causing the better comprehension, despite a high correlation between the two. Moreover, it is even possible that some characteristics of classrooms that produce relatively strong comprehenders may undermine comprehension and/or could be improved in important ways. For example, in the past, at least, many primary classrooms that produced relatively better comprehenders (as compared to other classrooms) likely used very little informational text (Duke, 2000), but we wouldn't want to conclude from this characteristic that using little informational text causes better comprehension development! It is probable that including more informational text would make these relatively successful classrooms *even better*. So we need to be cautious when interpreting this kind of research as well and continue to strive in our research and practice to find *even better* ways to develop children's all-important reading comprehension.

RESEARCH-TESTED INSTRUCTIONAL PRACTICES FOR IMPROVING READING COMPREHENSION IN THE PRIMARY GRADES

Despite the rapid growth of research on comprehension instruction in the primary grades, there are still very few comprehension strategies with large numbers of empirical studies to support their use. Some of the strategies we present in this section have not yet been the subject of many studies (though all have been the subject of some research). Some people hesitate to recommend practices without a substantial number of studies to support them (e.g., National Reading Panel, 2000), but we have decided to include such practices because we believe that some studies are better than none. We just can't wait out the long process of building a larger research base before providing recommendations for practice; we risk missed opportunities for learning for the current generation.

Text-Structure Instruction

One strategy that has been successful in increasing comprehension of text is deliberate instructional attention to the structures of text. Although text-structure instruction is typically associated with the upper and middle grades, research has shown that children as young as kindergarten (Garner & Bochna, 2004) and first grade (Baumann & Bergeron, 1993; Williams, 2005) can benefit from instruction on, and knowledge of, text structure. Those who doubt the efficacy of text-structure instruction argue that authentic texts have such a wide variety of structures that teaching all of them is both time-consuming and poses an unreasonable dedication of effort and memory for students, especially those who are learning disabled (Anderson & Roit, 1993). Expository text structures alone comprise a formidable list (e.g., compare–contrast, enumerative, persuasive, procedural, cause–effect, description). In addition, the tendency of some texts to mix genres complicates matters by producing a myriad of possible hybrid structures (Meyer & Poon, 2001). However, proponents of the strategy contend that (1) the knowledge that texts are structured can help students identify and utilize even uninstructed structures, and (2) when students encounter authentic texts (i.e., in this context, not researcher-created texts) that do not exactly follow the structures they are taught, they may be able to mentally organize the information according to the structures with which they are familiar (Williams, 2005).

A series of experiments with second graders set out to test these assumptions (Williams, 2005). In the first study, classroom teachers taught their students to identify clue words signaling compare–contrast structure (i.e., *alike, both, and, compare, but, however, than,* and *contrast*) and to use graphic organizers to outline relevant information from the text. They then followed up instruction with a series of questions to help students focus on the most important information in the text. In comparison to students who were taught content through more traditional content-area instruction or who were not instructed at all, the students who received text-structure instruction were better able to summarize researcher-created paragraphs about the content that they had learned (orally and in writing) using the compare–contrast structure, and were also better able to perform these tasks on transfer tests of uninstructed material following the same structure. However, when asked to use a different, uninstructed text structure (pro–con), the students who had been taught to use the compare–contrast text structure did not perform significantly differently from the content- or no-instruction groups, indicating that although successful use of one structure transferred to uninstructed content, it did not transfer to use of an uninstructed structure.

Two subsequent experiments, also with second graders, produced mixed results (Williams, 2005). In one experiment, researchers found that the children who were taught with dual foci of content and text structure performed significantly better on measures of text structure use and performed as well as the content-only comparison group on measures of content learning. This experiment also indicated that learning transferred to authentic texts. In the other experiment, text-structure instruction was reduced and replaced with more content instruction. Again, these students were compared to a group that was taught the same content, but not taught to use text structure. The results of this study indicated that, with less time dedicated to text-structure instruction, the students were still able to learn about text structure and outperform control students on text structure models, but did not perform significantly better on measures of content knowledge or transfer to authentic text.

Although the above experiments used only expository texts, positive results have also been found for narrative texts. Baumann and Bergeron (1993) conducted a study with first graders using authentic narrative texts. They found that teaching students to attend to story structure elements (i.e., characters, setting, problem, events, and resolution) increased student comprehension of both independently read stories and stories that were read aloud by teachers. Narrative story structure instruction has also been embedded in retelling instruction and used to successfully increase listening comprehension of students as early as kindergarten (Morrow, 1984).

Retelling

In comparison to answering questions after reading or listening to a text, it is believed that retelling may be more effective for stimulating deep processing of information. This is because retelling requires readers to integrate information and reconstruct the text independently, as opposed to simply responding to teacher/caregiver-initiated questions, which often inadvertently give clues that direct thinking (Hansen, 1978).

The strategy also requires little or no preparation and relatively little time, which contribute to its practicality and help to explain its widespread use in classrooms (Stahl, 2004). Although retelling, like most other comprehension practices, has been studied more widely in older grades (National Reading Panel, 2000), it does have some history of being implemented successfully in the primary grades, as early as kindergarten and first grade (Baumann & Bergeron, 1993; Morrow, 1985; Morrow, Tracey, Woo, & Pressley, 1999). Because the strategy is oral and can be used with equal ease with independently or teacher-read stories, it lends itself particularly well to emergent and early readers.

In a two-study series, Morrow (1985) studied the differences in comprehension between kindergarteners who engaged in guided retellings after listening to a story and their peers who drew pictures about the story after listening to the same story. In the first study, a half hour after listening to the story, all students were asked a series of literal, inferential, and story structure questions (i.e., one question each about plot, resolution, and theme; two about setting). In this study the intervention only spanned 3 sessions over 3 days, yet a statistically significant advantage was found favoring the guided retelling group over the drawing pictures group as measured by their total comprehension (but not by individual question type).

Theorizing that a greater impact could be found with a longer intervention, Morrow (1985) conducted the second study, lengthening instruction to 8 sessions over 8 weeks. In addition to the comprehension measure described above, all participants in the second study engaged in an independent retelling at the end of the intervention period. These retellings were recorded and analyzed for story structure elements, length, and syntactic complexity. The results of this study showed that children in the guided retelling group scored significantly higher on each type of comprehension question as well as overall (recall that in the shorter-term study they scored higher only overall). Retellings by students in the guided retelling group also contained significantly more story elements, were significantly more syntactically complex, and contained significantly more episodes in the correct chronological order.

Visual Imagery Training

Visual imagery training (also called *mental imagery* or *visualization*) aims to teach children how to create mental pictures of the text they listen to or read, which in turn encourages children to think actively about the text—a hallmark of good readers/comprehenders (Duke, Pressley, & Hilden, 2004; RAND Reading Study Group, 2002). Instruction in visualization typically involves teaching children specific procedures to translate words (read or listened to) into mental images. In order to make this process transparent, many teaching models involve the teacher drawing on paper what he or she is "seeing" in his or her head while thinking about the text. From there, students are transitioned into imagining still or moving images in their heads. Creation of mental images likely facilitates comprehension in two ways: (1) Creating mental images requires readers to think about the meaning of what they are reading—they cannot create mental images if they process text only in terms of decoding; and (2) when reading (verbal) or creating mental images (nonverbal), information is stored in two distinct but interconnected parts of memory, the sum of which is greater than either alone (Paivio, 1991).

When teachers teach students to create mental images, does their comprehension improve? Center, Freeman, Robertson, and Outhred (1999) addressed this question in their study of year 2 (mean age, 7 years, 8 months) Australian students. In this investigation, all children received high-quality comprehension instruction that included discussion of story elements (i.e., setting, problem, resolution, and characters), setting a purpose, prereading prediction discussions, literal and inferential questioning during reading, and story mapping after reading. However, for some of the children part of the discussion time was replaced by instruction on mental imagery, in which the teacher modeled and scaffolded the creation of mental images through a progression of increasingly less concrete tasks. In the first session, students were given a familiar object to examine carefully and then asked to "paint a picture in their minds" of that object. They were then shown a picture of a barnyard and asked to close their eyes and visualize what they had just seen. Next the teacher asked several students to describe the images in their heads. The teacher then read the students a simple sentence and modeled drawing the "picture" in her head on paper for the students. Finally, the students were read a passage that was the object of the comprehension lesson and were encouraged to utilize the visualization strategy. These last two steps were repeated as a part of six subsequent comprehension lessons. In the remaining five sessions, students were reminded to use the strategy, but there was no further scaffolding or modeling. In comparison to peers who did not receive instruction in visualization, the students who did receive such instruction scored significantly higher on a curriculum-based listening comprehension assessment, a standardized reading comprehension assessment, and a measure of story structure knowledge.

Admittedly, there is a need for further study of visualization, especially with young children. However, the positive results of studies conducted with older children (e.g., Gambrell & Bales, 1986; Gambrell & Jawitz, 1993) in combination with limited evidence of effectiveness with younger children (e.g., Borduin, Borduin, & Manley, 1994; Center et al., 1999) are compelling and give us reason to believe that teaching visual imaging is a successful instructional technique that can benefit even very young students.

Activation and Use of Prior Knowledge

All readers use their prior knowledge to bring meaning to texts (Anderson & Pearson, 1984). Therefore, it stands to reason that the more relevant prior knowledge a reader possesses, and the greater his or her ability to access and use that knowledge, the greater the likelihood of successful comprehension. Prior knowledge plays a role in understanding what to expect within certain genres' text structures (Meyer, Brandt, & Bluth, 1980), when drawing inferences (Duke et al., 2004; Hansen, 1981), and when making accurate predictions (McIntyre, 2007). In short, children's prior knowledge related to a text determines, at least in part, how they read and the strategic decisions they make (Pressley et al., 1994).

In her study of students' comprehension of basal text stories, Hansen (1981) investigated the impact of different instructional strategies utilizing prior knowledge. She randomly assigned second graders who were reading at or above grade level to one of three groups: control, in which students were given traditional story introductions and asked literal and inferential questions about the story; strategy, in which students were taught to use their prior knowledge to predict the content of text; and question, in which students practiced answering inferential questions using the text and their own prior knowledge. On both standardized assessments and questions asked immediately after students read the texts, the strategy and question groups outperformed the control group in answering inferential questions, indicating that the use of prior knowledge, either to drive predictions or help answer specific questions, improved comprehension.

One caveat about activating and using prior knowledge is that, in order for it to be effective, teachers must teach students both to select *relevant* prior knowledge and to *apply* that knowledge judiciously to the text in question. If these conditions are not met, it is possible for prior knowledge to interfere with comprehension. Readers may become deeply involved with thinking about information that is only tangentially related to the text and does not aid in text comprehension. Further, there are references in practice and in research to situations in which readers refuse or are unable to synthesize new and old information (Keene & Zimmerman, 2007; Otero & Kintsch, 1992). In some cases, readers should modify their schema to accommodate the new information, but instead they may reject the information. Thus, even though there is considerable research supporting instruction in activating and applying background knowledge for older students, and even some research supporting this for primary-grade learners, there are also potential pitfalls of which to be aware.

Multiple Strategy Instruction

All of the strategies outlined above are powerful in and of themselves, but there is reason to think it may be more powerful to teach strategies in a combined fashion, so that readers learn from very early on to coordinate use of multiple strategies and select and apply appropriate strategies as they read. The work of reading is messy and complicated, and good readers flexibly and strategically employ a wide range of strategies, depending on the text and context, especially when faced with challenging texts (e.g., Brown, Pressley, Van Meter, & Schuder, 1996; Duke et al., 2004; Guthrie, Wigfield, Barbosa et al., 2004; Pressley & Afflerbach, 1995).

In a comparison of one-at-a-time versus multiple-strategy instruction approaches with second-grade students, Reutzel, Smith, and Fawson (2005) did find that students who were taught to use multiple strategies when reading science texts showed better memory of the science text (as evidenced by their abilities to retell what they had read) and content (as evidenced by a multiple choice test on the content of the text), and they performed better on curriculum-based reading assessments (they performed the same on some other measures, including motivation surveys and standardized tests). Below we will describe three examples of multiple-strategy instruction approaches that have been shown to have positive impacts on the comprehension of students in the primary grades.

Transactional Strategy Instruction

In transactional strategy instruction (TSI; Brown et al., 1996; Pressley et al., 1992, 1994), teachers introduce, model, and scaffold the use of a variety of strategies, including use of prior knowledge, visualization, summarization, prediction, identifying and adjusting to purpose, thinking aloud, question generation, identification of important information, and active interpretation of text (Brown et al., 1996). In addition,

> the usefulness of strategies is emphasized, with students reminded frequently about the comprehension gains that accompany strategy use. Information about when and where various strategies can be applied is commonly discussed. Teachers consistently model flexible use of strategies; students explain to one another how they use strategies to process text. (Brown et al., 1996, p. 19)

Inherent in the process are teacher think-alouds as well as an ongoing focus on students' metacognition—their ability to talk about which strategy they are choosing, why they made that particular selection, and how it is (or is not) helping them. The following excerpt is typical of discussions about text in TSI classrooms. In this particular discussion, the teacher and students have been reading a book about the medical profession, and the teacher (Randall) is responding to a connection that she has prompted a student to make:

> "That's exactly right. You're brilliant. Have you ever had that happen to you? See, that's what makes reading so important is that when you're reading an information book like this one and you've had some experiences, like wheezing with bronchitis, then when you read the word 'stethoscope' and we talk about this sentence, it means a lot to you because you've had it happen to you." (Pressley et al., 1992, p. 523)

Studies on the ability of TSI to increase comprehension showed that first-, second-, and fourth-grade students who participated in TSI instruction performed significantly better on standardized tests of comprehension than demographically comparable peers in classrooms that did not utilize the instructional model (Brown et al., 1996; Pressley et al., 1994). In addition, second graders in TSI classrooms were significantly more interpretive in their recollection of stories (Brown et al., 1996).

Concept-Oriented Reading Instruction

Concept-Oriented Reading Instruction (CORI; e.g., Guthrie et al., 1996; Guthrie, Wigfield, & Perencevich, 2004) is a model that teaches students to use multiple cognitive strategies (i.e., activating prior knowledge, questioning, searching for information, summarizing, organizing graphically, and using story structure) in combination with motivational strategies and practices to increase their comprehension, content learning, and motivation. CORI has a rich research base (see, e.g., Guthrie, McRae, & Klauda, 2007; Guthrie, Wigfield, & Perencevich, 2004), with studies showing that the approach improves reading comprehension as well as related constructs such as reading motivation. Unfortunately, CORI has not been tested against a comparison condition below third grade, a point we consider in the concluding section of this chapter.

Directed Reading–Thinking Activity

Directed Reading–Thinking Activity (DR-TA; Stauffer, 1969) typically combines strategies of activating prior knowledge, prediction, and text structure use, though other strategies may also be used. This combination of strategies may also be used by students listening to a text, as in the Directed Listening–Thinking Activity or DL-TA (Stauffer, 1976). The typical instructional pattern involves the teacher leading a discussion that elicits predictions from students, which they are then asked to justify before reading or listening to part of the text to confirm or disconfirm. This cycle continues as students verify/modify predictions and make new ones throughout the reading of the text (Baumann & Bergeron, 1993).

Thus far, empirical research on DR-TA with primary-grade students is encouraging. In Baumann and Bergeron's (1993) study of first graders' use of story mapping, DR-TA, and traditional instructional conditions, they found that the comprehension of participants in the DR-TA group was superior to the traditional group at a statistically significant level on measures of ability to identify central story elements and ability to answer questions about story structure elements (i.e., main characters, setting, problem, major events, and solution). In Stahl's (2008) study of DR-TA with second graders reading informational text, she found that it had statistically significant effects on reading comprehension, though with instructed texts, and science learning. DR-TA can be added to CORI, TSI, and instruction in activation and use of background knowledge, visual imagery, retelling, and text structure as approaches having positive impacts on primary-grade students' reading comprehension development.

CHARACTERISTICS OF CLASSROOMS WITH RELATIVELY GOOD COMPREHENDERS

The studies described above give us insight into comprehension instruction via interventions. Another source of information on fostering comprehension in primary-grade classrooms comes from the classrooms themselves. Studying existing classrooms that have a relatively greater number of good comprehenders or relatively stronger comprehension growth provides us with a picture of what a supportive environment for building comprehension looks like, and can give us clues about what might help build comprehension in all classrooms. Several conditions and practices are present in classrooms in which students develop well as comprehenders.

There Is a Focus on Comprehension

Not surprisingly, teachers who develop better comprehenders spend time working on comprehension. Teaching other constructs, such as decoding and vocabulary, can certainly improve comprehension, but this alone is not enough (Pressley et al., 2008). Teachers of strong comprehenders intentionally teach their students how to comprehend (Taylor, Pearson, Clark, & Walpole, 2000). This relationship between the intentional teaching of comprehension and positive comprehension outcomes may seem obvious, but it must not be, given that comprehension instruction is not nearly as common in the younger grades as more isolated skill instruction (Taylor et al., 2000)—a fact that is mirrored in the research community by disproportionate amounts of research in the primary grades on lower-level skills (phonics, letter knowledge, phonemic awareness) as compared to comprehension (e.g., National Reading Panel, 2000).

A focus on comprehension should not be mistaken for prolonged teacher lecture, demonstration, and quizzing of students in the area of comprehension—something we observe in too many classrooms. Research by Smith, Lee, and Newmann (2001) is instructive on this point: They found that growth in reading/language arts achievement in second- through eighth-grade classrooms in the Chicago School District was greater in classrooms in which teachers used a less didactic, more interactive approach. Among other tendencies, teachers with a more interactive approach are more likely to coach, listen to, and guide students, whereas those with a more didactic approach are more likely to lecture or demonstrate to students (p. 11).

Of course, being less didactic should not mean being less involved in instruction. In fact, in a study of third graders, those with average to low comprehension scores who were placed in classrooms in which teachers were more actively involved in managing learning activities (e.g., leading discussions, modeling think-alouds, conferring) experienced greater comprehension growth than students of similar ability in classrooms that favored more student-managed activities (e.g., sustained silent reading, independent worksheets) (Connor, Morrison, & Petrella, 2004). It seems that the amount and nature of teacher–student interaction is related to comprehension growth, a relationship that may be magnified for less skilled comprehenders.

Students and Teachers Talk about Text

Providing frequent opportunities for students and teachers to discuss text is associated with greater comprehension growth. Talking about text has a strong base in the research (Murphy, Wilkinson, Soter, Hennessey, & Alexander, in press; Nystrand, 2006). Encouraging children to talk with others about the text and their understandings or to engage in conversation with others before, during, and/or after the reading of text can foster comprehension, likely due to the accountability inherent in saying something oneself and the opportunity to hear the interpretations of others. This theory of socially constructed knowledge through talk has roots in Vygotsky's (1978) theory of sociogenesis, in which growth is seen as "more likely when one is required to explain, elaborate, or defend one's positions to others as well as to oneself; striving for an explanation often makes the learner integrate and elaborate knowledge in new ways" (p. 158).

Much of the research on discussion and reading comprehension is conducted with older students. However, even in a study with 4-year-olds from low-income homes, Dickinson and Smith (1994) found a relationship between teacher and student talk about a book and the children's vocabulary and comprehension growth. Children whose teachers encouraged and engaged students in analytic discussion performed modestly better than peers in classrooms in which children answered factual questions about the stories or recited portions of the text in unison when answering comprehension questions.

One concern we often hear from teachers is that they doubt the abilities of their young students to engage in discussions that require higher-level thinking skills. There is, however, research that directly refutes this point. As the Dickinson and Smith (1994) study suggests (see also, e.g., Tower, 2002; Whitehurst et al., 1994), even preschool children can talk about text in sophisticated ways. In the primary grades more effective classrooms are characterized by teachers who engage students in discussion of higher-level questions and themes related to text (Taylor et al., 2000; see Taylor & Pearson, 2002, for a review of research on effective schools).

Teachers and Children Read a Lot

One characteristic common to most, if not all, classrooms in which there is higher growth in comprehension is that there is *a lot* of reading. This isn't surprising, and we probably don't need research to convince us that good readers spend time reading, although it's certainly out there in abundance (e.g., Cunningham & Stanovich, 1997; Guthrie, 2004; Stanovich 1986, 2004). In these classrooms, there are frequent opportunities for students to listen to and interact with text during read-alouds and guided reading (e.g., Morrow et al., 1999; Taylor et al., 2000) as well as during paired and independent reading (e.g., Morrow et al., 1999), and to read across the content areas (e.g., Guthrie, Anderson, Solomon, & Rinehart, 1999). In short, good comprehenders spend time reading and listening to others read in a variety of formats and contexts.

There Are Authentic Purposes and Texts for Reading

In addition to how much reading is occurring, the purposes for reading can be important factors in comprehension development. In a recent study researchers found a relationship between comprehension growth and the authenticity of reading and writing activities in second- and third-grade classrooms (Purcell-Gates, Duke, & Martineau, 2007). More authentic reading and writing activities were defined as those in which children read and wrote texts the same as, or very much like, texts children read and write outside of school, and children read and wrote texts for reasons that went beyond just learning how to read and write. For example, in one classroom the teacher engaged students in reading informational text to answer questions they had about a classmate's broken arm (Duke, Purcell-Gates, Hall, & Tower, 2006/2007). Across classrooms, researchers found that the students of teachers who established more authentic reading and writing activities for informational and procedural texts in science showed higher growth in comprehension (as well as writing).

SUMMARY

Although there is relatively little research on comprehension instruction in the primary grades, the research that does exist suggests that there is much that teachers can do to improve young children's developing reading comprehension. Compared to classrooms without these activities, greater comprehension gains were observed when teachers engaged in text-structure instruction, elicited and guided retellings, provided visual imagery training, prompted children to activate and use prior knowledge, and used multiple-strategy instruction approaches, including TSI, CORI, or DR-TA. In addition, studies have found that young children's comprehension growth is greater in classrooms in which teachers and students read a lot, there are authentic purposes and texts for reading, students and teachers talk about text, and, of course, in which there is a focus on comprehension.

NEXT STEPS

We close the chapter by offering some thoughts about next steps in research and practice in primary-grade comprehension.

More Research on, and Dissemination of, Already Developed Techniques

In most cases the practices and insights shared in the preceding sections have been shown to be effective in only one or a few studies, and often with students at only one or two grade levels. We need replication studies (additional studies that mimic closely studies that have already been conducted) in order to evaluate whether strategies are widely beneficial or are bound to some other, less visible, characteristics of the context in which the original studies were performed. We also need to expand studies to new grade levels, populations, and contexts. For example, it would be valuable to find out whether approaches tested only at second grade can be modified to be effective for children in first grade. It is important to learn whether approaches tested only with monolingual speakers are equally, more, or less effective with children who are or are becoming bilingual. It would be very helpful to learn whether approaches tested in one content area—for example, CORI for science—can be modified to be effective in others. And it would be interesting to examine whether approaches tested exclusively with print texts can be modified to support children's developing comprehension with digital texts (as in research discussed by Leu et al., 2008, with older students).

Equally important is dissemination of existing techniques. Many teachers, coaches, and other school personnel have not even heard of many of the techniques—for example CORI or TSI—that have been shown to be so effective in research. It behooves us to get strategies that have been proven to work, at least under certain conditions, into classrooms where better instruction is badly needed. Getting these strategies into wider practice also provides the possibility that practitioners will use their experiences and expertise to suggest potential improvements in the techniques and next steps for research

Research and Development on Innovative Techniques

At the same time, we should not limit research and development to already-developed approaches. Surely there is room for the development and subsequent testing of innovative techniques. For example, we are interested in the development of ways to teach reading comprehension strategies to young children being instructed through a project-based curriculum (Katz, 1994), in which literacy instruction is embedded within an investigation of a particular topic, and in the development of interventions to help parents build children's comprehension through book reading at home. There are myriad ways that new technologies might be used to develop reading comprehension in our children. And we routinely encounter interesting new ways teachers have developed for talking about comprehension strategies with young children. We need a substantial program of research and development to make today's innovations tomorrow's research-tested techniques.

Creating More and Better Assessments

One barrier to both research and practice in comprehension in the primary grades is the relative lack of appropriate assessments. We need to develop more effective means to assess developing reading comprehension, particularly before children are reading independently. We have developed two such assessments of informational text comprehension appropriate for children as early as first grade (Billman et al., 2008; Hilden et al., 2008; see also Paris & Paris, 2003, with narrative text) and can attest to both the challenge and to the sense that any single assessment will be limited in a number of ways. It is clear that entire systems of assessment in this area need to be developed in the near future (RAND Reading Study Group, 2002).

Assessment will help us to flag much sooner children like the student in our opening vignette, who sound like good readers but who are not comprehending. Assessment—both formal and informal—can also provide insights as to *what* to instruct. Instruction of the kinds featured in the studies reviewed for this chapter and throughout much of this book hold the promise of putting this student (and all children) in the best possible position to jump start their reading comprehension.

REFERENCES

Anderson, R. C., & Pearson, P. D. (1984). A schema-theoretic view of basic processes in reading. In P. D. Pearson (Ed.), *Handbook of reading research* (pp. 255–292). New York: Longman.

Anderson, T. H., & Roit, M. (1993). Planning and implementing collaborative strategy instruction for delayed readers in grades 6–10. *Elementary School Journal, 94,* 121–137.

Baumann, J. F., & Bergeron, B. S. (1993). Story map instruction using children's literature: Effects on first graders' comprehension of central narrative elements. *Journal of Reading Behavior, 25,* 407–437.

Billman, A. K., Duke, N. K., Hilden, K. R., Zhang, S., Roberts, K., Halladay, J. L., et al. (2008). *Concepts of Comprehension Assessment (COCA)*. Retrieved June 18, 2008, from *www.msularc.org/html/project_COCA_main.html/*.

Borduin, B. J., Borduin, C. M., & Manley, C. M. (1994). The use of imagery training to improve reading comprehension of second graders. *Journal of Genetic Psychology, 155*(1), 115–118.

Brown, R., Pressley, M., Van Meter, P., & Schuder, T. (1996). A quasi-experimental validation of transactional strategies instruction with low-achieving second grade readers. *Journal of Educational Psychology, 88*, 18–37.

Center, Y., Freeman, L., Robertson, G., & Outhred, L. (1999). The effect of visual imagery training on the reading and listening comprehension of low listening comprehenders in year 2. *Journal of Research in Reading, 22*, 241–256.

Chall, J. S. (1983). *Stages of reading development.* New York: McGraw-Hill.

Connor, C. M., Morrison, F. J., & Petrella, J. N. (2004). Effective reading comprehension instruction: Examining child × instruction interactions. *Journal of Educational Psychology, 96*, 682–698.

Cunningham, A. E., & Stanovich, K. E. (1997). Early reading acquisition and its relation to reading experience and ability 10 years later. *Developmental Psychology, 33*, 934–945.

Dickinson, D. K., & Smith, M. W. (1994). Long-term effects of preschool teachers' book readings on low income children's vocabulary and story comprehension. *Reading Research Quarterly, 29*, 104–122.

Duke, N. K. (2000). 3.6 minutes per day: The scarcity of informational texts in first grade. *Reading Research Quarterly, 35*, 202–224.

Duke, N. K., & Pearson, P. D. (2002). Effective practices for developing reading comprehension. In A. E. Farstrup & S. J. Samuels (Eds.), *What research has to say about reading instruction* (3rd ed., pp. 205–242). Newark, DE: International Reading Association.

Duke, N. K., Pressley, M., & Hilden, K. (2004). Difficulties with reading comprehension. In C. A. Stone, E. R. Silliman, B. J. Ehren, & K. Apel (Eds.), *Handbook of language and literacy development and disorders* (pp. 501–520). New York: Guilford Press.

Duke, N. K., Purcell-Gates, V., Hall, L. A., & Tower, C. (2006/2007). Authentic literacy activities for developing comprehension and writing. *Reading Teacher, 60*, 344–355.

Gambrell, L. B., & Bales, R. J. (1986). Mental imagery and the comprehension-monitoring performance of fourth- and fifth-grade poor readers. *Reading Research Quarterly, 21*, 454–464.

Gambrell, L. B. & Jawitz, P. B. (1993). Mental imagery, text illustrations, and children's story comprehension and recall. *Reading Research Quarterly, 28*, 264–276.

Garner, J. K., & Bochna, C. R. (2004). Transfer of a listening comprehension strategy to independent reading in first-grade students. *Early Childhood Education Journal, 32*, 69–74.

Gersten, R., Fuchs, L. S., Williams, J. P., & Baker, S. (2001). Teaching reading comprehension strategies to students with learning disabilities: A review of research. *Review of Educational Research, 71*, 279–320.

Gough, P. B., Hoover, W. A., & Peterson, C. L. (1996). Some observations on the simple view of reading. In C. Cornoldi & J. Oakhill (Eds.), *Reading comprehension difficulties: Processes and interventions* (pp. 1–13). Mahwah, NJ: Erlbaum.

Guthrie, J. T. (2004). Teaching for literacy engagement. *Journal of Literacy Research, 36,* 1–30.

Guthrie, J. T., Anderson, E., Solomon, A., & Rinehart, J. (1999). Influences of Concept-Oriented Reading Instruction on strategy use and conceptual learning from text. *The Elementary School Journal, 99,* 343–366.

Guthrie, J. T., McRae, A., & Klauda, S. L. (2007). Contributions of Concept-Oriented Reading Instruction to knowledge about interventions for motivations in reading. *Educational Psychologist, 42,* 237–250.

Guthrie, J. T., Van Meter, P., McCann, A. D., Wigfield, A., Bennett, L., Poundstone, C. C., et al. (1996). Growth of literacy engagement: Changes in motivations and strategies during Concept-Oriented Reading Instruction. *Reading Research Quarterly, 31,* 306–332.

Guthrie, J. T., Wigfield, A., Barbosa, P., Perencevich, K. C., Taboada, A., Davis, M., et al. (2004). Increasing reading comprehension and engagement through Concept-Oriented Reading Instruction. *Journal of Educational Psychology, 96,* 403–423.

Guthrie, J. T., Wigfield, A., & Perencevich, K. C. (Eds.). (2004). *Motivating reading comprehension: Concept-Oriented Reading Instruction.* Mahwah, NJ: Erlbaum.

Hansen, C. L. (1978). Story retelling used with average and learning disabled readers as a measure of reading comprehension. *Learning Disability Quarterly, 1,* 62–69.

Hansen, J. (1981). The effects of inference training and practice on young children's reading comprehension. *Reading Research Quarterly, 16,* 391–417.

Hilden, K. R., Duke, N. K., Billman, A. K., Zhang, S., Halladay, J. L., Schaal, A. M., et al. (2008). *Informational Strategic Cloze Assessment (ISCA).* Retrieved June 18, 2008, from *www.msularc.org/html/project_ISCA_main.html.*

Katz, L. (1994). The project approach [Electronic Version]. *ERIC Digest,* 1–6. Retrieved January 27, 2008.

Keene, E. O., & Zimmerman, S. (2007). *Mosaic of thought: The power of comprehension strategy instruction* (2nd ed.). Portsmouth, NH: Heinemann.

Leu, D. J., Coiro, J., Castek, J., Hartman, D. K., Henry, L. A., & Reinking, D. (2008). Research on instruction and assessment in the new literacies of online reading comprehension. In C. C. Block & S. Parris (Eds.), *Comprehension instruction: Research-based best practices* (pp. 321–345). New York: Guilford Press.

McIntyre, E. (2007). Story discussion in the primary grades: Balancing authenticity and explicit teaching. *Reading Teacher, 60,* 610–620.

Meyer, B. J. F., Brandt, D. M., & Bluth, G. J. (1980). Use of top-level structure in text: Key for reading comprehension of ninth-grade students. *Reading Research Quarterly, 16,* 72–103.

Meyer, B. J. F., & Poon, L. W. (2001). Effects of structure on strategy training and signaling on recall of text. *Journal of Educational Psychology, 93,* 141–159.

Morrow, L. M. (1984). Reading stories to young children: Effects of story structure and traditional question strategies on comprehension. *Journal of Reading Behavior, 16,* 273–288.

Morrow, L. M. (1985). Retelling stories: A strategy for improving young children's comprehension, concept of story structure, and oral language complexity. *Elementary School Journal, 85,* 647–651.

Morrow, L. M., Tracey, D. H., Woo, D. G., & Pressley, M. (1999). Characteristics of exemplary first-grade literacy instruction. *Reading Teacher, 52,* 462–476.

Murphy, P. K., Wilkinson, I. A. G., Soter, A. O., Hennessey, M. N., & Alexander, J. F. (2009). Examining the effects of classroom discussion on students' high-level comprehension of text: A meta-analysis. *Journal of Educational Psychology, 101,* 740–764.

National Reading Panel. (2000). *Report of the National Reading Panel.* Washington, DC: Government Printing Office.

New Standards Primary Literacy Committee. (1999). *Reading and writing grade by grade: Primary literacy standards for kindergarten through third grade.*Pittsburgh: National Center on Education and the Economy and the University of Pittsburgh.

Nystrand, M. (2006). Research on the role of classroom discourse as it affects reading comprehension. *Research in the Teaching of English, 40,* 392–411.

Otero, J. C., & Kintsch, W. (1992). Failures to detect contradictions in a text: What readers believe versus what they read. *Psychological Science, 3,* 229–235.

Paivio, A. (1991). Dual coding theory: Retrospect and current status. *Canadian Journal of Psychology, 45*(3), 255–287.

Paris, A. H., & Paris, S. G. (2003). Assessing narrative comprehension in young children. *Reading Research Quarterly, 38,* 36–76.

Pearson, P. D., & Duke, N. K. (2002). Comprehension instruction in the primary grades. In C. C. Block & M. Pressley (Eds.), *Comprehension instruction: Research-based best practices* (pp. 247–258). New York: Guilford Press.

Pressley, M. (2005). *Reading instruction that works* (3rd ed.): *The case for balanced teaching.* New York: Guilford Press.

Pressley, M., & Afflerbach, P. (1995). *Verbal protocols of reading: The nature of constructively responsive reading.* Hillsdale, NJ: Erlbaum.

Pressley, M., Almasi, J., Schuder, T., Bergman, J., Hite, S., El-Dinary, P. B., et al. (1994). Transactional instruction of comprehension strategies: The Montgomery County, Maryland, SAIL program. *Reading and Writing Quarterly: Overcoming Learning Difficulties, 10,* 5–19.

Pressley, M., Duke, N. K., Gaskins, I. W., Fingeret, L., Halladay, J., Hilden, K., et al. (2008). Working with struggling readers: Why we must get beyond the simple view of reading and visions of how it might be done. In T. Gutkin & C. R. Reynolds (Eds.), *The handbook of school psychology* (4th ed.). New York: Wiley.

Pressley, M., El-Dinary, P. B., Gaskins, I. W., Schuder, T., Bergman, J., Almasi, J., et al. (1992). Beyond direct explanation: Transactional instruction of reading comprehension strategies. *Elementary School Journal, 92,* 513–555.

Purcell-Gates, V., Duke, N. K., & Martineau, J. A. (2007). Learning to read and write genre-specific text: Roles of authentic experience and explicit teaching. *Reading Research Quarterly, 42,* 8–45.

RAND Reading Study Group. (2002). *Reading for understanding: Toward an R & D program in reading comprehension.* Santa Monica, CA: RAND.

Reutzel, D. R., Smith, J. A., & Fawson, P. C. (2005). An evaluation of two approaches for teaching reading comprehension strategies in the primary years using science information texts. *Early Childhood Research Quarterly, 20,* 276–305.

Schneider, B., Carnoy, M., Kilpatrick, J., Schmidt, W. H., & Shavelson, R. J. (2007). *Estimating causal effects using experimental and observational designs.* Washington, DC: American Educational Research Association.

Smith, J., Lee, V., & Newmann, F. (2001). *Instruction and achievement in Chicago elementary schools.* Chicago: Consortium on Chicago Schools Research.

Snow, C. E., Burns, M. S., & Griffin, P. (Eds.). (1998). *Preventing reading difficulties in young children.* Washington, DC: National Academy Press.

Stahl, K. A. D. (2004). Proof, practice, and promise: Comprehension strategy instruction in the primary grades. *Reading Teacher, 57,* 598–610.

Stahl, K. A. D. (2008). The effects of three instructional methods on the reading comprehension and content acquisition of novice readers. *Journal of Literacy Research, 40,* 359–393.

Stanovich, K. E. (1986). Matthew effects in reading: Some consequences of individual differences in the acquisition of literacy. *Reading Research Quarterly, 21,* 360–407.

Stanovich, K. E. (2004). Matthew effects in reading: Some consequences of individual differences in the acquisition of literacy. In R. B. Ruddell & N. J. Unrau (Eds.), *Theoretical models and processes of reading* (5th ed., pp. 454–516). Newark, DE: International Reading Association.

Stanovich, K. E., Cunningham, A. E. (2004). Inferences from correlational data: Exploring associations with reading experience. In N. K. Duke & M. H. Mallette (Eds.), *Literacy research methodologies* (pp. 28–45). New York: Guilford Press.

Stauffer, R. G. (1969). *Directing reading maturity as a cognitive process.* New York: Harper & Row.

Stauffer, R. G. (1976). *Teaching reading as a thinking process.* New York: HarperCollins.

Taylor, B. M., & Pearson, P. D. (Eds.). (2002). *Teaching reading: Effective schools, accomplished teachers.* Mahwah, NJ: Erlbaum.

Taylor, B. M., Pearson, P. D., Clark, K., & Walpole, S. (2000). Effective schools and accomplished teachers: Lessons about primary-grade reading instruction in low-income schools. *Elementary School Journal, 101,* 121–165.

Tower, C. (2002). "It's a snake, you guys!": The power of text characteristics on children's responses to information books. *Research in the Teaching of English, 37,* 55–88.

Vygotsky, L. S. (1978). *Mind in society: The development of higher psychological processes.* Cambridge, MA: Harvard University Press.

Whitehurst, G. J., Arnold, D. H., Epstein, J. N., Angell, A. L., Smith, M., & Fischel, J. E. (1994). A picture book reading intervention in daycare and home for children from low-income families. *Developmental Psychology, 30,* 679–689.

Williams, J. P. (2005). Instruction in reading comprehension for primary-grade students: A focus on text structure. *Journal of Special Education, 39,* 6–18.

3

Comprehending in the Subject Areas

The Challenges of Comprehension, Grades 7–12, and What to Do about Them

Elizabeth Birr Moje

COMPREHEND THIS: INTRODUCING THE PROBLEM

Day in and day out, most people comprehend texts of one kind or another. Despite, or perhaps because of, the omnipresence of comprehension tasks in daily life, very few people can offer a clear definition of just what it means to comprehend something. Even people who have studied comprehension for years find it difficult. The question becomes even more complicated when we consider the many different forms of representation to be comprehended, including print texts, oral texts, images, and charts or other graphics. Even more complex: The integration of all of them. And just to put the final bit of icing on the cake, consider what is required to comprehend texts of different domains. Is there a difference, for example, between the comprehension of a mathematics word problem and the comprehension of a newspaper article? A journal entry from the 17th century? A lab report? An excerpt of a novel?

Conversely, think about the act of comprehension required across different types of texts all within one domain of learning. For example, different reading practices and skills may be required to read a science textbook compared to a report written by a scientist, even when the concepts of study are at the same conceptual level. More to the point, do experts read differently from novices precisely because they are experts (i.e., they have the knowledge, skills, and strategies they need to read proficiently in their domains)? If so, then why would anyone imagine that secondary school students could or should read subject-area domain texts in order to learn the knowledge, skills, and strategies of the domain?

Although we have a strong research base around a number of these questions, many remain largely unanswered in specific ways. In particular, questions of reading in the subject-matter domains have been largely unattended in research on middle and high school literacy until recently.[1] Even more critical, there is little research or practical experience with how to *teach* within and across those differences in ways that support a novice's developing competence with more and more sophisticated texts of different domains. And yet educators in a range of contexts ask young people to comprehend print texts in multiple domains of secondary school learning on a regular basis. Add to this demand the fact that as young people move through schooling, they experience more and more complex texts. Moreover, it is often the case that very little instruction in how to read text is offered beyond the upper elementary grades, even as texts become more complex. Finally, the possibilities for engagement in nonschool texts and experiences increase as children move into adolescence because they are more independent (Eccles et al., 1993; Moje, 2002).

This is the challenge I address in this chapter. *Answering* these questions is beyond the scope of this chapter (or even my life's research and teaching agenda), but the chapter touches on a number of these issues. To begin, I provide a working definition of comprehension. Next, an example drawn from a real-world science text helps to distinguish comprehension at the elementary level from what we ask young people to do at the secondary level. To conclude the chapter, I offer planning and teaching practices that can support young people not only in comprehending sophisticated texts of different domains, but also in *learning to comprehend* texts that challenge their working knowledge and, at times, their interest and engagement.

A WORKING DEFINITION OF COMPREHENSION

Comprehension—whether of oral or written text—is at its core about understanding what a speaker or author is trying to say. Even this simple definition, however, could easily inspire controversy. Is comprehension a matter of figuring out what an author is trying to say or about making meaning of concepts for one's own purposes? Should one try to get at the author's intentions or is that impossible? Does all meaning reside in the text or in an interaction between text and reader? Is comprehension about determining the main or primary idea(s) being expressed or communicated in the text and understanding the relationship of supporting details to the main idea? Or is comprehension the full range of processes—information extraction, critique, summarization, synthesis, and application? A full review of the many ways of thinking about this complex phenomenon cannot be offered here (but see Pearson, Chapter 13, this volume, for more detailed analyses of comprehension research). However, I do offer a brief survey of a few definitions and components of comprehension.

In this chapter, I work from a well-established theoretical and empirical model of comprehension as the interaction of a reader and text (Rumelhart, 1994) immersed in particular activities, situated in specific and broad contexts, reading for particular purposes (Moje, Dillon, & O'Brien, 2000; Tierney & Pearson, 1981, 1992; Scribner & Cole, 1981; Snow, 2002). The elements that a *reader* brings to a text include word recognition knowledge, vocabulary knowledge, background knowledge, linguistic and textual knowledge, ability to infer meanings, the ability to use strategies to make sense when comprehension is challenged, and motivation and interest to engage with a given text (Guthrie & Wigfield, 2000; Snow, 2002; Tierney & Pearson, 1981, 1992).

Readers read for particular purposes in particular activities, as well (Scribner & Cole, 1981). After conducting a long-term, large-scale ethnographic and experimental study of readers and writers in Western Liberia, for example, Scribner and Cole (1981) concluded that literacy was not just a set of skills that people learned, but regular practices situated in the tasks people needed to accomplish on a daily basis. This point can be extended to comprehension: Understanding a text does not occur outside the purpose for which one is reading it. Think about the difference in your comprehension were you to read this chapter to guide your own teaching, versus reading it because you have to lead a discussion on it in a literacy course, versus reading it to present to colleagues across the subject-matter areas at your school. You might draw on the same concepts from the chapter, but your different purposes and applications would shape the sense you might make of the concepts as well as how you represent them to others. Similarly, think back over times when you have read something at one point in your life and then read it again several years later. Both changes in knowledge and purpose for reading may intervene on the example, reinforcing the idea that not only does purpose matter, but the specific context (whether time or space) of the act of reading may be crucial to comprehension.

The possible *contexts* that can shape a reader's meaning making are vast. For secondary school students, the contexts are potentially vaster than for young children, simply by virtue of the nature of secondary schools and of adolescence. Contexts for an adolescent can include the academic subject area in which he or she is reading (e.g., science), a context that changes from hour to hour throughout the adolescent's day; his or her ethnic background; the social situation in which he or she is reading; a broad, sociopolitical context; a family situation; peer groups; extracurricular activities; and even variations in environmental factors such as temperature or noise around a person when reading. (Moje et al., 2000).

Finally, the *text* contributes to the reading process because texts are written in a variety of ways. Texts can tell stories (i.e., narrative) or explain information (i.e., exposition), and some texts do both. Texts can pose problems to be solved or can lecture readers on methods to solve problems. Texts can be written in many different styles, relying heavily on technical language and particular ways of phrasing ideas, or they can be written to appeal to more general audiences.

HOW COMPREHENSION DEMANDS DIFFER IN ELEMENTARY AND SECONDARY SCHOOL

What makes comprehension a different task in middle and high school learning activities from the task of reading in elementary school activities? Many of the questions raised in the introduction of this chapter foreshadowed the answer to this question: In short, reading at the secondary school level is more demanding, in part because the texts are longer and more complex, in part because the expectations for prior knowledge are so high, and in part because the concepts become more abstract and complex. Complexity increases as a function of domain specificity, of the nature of concepts addressed in the upper levels of schooling, and as a function of the length and quality of texts (Alexander & Jetton, 2001; Alexander, Kulikowich, & Jetton, 1994; Snow, 2009).

These points are coupled with two other extremely important observations. One is that we know that regular and explicit literacy instruction tends to diminish around grade 6. Students may pick up "tips" on how to read certain kinds of texts on an occasional basis, but sustained instruction in literate processes and practices is rare (Biancarosa & Snow, 2004).

Equally important, many claim that students' interest in "voluntary reading" also diminishes at about the same time period, arguing that as students go through school from upper elementary through high school, they become less intrinsically motivated to read or have less curiosity about new books and topics, and they spend less time immersed in reading longer and more complicated texts (Guthrie, Hoa, Wigfield, Tonks, & Perencevich, 2006).[2] Nonschool texts and experiences are often more engaging than the texts youth are asked to read in school (Alvermann, Young, Green, & Wisenbaker, 1999; Leander & Lovvorn, 2006; Moje, Overby, Tysvaer, & Morris, 2008). Simultaneously, these same researchers argue, students become more extrinsically motivated to read school-based texts because they become more grade-oriented, competitive, and driven by conceptions of their abilities as readers (Guthrie & Davis, 2003). Although all students lose some of their intrinsic motivation for reading between grades 4 and 7, proficient readers tend to maintain more of a balance between intrinsic and extrinsic motivation (Guthrie & Davis, 2003).

Another way to think about what some label as "lack of motivation to read" is that as young people age, they meet competing demands on their time. They are often expected to complete more school homework, extracurricular activities increase, domestic responsibilities (e.g., care-taking of younger siblings or working outside the home) increase, and they have more access to peers. In fact, among the most common reasons given by adolescents for *not reading* outside of school are time, noise and other distractions, and too much homework (Moje et al., 2008).

In a digital age, young people also have access to a global network of peers, texts, and activities (e.g., massive, multiuser computer games) that are often more compelling or engaging than are the texts of schools. When one considers each of these changes, together with the probable lack of change in young people's overall literacy skill (due to lack of continued, sustained literacy instruction), it should be clear that secondary school comprehension is a difficult task. Indeed, attending to these issues puts a different spin on recent test results: Perhaps we should be surprised that so many youth in secondary school read at even basic levels.

The argument that youth, who are increasingly disengaged in school, encounter increasingly complex texts with little instructional support suggests that we need to tackle the problem of text (all kinds, from print-based to image-based) in subject-matter instruction at the secondary level. Tackling that problem requires some insight into what makes the texts of secondary school more challenging. As noted previously, secondary school texts are usually longer than elementary school texts and are typically written in a smaller font than children are accustomed to reading in elementary school. The change even in format can be dramatic and abrupt. More challenging, however, are assumptions about the knowledge young people bring to the reading task, from world knowledge to subject-matter domain knowledge, discursive knowledge, semantic knowledge, and pragmatic knowledge, to name just a few (Moje & Speyer, 2008).

Consider, for example, a text titled, "Top U.S. Warship delivers aid to Georgia" (CNN.com, September, 2008),[3] distributed in a sixth-grade social studies class in the first week of school. Students were asked to write a summary of the article, using the categories of who, what, where, when, and how as guides. The text consisted of 21 "paragraphs," each one to three lines long, with none more than one sentence in length. Here, for example, are just the first three paragraphs:

> (CNN)—A U.S. Navy command ship arrived in the Georgian port of Poti on Friday to deliver humanitarian supplies following the republic's war with Russia last month.
>
> The *USS Mount Whitney* will also coordinate the work of a group of NATO ships currently in the Black Sea, the Russian news agency Interfax reported.
>
> Two other U.S. vessels have already arrived in the Georgian port of Batumi, south of Poti, delivering humanitarian supplies, the U.S. Navy said.

One sixth-grader who read the article proclaimed it to be "the worst writing" she had ever read because it was "just a list of random statements." Then she asked, "And which *who* am I supposed to name? Russia? Georgia? The United States? Dick Cheney?"

This young person's legitimate questions reveal her lack of prior knowledge about the Russian–Georgian conflict (knowledge of which *might* have simplified the task of deciding on a particular subject—or *who*—for the summary), but also her lack of knowledge about how to handle complex who–what–where–when–how tasks. This particular young person had experience with such tasks in elementary school, but they were tightly constrained reading tasks, with clear subjects, foci, locations, time periods, and processes controlled by the teacher and text made available (e.g., there was usually only one *who* in a text). The jump from relatively simple texts and tasks to relatively complex texts and tasks was massive, abrupt, and unscaffolded in this instance, emphasizing the need for teachers to acknowledge and mediate several factors, including the demands of secondary level texts and the legitimate lack of preparation young people might have for such texts. I use the word *legitimate* to refer to lack of preparation because I do not wish to play into the popular assumption that when young people come to middle or high school without the skills necessary to handle advanced texts and tasks, it is somehow the fault of prior teaching. In some situations that may certainly be the case, but more often than not, it is the task or text that is new and demanding. This newness requires instruction by the people who assign the texts and tasks, that is, by the secondary school teachers in the subject-matter domains. Secondary school subject-area teachers are the people who know their subject areas best and thus are best equipped to teach students how to read and write in the accepted ways of specialized domains. But what will that take?

First, the field needs a better understanding of the knowledge and skills demanded in subject-area domains. Second, it would be helpful for teachers to consider how to select, analyze, and use the texts of respective domains, rather than simply using the assigned textbook or locating isolated pieces and assigning them with little or no instruction. Finally, teachers and researchers alike could advance work in this area by thinking in terms of regular teaching *practices* (Moje & Speyer, 2008) or *routines* (Deshler & Schumaker, 2005; Schoenbach, Greenleaf, Cziko, & Hurwitz, 1999) and accompanying subject-area literacy strategies (Buehl, 2002; Vacca & Vacca, 2004).

TYPES OF KNOWLEDGE AND SKILL NECESSARY FOR COMPREHENSION

A previous analysis I conducted with a colleague in a high school classroom indicated that at least four types of knowledge and/or skill are necessary to comprehend advanced texts of the secondary school subject areas (Moje & Speyer, 2008). These knowledge types include (1) semantic, (2) discipline-specific (historical, scientific, mathematical, literary, geographical, etc.), (3) discursive, and (4) pragmatic. We further illustrated that at times the working knowledge and skill from one subject area are required for comprehension within a different subject area. Reading statistics germane to the social studies or natural sciences, for example, requires mathematical knowledge and skill. Understanding the import of a particular mathematical concept may require historical knowledge, and so on. Indeed, the more advanced the subject matter concepts, the more likely it is that disciplinary knowledge and skill from multiple areas will be required to make sense of texts (see Moje & Speyer, 2008, for a simple example).

I refer readers to that analysis for social studies knowledge and skill demands; in this chapter, I examine an excerpt of a text that a student might encounter in a typical high school science classroom to demonstrate how different knowledge and skills are demanded for the comprehension and interpretation of text. Assume, for example, that a teacher is interested in teaching a unit on genetics to high school students in a biology class, and decides to use the following article from a popular science website (*www.scienceagogo.com*, October 27, 2008) to demonstrate the application of content concepts, reinforce vocabulary the students are learning, and to show students that the classroom concepts have meaning in the real world (only a brief excerpt is provided here).

**Immune system overdrive responsible for cold symptoms
by Kate Melville**

The human rhinovirus (HRV) cops most of the blame for the sneezing and runny nose that we associate with the common cold, but in reality, it's not the virus but its ability to manipulate our genes that causes the most annoying cold symptoms. Now, for the first time, researchers have revealed how HRV hijacks our genes to trigger this overblown immune response, possibly opening the door for new therapeutic treatments for the common cold. "The study's findings are a major step toward more targeted cold prevention and treatment strategies while also serving as a valuable roadmap for the broader respiratory science community," the University of Calgary's David Proud, lead author of the study, told the *American Journal of Respiratory and Critical Care Medicine....*

Source: American Thoracic Society, Procter & Gamble

Semantic Knowledge

That semantic—or word—knowledge is needed to make sense of this passage may seem rather obvious and is often the first factor considered by teachers and reading theorists alike. In the first paragraph alone excerpted above, the passage is ripe with technical language, including *human rhinovirus (HRV), genes,* and *lead author.* The piece goes on to include language about *inoculations, immune response, nasal mucosa, antiviral proteins, viperin,* and *pro-inflammatory cytokines.*

These technical terms are important because we quickly home in on them as educators, worrying that youth readers will be tripped up by such terms. What is interesting, however, is that although these technical terms are often daunting to adolescent readers, they are not usually the most problematic in terms of comprehension because readers are aware that they do not know the meaning of these terms, and they recognize that one point of the passage or larger unit of study is to be introduced to such terms. There is, then, no shame in not knowing the terms.

Technical terms are important, but equally problematic are everyday terms that readers think they know but whose meanings are specialized in the context of the passage and domain. *Subjects* is such a term. In most cases, the average adolescent will be able to decode and/or quickly recognize the word *subjects* but may not understand that it functions as a reference to research participants studied under particular conditions in the context of science and of this passage. *Therapeutic* is another example of an everyday word that many young people may have read or heard, but perhaps not in the context of a drug regimen. More interesting is the fact that the word *genes* may actually seem to be an everyday word to youth readers, given its everyday parlance on popular crime shows or in the news media. But the likelihood that readers really know the scientific meaning of *gene* is slim.

Finally, the passage also includes *everyday* terms that might be especially challenging to adolescent readers due to their unusual syntactical use in this passage. The phrase, "human rhinovirus (HRV) cops," for example, may demand a second look even of adult readers, especially with *cops* following a technical term that may throw off readers. These terms are not words that will pose decoding or word recognition challenges, but their syntactic use changes semantics, implicating the role of syntactic knowledge intertwined with semantic knowledge in passages of this complexity. Most youth will be likely to have heard many of these terms before; however, the difference between their casual use and their meaning in this passage may be critical.

It is also worth noting that the author of this piece has used a number of verbs (e.g., *cops, hijacks, manipulates*) that suggest a strategic orientation on the part of the *HRV*. Is this move intentional on the part of the journalist, signaling the active debate in biological science communities over whether viruses are intelligent life forms, or is it simply a matter of rhetorical device on the part of the journalist? Such a question reveals the way that deep comprehension is dependent on the intersection of semantic knowledge (recognizing that such words signal a strategic—and perhaps even *sly*—orientation), rhetorical and discursive knowledge (the understanding that authors write with an audience in mind and that writing conventions differ from one discourse community to another—i.e., the news media to the scientific community), and disciplinary knowledge (the knowledge of the contested status of the virus in biological science).

The mention of disciplinary knowledge takes us from the discussion of semantic knowledge, or knowledge of words and word phrases, to that broader of category of disciplinary knowledge: What does it mean to *know* something from a disciplinary standpoint, and how does that knowledge shape one's comprehension?

Disciplinary Knowledge

One dilemma of reading comprehension at the secondary school level is that although the relationship between comprehension and prior knowledge is extraordinarily well documented (e.g., Alexander et al., 1994;

Anderson & David, 1984; Kintsch & Van Dijk, 1978), most teachers expect young people to read and *learn from* texts on subjects they have not yet encountered. The idea that anyone could really *learn from* the text above with only a layperson's knowledge of genetics and epidemiology is rather farfetched. And yet, we expect that of young people on a daily basis because they are assigned texts to read regularly, whether textbooks or other kinds of text materials.

For example, in the HRV passage shown previously, the reader must know something about how viruses work, both to understand the content of the text and to be able to question the author's use of language that makes a virus seem like a sentient life form. Moreover, the many technical terms and phrases used in the passage require disciplinary knowledge. What, for example, does it mean when the author refers to an "immune response"? How are "therapeutic treatments" unique from other kinds of treatments? As the text progresses (not included here), it becomes equally important to understand how scientific experiments are conducted because the text refers to "sham inoculation," obtaining "cell scrapings from the nasal passages," the passage of time (a key ingredient in growing bacteria), and "control" and "HRV-inoculated" groups. The text becomes more and more dependent on scientific domain knowledge as one continues reading—a fact that might be missed by a teacher searching for a real-world piece to exemplify concepts about viruses. Of note is the fact that the passage becomes more domain-specific not only because of the increasing use of technical vocabulary (e.g., "antiviral proteins," "viperin," "pro-inflammatory cytokines," "chemotaxis"), but also because it assumes an understanding of the cause–effect relationships in scientific experimentation, of inquiry processes, and of ways of communicating ideas (more on that to come). These are all aspects of disciplinary knowledge that need to be taught even as we engage students in reading about these concepts. In short, we cannot expect young people to learn independently from these disciplinary texts, because these texts are written inside the discourse community of science and thus depend on readers already possessing some working knowledge of the domains, their epistemological assumptions, and the resulting discourse and terminology.

Some readers might appropriately wonder at this juncture whether, in fact, this knowledge dependence claim is really true of *textbooks*. Textbooks are, after all, written to be readable for learners and thus should not require extensive disciplinary knowledge, at least in theory. They are meant to impart disciplinary knowledge, are they not? This is a reasonable question, but research on textbooks demonstrates that, in fact, textbooks suffer from two problems: They are often poorly organized, and they make extensive prior domain knowledge demands on readers (Anderson & Armbruster, 1984; Armbruster & Anderson, 1985; Chambliss & Calfee, 1998). Even introductory textbooks make domain knowledge demands; indeed introductory texts in their attempt to only survey the domain landscape, may make even more domain knowledge demands than more subject-specific texts. It is often the case that in the attempt to provide a scan of basic facts about a topic, introductory textbooks leave out key ideas that would help the reader understand relationships between key concepts. Consider, for example, this passage on the 1920s drawn from an eighth-grade history textbook (Davidson, 2005):

> ### The Prosperous Twenties
>
> The auto industry was important in the booming economy. Factories turned out new consumer goods such as radios, vacuum cleaners, and refrigerators. Many people also invested in the stock market for the first time. Stock prices rose steadily. Women could now vote. More women also joined the workforce. Young women known as flappers shocked older Americans with their short skirts and reckless behavior. (p. 553)

Much could be said about this particular passage, but in this case I use it simply to illustrate how much making an inference about prosperity in the 1920s depends on having some knowledge about the 1920s. Adult readers with extensive background knowledge can, with some effort, make connections among these ideas (although in my professional development work with groups of teachers, I have noted that most adults come up with variations on what they consider to be the main idea of this passage). The typical eighth-grade student, however, reads this text as a series of disconnected or tenuously connected statements (Moje, 2007).

Consequently, secondary school content teachers find themselves in a bit of a bind: They cannot rely on textbooks alone because textbooks often contribute to the reading challenge for young people and because many youth find textbooks less than stimulating (Stockdill & Moje, 2007), but real-world and primary source texts also present reading challenges for young people because these texts also make disciplinary knowledge demands. The *Scienceagogo* site, for example, can assume that its readers know and care about science concepts; why would anyone who did not know or care about science search a popular science website?

Discursive Knowledge

Discursive knowledge refers to an understanding of the ways texts are constructed in the domain in which they are written and how they are tied to the purposes for which they were originally written. Secondary school students need both the general knowledge that domains have different discursive demands—which the New London Group (1996) referred to as *metadiscursivity*—and the specific knowledge of particular domain discourses. For example, as many analysts of scientific text and discourse have noted (e.g., Gee, 2001; Hand, Wallace, & Yang, 2004; Hicks, 1995/1996; Lemke, 1990), scientific writing typically removes the subject from an action, turning actions or processes into things and phenomena (e.g. "we studied three processes" becomes "the study of three processes"). Scientific writing also requires precision in language use, thus proliferating technical terms that capture as closely as possible the precise meaning of a phenomenon. Furthermore, scientific writing uses what might seem to be common, everyday words in particular ways (e.g., *significant* has a statistical meaning in science and would not be used to mean *important* or *noteworthy*, although statistically significant findings are both important and noteworthy). Finally, as Lemke (1990) noted, scientific writing is based on certain assumptions about the world, which he referred to as "thematic formations." In particular, scientific experimentation rests on the idea that phenomena can be identified, studied, and known; that correlations between phenomena do not equal causation, and that variation can and must be controlled in order to determine causation. Thematic formations of science as a discipline and profession, for example, revolve around deepening, and often challenging, everyday knowledge. Scientific themes also focus on controlling the natural world in the attempt to produce innovations, tools, or solutions that improve human life. Thematic formations differ for each discipline or domain of study, thus producing different ways of talking, reading, and writing in the different subject-matter areas.

With these discursive points in mind, the HRV text illustrated in this chapter poses an additional challenge to adolescent readers because it actually represents a kind of hybrid between scientific and everyday discourses. The conflicting uses of terms discussed previously underscore this hybrid by illustrating that viruses are represented as agents that can manipulate, when in actual practice, scientists cannot determine whether viruses "think" or simply "act." What's more, the discourse of the piece, written in somewhat friendly or everyday language, might send mixed messages to young readers about the quality of the science therein or about conventions for writing scientific findings. Furthermore, as noted previously, the piece becomes more and more "scientific" as it progresses, demanding that the reader navigate the discourse communities of everyday or news articles and the discourse of science.

Pragmatic Knowledge

Making sense of this text also requires another kind of knowledge that is tied to the question of purpose. In short, why has this text been written, and why is the reader reading it? *Pragmatic knowledge* involves the reader's recognition that he or she should get information, ideas, or perspectives from texts. The question, however, is which information, ideas, or perspectives are to be taken away from the text, and once one has them, what is to be done with them? Studies of expert readers (Leinhardt, 1989; Wineburg, 1998) have demonstrated that they either ask for, articulate, or have in their minds an explicit purpose when approaching a text. How many high-school-aged readers approach texts such as the human rhinovirus newspaper article with a specific purpose in mind? How many high school teachers help readers set a purpose for the various texts they read? And when we do set purposes for student readers, how clear and specific are they? Equally important, do the purposes match those of the discipline? A scientific researcher who studies HRV would be likely to read the HRV text with his or her own investigations in mind. How often do we use texts in secondary school classrooms as ways of launching investigations, framing problems, or expanding on findings? More often than not, we assign texts to be read and ask students to answer "comprehension questions" about the text or to have a class discussion of them. How might comprehension of the text change if students were asked to read domain-specific texts for domain-specific purposes?

The mention of questions leads to yet another type of pragmatic knowledge useful for comprehension: the recognition that texts can be questioned. Many of the youth with whom I work on a regular basis seem to struggle with asking and answering analytic and critical questions. My analysis of their discussion practices does not suggest a lack of cognitive skill or even of understanding of the text's main ideas. Rather I have observed a lack of movement to higher or deeper levels of comprehension, meaning making, or understanding. As illustrated in a previous analysis of young people reading the Emergency Quota Act of 1921, not one student questioned what the "emergency" was or why the law relied on U.S. Census data from 1910 rather than from 1920, the Census closest to the enactment of the law (Moje & Speyer, 2008). When prompted to question these things, students were able to generate reasonable hypotheses, but they did not ask those questions of the texts themselves.

In addition, readers need to be able to recognize when they need more information than is available in a text. In order to obtain that information, however, readers need additional knowledge or skill, specifically, *search* and *analytical* skills and knowledge. Let us assume that high school readers possess all of the different kinds of knowledge described above. They still need to build relevant knowledge or information (we can assume that they do not possess it in depth, or we would not be teaching them). Thus, they either need the information handed to them (say, in the form of a lecture), or they require knowledge of how to access relevant information. Once they have access to the relevant information, they must be able to make sense of it. The demand for additional knowledge directs attention to the kind of search skills needed in a digital age, where obtaining information is a relatively simple task, but sorting through it, analyzing its validity, and making sense of the information and its relationship to the topic and texts under study is challenging. Not all texts are equally valid; learning how to analyze the validity of a text has always been central to good teaching, but is even more imperative in a digital world (Coiro, 2003).

This brief analysis of the types of knowledge and skill necessary for reading even a short piece of text should reveal the complexity of what it means to comprehend something at the secondary school level. Indeed, this list is quite probably incomplete, particularly as one considers all the different types of text that secondary school teachers and students encounter (or should encounter) on a daily basis. The analysis may make the task of teaching students to understand and use complex texts in complex ways seem daunting, even impossible. Many subject-area teachers recognize how much young people struggle with the texts of the discipline, and in frustration, they simply avoid using texts in their classrooms.

Avoiding texts, however, just sidesteps the challenges and potentially disenfranchises young people, especially those who do not have access to disciplinary text knowledge and skills in other contexts of their lives. National test scores seem to bear out this concern: Data from the National Assessment of Educational Progress (Lee, Grigg, & Donahue, 2007) show that although a reasonable number of youth can read at "basic" levels, few can read with proficiency *or* at advanced levels. Similarly, a recent report of the American College Testing service (ACT, 2006) posited that 51% of youth who took the ACT test were not prepared to deal with the reading demands of the college or university. These statistics, together with the analysis provided here, suggest that secondary school teachers need to mediate text reading for their students. Reading in specialized domains requires that people be taught to read in those domains. Reading in the domains *is* reading to learn, but it nevertheless requires that young people also learn to read these specialized texts. Subject-matter teachers are the best people to teach youth how to make sense of the texts of those domains. But where does one begin?

IMPLICATIONS FOR TEACHING

In this section I focus on two aspects of teaching demanded by the recognition that comprehension is a complex process and that the texts of the upper-level subject areas are challenging to all adolescent readers. One is the importance of thinking about how texts are chosen for use in the classroom. The second addresses the teaching practices used to support students in working with those texts.

Selecting and Analyzing Texts of Instruction

Too often, middle and high school teachers assume that the course textbook should serve as the unquestioned textual resource for classroom instruction. Not only do I want to provide ideas for analyzing classroom texts, but I want also to encourage teachers to seek out other kinds of texts (cf. Bain, 2005; Lee & Spratley, 2006; Snow, 2009). Students across the different subject areas can benefit from encountering many different types of texts that cast subject-area concepts in different ways (Lee & Spratley, 2006; Solomon, van Der Kerkhof, & Moje, in press). Using both the textbook and many other types of texts, however, requires that teachers analyze the texts so that they know where and when they will need to scaffold students' comprehension, where they work in particular kinds of literacy strategy instruction, and where and when they can assign texts to be read independently. The questions shown in Figure 3.1 could be useful in such an analysis, although they are just a starting place for analysis. Once one analyzes possible texts, then one must make decisions about which texts will be used to do what and about how the texts will be used. It is particularly important to decide whether texts need to be scaffolded in terms of vocabulary, prior knowledge, and discourse. At times, however, one text can scaffold another.

Bain (2005) provides a helpful illustration of the process of text scaffolding in an analysis of his teaching of Columbus's exploration of the world in a high school history class. His first step was to determine the historical problem of how explorers viewed the world as flat or spherical in the late 1400s; Bain—a historian and 25-year veteran of teaching high school history—knew that many people of Columbus's time actually believed the world to be round, not flat, as the popular myth suggests. The problem he wanted students to investigate then was whether Columbus was, indeed, the only brilliant fellow to posit that the world was round—a point that might lead students to question other taken-for-granted historical "truths." He thus selected texts by historians to support students' speculations that everyone but Columbus thought that the world was flat in 1492. He presented these texts to students, fol-

1. For what purposes am I using the text?
2. How will I set a purpose for the students? What kind of purpose will help them learn the content best?
3. What can I assume students already know or believe about the concept I want them to learn from this text?
4. What seems to be the main idea the author wants to put forward? What other ideas in the text might get in the way of the main idea?
5. What are the key ideas or concepts in the text that support the author's intention?
6. Is any key information missing? If so, how might the missing pieces interfere with students' comprehension?
7. Is any of the information extraneous? How could I address the extra information? Why might the author have included it?
8. What challenges does the text pose for me, as an adult reader with relatively deep knowledge of this subject?
9. What challenges might the text pose for adolescent readers of this text?
10. What knowledge does the author seem to assume a reader will bring to this text?
11. What aspects of the text would my students find most interesting?
12. What aspects of the text would my students find most difficult?
13. What cultural, racial/ethnic, or gendered connections might my students make to this text?
14. How would I describe the structure and tone of this text?
15. What are the key words or technical terms in the text?
16. How do I assess the organization and flow of ideas within this passage?
17. What, if any, texts are embedded within this text?
18. What other texts could accompany and expand on this one?

FIGURE 3.1. Questions to guide analyses of disciplinary texts and textbooks.

lowed by a text with a radically different message: a picture of Greek Titan Atlas holding a globe. This image-based text served to contest the other sources, given that the Greek civilization existed just a few centuries before Columbus, and so confounded the students. In creating that confound, Bain produced cognitive dissonance, which opened a space for new learning to occur (i.e., it sets a purpose for examining other texts), all by simply offering multiple print- and image-based texts.

Bain then provided his students with more texts to support, extend, or challenge their thinking and comprehension, supporting their comprehension of individual texts when necessary, based on his analysis of whether and how the students could read them. Bain's example demonstrates that selection and use of texts to support content learning and reading comprehension has to be done in the service of particular cognitive and pedagogical functions and most definitely in the service of subject-area learning. He also illustrated that the question of selecting texts is less about the length or density of text (although he edited text length as he judged necessary), and is instead more about the juxtaposition of one text to others and to what he knew about his students' thinking and prior experiences.

Teaching Practices for Enhancing Comprehension in the Secondary School Subject Areas

The usual answer for addressing the challenges of comprehension at the secondary school level has been to offer content-area literacy teaching "strategies" that build on what we know good readers do when they read. These strategies are intended to teach readers both the skills they need for making sense of content texts and the strategies they can use when their comprehension breaks down. The idea of using strategies is critical for secondary school students because regardless of how proficient a reader is, the possibility for comprehension skills to be challenged in secondary school is high simply because the content and accompanying texts become more and more domain-specific and thus less and less likely to have been encountered previously. In other words, if proficient comprehension is dependent in large part on prior knowledge, then the more obscure or specialized the topic or concept being read, the less likely the reader will have extensive prior knowledge. Thus, readers need to be equipped with the ability to recognize their own comprehension challenges and then strategize about how to address them. Enter the teaching of content literacy comprehension strategies. The problem that arises, of course, is one that has already been mentioned: Even strategy use is dependent on knowledge. Thus, if the reader is already struggling with a piece of text because prior knowledge is minimal, then how does he or she know which strategies will work best?

Another problem in considering the teaching of content-literacy strategies as a solution to the challenges of comprehension is that historically these strategies have been taught in generic ways, as if previewing a text, for example, is done in the same way regardless of the text itself, the needs of the learners, or the purpose of the activity for which the text is being read.

Content-area literacy teaching strategies provide a framework for thinking and an organization for instruction, but they may not address the greatest challenges presented by advanced content-area texts being read by a wide variety of youth (i.e., who may or may not care). We need to continue to use literacy teaching strategies, but those strategies appear to work best if embedded in content teaching *practices* that make working with texts central to the work of content learning (Greenleaf, Schoenbach, Cziko, & Mueller, 2001; Sutherland, Moje, Cleveland, &

Heitzman, 2006). In what follows, I recommend teaching practices and related literacy teaching and learning strategies. The practices are activities that should frame subject-area pedagogy on a daily basis, with literacy teaching and learning strategies inserted as tools for engaging in the practices.

Knowledge Building and Purpose Setting

To address the quite reasonable lack of prior domain-specific knowledge that young people bring into subject-matter classrooms, it is crucial to engage in knowledge building. However, it is also crucial that this knowledge building does not take only the form of lecturing to students. The practices suggested in what follows are ways to engage students in constructing the knowledge they need to make sense of texts. These activities also serve to set purposes or frame problems for reading, thus enhancing the possibility that students will be motivated to read and will be able to locate and analyze information and concepts offered in texts.

• Preview texts with strategies such as K-W-L, anticipation guides, preview guides, and advanced organizers. When previewing, keep in mind the purpose you have set for the reading. It is easy to lose focus when previewing, especially if students have a great deal to say about the topic. Equally important, staying focused on your purpose will allow you to make decisions about how much to preview, how long to continue the previewing activity, and what aspects to take up in later phases of instruction. Too often, previewing activities take up the bulk of instructional time, and we fail to revisit the previewing to assess what was learned. In addition, make explicit what you expect your students to do with the text (whether to ask questions, to use it in an essay, to link it to another text, and/or to critique or question its purpose in history).

• Contextualize texts. Discuss with students the purpose of the text for the context in which it was written. Who was its author? What did the author intend? To whom was the author writing? Although these are questions that historians routinely ask of texts in their work (Wineburg, 1991; Bain, 2006), they are relevant for students reading texts in any content area, because no matter what the text is, students are reading it outside of the context in which it was written. Often mathematics and science teachers will argue that context does not matter for the texts of mathematics and science, but all texts are produced in and for particular contexts and purposes, and students benefit from knowing what those are or knowing how to ask what they are and how to find out and assess those contexts and purposes.

• Talk about the texts using text discussion strategies such as close reading, dictionary searches, concept mapping of ideas in texts, and text–self/community/world connections. As you talk about texts, define words together and talk about nuances in meaning. Model for students how to ask questions even at the word level.

  • Make texts visible. Too often teachers introduce new concepts by using new words that secondary school students have never seen written. They hear the word and make it part of their oral vocabulary, but they do not get to connect the written form with the word they heard pronounced. Project sections of text on an overhead screen so that students can see and hear words read and so that you can point to words as you read. Look up important words together in the dictionary while also pointing to them on a common text. Similarly, teachers often talk about places and concrete things, but rarely make them visible for an entire class to see, critique, and discuss. One of my teaching colleagues, Tom Hoetger at Western International High School in Detroit, Michigan, uses political cartoons and other images in all of his lectures to ensure that young people are not only reading words but also reading images. He does not just flash the images at his students; he asks them to analyze the images as a whole group.

  • Read charts and tables. Mr. Hoetger makes the same move with charts and tables that students often encounter in texts. Rather than simply ignoring the charts and tables—many of which are often central to meaning making around certain concepts (see Moje & Speyer, 2008), he engages students in analyzing the trends or patterns represented in the charts and tables. At times this work requires teaching students how to read the charts and tables, a skill that is absolutely necessary in social sciences, natural sciences, and mathematics, but that is not typically taught in explicit ways.

Questioning

In the tradition of Palincsar and Brown's (1984) teaching practice of Reciprocal Teaching, I suggest that secondary school teachers model good questions about texts and subject-area concepts for their students in whole-group, small-group, and individual activities. This requires more than posing questions on a study guide, but instead involves showing students how to question texts. A model for this kind of work at the secondary level can be found in Bain's (2005, 2006; Bain, Lander, Hines, & Mercado, 2008) work in history classrooms. Bain models questioning from the very first stages of a unit by framing problems for students to tackle. He also helps to maintain motivation to continue questioning by selecting texts that challenge previously held notions of the concepts.

Visualization

Visualization is often suggested as a literacy teaching strategy in supporting students as they read literature (e.g., see Roberts & Duke, Chapter 2, this volume). In the case of social science, natural science, and mathematics, visualization teaching practices may take a different form. For example, Speyer and I (Moje & Speyer, 2008) found that we had to provide images of immigrants from the late 1800s/early 1900s to help students understand the role of racist and classist ideologies in the immigration laws that were passed during the time period. We read together, we discussed, we looks at tables of immigration statistics, but it was not until our students saw images of Italians, Poles, and Romanians that they began to understand the assumptions being made about these groups in that period. In a different way, seeing an image of a bacteria colony can help science students who are learning to investigate and understand the spread of communicable disease. Seeing a graphic representation of the slopes of two lines may help mathematics students understand how the intercept functions to signal key mathematical information to both the mathematician and to someone applying mathematic concepts (e.g., an economist or business person). In short, visualization may be about encouraging students to imagine and visualize scenes or interactions, but it may also be about providing visual images *and linking those with print and numerical information* in a way that furthers conceptual understanding.

Summarization and Synthesis

In my own teaching I sometimes use a great deal of time previewing texts or activities of a unit and, quite simply run out of time for summarizing what has been learned. Summarization, however, is a key teaching practice for helping adolescent readers learn to integrate ideas across texts. National test data (i.e., the National Assessment of Educational Progress [NAEP]) suggest that adolescent readers can generally extract main ideas from single texts, but are less proficient synthesizing ideas across texts (Lee et al., 2007). Consequently, it is critical that we engage in instruction that not only encourages summarization within, and synthesis across, texts and ideas, but that teaches students how to summarize and synthesize. Phyllis Blumenfeld (Blumenfeld, Kempler, & Krajcik, 2006) has written extensively on the importance of what she refers to as "coming back around" to concepts and ideas. Teachers can help students weave connections to other texts and to broader unit concepts throughout each unit. More important in relation to text comprehension, teachers need to "come back around" by referring back to texts in both general and highly specific ways. Comparing words used across texts, examining different kinds of sentence structures and language used (i.e., "discourse") in various text types, and highlighting points of similarity and contradiction can model for students how to look strategically across texts while also helping to develop metadiscursive skills. With regular opportunities to engage in intertextual analyses, summarization, and synthesis of texts, young people can learn to enact such practices independently and regularly, any time they read any type of text. In other words, although making intertextual connections may be an automatic, taken-for-granted practice for those of us who are proficient readers, teachers should recognize that making intertextual connections may not be the norm for our students, especially if they do not typically see how texts connect to each other in the study of a given concept. Teachers have to teach them, both by modeling and by explicitly pointing out areas of overlap and differences between and among texts of instruction. And, as Bain's (2005) work on teaching students to question commonly held historical assumptions demonstrates, we need to consider these intertextual connections *as we plan* for instruction, in order to choose the texts that will provide the most generative opportunities for dissonance and synthesis.

WHAT DOES SECONDARY SCHOOL COMPREHENSION INSTRUCTION REQUIRE OF TEACHERS?

The short answer is "a lot." Teaching young people the central concepts and practices of the subject areas is extremely challenging work. Just as comprehending the complex texts of high school classrooms makes many knowledge and skill demands on adolescent students, comprehension instruction at the high school level makes comparable knowledge and skill demands of teachers. First, teachers need to know about students' interests, knowledge, and skills. To learn about students, teachers need to develop relationships with them.

A second and related kind of knowledge is the knowledge of how to maintain student engagement in concept learning and text reading once the initial, situated interest (Renninger, Hidi, & Krapp, 1992) starts to wane. The example drawn from Bain (2005) provides one example of how such work can be done, but it also emphasizes how much careful forethought this kind of instruction takes. In addition, teachers who seek to build on students' interests as a way of engaging them must then possess skill in how to help students learn to examine their own beliefs and to develop strong arguments for or against issues. Learning to carefully consider data and assess the validity of one's own beliefs is hard work even for adults who have honed their research and analysis skills; teaching 16-year-olds to do it when they do not possess the range of experience adults possess is even harder.

The third and rather obvious kind of knowledge and skill teachers must develop to do this work is deep disciplinary knowledge and skill. Teachers need not only to know the information and concepts of the subject areas they teach in order to choose texts, analyze them, and teach them, but they also need to have a sense of how members of the discipline engage in reading and writing as an aspect of knowledge production. As Brian Hand and colleagues (Hand, Hohenshell, & Prain, 2004; Hand, Prain, & Yore, 2001; Hand, Wallace, et al., 2004) have demonstrated in multiple studies, when teachers engage students in the discourse practices of the discipline, young people learn the concepts and the writing and reading skills to a greater degree of proficiency than when taught concepts apart from disciplinary practices.

A fourth kind of knowledge is knowledge of how to support adolescents of varying skill and interest levels in building relevant knowledge or in developing skills for finding and interpreting information. Teachers also need to know not only how to develop reasoned critiques of issues, but how to teach novices to do so. For example, simply knowing that young people may never think to ask questions such as "Who lived in the United States in 1910?" is key to knowing that the question must be posed and methods for answering the question modeled. Teachers may likewise need to model how to make sense of the data they find. Teachers in the 21st century further need to hone their skills of searching and critiquing texts available on the Internet. Learning how to support young people in navigating and comprehending Internet texts (Afflerbach & Cho, 2008; Coiro, 2003; Coiro, Knobel, Lankshear, & Leu, 2008) will be increasingly important as more and more schools and homes achieve reliable access to digital sources.

It may be that subject-area teachers will read this and say, "Wait a minute; isn't it enough that I have to teach all of this content? Now you want me to teach comprehension of text as well?" This is a common question in secondary school literacy work. However, if I have performed my task well in this chapter, then it should be clear that comprehension of text is part and parcel of learning in the subject areas of the secondary school. Proficient learning in the upper levels of schooling becomes increasingly dependent on being able to access, navigate, and comprehend many different kinds of text. Thus, to teach young people how to navigate texts in secondary school should be everyone's task because it is really the process of teaching the key concepts of the subject areas.

NOTES

1. Patricia Alexander and colleagues have done groundbreaking work in domain-specific reading, but primarily focused on college-age students. Still, this work has been and will continue to be extremely useful in applications of comprehension teaching practices for older youth.
2. It should be noted that these findings refer largely to "school-like" reading.
3. The exact story is no longer retrievable on *www.CNN.com*. It should also be noted that no specific data was given on the text distributed in class, which could be considered antithetical to the work of reporting on "current events," particularly because references are made in the text to "Friday," etc. As Wineburg (1998) has noted, one of the key reading tasks of social scientists, particularly historians and political scientists, is to contextualize the sources of information they read. Without access to temporal information, the youth in this sixth-grade class would be unable to engage in historical or civic reading strategies.

REFERENCES

ACT, Inc. (2006). *Reading between the lines: What the ACT reveals about college readiness in reading.* Iowa City, IA: Author.

Afflerbach, P., & Cho, B.-Y. (2008). Identifying and describing constructively responsive comprehension strategies in new and traditional forms of reading. In S. E. Israel & G. G. Duffy (Eds.), *Handbook of research on reading comprehension* (pp. 69–90). Mahwah, NJ: Erlbaum.

Alexander, P. A., & Jetton, T. L. (2001). Learning from text: A multidimensional and developmental perspective. In M. Kamil, P. D. Pearson, R. Barr, & P. Mosenthal (Eds.), *Handbook of reading research* (pp. 285–310). Mahwah, NJ: Erlbaum.

Alexander, P. A., Kulikowich, J. M., & Jetton, T. L. (1994). The role of subject-matter knowledge and interest in the processing of linear and nonlinear and nonlinear texts. *Review of Educational Research, 64,* 201–252.

Alvermann, D. E., Young, J. P., Green, C., & Wisenbaker, J. M. (1999). Adolescents' perceptions and negotiations of literacy practices in after-school read and talk clubs. *American Educational Research Journal, 36,* 221–264.

Anderson, R. C., & David, P. P. (1984). A schema-theoretic view of basic processes in reading comprehension. In P. D. Pearson, R. Barr, M. L. Kamil, & P. Mosenthal (Eds.), *Handbook of reading research* (pp. 225–253). New York: Longman.

Anderson, T. H., & Armbruster, B. B. (1984). Content area textbooks. In R. C. Anderson, J. Osborne, & R. J. Tierney (Eds.), *Learning to read in American schools: Basal readers and content texts* (pp. 193–226). Hillsdale, NJ: Erlbaum.

Armbruster, B. B., & Anderson, T. H. (1985). Producing "considerate" expository text: Or easy reading is damned hard writing. *Journal of Curriculum Studies, 17*, 247–263.

Bain, R. B. (2005). "They thought the world was flat?" HPL principles in teaching high school history. In J. Bransford & S. Donovan (Eds.), *How students learn: History, mathematics, and science in the classroom* (pp. 179–214). Washington, DC: National Academies Press.

Bain, R. B. (2006). Rounding up unusual suspects: Facing the authority hidden in the history classroom. *Teachers College Record, 108*, 2080–2114.

Bain, R. B., Lander, A., Hines, M., & Mercado, G. (2008, April). *Working toward a problem-centered history classroom: Using historical inquiry and literacy to teach American history.* Paper presented at the National Council of History Education Annual Conference, Louisville, KY.

Biancarosa, G., & Snow, C. E. (2004). *Reading next: A vision for action and research in middle and high school literacy.* A report to the Carnegie Corporation of New York. Washington, DC: Alliance for Excellent Education.

Blumenfeld, P. C., Kempler, T. M., & Krajcik, J. S. (2006). Motivation and cognitive engagement in learning environments. In K. Sawyer (Ed.), *The Cambridge handbook of the learning sciences* (pp. 475–488). New York: Cambridge University Press.

Buehl, D. (2002). *Classroom strategies for interactive learning.* Newark, DE: International Reading Association.

Chambliss, M. J., & Calfee, R. (1998). *Textbooks for learning: Nurturing children's minds.* Boston: Blackwell.

Coiro, J. (2003). Rethinking comprehension strategies to better prepare students for critically evaluating content on the Internet. *NERA Journal, 39*, 29–34.

Coiro, J., Knobel, M., Lankshear, C., & Leu, D. J., Jr. (2008). Central issues in new literacies and new literacies research. In J. Coiro, M. Knobel, C. Lankshear, & D. J. Leu, Jr. (Eds.), *Handbook of research on new literacies* (pp. 1–21). New York: Erlbaum.

Davidson, J. W. (2005). *The American nation: Beginnings through 1877.* Upper Saddle River, NJ: Pearson Prentice Hall.

Deshler, D. D., & Schumaker, J. B. (2005). *High school students with disabilities: Strategies for accessing the curriculum.* New York: Corwin Press.

Eccles, J. S., Midgley, C., Wigfield, A., Miller-Buchannan, C., Reuman, D., Flanagan, C., et al. (1993). Development during adolescence: The impact of stage–environment fit on young adolescents' experiences in schools and families. *American Psychologist, 48*, 90–101.

Gee, J. P. (2001, December). *Reading in "new times."* Paper presented at the National Reading Conference, San Antonio, TX.

Greenleaf, C., Schoenbach, R., Cziko, C., & Mueller, F. L. (2001). Apprenticing adolescent readers to academic literacy. *Harvard Educational Review, 71*, 79–129.

Guthrie, J. T., & Davis, M. H. (2003). Motivating struggling readers in middle school through an engagement model of classroom practice. *Reading and Writing Quarterly, 19*, 59–85.

Guthrie, J. T., Hoa, L. W., Wigfield, A., Tonks, S. M., & Perencevich, K. C. (2006). From spark to fire: Can situational reading interest lead to long-term reading motivation? *Reading Research and Instruction, 45,* 91–113.

Guthrie, J. T., & Wigfield, A. (2000). Engagement and motivation in reading. In P. B. Mosenthal, M. L. Kamil, P. D. Pearson, & R. Barr (Eds.), *Handbook of reading research* (Vol. III, pp. 403–419). Mahwah, NJ: Erlbaum.

Hand, B., Hohenshell, L., & Prain, V. (2004). Exploring students' responses to conceptual questions when engaged with planned writing experiences: A study with year 10 science students. *Journal of Research in Science Teaching, 41,* 186–210.

Hand, B., Prain, V., & Yore, L. D. (2001). Sequential writing tasks' influence on science learning. In P. Tynjala, L. Mason, & K. Lonka (Eds.), *Writing as a learning tool: Integrating theory and practice* (pp. 105–129). Dordrecht, The Netherlands: Kluwer.

Hand, B., Wallace, C., & Yang, E. (2004). Using the science writing heuristic to enhance learning outcomes from laboratory activities in seventh grade science: Quantitative and qualitative aspects. *International Journal of Science Education, 26,* 131–149.

Hicks, D. (1995/1996). Discourse, learning, and teaching. In M. W. Apple (Ed.), *Review of research in education* (Vol. 21, pp. 49–95). Washington, DC: American Educational Research Association.

Kintsch, W., & Van Dijk, T. A. (1978). Toward a model of text comprehension and production. *Psychological Review, 85,* 363–394.

Leander, K. M., & Lovvorn, J. F. (2006). Literacy networks: Following the circulation of texts, bodies, and objects in the schooling and online gaming of one youth. *Cognition and Instruction, 24,* 291–340.

Lee, C. D., & Spratley, A. (2006). *Reading in the disciplines and the challenges of adolescent literacy.* New York: Carnegie Corporation of New York.

Lee, J., Grigg, W., & Donahue, P. (2007). *The nation's report card: Reading 2007.* Washington, DC: National Center for Education Statistics, Institute of Education Sciences, U.S. Department of Education.

Leinhardt, G. (1989). Math lessons: A contrast of novice and expert competence. *Journal for Research in Mathematics Education, 20,* 52–75.

Lemke, J. L. (1990). *Talking science: Language, learning, and values.* Norwood, NJ: Ablex.

Moje, E. B. (2002). But where are the youth: Integrating youth culture into literacy theory. *Educational Theory, 52,* 97–120.

Moje, E. B. (2007, April). *Social and cultural influences on adolescent literacy development.* Paper presented at the American Educational Research Association, Chicago.

Moje, E. B., Dillon, D. R., & O'Brien, D. G. (2000). Re-examining the roles of the learner, the text, and the context in secondary literacy. *Journal of Educational Research, 93,* 165–180.

Moje, E. B., Overby, M., Tysvaer, N., & Morris, K. (2008). The complex world of adolescent literacy: Myths, motivations, and mysteries. *Harvard Educational Review, 78,* 107–154.

Moje, E. B., & Speyer, J. (2008). The reality of challenging texts in high school science and social studies: How teachers can mediate comprehension. In K. Hinchman & H. Thomas (Eds.), *Best practices in adolescent literacy instruction* (pp. 185–211). New York: Guilford Press.

New London Group. (1996). A pedagogy of multiliteracies: Designing social futures. *Harvard Educational Review, 66,* 60–92.

Palincsar, A. S., & Brown, A. L. (1984). Reciprocal teaching of comprehension fostering and comprehension-monitoring activities. *Cognition and Instruction, 1,* 117–175.

Renninger, K. A., Hidi, S., & Krapp, A. (Eds.). (1992). *The role of interest in learning and development.* Hillsdale, NJ: Erlbaum.

Rumelhart, D. (1994). Toward an interactive model of reading. In R. B. Ruddel, M. R. Ruddell, & H. Singer (Eds.), *Theoretical models and processes of reading* (4th ed., pp. 864–894). Newmark, DE: International Reading Association.

Schoenbach, R., Greenleaf, C., Cziko, C., & Hurwitz, L. (1999). *Reading for understanding: A guide to improving reading in middle and high school classrooms.* San Francisco: Jossey-Bass.

Scribner, S., & Cole, M. (1981). *The psychology of literacy.* Cambridge, MA: Harvard University Press.

Snow, C. B. (2002). *Reading for understanding: Toward a research and development program in reading comprehension.* Santa Monica, CA: RAND.

Snow, C. B. (2009). *Time to act: An agenda for advancing adolescent literacy.* New York: Carnegie Corporation of New York.

Solomon, T. C., van Der Kerkhof, M., & Moje, E. B. (in press). When is a detail seductive?: Examining text and the role of interest in middle-school students' scientific literacy development. In A. Rodriguez (Ed.), *Science education as a pathway to teaching language literacy.* Rotterdam, The Netherlands: Sense Publishers.

Stockdill, D., & Moje, E. B. (2008, April). *Adolescents as readers of culture, history, economics, and civics: The disconnect between student interest in their world and social studies schooling.* Paper presented at the American Educational Research Association, New York.

Sutherland, L. M., Moje, E. B., Cleveland, T. E., & Heitzman, M. (2006).*Incorporating literacy learning strategies in an urban middle school chemistry curriculum: Teachers' successes and dilemmas.* Paper presented at the American Educational Research Association, San Francisco, CA.

Tierney, R. J., & Pearson, D. P. (1981). Learning to learn from text: A framework for improving classroom practice. In E. K. Dishner, T. W. Bean, J. E. Readence, & D. W. Moore (Eds.), *Reading in the content areas: Improving classroom instruction* (pp. 496–513). Dubuque, IA: Kendall/Hunt.

Tierney, R. J., & Pearson, D. P. (1992). A revisionist perspective on "learning to learn from text": A framework for improving classroom practice. In E. K. Dishner, T. W. Bean, J. E. Readence, & D. W. Moore (Eds.), *Reading in the content areas: Improving classroom instruction* (3rd ed., pp. 82–86). Dubuque, IA: Kendall/Hunt.

Vacca, R. T., & Vacca, J. (2004). *Content area reading: Literacy and learning across the curriculum* (8th ed.). New York: Allyn & Bacon.

Wineburg, S. S. (1991). On the reading of historical texts: Notes on the breach between school and the academy. *American Educational Research Journal, 28*(3), 495–519.

Wineburg, S. S. (1998). Reading Abraham Lincoln: An expert/expert study in the interpretation of historical texts. *Cognitive Science, 22,* 319–346.

Part II

CLASSROOM AND SCHOOL APPLICATIONS

4

Comprehension in the Primary Grades

Diane Barone

An enormously important influence on the development
of comprehension in childhood is what happens after we
remember, predict, and infer: we feel, we identify, and in the
process we understand more fully and can't wait to turn the
page.
—WOLF (2007, p. 132)

As I began composing this chapter, I was constantly reminded
of the conversations I have with primary teachers centered on comprehension. We often strategize on how we can better support students in
developing their understandings of text, both fiction and nonfiction. We
worry that although decoding or word level instruction is important to
young readers, too much time is allotted for it without a similar focus on
comprehension. We contemplate the use of organizational worksheets
to develop comprehension and wonder if they are seen as the result of
comprehending or a method to further refine understanding. Through
these conversations and the subsequent adaptations with students, we
have come to learn that:

- Comprehension is not an end destination; rather it is a process
  wherein understanding is constantly refined (Serafini & Youngs,
  2008).

- Comprehension is developed through listening, writing, talking, and drawing (Wilhem, 2008).
- Comprehension occurs throughout a school day in all content areas (Stead, 2006).

This chapter is grounded in these beliefs and how, through being read to, reading with others, or reading independently, comprehension or understanding can develop and be nurtured. The chapter begins with an exploration of the critical element of comprehending—wonderful books and access to them and the foundations necessary for comprehension to occur. From this foundation, aspects centered on comprehension are shared such as types of comprehension and strategies. The chapter ends with an overview of more general ways to develop understanding through reading and rereading, talking, writing, and drawing.

FOUNDATIONS FOR COMPREHENSION

Children's Literature

Literature offers possibilities and takes us beyond space, time, and self.
—WILHEM (2008, p. 53)

Exemplary literacy instruction, especially in comprehension, occurs in classrooms where a literate environment has been created even before students arrive. When students first enter, they are enfolded in an environment that supports literacy—a room filled with children's books (Barone & Youngs, 2008; Pressley et al., 2003). In such classrooms, students are immediately aware of the importance of books and reading to their teacher. They may see an inviting bookcase filled with books, book tubs with leveled text or text grouped by topic, or books on a table collected because of a similar author, illustrator, or topic.

It is difficult to develop comprehension if students are in rooms where the core reading program and its related materials are the only available texts. Most selections within core programs are fine for modeling comprehension strategies and teacher thinking; however, for many students these selections are beyond their current reading abilities and therefore too difficult for independent reading. Even though core reading programs provide quality literary selections and leveled text, these materials are not sufficient by themselves to develop comprehension. They provide occasions for teachers to model instructional strategies and for students to practice them immediately.

Teachers, through read-alouds and opportunities to participate with literature, offer students the materials and time for developing comprehension and understanding (Barone & Youngs, 2008). Throughout a day, week, or longer, students revisit themes, genres, or topics in a variety of children's literature and through these multiple exposures develop an understanding of various texts and connections across them (Wolf, 2004).

The ways in which teachers mediate literature with students has a profound effect on the kinds of readers they become (Wilhem, 2008). Across a day teachers provide direct instruction to support students in developing reading competencies; however, these directed lessons are only a part of reading instruction. Students need multiple reasons to engage with text throughout a day to refine and extend this learning. These reasons could include reading to find answers; reading to learn more about a character or plot; reading to know about a topic; reading to find information in books and on the screen; reading to learn about a genre; reading to discover more about an author or illustrator; reading to better understand the visual representations within a text; or reading for the joy of it.

While it is critical for teachers to know how to develop students' comprehension strategies, and create activities to support comprehension, it is equally important for teachers to have current knowledge of available children's literature to support the teaching of comprehension. Several websites offer assistance to teachers in choosing children's literature. A few of these websites include:

- *www.carolhurst.com*. This site organizes children's books by theme.
- *www.ala.org*. This site provides links to many websites focused on children's literature.
- *www.reading.org*. This is the site of the International Reading Association. Each year they publish teachers', parents', and children's choices of children's literature.

Background Knowledge

Building Content Background

The more students know about a topic, the more deeply they can think about it.
—GUNNING (2008, p. 33)

As students approach a new text, comprehension can be aided if they have background about the content of the piece, the genre of the piece, and its vocabulary (Gunning, 2008). Knowing a bit about the content of what is being read scaffolds comprehension (Anderson & Pearson,

1982). For some students this background might be built through discussion, wherein the teacher quickly provides necessary information and
students supply relevant personal life experiences. In other circumstances
photos supply critical background information by providing an image to
support content. For instance, I observed a second-grade teacher use
photos to help students understand the differences among lakes, oceans,
and rivers. In other classrooms I have seen teachers utilize the Internet
to build this background by having students explore various websites to
learn pertinent information. For example, students studying frogs visited numerous websites to listen to how different frogs sound and to
watch short videos of a variety of frogs.

A traditional way to support students in bringing background to
a text, especially for informational text, is through the K-W-L strategy
(what you already *know*, what you *want* to know, and what you *learned*
from your reading) (Ogle, 1986). In this strategy the teacher encourages
students to offer what they know about a topic, character, and so on,
what they want to know, and then after reading, what they learned.
Although this strategy is commonly used in schools, many teachers
notice that children often have misperceptions that they think are facts.
Teachers are reluctant to disconfirm these ideas because they want to
convey a valuing of student comments. Unfortunately, many students
consider their misperceptions to be truths even when the text does not
validate them. A variation of the K-W-L strategy is the reading and analyzing nonfiction strategy (RAN; Stead, 2006). When using this strategy,
students record as column labels "What I think I know," "Confirmed,"
"Misconceptions," "New Information," and "Wonderings." Through
this shift, students can suggest what they believe to be accurate, but no
such proffered "fact" is considered trustworthy until confirmed by the
text. There is also a place to record misconceptions. The other difference
is that students can acknowledge what they are still pondering about a
topic.

Building Genre Background

In order to understand a genre, students must first read widely within it
as they determine particular genre characteristics.
                    —YOUNGS AND BARONE (2007, p. 14)

While teachers are familiar with building background knowledge, they
are often not as aware of the importance of knowledge about genres to
comprehension (Youngs & Barone, 2007). A genre constitutes a kind of
roadmap regarding expectations that support comprehension of informational or narrative text. For instance, when reading a fairytale, stu-

dents know that there will be fanciful elements such as talking animals, magic coaches, and so on; they know that there will be good characters and evil characters; and they know that the story will end with a happy resolution. To facilitate genre knowledge, teachers can organize units of instruction centered on a particular genre. Young students can easily learn about fairytales and legends, among other genres. As teachers explore a genre with students, they create posters that identify the critical elements. Using fairytales, students might include some of the descriptors provided in this paragraph on their chart. As they read additional fairytales, they add new details to their chart, thus developing their understanding of fairytales, and, through using this process with other genres, deeper knowledge of those as well.

This process is similar for informational genres for which students focus on their organization as well as genre type. They learn that some text is organized via description, comparison, cause–effect elements, time line, or problem–solution elements. Eventually, they discover that a single text can have all of these organizational patterns within it. In addition, they learn about biographies, persuasive writing, and informational text in various content areas.

Table 4.1 lists some of the possible genres that young students explore.

Building Vocabulary Background

We consider the best sources for new vocabulary to be trade books that teachers read aloud to children rather than the books children read on their own.
—BECK, MCKEOWN, AND KUCAN (2002, p. 27)

The connections between vocabulary knowledge and comprehension are well documented in research (Beck, McKeown, & Kucan, 2002). For young students, new words, even rare or unusual words, come from read-alouds, during which students' word meaning knowledge is expanded. Teachers often pause in their reading and offer quick, student-friendly definitions of words to help with this development. For instance, they may stop when reading *A Pocket for Corduroy* (Freeman, 1978), so that students learn what *reluctant* and *insisted* mean in the sentence "Lisa was reluctant to leave without Corduroy, but her mother insisted" (unpaged). A great source for student-friendly definitions is the Longman Online Dictionary (*www.ldoceonline.com*). To further support students in learning the meaning of these words, teachers provide multiple opportunities for practice throughout the day.

To develop vocabulary knowledge with students teachers also use

TABLE 4.1. Possible Student Genres

Narrative genres	Informational genres
• Poetry	• Biography
• Nursery rhyme	• Science
• Picture storybook	• Social studies
• Wordless book	• Reference
• Myth	• Photo essay
• Legend	• Map
• Fable	• Newspaper
• Mystery	• Brochure
• Realistic fiction	• Animal book

numerous strategies that might involve talking, writing, acting, drawing, and so on. They understand that a rich repertoire of words and their associated words or concepts facilitate children's comprehension (Wolf, 2004), as does easy access to a well-stocked bookcase of high-quality books.

LEVELS OF COMPREHENSION

Simply being able to decode and answer low-level literal questions about a piece of text is no longer sufficient. Becoming fully literate has come to mean, among other things, using strategies independently to construct meaning from text, using text information to build conceptual understanding, effectively communicating ideas orally and in writing, and developing the intrinsic desire to read and write.

—GAMBRELL, MALLOY, AND MAZZONI (2007, p. 13)

As students develop comprehension, they learn that there are levels to it from explicit to inferential to critical. Even young students can explore and come to understand each of these levels. There is no specific hierarchy to levels of comprehension based on grade level. Students typically grasp literal understanding before inferential or critical understandings, however. Pragmatically, it is difficult to impossible to understand how the setting contributes to a story without first recognizing what the setting is.

A strategy that helps students learn about the levels of comprehension is the question–answer relationship strategy (QAR; Raphael, 1986). When teachers support students in using QAR, they identify the expectations of a question and the corresponding level of comprehension. The following represents the types of possible answers:

- *Right there:* The answer is right in the text—literal comprehension
- *Putting it together:* The answer is in the text but it might be located in several places—literal comprehension
- *On my own:* The answer comes from the student's background knowledge—inferential and/or critical comprehension
- *Writer and me:* The answer comes from inferring and using background knowledge plus knowledge from the text—inferential and/or critical comprehension

Literal Comprehension

Literal comprehension includes the basics of the plot, setting, or information about characters in narrative text; in informational text it includes important details. There are numerous ways for teachers to develop students' literal comprehension. Following are a few ideas:

Narrative Text

- Students write or sketch the beginning, middle, and end to support knowledge about the basic plot.
- Students do a quick drawing of a major character and then write words to describe this character.
- Students retell a story.

Informational Text

- Students list some facts they learned, as designated by the teacher.
- Students create a time line identifying what happened at each point of time.
- Students complete a graphic organizer with appropriate details.

Most core reading programs provide an abundant amount of literal-based questions. I have observed many well-meaning teachers ask individual students for answers to these questions. As each student answers, other students lose focus and engagement with the text. A more engaging way to think about these questions is that if the answer is short, all students can respond chorally. Through choral response, even students who are not quite sure of the answer have a chance to participate. If questions require longer responses, it is best if students share with a partner and the teacher listens in during this collaboration. In this way the old pattern of teacher question, individual student response, back to teacher question shifts to one in which *all* students are expected to participate *all* of the time. Additionally, teachers may decide to whittle down the number of literal questions to save time and thinking for more consequential discussion.

Inferential Comprehension

Inferential comprehension requires readers to move beyond what is explicitly written in a text. For instance, in the book *The Pigeon Wants a Puppy* (Willems, 2008), the reader understands that the pigeon wants a puppy, but nowhere in the text does it discuss the complications of a pigeon owning a puppy or why a pigeon would want a puppy. These ponderings are left to the reader. In an uncomplicated informational book about astronauts, *Astronauts in Space* (Spencer, 2003), children learn simple facts about astronauts. Once the book is read, children might move beyond the explicit text to consider what it means to live without gravity or other issues related to being an astronaut in space.

Students must be supported in moving from literal comprehension to inferential understandings. For instance, teachers might ask students to create a list of facts from *Astronauts in Space* as it is read. From this list, students might then be asked to step back and consider what is important about being an astronaut.

In a third-grade classroom I observed a teacher's exemplary practice of supporting students' growing ability to form inferential understandings. During each small-group reading session, she asked students to write one fact they knew about a character on a sticky note. Students shared their facts orally. Then she asked students to think about what they read, wrote, and heard from other students about the character. After students had a chance to think, they shared their new understandings about the character. For example, a small group of boys was reading *Game Day* (Barber & Barber, 2005). The students chose Tiki Barber as the character on which they would focus. They each wrote details about him—he knew plays by heart, he did his homework with his brother, he was a fast runner, and so on. Then they reflected on what they might conclude about Tiki Barber beyond these details but based on them. During discussion they decided that Tiki liked to play football, worked hard at it, and was a good brother. For each of their inferences about

Tiki, they provided supporting details. This process, which goes beyond the typical asking of questions to elicit fact-based answers, helped students learn how to infer additional understandings that are based on text details.

Critical Comprehension

Critical comprehension requires readers to evaluate and critique a text with evidence from it (Gunning, 2008). This level of understanding requires more from students than saying merely that they liked or did not like the text. Typically a student evaluates the writer's craft by focusing on how the author presented a character and plot or how accurate or objective the information was. Keene and Zimmermann (2007) describe critical comprehension as an infrequent focus in classrooms because teachers focus more on literal understandings.

I remember a vivid example of a second-grade teacher, Mrs. Cambell, who routinely engaged her students in critical comprehension (Barone, 1999). During her read-alouds, she had the children put on visors to help them think. She told the children that the visor gave them "extra-special thinking powers"—and the children responded as if they did have special thinking powers. On one occasion, she had just finished reading *Miss Nelson Is Missing* (Allard, 1977) and asked her students to decide if Miss Nelson were a good teacher. To answer this question, children had to consider what qualities a good teacher has and the degree to which Miss Nelson matched this description. As the discussion became animated, Mrs. Cambell created a chart listing the behaviors of good teaching provided by her students. The students then compared Miss Nelson to this list and decided that she was not a good teacher. In this example, the children were challenging the author's opinion that she was a good teacher. Although Mrs. Cambell did not have a specific name for this strategy, it is similar to the thinking–reading lesson (Commeyras, 1990) wherein students debate complex questions about text with no clear right or wrong answer.

To support students in critical comprehension discussions such as the above, teachers might use a graphic organizer (McLaughlin & Fisher, 2005). Figure 4.1 presents an example that can be used by students to guide them in this process. Students can work with such an organizer alone, with a partner, or in a small group. I have seen teachers use this type of graphic organizer wherein they assign the yes or no position to groups and then have them build an argument for it. The groups engage in discussion to convince each other of the saliency of their arguments.

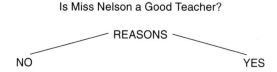

FIGURE 4.1. Critical thinking graphic organizer.

STRATEGIES TO SUPPORT COMPREHENSION

Comprehension strategies are the tools with which we leverage deeper understanding.

—KEENE (2008, p. 5)

In most core reading programs similar comprehension strategies are shared in each grade level, so that students have continued experiences with this small set of strategies through the elementary grades. The strategies group around prediction, monitoring and clarifying, questioning, summarizing, and visualizing (Smith & Read, 2009). These strategies are explicitly taught so that students automatically use them when they read independently. In fact, the goal is for these strategies to become skills, so that students use them effortlessly and without conscious thought in their reading (Afflerbach, Pearson, & Paris, 2008). Following are brief descriptions of each strategy:

- *Prediction.* Students use background knowledge, cover illustration, and/or text to predict what might happen in a story.
- *Monitoring and clarifying.* Students realize that they are confused by the text and reread to clarify passages that do not make sense.
- *Questioning.* Students spontaneously form questions about the content of text before, during, and after reading.
- *Summarizing.* Students understand the most important content shared in a passage or text.
- *Visualizing.* Students create mental images of the text during and after reading.

Two of the fundamental ways in which teachers share these strategies is with the think-aloud and rereading of text (Keene, 2008; Peterson

& Eeds, 2007). In the think-aloud, teachers plan ahead where to stop in text to effectively share their thinking as a model of the process for students. For instance, a teacher who is reading *Skippyjon Jones* (Schachner, 2003) might pause after Skippyjon's mother asks him to think about what it means to be a Siamese cat. The teacher might say, "I am wondering why Skippyjon likes to sleep with birds and eat worms. So far in the story, the author hasn't told us, so I need to think about this as we read ahead. I predict that Skippyjon might like other animals as well, not just birds." In this example, students learn how their teacher uses prediction to enhance the reading experience and deepen comprehension as he or she makes explicit to students that this was the strategy modeled and why he or she used it.

Some teachers think that young students need visual clues as well when they think aloud. They want to make sure that students are listening closely and are active during this process. These teachers may designate a special place in the room for think-alouds; some teachers even have a "think bubble" on a bulletin board that they stand near when they engage in a think-aloud. Teachers also prompt students to listen for a purpose before a think-aloud. They might say, "I am going to ask some questions about this text. I want you to listen carefully to my questions." Then, after the think-aloud experience, students share the questions they heard with a partner.

Rereading text offers students multiple opportunities to engage with it in ways that support comprehension. On the first read, they might focus on gaining meaning about the plot. Their teacher would model strategies to help them acquire this fundamental understanding—strategies such as prediction, monitoring and clarifying, asking questions, summarizing, and/or visualizing.

On the second read, students might look more deeply into the plot for possible points of tension in text, setting, or characters (Peterson & Eeds, 2007). For instance, I listened in as two first-grade boys explored the wordless book *The Grey Lady and the Strawberry Snatcher* (Bang, 1980), a very complicated wordless book in plot and illustration. At first, the children commented:

> MICAH: It is an award winner. I see cherries, grapes, cucumbers, oranges, red apples, garlic, onions, broccoli, watermelons, lettuce.
>
> GABRIEL: Where are the words? I see the Strawberry Snatcher going after berries.
>
> MICAH: He looks like a zombie.
>
> GABRIEL: She is blending in with the trees.

Their conversation continued in this fashion as they were trying to determine what was happening, and they only had illustrations to use. After their first visit through the entire book, they returned to various pages throughout to monitor and clarify their understandings.

> MICAH: He tried to get the strawberries, but he didn't. She is having a party, and he is eating blackberries. They are all dressed up for the party in colorful clothes.
>
> GABRIEL: I have no idea why the bus is in the book—they don't get on. Look, he is on a skateboard. The lady was on that before (*turning pages to find the illustration*). I wonder how he got it. Look at this page, she is hiding but it is a reflection; that is why she looks like she is upside down.

In the boys' first comments, they were glued to the illustrations in their efforts to comprehend the plot. On their second reading, they began to more fully understand the plot as shown in their comments and how they returned to text to clarify places where they were confused. It could be surmised that if they returned to this book again, they would find additional details in the illustrations that would shape clearer inferential understandings of text.

Perhaps the most important point for teachers to understand about comprehension strategies is that they are only important *if* teachers expect more from their students than answers to literal comprehension questions (Keene, 2008). In addition to learning about the strategies, students need multiple opportunities, during guided and independent practice, to apply each strategy and to see how it contributes to their reading experience (Routman, 2003).

MODES TO SUPPORT COMPREHENSION

Listening and Talking

Creating community in read-alouds means [creating] a place where children want to live as well—where they'll feel heard and respected, and where they'll want to spend time everyday.
—WOLF (2004, p. 99)

The read-aloud provides the perfect opportunity for teachers to nurture novice comprehension skills in young students, for these books are just beyond their independent reading capability (Lehman, 2007). McGee and Richgels (2008, p. 164) provide directions for teachers to use during a read-aloud to encourage and elicit more analytical discussion. These include:

1. Before reading, teachers provide short introductions to identify the main character or problem readers will encounter. These conversations build background knowledge. For informational text, teachers identify the topic that was being shared.
2. Teachers make comments as they read—that is, they think aloud.
3. During reading teachers pose a few questions in their think-alouds that help children recall what has happened so far.
4. During reading teachers highlight the meaning of a few important words and provide student-friendly definitions.
5. After reading, teachers lead students in recalling the main events or ideas and then pose a question that stimulates conversation regarding the main event or a character's motives.
6. Teachers reread the book to stimulate deeper exploration of the ideas.

As students listen to their teacher read, and as they engage in discussion, they learn new ideas. The think-alouds and discussion expand their vocabulary and provide the foundation for independent comprehension.

Teachers often modify what students are expected to do during read-alouds. On some days a teacher might stay close to the process described by McGee and Richgels (2008); on other days he or she might expect students to write or draw during the pauses in reading. For example, when reading about sharks, the teacher might give students an anticipation guide (Wood, Lapp, Flood, & Taylor, 2008). Before reading students mark their predictions; during reading they verify their predictions. See Figure 4.2 for an example. Using such a guide engages students in listening carefully to what their teacher is reading. Teachers typically include facts in the guide that they expect students to learn to build their knowledge about a topic.

At other times, teachers may have students create a quick sketch that is expanded when the teacher pauses. For instance, before reading *Skippyjon Jones* (Schachner, 2003), the teacher asks students to create a quick sketch of a Siamese cat. When the teacher pauses during the reading, students are told to add words that describe Skippyjon. At the end of reading children can share their descriptions of Skippyjon, grounded in information from the text. Teachers can also push students beyond literal descriptions and ask them, for example, of how they would describe

Put a Y for *Yes* and an N for *No*.

	Before	During
1. Sharks are fast swimmers.	_____	_____
2. Sharks have teeth that replace themselves when they fall out.	_____	_____
3. Sharks are fish that eat meat.	_____	_____
4. Sharks don't have bones.	_____	_____

FIGURE 4.2. Anticipation guide about sharks.

Skippyjon—their responses might include that he is creative because of his imagination, especially when he thought he was a chihuahua.

The most natural response during a read-aloud is discussion about what is being read (Tunnell & Jacobs, 2008). Teachers can easily move beyond the typical questions by engaging students in more substantial discussion that might include the following questions: "When you first saw the cover of this book, what did you think it would be about? How did you know?" Or "Tell me what you notice about this book?" Questions such as these allow students to participate as expert readers where ideas are valued and nourished.

Reading and Writing

Students should spend most of their time actually reading rather than on useless seatwork or other activities that do not directly support learning to read.

—STRICKLAND (2002, p. 79)

Although the idea of having students read to become better readers seems obvious, in fact students spend little time in classrooms really reading (Allington & Cunningham, 2002). In the primary grades students spend time in whole-class instruction and then guided reading groups. During their time away from their teacher, as he or she is working with a small group, many students are busy with seatwork, often worksheets. However, this time away from direct instruction is a perfect time for students to practice the comprehension strategies their teachers have taught them through independent reading. The issue during independent reading is students' accountability, as it is not a time to just look at books, never engaging with the words. There are numerous ways for students to read and remain accountable. They might be asked to read three books first, pick the one they liked best, and then write a summary or retelling of it.

During independent reading students can respond on a bookmark that can be directed to any specific strategy teachers want students to practice. For example, the bookmark might guide students to write:

- The most interesting part was ...
- Something that confused me was ...
- The illustrations helped me understand ...
- The map or graph helped me understand ...
- I wonder about ...

Teachers can also use graphic organizers to guide student responding as well as direct students' comprehension as they read independently. They might complete a web to describe a character or a semantic question map where, in each bubble, they respond to a question about a topic. Other graphic organizers might include a comparison chart, Venn diagram, cause–effect chart, time line, or problem–solution chart. Students require teacher modeling of these various charts before they can successfully use them independently.

Additionally, for informational text, students can create a fact–think chart either by putting a line down a paper or folding it in half. One side is labeled *Fact* and the other side *This Makes Me Think*. The student records a fact and then writes what he or she thinks about it. For example, if the child wrote that spiders have eight legs, he or she might think "It must need so many legs to build webs" (Stead, 2006). This form allows students to think beyond just a list of facts about a topic.

A less structured writing practice is to have students write in a response journal about what they are reading. Teachers thereby learn what was important to students as they read their comments. For example, two second graders read *Diary of a Fly* (Cronin, 2007) and wrote:

I think I am like the fly I was scared about the first day of school.
I hate my school picture just like the fly did.

These comments show the personal connections students made with the text; other comments may be closer to literal comprehension.

It is important to remember that writing about reading is first-draft writing, so it can be messy, have spelling errors, and show limited use of convention. Young students are focused on meaning, and it is often difficult to focus on meaning and get all the other important details correct. I recommend that teachers consider only the message and have confidence that their teaching will help students become automatic with spelling and writing conventions.

Viewing

Artistic response encourages risk-taking because it is traditionally freer from judgment than the answering of authority-generated questions about reading.
—WILHEM (2008, p. 181)

Although the picture book is the mainstay of primary-grade reading curriculum, teachers most often focus only on the words, not the illustrations. Arizpe and Styles (2003) write that in a picture book it is the interaction between the text and image that renders meaning. Although teachers are familiar with ways to help students understand text, they are less aware of how to support students in gaining meaning from illustrations. Nikolajeva and Scott (2001) provide ways for teachers to facilitate visual understanding. When viewing a picture book, teachers and students first consider the way text and illustrations relate to each other: They can tell the same story; they can complement each other; either can tell more of the story—the text is dominant or the image is dominant; they share what is beyond the text or image when viewed alone; or they each tell a different story. Once students are comfortable understanding how text and illustration generally work together, they can focus on more artistic elements such as line, color, placement of image, and so on (Albers, 2007).

To explore these relationships I asked a first grader to read and reread *Voices in the Park* (Browne, 2003). This book is considered to be a postmodern picture book as the author/illustrator includes variations in font and unusual images in illustrations like Santa Claus and Romeo and Juliet. Within it, four characters share a similar experience although each has a unique perspective. On the first reading, Micah focused on the illustrations; he was impatient with the text and turned the pages before I could read. Following are a few of his comments on this first excursion into this book:

- "The dog wants to see another dog."
- "Why does a gorilla have a monkey child?"
- "It looks like winter. There are no leaves."

On the second visit through the book, he noted:

- "The kids liked each other, but the mom didn't like the other kid."
- "The man is sad, and he is looking for a job."
- "They are climbing a tree, and it looks like a maze."
- "When the boy is near his mother, he is in her shadow."

Even on the second read, Micah was glued to the illustrations. Whereas he poured over the illustrations and gained deeper meaning, he found it hard to listen to the text. If he is offered more opportunities to explore this text, he may learn that the text and illustrations tell different stories, that each character sees the same scene differently, and finally how these stories connect. He might also expand his beginning understandings about the boy and his mother and Browne's interesting use of shadow.

This example shares conversation around a book that draws attention to illustration. Conversation is certainly one way to heighten students' understanding about the relation between text and illustration. I share a few other ways for teachers to support students' understanding of the visual as well as the text within books.

A simple way for teachers to draw students' attention to the visual component and its implications for understanding is to read a picture book wherein students only listen to the words and chat about what they know. Then on a second reading, the teacher might only show the illustrations so that students add what they learned from the reading to their impressions of the illustrations. This process can be reversed such that students view illustrations before listening to the text (Barone & Youngs, 2008). Through this process, students become aware of the contribution of the text and the illustrations to the story.

Teachers can also support students in their efforts to comprehend text by having them create quick sketches of their connections or images that come to mind about the text (McLaughlin & Fisher, 2005). Once again, the strategy is made explicit by asking students why this sketch helps them comprehend the text they are reading. They can either share their reasons orally or in writing. Figure 4.3 shows Mark's image from the story his kindergarten teacher was reading. From viewing this quick sketch, it is clear that Mark has a relatively accurate image of a T-rex.

The previous examples have centered on narrative text. Similar visual understanding can occur with informational text. For instance, Figure 4.4 shares one example from a young student who explored the Internet to find images of planets, which he wrote about to extend his in-class learning about space and the planets. Whereas his images are from the Internet, students could also sketch their own to further understand a topic.

A final type of visual understanding that can occur as students read supports prediction or more literal comprehension. Students sketch their prediction and then write it. The drawing helps young readers and writers remember the details of their prediction as they engage in the more laborious process of writing.

Comprehension is a road with no final destination—we can always

FIGURE 4.3. Mark's image of T-rex.

Jupiter's red spot is a hurricane.

FIGURE 4.4. Image of a planet.

get better at it. Throughout this chapter numerous methods have been shared of ways in which students and teachers can engage in lively conversations about the reading to support comprehension. As teachers work with young readers, it is important to *not* get stuck on the decoding part and to help engage joyfully with text as they simultaneously learn to comprehend.

RECOMMENDED ADDITIONAL READING

Barone, D., & Youngs, S. (2008). *Using your core reading program and children's literature: Effective strategies for using the best of both K–3.* New York: Scholastic.

Keene, E. (2008). *To understand.* Portsmouth, NH: Heinemann.

McLaughlin, M., & Fisher, L. (2005). *Research-based reading lessons for K–3.* New York: Scholastic.

REFERENCES

Afflerbach, P., Pearson, P. D., & Paris, S. (2008). Clarifying differences between reading skills and reading strategies. *Reading Teacher, 61,* 364–373.

Albers, P. (2007). *Finding the artist within.* Newark, DE: International Reading Association.

Allington, R., & Cunningham, P. (2002). *Schools that work* (2nd ed.). Boston: Allyn & Bacon.

Anderson, R., & Pearson, P. D. (1982). A schema-theoretic view of basic processes in reading. In P. D. Pearson (Ed.), *Handbook of reading research* (pp. 255–291). New York: Longman.

Arizpe, E., & Styles, M. (2003). *Children reading picture: Interpreting visual text.* New York: Routledge.

Barone, D. (1999). *Resilient children: Stories of poverty, drug exposure, and literacy development.* Newark, DE: International Reading Association.

Barone, D., & Youngs, S. (2008). *Using your core reading program and children's literature: Effective strategies for using the best of both K–3.* New York: Scholastic.

Beck, I., McKeown, M., & Kucan, L. (2002). *Bringing words to life.* New York: Guilford Press.

Commeyras, M. (1990). Analyzing a critical-thinking reading lesson. *Teaching and Teacher Education, 6,* 201–214.

Gambrell, L., Malloy, J., & Mazzoni, S. (2007). Evidence-based best practices for comprehensive literacy instruction. In L. Gambrell, L. Morrow, & M. Pressley (Eds.), *Best practices in literacy instruction* (pp. 11–29). New York: Guilford Press.

Gunning, T. (2008). *Developing higher-level literacy in all students.* Boston: Pearson.

Keene, E. (2008). *To understand*. Portsmouth, NH: Heinemann.

Keene, E., & Zimmermann, S. (2007). *Mosaic of thought*. (2nd ed.). Portsmouth, NH: Heinemann.

Lehman, B. (2007). *Children's literature and learning*. New York: Teachers College Press.

McGee, L., & Richgels, D. (2008). *Literacy's beginnings: Supporting young readers and writers*. (5th ed.). Boston: Pearson.

McLaughlin, M., & Fisher, L. (2005). *Research-based reading lesson for K–3*. New York: Scholastic.

Nikolajeva, M., & Scott, C. (2001). *How picturebooks work*. New York: Garland.

Ogle, D. (1986). K-W-L: A teaching model that develops active reading of expository text. *Reading Teacher, 39*, 564–570.

Peterson, R., & Eeds, M. (2007). *Grand conversations: Literature groups in action*. New York: Scholastic.

Pressley, M., Dolezal, S., Raphael, L., Mohan, L., Roehrig, A., & Bogner, K. (2003). *Motivating primary-grade students*. New York: Guilford Press.

Raphael, T. (1986). Teaching question/answer relationships revisited. *Reading Teacher, 39, 516–522*.

Routman, R. (2003). *Reading essential: The specifics you need to teach reading well*. Portsmouth, NH: Heinemann.

Serafini, F., & Youngs, S. (2008). *More (advanced) lessons in comprehension: Expanding students' understanding of all types of texts*. Portsmouth, NH: Heinemann.

Smith, J., & Read, S. (2009). *Early literacy instruction: Teaching reading and writing in today's primary grades* (2nd ed.). Boston: Allyn & Bacon.

Stead, T. (2006). *Reality checks: Teaching reading comprehension with nonfiction K–5*. Portland, ME: Stenhouse.

Strickland, D. (2002). *The importance of early intervention*. In A. Farstrup & J. Samuels (Eds.), *What research has to say about reading instruction* (pp. 69–86). Newark, DE: International Reading Association.

Tunnell, M., & Jacobs, J. (2008). *Children's literature briefly* (4th ed.). Upper Saddle River, NJ: Pearson.

Wilhem, J. (2008). *"You gotta be the book": Teaching engaged and reflective reading with adolescents* (2nd ed.). New York: Teachers College Press and Urbana, IL: National Council of Teachers of English.

Wolf, M. (2007). *Proust and the squid: The story and science of the reading brain*. New York: HarperCollins.

Wolf, S. (2004). *Interpreting literature with children*. Mahwah, NJ: Erlbaum.

Wood, K., Lapp, D., Flood, J., & Taylor, D. B. (2008). *Guiding reading through text: Strategy guides for new times*. Newark, DE: International Reading Association.

Youngs, S., & Barone, D. (2007). *Writing without boundaries: What's possible when students combine genres*. Portsmouth, NH: Heinemann.

CHILDREN'S BOOKS

Allard, H. (1977). *Miss Nelson is missing!* Boston: Houghton Mifflin.

Bang, M. (1980). *The grey lady and the strawberry snatcher.* New York: Four Winds Press.

Barber, T., & Barber, R. (2005). *Game day.* New York: Scholastic.

Browne, A. (2003). *Voices in the park.* New York: DK Publishing.

Cronin, D. (2007). *Diary of a fly.* New York: Joanna Cotler Books.

Freeman, D. (1978). *A pocket for Corduroy.* New York: Viking Press.

Schachner, J. 2003). *Skippyjon Jones.* New York: Puffin.

Spencer, W. (2003). *Astronauts in space.* Washington, DC: National Geographic.

Willems, M. (2008). *The pigeon wants a puppy.* New York: Hyperion

5

Active Thinking
and Engagement

Comprehension in the
Intermediate Grades

Kathy Ganske

Much has been said and written about the "activeness" of good readers. Among other things, they draw on background knowledge; make predictions and inferences; create mental images; monitor for meaning; make connections; ask questions; recognize the organization and structure of text; determine what's important; and synthesize, summarize, and evaluate what they've read (Duke & Pearson, 2002; Harvey & Goudvis, 2007; Keene & Zimmerman, 2007; National Institute of Child Health and Human Development, 2000; Pressley & Afflerbach, 1995)—and, we hope, enjoy what they are reading. We get glimpses of what active reading looks like through journal excerpts written by a proficient fifth-grade reader, Kelly, who is beginning Mildred Taylor's (1981) *Let the Circle Be Unbroken* (Figure 5.1).

Clearly, Kelly is an engaged and active reader. She immediately makes known her enjoyment of *Let the Circle Be Unbroken*, drawing a text-to-text comparison to another book by the same author: "I am enjoying this book as much as *Roll of Thunder Hear My Cry* [Taylor, 1976]. It has just as many intense and tear-jerking events and thoughts." Then she shares her thinking about possible interpretations of the book's title, clarifying and elaborating her predictions with drawings and by con-

April 6

I am enjoying this book as much as <u>Roll of Thunder, Hear My Cry</u>. It has just as many intense and tearjerking events and thoughts.

I think the title refers to the family being in a circle and connecting the people would be love, caring and understanding. This is what a diagram or picture might look like:

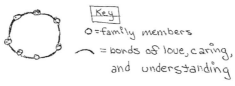

There is another possibility that it could be a song. I just thought of that because everytime my brother sees the book he sings the words of the title. Do you know if it is a song? Maybe they sing the song (if it is a song) if they are going through really hard times, or it could be my two ideas put together. I think it is both because it sounds like a song you sing and it would be hard times if the circle was broken. This is how it could break:

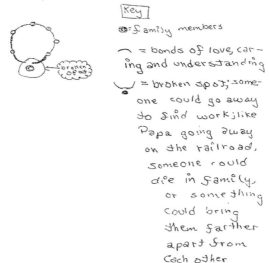

It wouldn't be too likely for someone to die in the family, because all of the characters are so developed and give the story more deep feelings. Everyone in the family could die except for Cassie, because she tells the story, but the author can make-up more ways to add sadness then letting a family member die. I would prefer the author to keep the family alive.

FIGURE 5.1. A fifth grader's journal entry excerpts for *Let the Circle Be Unbroken.*

necting the text to both a personal experience she had with her brother and to her knowledge of the world, "hard times." Uncertain whether a song with the title words actually exists, she questions her reader, in this case the classroom teacher ("Do you know if it is a song?").

In her final paragraph Kelly shows sophisticated understanding of the structure of stories and how they work and provides a personal evaluation of what she thinks the author can and should do as a writer: "The author can make-up more ways to add sadness then letting a family member die. I would prefer the author to keep the family alive." The student reveals her deep engagement with the book through drawing and her journal writing, which resonates as a think-aloud written down. After finishing *Let the Circle Be Unbroken* she created a visual representation depicting her overall assessment of the book (Figure 5.2).

For this fifth grader and this book, the act of reading was clearly a pleasurable and absorbing one, a *flow* experience (Csikszentmihalyi, 1991) that totally captured her attention. This sort of engagement is a critical factor in reading because how motivated students are impacts the extent and manner in which they use comprehension strategies (Guthrie et al., 1996), and according to Guthrie and Wigfield (1997), whether or not readers are motivated depends on how they perceive themselves relative to the reading task, namely:

1. *Do they feel a sense of self-efficacy, in other words, are they self-confident?*? Readers who are confident of success are more likely to

FIGURE 5.2. Rating pot for *Let the Circle Be Unbroken*.

put forth effort and persist when they encounter difficulties. Texts that challenge readers without frustrating them facilitate this willingness to persevere, as does teaching that builds on strengths.

2. *When faced with roadblocks, do readers feel personally inadequate, or do they believe that they have not succeeded because their approach to solving the problem was simply not the right one?* Those with the former attitude are likely to give up and very well may not choose to read when provided time to do so. Overcoming hurdles during reading requires that readers monitor their understanding as they read so that they quickly realize when they run into a problem that breaks down their comprehension. Further, once aware of a problem, they need to know what to do to fix it: for example, reread, look ahead, and so on.

3. *Do they gain pleasure, fulfillment, or practical benefits from the reading experience* (Baumann & Duffy, 1997)? Whether or not readers are interested in what they are reading may depend on the topic, genre, or reading situation. Choice, prior experiences with books, book access, and opportunities to interact socially with others are motivating factors for readers in the upper elementary grades (Gambrell, 1996; Palmer, Codling, & Gambrell, 1994; Worthy, 1996). Even situational motivation, such as using informational books in conjunction with hands-on science observations and experiments, can encourage reading interest (Guthrie et al., 2006).

This chapter focuses on ways to promote active, engaged reading in the intermediate grades. We'll explore strategies that encourage readers to monitor for meaning, activate background knowledge, visualize, develop a thinking-and-questioning stance, and summarize. But first, let's take a brief look at the role of metacognition in comprehending text.

THE IMPORTANCE OF METACOGNITION

Good drivers keep a careful eye on the road, monitor the situation, and modify their actions as needed. They observe not only what is directly in front and behind them but also relevant events and objects in surrounding areas—a car approaching an intersection from the side; a passing vehicle; signs indicating an upcoming curve, construction area, exit, tunnel, or bridge; and sometimes even a deer or other animal threatening to dart across the road. This approach helps good drivers avoid pitfalls and makes it more likely that when they do encounter a problem, they will be ready to react. The sort of conscious awareness that enables a person to monitor, adjust, and direct attention to a desired end is known as *metacognition* (Harris & Hodges, 1995).

Proficient readers use metacognition to track whether their reading makes sense and when it does not they know what to do to improve the situation. Unfortunately, students who struggle with reading often do not have strategies for improving their understanding. By contrast, proficient readers use a variety of metacognitive strategies to monitor and adjust. They draw on what they already know (background knowledge), create mental pictures, question, sift out what's important from what's not, summarize and synthesize. For the fifth grader featured at the onset of this chapter, application of several of these strategies was likely fluid and automatic; however, the process of gaining that automaticity probably involved active learning and active teaching.

MONITORING FOR MEANING

When I'm tired, distracted from the day's events, or confronted with a text that either does not hold my interest or that I am forced to read and feel no connection to, I can find myself at the end of a paragraph or even a whole page having "read" every word but knowing more about whatever was on my mind at the time than what the text was about. Clearly, I was neither actively thinking about the reading nor noticing whether I grasped what the author was trying to communicate, much less considering whether I agreed or disagreed with what was said or whether I might be able to relate to it in some way. Although this is an extreme example, it is probably a situation we have all experienced at some time or other and certainly an event that happens all too often with students who don't know how to monitor for meaning and who tell us they've read everything they were supposed to but show us they've understood nothing.

Monitoring for meaning requires close, thoughtful reading. Without close reading, comprehending text can be a slippery slope. Let one text segment go by without understanding it and the next, which likely builds on the first, may go sliding by as well, and soon the reader is mired in confusion. As proficient readers we carry on silent conversations in our heads as we read and monitor for meaning, sometimes directing comments to the author or a character. Teachers who use think-alouds to make these conversations transparent to students can help them realize that proficient readers do more than just look at or call out words when they read. Proficient readers critically consider the text, question the author, solve problems, enjoy humor, savor interesting language, marvel over fascinating facts, wonder what may happen next, and myriad other things. In my experience the beginning of a book is one good place to think aloud. Characters, setting, actions—everything about the story is virtually unknown at this point, and a think-aloud can illustrate how good readers sift through information to get focused on who and what are likely important. Let's consider the following example based on the beginning lines of a picture book by Paul Fleischman (1999) called *Weslandia*. The story is about a young boy with a vivid imagination and a keen curiosity who would rather read a book or try out a science experiment than eat pizza or watch football. Because he is different than other boys his age, Wesley is rejected by his peers until he creates a new civilization in his backyard and becomes the envy of all his classmates. The teacher begins reading:

> "*Of course he's miserable,*" *moaned Wesley's mother.* "*He sticks out.*"
>   "*Like a nose,*" *snapped his father.* [Stops reading.] So ... a boy named Wesley is probably the main character in this story. Wesley must be different from other kids, since his mother says "He sticks out." She feels bad for him, maybe because being different is making him really unhappy—"miserable" in her words. And the dad seems angry about the whole business, or maybe he's just feeling really hurt by it all, and that's why he "snapped."
>   [Resumes reading.] *Listening through the heating vent, Wesley knew they were right. He was an outcast from the civilization around him.* [Stops reading.] I wonder why he's listening through the vent? I did that once to try to hear a funny story. This doesn't seem like a funny situation, though, so maybe Wesley's wondering what his parents are going to do. It says he's an "outcast." *Outcast* means somebody who is *cast out*, rejected. I'm not exactly sure what *civilization* means. I've seen the word in books about the Greeks and Romans, like the "Greek civilization." I thought it meant "Greek life." Maybe Wesley feels cast out from the life around him because he's different. But how's he different? And what will happen to him? I'll read on to see what I can find out. [Resumes reading.]

Thoughts and wonderings that help students monitor for meaning, such as those revealed in the preceding think-aloud, can also be recorded on sticky notes or in a journal and serve as springboards for discussions (see Figure 5.3). To ensure that students understand the process, teachers:

- Demonstrate with a think-aloud.
- Distribute a stack of sticky notes to each student.

FIGURE 5.3. Monitoring for meaning with sticky notes.

- Ask students to jot down their reflections, questions, and unfamiliar words on sticky notes and post them on relevant pages as they read a few pages of text.
- Lead students to deeper understanding of the text and broader perceptions about the kind of musings they might record by providing time for them to share their thinking, either with a partner or as part of a whole-group discussion.

Because some students may be overwhelmed by the task of determining what to write down and where to begin, it often works well initially to determine a specific focus for the recording—for example, unfamiliar words—or provide students with a prompt to guide their note taking, such as "I was confused when … " "I stopped reading to think about … " "When I read I thought about … " or "I'd like to ask the author …" (Strickland, Ganske, & Monroe, 2002). Be careful not to inadvertently cause students to become overreliant on prompts of this sort. The quiet talk in which we engage with ourselves as we read is a conversation, not a fill-in-the-blank question-and-answer session. Guide and encourage students to put down what they notice and what they think about it. Let them know you are not looking for a "right answer," but rather you want them to share their thinking. Because our experiences influence our thinking, and the experiences we've had differ from person to person, everyone's musings will be somewhat different.

USING SCHEMAS TO MAKE CONNECTIONS

Being able to recognize and understand words is essential for reading; the more words you know the easier it is to make sense of the text (National Institute of Child Health and Human Development, 2000). Although the importance of vocabulary knowledge in reading can hardly be overstated, comprehension isn't just a matter of "adding up" the meanings of words to understand the whole. "The click of comprehension occurs only when the reader evolves a schema that explains the whole message" (Anderson, 2004, p. 596). A *schema* is our stored memory representation for an object, event, or relationship (Harris & Hodges, 1995). Our personal experiences, knowledge of the world, and knowledge of texts contribute to schema development. As we gain new knowledge related to a concept, our schema changes and becomes enriched, with links forged to other schemas. For example, my schema for *reading* is much different now than the schema I had when I was a toddler and "read" back stories to my mother by pointing to pictures. In fact, my schema continues to change. While working on the manuscript for this book, my review of Chapter 10 by Lapp and Gainer, which is about multiliteracies, further developed my *reading/literacy* schema.

Being able to link new information to what we already know aids comprehension and memory, but children do not automatically do this as they read; and due to differences in age, gender, race, religion, nationality, occupation, and so forth, a particular schema will not necessarily be activated (Anderson, 2004). Another factor to consider about schema activation is that at times readers may not have relevant experiences to activate, as, for instance, might be the case if we were asked to read an article on *histology* (the study of the microscopic structure of plant and animal tissues). Lack of prior knowledge would likely negatively impact our interest and comprehension. We see evidence of the critical role that background knowledge plays in engagement and understanding in the series of dialogue journal entries, with teacher response, written by a proficient intermediate-grade reader and shown in Figure 5.4. The story *Monkey Island* by Paula Fox (1991) features an 11-year-old boy growing up in New York City who becomes homeless after his family falls into economic difficulties.

Classroom dialogue, such as occurs during read-alouds and small-

Dear Mr. K.,

I just started reading Monkey Island by Paula Fox. Here's what's happened so far.

The main character is a boy named Clay. He lives with his mom in a hotel in some city but she's been missing for five days. Clay's dad's gone too. He left to look for work after he lost his job and Clay's mom is looking for him. Clay has quit going to school and he has to find his food in other people's garbage. That's about it, not much happening. It might pick up but this first chapter reminds me of my sister before she learned to walk. It just creeps on and on and on and on and on. You know how in Writing Workshop we talk about hooking the reader? Well, I think the author forgot the hook. I hope it will get better; I don't like quitting a book.

Your friend,

T. R.

Dear T. R.,

I wonder if Monkey Island hasn't grabbed your attention because Clay's life in a big city is so tremendously different from our experiences in the country. I read the book aloud last year. We talked about the book as I read it and overall, everyone really enjoyed the story. What do you think? At any rate, if your opinion of the book doesn't change, pick another one. Reading should be fun!

Your friend,

Mr. K.

Dear Mr. K.,

I quit reading Monkey Island after the second chapter. There was nothing pulling me to read on. I had to drag myself to read it. It was just about Clay wandering around in the city. No snapshots no thoughtshots, just boring, boring, boring. I think Paula Fox was in a hurry to get done. Clay isn't a round character at all. He's as flat as a pancake. I'll look for a better book.

Your friend,

T. R.

Dear Mr. K.,

I just read your letter. You're right about Clay's life being different from mine. It's another world! Clay lives in New York where there are a zillion people and lots of noise. In the country where I live everything is quiet, without many people, and my parents aren't missing. I've decided to read My Side of the Mountain instead. I think I'll like this story better.

Your friend,

T. R.

FIGURE 5.4. Student dialogue journal entries with teacher response.

group discussions, would likely have done much to increase T. R.'s engagement with *Monkey Island*. Differences between living in a rural area versus an urban area, and all that that may mean for everyday living experiences, could have been bridged, to some extent, through talk, questioning, and the sharing of experiences, as likely occurred the year the teacher read aloud the story to the class. Encouraging such dialogue in the classroom is not only desirable, it is imperative if students are to deeply understand texts (Hacker, 2004).

There are many ways to activate background knowledge and get students thinking about their reading both before and while they read, including sharing and discussing artifacts related to a reading, brainstorming about the topic, and examining a relevant picture. Involving students in picture walks or text walks by previewing the pictures or headings and captions provides them with a kind of roadmap for the upcoming reading, so that they can capitalize on what they know. Previewing also encourages speculation and prediction making (What's happening to a character? How will the event turn out? What might have happened since the previous picture or subheading?), and it can increase students' engagement for the reading. To activate or build background knowledge in preparation for reading a textbook topic, teachers often provide opportunities for students to explore the event, culture, or phenomenon by reading a trade book, chapter book, or picture book. These have the added advantage of enabling students to engage with texts that are of appropriate reading difficulty. Two other possibilities for activating background knowledge are anticipation guides (Readance, Bean, & Baldwin, 1985) and double-entry drafts (Barone, 1990; Berthoff, 1981).

Anticipation Guide

Anticipation guides work well with informational text (including textbook passages) to help activate students' background knowledge and to ignite their interest; they can also be used with fiction. They are easily constructed. Each guide consists of a series of statements (typically 6–10 statements), some of which the reading will reveal to be true and some false. Students indicate their agreement or disagreement with each statement before reading and then check off the correct category as they come across relevant information in their reading. Figure 5.5 shows an example based on Cathy Camper's (2002) informational book *Bugs before Time: Prehistoric Insects and Their Relatives*, which includes some pretty incredible facts about various ancient members of the insect class. Whereas students generally believe that cockroaches existed before humans, and they tend to doubt that cockroaches were ever very differ-

Before		*Bugs before Time* by Cathy Camper	After	
Yes	No		Yes	No
√		There were cockroaches before there were humans.	√	
	√	Fossils show us that ancient cockroaches were very different than the cockroaches of today.		√
	√	A cockroach has a kind of brain in its head and its tail.	√	
	√	If we could run as fast as a cockroach, we could run 200 miles per hour.	√	

FIGURE 5.5. Part of an anticipation guide.

ent, most are surprised or even shocked to discover the speed at which a cockroach can run *and* that with a brain at both ends of its body, it can survive even after losing its head or tail!

Double-Entry Drafts

Double-entry drafts (DEDs) are an effective way to encourage students to activate schema and make connections as they read. Students fold a notebook page in half, lengthwise. At the top of the inner half of the page they record the book's title and author and beneath it a quote from the reading that captured their interest. (The page number can also be included for easy reference during discussion.) On the right half of the page students respond to the quote. Although responses can be text-to-text or text-to-world associations, they are often text-to-self connections. Good readers attend carefully to characters and setting as they read (Duke & Pearson, 2002). Making personal connections can help students relate to an incident or draw students into a story by creating empathy for a character, and thus promote comprehension (see Figures 5.6 and 5.7).

Another advantage of DEDs is that they are extremely adaptable. Besides being used by students to record quotes and their reactions, DEDs can also be used to encourage other types of thinking—as, for example, with the heading titles: "I Predict/I Learned," "I Learned/I Wonder," "What I Know/What I Want to Know," "My Connection/ What Kind Is It?" and so on. DEDs can also be used to foster comprehension in math ("The Problem/My Solution," "What I Know/The Problem,") and other content areas.

Despite the importance of prior knowledge in comprehending text, there is a caveat to bear in mind: Readers can be overly influenced by

Sideways Stories from Wayside School by *Louis Sachar* *"I don't believe it," said Mrs. Jewls. "It's a room full of monkeys!"*	*It reminds me of when my dad, brother, and I were whoching TV one time and some monkeys came on and my dad would say "Hey look theirs Lauren and Andy on T.V. And say when we are in the car "I have two little monkeys in the back of my car. And he still says that!*

FIGURE 5.6. Double-entry draft by an intermediate-grade student—Example 1.

their prior knowledge and as a result fail to construct a meaning that is congruent with the text. Also, students sometimes make connections that are inconsequential to understanding the gist of the story. The two intermediate-grade student responses shown in Figures 5.6 and 5.7 reveal meaningful connections that help the students connect to characters in their stories, but this is not always the case. For example, a reader might know someone by the name of Mrs. Jewls and comment on this fact, but the Mrs. Jewls the reader knows may have nothing in common with the character in the story, besides their names, and because the real Mrs. Jewls has different character traits, the background knowledge may actually lead to confusion and misinterpretation during reading. Teacher modeling, opportunities for students to talk about their readings, and thoughtful reading of students' DEDs help teachers identify when redirecting or clarifying is needed for understanding.

The Fellowship of the Ring by J. R. R. Tolkien "There was a sudden silence in which his heart was thumping hard."	Sometimes when you say something dumb and everyone looks at you like huh? and it seems like it is silent forever and in that time you can almost see your heart thumping under your skin. That happened to me one time when I had finished a speech and no one knew it was over, so they gave me the go on look. In that time I felt like my heart was going to tear through my skin and through the air somewhere.

FIGURE 5.7. Double-entry draft by an intermediate-grade student—Example 2.

VISUALIZING: READING WITH THE MIND'S EYE

After viewing the movie version of a book they have previously read, careful readers often make comments like "It wasn't as good as the book." Readers who experience flow (Csikszentmihalyi, 1991) have little trouble creating mental images of the actions and descriptions in the text or feeling the emotions of the characters, whether sad, happy, frightened, angry, or surprised. They are living the experience vicariously. In general, movies just do not have the space or time (or the budget that would be required) to render scenes and events as authors depict them. Also, because as readers we bring our personal experiences to bear as we read, the images we form necessarily differ, at least somewhat, from person to person. Consider, for instance, the following paragraph; as you read it, concentrate on making mental images of the event taking place, especially: Who are the "we" the author speaks of? What is the loop area like where huckleberries are being sought? What do the containers look like that are being used for the berries? Where is home? And what's the desired result?

> On our long trek through the loop area, we finally found a spot to get our much-desired huckleberries. Our sacks were bulging as we left, ready for the long drive home. We were satisfied when we imagined our end result.[1]

Depending on your experiences and which part of the country you live in, you may have pictured very different scenes. Did you picture a family traipsing through the woods on a brambles-ridden path carrying burlap sacks in search of huckleberries, like many readers/listeners do? Or like the author of the paragraph, who grew up in Chicago, did you perhaps envision a couple of adults driving along Chicago's downtown Loop in search of a health-food store to get some huckleberries? The bags are the green, nylon variety. The long drive home is back to the suburbs, and the end result? In my experience with using this paragraph there is less regional distinction here—pie, jam, pastries, we all like our sweets!

Good authors (whether professional or intermediate-grade writers) create wonderful snapshots in their writing, and though some authors may focus more on describing action and others on character and setting, the snapshots create visual images that draw readers into and through the text. For example, consider the flashback that Betsy Byars (1968) uses to open *The Midnight Fox*. We are introduced to Tommy, the main character and storyteller, as he closes his eyes recalling the black fox he has come to know and love. Sometimes he pictures the first time he saw her leaping over the green grass with a quick and easy gait, and

> Sometimes it is that last terrible night, and I am standing beneath the oak tree with the rain beating against me. The lightning flashes, the world is turned white for a moment, and I see everything as it was—the broken lock, the empty cage, the small tracks disappearing in the rain. Then it seems to me that I can hear, as plainly as I heard it that August night, above the rain, beyond the years, the high, clear bark of the midnight fox. (p. 9)

Passages such as the one above and those that follow are excellent for engaging students in the skill of visualizing. Ask them to close their eyes and create pictures of the scene, character, or action as you read the passage expressively aloud. After the reading, ask listeners to draw a quick sketch to capture as many details from the reading as possible or invite them to retell the passage to a partner and then listen while the partner tells it back, adding anything that might have been missed.

Roald Dahl was a master at using description to captivate his readers, describing characters, settings, and events in picture-making language, sometimes even going so far as to ascribe names to his characters that captured a physical or personality trait, as he did in *James and the Giant Peach* (1996) with Aunts Sponge and Spiker who, as the author tells readers, "were both really horrible people" (p. 2).[2]

> Aunt Sponge was enormously fat and very short. She had small piggy eyes, a sunken mouth, and one of those white flabby faces that looked exactly as though it had been boiled. She was like a great white soggy overboiled cabbage. Aunt Spiker, on the other hand, was lean and tall and bony, and she wore steel-rimmed spectacles that fixed onto the end of her nose with a clip. She had a screeching voice and long wet, narrow lips, and whenever she got angry or excited, little flecks of spit would come shooting out of her mouth as she talked. (p. 6)

Later in the story, as James and his motley creature crew fly high in the sky on the peach, Roald Dahl depicts an ominous scene:

> Clouds like mountains towered high above their heads on all sides, mysterious, menacing, overwhelming. Gradually it grew darker and darker, and then a pale three-quarter moon came up over the tops of the clouds and cast an eerie light over the whole scene. (p. 86)

Dahl also cast actions in a vivid manner, sometimes using similes and onomatopoeia, as in the following scene in which Cloud-Men respond to a challenge by Centipede:

A large hailstone can hurt you as much as a rock or a lump of lead if it is thrown hard enough—and my goodness, how those Cloud-Men could throw! The hailstones came whizzing through the air like bullets from a machine gun, and James could hear them smashing against the sides of the peach and burying themselves in the peach flesh with horrible squelching noises—*plop! plop! plop! plop!* And then *ping! ping! ping!* as they bounced off the poor Ladybug's shell because she couldn't lie as flat as the others. And then *crack!* as one of them hit the Centipede right on the nose and *crack!* again as another one hit him somewhere else. (pp. 91–92)

Nonfiction or informational text can also be used to develop visualization skills and to help increase reading motivation and comprehension. Picture, for example, the following from the opening paragraphs of "Dragonflies: Rulers of the Sky" in Cathy Camper's (2002) *Bugs before Time: Prehistoric Insects and Their Relatives:*

It's three hundred million years ago, the world is swampy, the air is hot and humid. There are no people or dinosaurs. A few huge amphibians doze in the warm mud. Horsetails, mosses, and ferns as big as trees bake in the still air.

Suddenly there's a loud whirring sound. What is it? Birds, bats, pterosaurs and planes don't exist in the ancient world.

Flying overhead is the biggest insect that ever lived! (n.p.)

To visualize nonfiction passages such as the preceding one, students need well-developed vocabulary knowledge, or they need to be introduced to critical vocabulary before the passage is read. In the dragonfly segment, lack of prior knowledge of *amphibians, horsetails,* or *pterosaurs,* as well as other words that may be unfamiliar, is likely to negatively impact readers'/listeners' abilities to visualize the scene and may possibly distract students from the amazing fact that ends the scene: Prehistoric dragonflies had wing spans of over 30 inches!

THINKING AND QUESTIONING

Students need to be able to generate questions in order to monitor for meaning and to engage with one another about the text. Strategies such as reciprocal teaching (Palincsar & Brown, 1986) and questioning the author (Beck, McKeown, Sandora, Kucan, & Worthy, 1996) help students to develop and internalize a questioning stance. Modeling the sorts of questions you want students to ask is an important part of the process of teaching students to question. If the kinds of questions you ask are primarily literal and require memory for what is read but little or no thinking, that's the kind of question you will likely find students generating. If, on the other hand, you want to encourage questions that involve inferring, evaluating, analyzing, interpreting, synthesizing, and so forth—in other words, questions that involve higher levels of thinking—then those are the kinds of questions you need to be modeling.

As readers, we sometimes ask ourselves literal questions to recall a bit of information we previously read in order to more fully understand a portion of text we are currently reading, but the bulk of our questions is comprised of the whys and hows that surface as we seek to understand and make connections. For example, consider the discussion of Pluto and its new classification in Seymour Simon's updated edition (2007) of *Our Solar System,* in particular, the sentence about the new definition of the solar system, which identifies that, among other objects, "there are eight planets, at least three minor, or dwarf, planets, and tens of thousands of much smaller Solar System objects, such as comets and asteroids" (p. 57) As a reader, I may recall that earlier in the book the phrase "minor planets" was explained, but I may not remember the term *asteroid* that was given to explain it and therefore ask myself the question: "What is another name for *minor planet*?" and look back to find the answer. With that understanding, a bigger, more provocative question comes to mind: "Although all minor planets seem to be asteroids, from the last part of the sentence, it's clear that not all asteroids are minor planets; why is that?" To try to resolve the matter, I would need to analyze text from the preceding page and make some inferences.

An engaging way to provide upper-elementary students with practice in generating questions and probing text (and graphics) is through the use of cartoons or nursery rhymes. Present students with a cartoon from the newspaper, a magazine, or a resource, such as *The Complete Cartoons of the New Yorker* (Mankoff, 2004), or with a nursery rhyme, which can easily be downloaded from the Internet, and ask them, individually or with a partner, to generate at least five questions about the cartoon or nursery rhyme, allowing one or none of the literal variety. Then ask individuals or partners to pair up and talk about their questions and possible responses to them. If time allows, ask each group to choose three questions from those already generated or new ones, and trade them with another group. Repeat the discussion process; then debrief as a group. Which questions were most engaging, which required the most thinking, which could be answered without ever looking at the cartoon or reading the nursery rhyme? Are the questions authentic; in other words, do they logically relate to the text?

Consider one or both of the following nursery rhymes and generate as many questions as you can; interrogate the text; ask the difficult questions. Poetry can be used to extend students' work with cartoons and/or nursery rhymes and encourage questioning as a habit of mind.

Jack and Jill	Humpty Dumpty
Jack and Jill went up the hill	Humpty Dumpty sat on a wall,
To fetch a pail of water.	Humpty Dumpty had a great fall.
Jack fell down and broke his crown,	All the King's horses, and all the
And Jill came tumbling after.	King's men
	Couldn't put Humpty together
	again!

Some possibilities for "Jack and Jill" include:

- Who are Jack and Jill? What's their relationship?
- A hill seems an unlikely place to fetch water; why are they going up the hill?
- Why do they need the water?
- What caused Jack to fall down—was he running? Did he trip?
- Which kind of crown did he break—his head, the kind worn by a king, part of his tooth, or something else?
- Why did Jill tumble after Jack? Did the same thing that caused Jack's fall cause hers?
- Is Jill hurt?
- What happened to the water? Or did Jack fall before they got the water?
- How will Jack and Jill get home?
- Should one or both of them go after the water one more time?

Some possibilities for "Humpty Dumpty" include:

- Who or what is Humpty Dumpty?
- Why was Humpty sitting on a wall?
- Where is the wall?
- How did Humpty get on the wall in the first place?
- What caused Humpty's fall?
- Was someone who could have prevented the fall negligent?
- How did the King's horses and men try to put Humpty together?
- What made anyone think that horses could put Humpty together again?
- How did people feel about the fact that Humpty couldn't be put together again?
- Which is Humpty Dumpty: Brave or foolhardy? Why do you think as you do?
- What additional questions could be generated that would relate the two texts?

Some online sources for nursery rhymes, such as *www.rhymes.org. uk/*, include the rhyme's origin as well as the lyrics. Discussion of the history can be an interesting follow-up to the question-generating activity. For instance, "Jack and Jill" originated in France, and Jack was none other than Louis XVI, who was beheaded ("broke his crown") during the French Revolution's Reign of Terror during 1793, as was his queen, Marie Antoinette ("and Jill came tumbling after"). "Humpty Dumpty" derives from the English Civil War (1642–1649). In 1648, Colchester, a walled town that had been fortified by the Royalists ("King's men"), was besieged by the opposition. Next to the wall was a church, which housed a Royalist fort. A huge cannon ("Humpty Dumpty") had been tactically placed on it. The opposition fired at the Royalists, damaged the wall, and Humpty Dumpty fell to the ground. The Royalists ("all the King's men and all the King's horses") tried to restore the cannon to another part of the wall, but it was too heavy ("couldn't put Humpy together again"). The loss of Humpty Dumpty had tragic consequences, as the town fell to the opposition.

SUMMARIZING: MAKE IT ACTIVE!

Being able to summarize information, to pare down what has been read to its gist, along with key supporting details, is an aid to comprehension and remembering. Students are frequently asked to summarize information, but if we want *all* students to be able to engage in the process, we need to precede the *asking* with *showing* students how to summarize. According to Hidi and Anderson (1986), summarizing involves (1) determining what's important, (2) condensing information by generalizing rather than specifying all the details, and (3) writing down the result in your own words.

Graphic Organizers

Graphic organizers can help students master the process of summarizing, and because there are lots of different types of organizers, they can be used with both narrative and informational text. Three good sources for downloadable graphic organizers include

> *Education Place: www.eduplace.com/graphicorganizer/* (Spanish option)
> edHelper.com: *edhelper.com/teachers/graphic_organizers.htm*
> Teacher Vision: *www.teachervision.fen.com/graphic-organizers/ printable/6293.html*

Story retelling frames and story maps can be used to guide students to include important elements when summarizing narrative text. These two types of graphic organizer typically include a space, or a prompt, for each story element—setting, characters, problem/goal, events/roadblocks, resolution, and conclusion. The categories draw students' attention to what is important, and the limited space for responding necessitates concise wording. Once the graphic is complete, the student has a template of information from which to draw for writing the summary.

Although an informational text usually involves multiple text structures (description, sequence, compare and contrast, problem and solution, and cause and effect), for a given topic one structure is likely to predominate or be more suitable for the portion to be summarized. For example, although the discussion in Seymour Simon's (2007) *Our Solar System* moves sequentially from planets closest to the sun to those farthest away, and information is presented that allows readers to compare and contrast the planets, the structure of the text for each planet discussion is that of description. So if a summary is being written for a particular planet, a graphic organizer for description would be most appropriate; however, if the aim is to examine relationships or order, a compare–contrast or sequence graphic organizer would be more suitable.

Sticky Notes

The sticky notes students use as they monitor for meaning can also be used to help them summarize. Students can write down in their own words key ideas for a given paragraph or section of text read and stick it on the page. A sentence or even a phrase can capture the essence of what was read in a portion of the text. To avoid confusing these sticky notes with others, students might label them with a code, such as *S* for summary. When finished with reading the chapter or part, students can compile their section stickies to create an overall summary.

Countdown Summaries

A final possibility for summarizing involves performance. This technique stems from a comedic improvisation activity called "Countdown," used by The MAD* Factory (music, art, and drama), a nonprofit theater arts organization for kids of all ages located in Oberlin, Ohio. Although grounded in improvisation, Countdown is well suited for summarization of text that has been listened to or read. It not only encourages students to focus on what's important and to be concise, but it's tremendously fun for everyone involved. The procedure, which involves a series of dramatizations and seems better-suited for fiction than nonfiction (other than perhaps history), works as follows:

After students have read or listened to a passage, ask for two volunteers to act out a summary of the reading. Because performance is used, some students may be reluctant to get involved at first. Work with volunteers initially, rather than choosing actors, until everyone feels it's safe for risk taking. Warming up the whole group with some theater games, and improv activities such as those in Viola Spolin's *Theater Games for the Classroom: A Teacher's Handbook of Techniques* (1986), or Carrie Lobman and Matthew Lundquist's *Unscripted Learning: Using Improv Activities Across the K–8 Curriculum* (2007), will make it easier for more students to volunteer. A third person serves as timer.

Initially, the pair of actors has 1 minute to perform a summary of the text just read. Before they begin, talk about the essence of the passage—What's important? What sort of movements will there be? Thinking about likely movements in advance is just as important as considering what's important from the text. Movement adds interest and helps students remember the summary. One minute passes by very quickly; to ensure that students get to the end of their summary, when there are about 10 seconds left, say something like "Find a way to end the scene."

For the second try reduce the time allowance to 30 seconds. The same two actors repeat their scene but with obvious consolidation of the events. Before they begin, discuss with students what's most important and should be maintained and what will have to be sacrificed due to the brevity of action. For the third trial, reduce the time to 15 seconds; and for the fourth cut it back to just 5 seconds. By this point, a classroom *mirthquake* is likely as students strive to capture the essence of the text in a flash of action. To culminate the sequence, actors have a go at a 1-second performance.

Though the activity may sound almost ridiculous, the action of repeating the scene while still striving to capture the core meaning of the passage of text makes it a valuable tool for working on summarizing and in a context that is both challenging and highly entertaining. After the action, students can write down the summary, perhaps even as a paired script (Strickland et al., 2002).

CONCLUSION

Comprehension is at the heart of reading. Many effective strategies can be used to help develop intermediate-grade students' comprehension. In this chapter I have focused on strategies and techniques that actively engage students and that also have the potential to be motivating. Writing, thinking, imagining, drawing, questioning, talking, and performing are avenues for deepening students' understanding of text. With teacher modeling and ample opportunities for students to construct understanding and monitor for meaning using activities that hook and hold their interest, it is my hope that students will develop habits of mind that enable them to comprehend deeply, purposefully, and with a sense of satisfaction.

NOTES

1. Many thanks to Barbara Guzzetti of Arizona State University, originator of the paragraph.
2. Selections from *James and the Giant Peach* by Roald Dahl, copyright 1961 by Roald Dahl. Text copyright renewed 1989 by Roald Dahl. Illustrations copyright 1996 by Lane Smith. Used by permission of Alfred A. Knopf, an imprint of Random House Children's Books, a division of Random House, Inc.

REFERENCES

Anderson, R. C. (2004). Role of the reader's schema in comprehension, learning, and memory. In R. B. Ruddell & N. J. Unrau (Eds.), *Theoretical models and processes of reading* (5th ed., pp. 594–606). Newark, DE: International Reading Association.

Barone, D. (1990). The written responses of young children: Beyond comprehension to story understanding. *New Advocate, 3,* 49–56.

Baumann, J. F., & Duffy, A. M. (1997). *Engaged reading for pleasure and learning: A report from the National Reading Research Center.* Athens, GA: National Reading Research Center (NRRC).

Beck, I. L., McKeown, M. G., Sandora, C., Kucan, L., & Worthy, J. (1996). Questioning the author: A yearlong classroom implementation to engage students with text. *Elementary School Journal, 96*(4), 385–414.

Berthoff, A. E. (1981). *The making of meaning.* Montclair, NJ: Boynton/Cook.

Csikszentmihalyi, M. (1991). Literacy and intrinsic motivation. In S. R. Graubard (Ed.), *Literacy: An overview by fourteen experts* (pp. 115–140). New York: Hill & Wang.

Duke, N. K., & Pearson, P. D. (2002). Effective practices for developing reading comprehension. In A. E. Farstrup & S. J. Samuels (Eds.), *What research has to say about reading instruction* (3rd ed., pp. 205–242). Newark, DE: International Reading Association.

Gambrell, L. B. (1996). Creating classroom cultures that foster reading motivation. *Reading Teacher, 50*(1), 14–23.

Guthrie, J. T., Van Meter, P., McCann, A. D., Wigfield, A., Bennett, L., Poundstone, C.C., et al. (1996). Growth of literacy engagement: Changes in motivation and strategies during concept-oriented reading instruction. *Reading Research Quarterly, 31,* 306–332.

Guthrie, J. T., & Wigfield, A. (1997). Reading engagement: A rationale for theory and teaching. In J. T. Guthrie & A. Wigfield (Eds.), *Reading engagement: Motivating readers through integrated instruction* (pp. 1–12). Newark, DE: International Reading Association.

Guthrie, J. T., Wigfield, A., Humenick, N. M., Perencevich, K. C., Taboada, A., & Barbosa, P. (2006). Influences of stimulating tasks on reading motivation and comprehension. *Journal of Educational Research, 99*(4), 232–245.

Hacker, D. J. (2004). Self-regulated comprehension during normal reading. In R. B. Ruddell & N. J. Unrau (Eds.), *Theoretical models and processes of reading* (5th ed., pp. 755–779). Newark, DE: International Reading Association.

Harris, T. L., & Hodges, R. E. (Eds.). (1995). *The literacy dictionary: The vocabulary of reading and writing.* Newark, DE: International Reading Association.

Harvey, S., & Goudvis, A. (2007). *Strategies that work: Teaching comprehension for understanding and engagement* (2nd ed.). Portland, ME: Stenhouse.

Hidi, S., & Anderson, V. (1986). Producing written summaries: Task demands, cognitive operations, and implications for instruction. *Review of Educational Research, 56,* 473–494.

Keene, E. O., & Zimmerman, S. (2007). *Mosaic of thought: The power of comprehension strategy instruction.* Portsmouth, NH: Heinemann.

Lobman, C., & Lundquist, M. (2007). *Unscripted learning: Using improv activities across the K–8 curriculum.* New York: Teachers College Press.

Mankoff, R. (Ed.). (2004) *The complete cartoons of* The New Yorker. New York: Advance Magazine.

National Institute of Child Health and Human Development. (2000). *Report of the National Reading Panel: Teaching children to read: An evidence-based assessment of the scientific research literature on reading and its implications for reading instruction.* Washington, DC: U.S. Government Printing Office.

Palincsar, A. S., & Brown, A. L. (1986). Interactive teaching to promote independent learning from text. *Reading Teacher, 39,* 771–777.

Palmer, B. M., Codling, R. M., & Gambrell, L. B. (1994). In their own words: What elementary students have to say about motivation to read. *Reading Teacher, 48*(2), 176–178.

Pressley, M., & Afflerbach, P. (1995). *Verbal protocols of reading: The nature of constructively responsive reading.* Hillsdale, NJ: Erlbaum.

Readence, J. E., Bean, T. W., & Baldwin, R. S. (1985). *Content-area reading: An integrated approach* (2nd ed.). Dubuque, IA: Kendall/Hunt.

Spolin, V. (1986). *Theater games for the classroom: A teacher's handbook of techniques.* Evanston, IL: Northwestern University Press.

Strickland, D. S., Ganske, K., & Monroe, J. K. (2002). *Supporting struggling readers and writers: Strategies for classroom intervention 3–6.* Portland, ME: Stenhouse.

Worthy, J. (1996). A matter of interest: Literature that hooks reluctant readers and keeps them reading. *Reading Teacher, 50*(3), 204–212.

CHILDREN'S BOOKS

Byars, B. (1968). *The midnight fox.* New York: Puffin Books.

Camper, C. (2002). *Bugs before time: Prehistoric insects and their relatives.* New York: Simon & Schuster Books for Young Readers.

Dahl, R. (1996). *James and the giant peach.* New York: Puffin Books.

Fleischman, P. (1999). *Weslandia.* New York: Scholastic.

Fox, P. (1991). *Monkey island.* New York: Dell Publishing.

Sachar, L. (2004). *Sideways stories from Wayside School.* New York: Harper Teen.

Simon, S. (2007). *Our solar system,* (updated edition). New York: HarperCollins.

Taylor, M. D. (1976). *Roll of thunder, hear my cry.* New York: Dial.

Taylor, M. D. (1981). *Let the circle be unbroken.* New York: Dial.

Tolkien, J. R. R. (1965). *The fellowship of the ring.* New York: Houghton Mifflin.

6

Promoting Comprehension in Middle School and High School

Tapping into Out-of-School Literacies of Our Adolescents

Xiufang Chen
Valarie G. Lee

Lanie, an eighth grader, settles in her desk in her second period English class. She drags the heavy textbook from her backpack as Mrs. Frazier asks for the class to turn to *The Miracle Worker,* Act I, scene ii. Lanie sighs, flips open her book, and retrieves her vocabulary notebook from her backpack, digging around her many magazines. Mrs. Frazier asks for someone to summarize what happened in the play in their reading yesterday. Lanie begins writing down the vocabulary words found in a textbook next to scene two. She knows Mrs. Frazier expects them to write the important vocabulary and definitions in their notebooks. After a short summary, Mrs. Frazier asks for volunteers to read the parts. Lanie does not raise her hand, but follows along in the play. After 30 minutes reading from the play, with intermittent questions from Mrs. Frazier, Lanie and the other students are assigned eight comprehension questions found at the end of the scene. Lanie sighs again and begins writing her answers.

Lanie is not the only adolescent in Mrs. Frazier's English/language arts class who is not motivated to read, not engaged in reading, and not prepared for the reading assignments in class. Kamil et al. (2008) found that motivation and engagement seem to decline as students enter adolescence. Thinking about Lanie's experience, years and years of frustration trying to make sense of literacy activities at school, you might understand how her disenchantment happens. Hinchman, Alvermann, Boyd, Brozo, and Vacca (2003) argue that literacy research supports instruction that "attends to older students' perceptions of competence, their ability to make personal connections, their participation, and their development of search and comprehension strategies that are embedded in context" (p. 308). Clearly, the instruction in Mrs. Frazier's classroom does not demonstrate an understanding of this research-proven instruction that would promote Lanie's reading comprehension and engagement.

As teachers and researchers, we know that adolescents' lack of motivation and engagement likely leads to poor comprehension. Additionally, it has been found that many of the middle and high school students who have basic reading and writing skills do not reach the necessary high level of literacy (Peterson, Caverly, Nicholson, O'Neal, & Cusenbary, 2000). When adolescent students' motivation for, and engagement with, literacy learning increases, they are more likely to become autonomous, self-directed, and strategic readers and learners (Alvermann, Phelps, & Ridgeway, 2007; Kamil et al., 2008).

Ironically, when talking about her out-of-school literacy activities, Lanie describes herself as an avid and competent reader. She enjoys reading fashion magazines and news events on the Internet and from magazines. Using a social networking site, she writes her own blog about what is happening in her life and uploads her life pictures and videos. She also frequently visits her friends' blogs, reading their written and digital stories and sometimes leaving her comments. She reads books recommended by her friends and trades these books with her other friends. Clearly, we see two different "Lanies" in and outside school and an inconsistency or maybe disconnection between in-school and out-of-school reading activities. In the new millennium, the term *adolescent literacy* is now more inclusive of what young people count as texts—for example, printed texts, digital texts, and hypertexts (Alvermann, 2001). Significantly, the International Reading Association/National Council of Teachers of English (IRA/NCTE; 2002) designates one of the major missions, if not the most important mission, of language arts as that of preparing students for the literacy requirements of the present and the future in a way that reflects technological advances and a changing society.

Like many of us, Mrs. Frazier wants to know how she can motivate Lanie and her other students to read and to engage them in the reading process while they acquire critical literacy skills. The key might be to look at the disconnection between Lanie's in-school and out-of-school literacies while rethinking the definition of adolescent literacy and the mission as an English/language arts teacher in the new millennium. As designated by IRA/NCTE (2002) and implied by Lanie's experiences, it is critical to value adolescent students' out-of-school literacy experiences.

Many of you have found ways to infuse out-of-school literacy experiences into your instruction and are looking for new ideas. Others may wonder, "How can I start making better connections between the language arts curriculum and adolescents' literacy activities?" In this chapter, we take three important aspects of language arts and show how you can infuse them with out-of-school literacies to increase students' motivation and engagement and thus improve their reading comprehension. These aspects are (1) setting a real purpose for reading through technology, (2) enhancing note taking and study skills through Web software programs, and (3) supporting critical thinking skills through multiple texts and Internet reading. For each aspect, we start with well-known strategies and show how we breathed life into them through technological applications and diverse texts. While the samples provided are from language arts, the information presented is appropriate for middle school and high school teachers of all content areas who are interested in incorporating students' out-of-school literacies to increase their motivation and engagement in literacy activities, leading to deeper understanding of concepts and skills.

SETTING A REAL PURPOSE
THROUGH TECHNOLOGIES

One way to increase adolescent students' motivation and engagement in reading is to set a real purpose for their reading. Purpose setting, which is critical to strategic reading, unfortunately has been overlooked as part of the instruction by many teachers (Allen, 2000), including Mrs. Frazier. Too often we fail to show students that there is a more significant reason to read than just to finish the text. There are many authentic purposes for reading. One such purpose is the creation of a product; that is, making something after reading a text. Some strategies used to create a product include drama/Readers' Theater performances and RAFT (role, audience, format, topic) writing. In the following sections, we show you how these strategies are enhanced through technological applications that many of our adolescents know and value.

Dramatizing/Moviemaking a Text

Chambers (1996) sends a very clear message that a reading teacher's work includes "helping children engage in the drama of reading, helping them become dramatist (rewriter of the text), director (interpreter of the text), actor (performer of the text), audience (actively responsive recipient of the text), even critic (commentator and explicator and scholarly student of the text)" (p. 5). When students script and act out a piece of literature, they must understand characters and other elements of the text and communicate the meaning and tone to others. Their comprehension of the text is thereby increased. Mitchell (2003) asserts that "creating and performing a script is fun and highly motivational because others will see our performance and respond to it" (p. 130). She also found that "drama not only enhanced [students'] engagement with text but also improved their interactions with the other students in the class" (p. 131). With students such as Lanie in mind, who are not motivated to do any literacy activities in class, some teachers choose moviemaking by using camcorders and moviemaking software to enhance the drama strategy. Vicki Sellers, an eighth-grade English/language arts teacher at Crosbyton Middle School, is one of those teachers who increases students' motivation for literacy learning through making a movie of a text. Students' critical thinking skills are also enhanced through the project. Let's look at the steps Mrs. Sellers takes to implement moviemaking in her classroom.

1. *Activating background knowledge and setting a purpose.* Mrs. Sellers introduced Mary Shelley's *Frankenstein* (1818/1981) by reviewing the horror stories students had read and themes such as friendship. She told students that they were going to read *Frankenstein,* and to set a real purpose, she explained that they would choose a theme expressed in the book and, working in small groups, they would make a camcorder movie to express that theme. The possibility of making a movie about the book—a real big-screen movie with themselves on the screen!—made the whole class anxious to read it.

2. *Reading the text.* Mrs. Sellers's students read an abridged version of *Frankenstein* together, stopping periodically to discuss, take notes, complete activities, etc. These activities further stimulated the class engagement with the book. Slowing down the reading process encouraged students to relate to the characters, events, and themes.

3. *Brainstorming topics and themes.* After reading *Frankenstein,* the class brainstormed a list of themes expressed in the book, including companionship, friendship, science versus religion, freedom, human versus nature, etc.

4. *Topic/theme selection.* Students chose topics/themes for their movie from the generated list. Those who selected the same theme became a team.

5. *Developing background knowledge.* In order to better understand the book and the theme before starting to write their scripts, students read the corresponding parts in its original version of *Frankenstein* and then researched background information on the book to develop their scripts.

6. *Scriptwriting.* Students wrote their scripts in small groups. To scaffold students' writing, Mrs. Sellers modeled how to write scripts based on texts and supported students through the process. Books such as *Readers Theatre for Young Adults: Scripts and Script Development* provide step-by-step guidance for producing scripts and include examples. As they wrote, students continually revisited their sources in order to render a more accurate interpretation, bearing in mind questions such as these: What message are we sending? Why do we want to send this message? Who is our audience? Will viewers have a different interpretation of this message? What's the relationship to the text?

7. *Peer critiques.* After the groups finished writing their scripts, each displayed its draft, along with any photographs to help communicate meaning, for the class to critique. Students read each others' scripts, asked questions, requested clarifications, and shared opinions and comments. Scriptwriters answered questions, provided further explanation or clarification, and took notes for possible revisions. Besides providing insights to refine writing, these feedback communications deepened students' understanding of the book. The process, which included teacher questioning as needed, enhanced students' critical thinking, writing skills, and ability to communicate effectively.

8. *Script revision.* Groups revised their scripts until satisfied.

9. *Recording preparation.* Once the script was finished, students prepared for the shooting. As a team students discussed and decided who would take which role and where they would shoot the movie. Mrs. Sellers's students finally chose a 1930-style hotel room in their city, Crosbyton, to record their movies. Once roles and location were determined they gathered materials, made costumes, and prepared to use equipment, such as learning how to make a video using a camcorder and software (e.g., Windows Moviemaker or Apple iMovie).

10. *Capturing the scenes.* Students recorded scenes using a camcorder. At times, the students in Mrs. Sellers's class were so involved that they redid a scene until each team member okayed the result. Mrs. Sellers asked the students to think about what techniques are used to attract attention as well as other clarifying or extending questions (e.g., see Step 6).

11. *Editing*. Students edited their movies using Windows Movie-Maker, I-Movie, etc. With teacher guidance they explored ways to add music and special effects. Websites that include detailed instruction and examples include *homepage.mac.com/torres21/* and *center.uoregon.edu/ISTE/uploads/NECC2006/KEY_13349523/Herzog_MovieMakerTutorial.pdf*.

12. *Presenting and responding*. Students presented their movies to the class and responded to their own and their peers' final products. Moviemaking from start to finish can take several weeks; Mrs. Sellers's students worked 4 weeks on their first movie.

13. *Reflection*. After the show students and teacher reflected on their moviemaking experience and what they gained from it. The reflections highlighted their new understandings of the book, the author, and the reading activity itself.

14. *New inquiries*. The moviemaking experience led students, especially those unmotivated adolescent readers, to want to know more about their own and/or other team's topics and ultimately to further reading.

Depending on the circumstances and confidentiality policies, some classes choose to put their movies on their class websites, and some even put their movies on YouTube (you can visit *www.techsoup.org/learningcenter/internet/page5876.cfm* to learn how to promote videos to a wider audience). The more people watch their performance and respond to it, the more likely students will be motivated to read more and perform better.

You can always adapt the steps of moviemaking a text, depending on the time and availability of equipment and students' motivation to read and engage. For example, you can simply ask students to dramatize a text in class or write and read a script as a Readers' Theater. Mrs. Sellers shared her feelings about their moviemaking project:

> "My kids are so excited ... they just enjoyed doing it! They learned the skills by doing them—reading, writing, moviemaking, cooperating, and so many other skills. They have a lot of planning ... lot of discussions. You must get used to an active classroom and will need to tolerate the noise. But I tell you: They are engaged! When they are engaged, the noise is different, and they are talking about business. They are giggling, good giggling; they are thinking, critically. ... As long as they have control, they will stay there and learn while having fun. This kind of learning is so important to me."[1]

RAFT: Rewriting a Text on Social Network Websites

RAFT (Santa, 1988) writing is another strategy for setting a real purpose for reading by creating a product after students have read a text. Shanahan (2004) emphasizes the importance of students taking a perspective when they write, moving past merely summarizing the events. Through RAFT students synthesize their learning and write a creative product to express their new knowledge. A RAFT requires that students consider the role of the writer (R), the audience (A), the format or genre (F), and the topic (T), thus leading them to think deeply about the concepts or main ideas of a reading.

In order to complete a RAFT, students select a topic to write about based on the reading, then consider a particular format or genre of writing, such as a letter, speech, recipe, breakup note, or biography. For instance, a RAFT using Guy de Maupassant's short story "The Necklace" might look like this:

R: Madame Mathilde Loisel
A: Young women at a French finishing school
F: Speech
T: Dangers of vanity

Writing a RAFT allows students to strengthen their comprehension of the text as they rethink the information they read, analyzing and synthesizing this knowledge into an engaging, creative product. Rethinking the text, taking another's perspective, allows for repeated, focused reading that encourages deeper comprehension. How can we connect this engaging writing strategy to our students' out-of-school literacies? We can easily encourage students to rewrite the text using formats they often enjoy, such as a social network page, blog, a discussion board, e-mails, and instant messaging. For instance, after reading the graphic novel *Persepolis,* a student might write an e-mail from 14-year-old Marjane to her parents in Iran, describing what it is like to attend school in Europe after fleeing the violence of the Islamic revolution in her country.

Other students may want to use technology such as MySpace (*www.myspace.com*) or Facebook (*www.facebook.com*) to create an actual Web-based RAFT product. For instance, if Romeo were to have his own social network page, who would he include on his "friends" list? Certainly Mercutio would be at the top. Also, what would he write in his profile? What music would he listen to? What would he describe as his interests and his dislikes? Family feuds? The interactive nature of a social network page allows students to add features or replace existing ones. In addition, students can search the Web for images to include on their page. You can visit the following site for a complete example of a Myspace page for Scout Finch, of *To Kill a Mockingbird*, designed by Nelson for his 10th-grade English class: *profile.myspace.com/index.cfm?fuseaction=user.viewprofile&friendid=303668723.* At this level, Nelson uses facts about Scout to make the page content authentic, and teachers can assess the logical as well as creative use of those facts. On a deeper level, Nelson creates a blog from Scout's point of view, much like the familiar RAFT strategy. As students create a blog for their character, they must think deeply about the character's motivations and personality, which requires students to make inferences. In Figure 6.1 we provide an example of Nelson's blog. In order for students to create a social network site for their character, they must create a profile using the character's information but their own e-mail address.

Concerns about the privacy and safety of students are warranted;

Tuesday, December 26, 1938

Disaster at Finch Landing

Have you ever had one of those awful days where things go bad quickly? This weekend I went to Finch's Landing to see my aunt and uncle for Christmas. My uncle Jack is a relative that I always want to see but I can't say the same about my Aunt Alex or my cousin Francis. We were having fun until Francis started bickering with me. Aunt Alex always favored Francis so I was the one who got into trouble. Francis was saying that Atticus was ruining the family for all of us and that he shouldn't be a part of it anymore. I was mad but then Aunt Alex stopped the fighting before anything happened. Then Aunt Alex left and Francis continued to bother me. He said that Atticus stood up for the wrong people and that he should be sent to jail for it and that was the last straw. When he called me the same ugly thing Cecil Jacobs did, I punched him as hard as I could in the mouth. I forgot all about my promise to Atticus. But can you blame me?
He went straight down and started yelling in pain. I couldn't believe that I had punched him and neither could Uncle Jack because he was mad. I didn't talk to anybody after that and when we went home I went straight to my room. Uncle Jack talked to me and I told him what Francis had said about Atticus ruin' the family and all. Uncle Jack was powerful mad, but Atticus told him I needed to control my anger more. He said I was going to have to deal with this more for awhile. I reckon he is talking about the trial and the Tom Robinson business. I get the feeling Atticus is trying to tell me something that I don't rightly understand yet. It was not a good day but I have to admit that the punch I got on Francis was a mighty good one.

9:26 pm   12 comments   Add a comment

FIGURE 6.1. Student's blog for *To Kill a Mockingbird*.

teachers must use caution in the use of Internet applications. Some teachers may not be comfortable having students use a social network website in a school setting or even requiring the use of one as homework. One way to address these concerns is for students to create a "webpage" using word processing to mimic the style of the webpage. We have included a blank template that students can fill in (see Appendix 6.1).

Another option is for teachers to create a class site for educational blogs such as a Nicenet (*www.nicenet.org*), which enables teachers to create a class site for free, allowing students to blog their responses to reading. This application creates a safer environment for students to be engaged in writing blogs from characters' points of view.

Rethinking text using a technology-based format, such as a social network page, allows students freedom to create a meaningful product, to further flesh out the characters by voicing characters' thoughts and feelings. Viewing the events of a story from a character's perspective also encourages students to connect with that character. We discovered that text rewrites using social networking applications such as blogs and discussion boards engage our students more effectively in interacting with the text. In many cases this is because they are creating a meaningful product using a format they enjoy outside of school. We have found that students read with more purpose and often refer back to the text for details to make their blog more authentic. As Nelson shared, "I am trying to get it to sound more like Scout. It needs to have her mannerisms and personality."

Using a popular genre such as a social networking site allows adolescents to write what they know in a familiar context. Hinchman et al. (2003) maintain that the "best practices are worthwhile only when viewed in context, embedded in information sources that are most familiar or interesting to students" (p. 308). As many classroom teachers are discovering, allowing the use of popular website formats in the classroom helps students apply their out-of-school literacy skills to create a meaningful product in school and can result in increased engagement.

ENHANCING NOTE-TAKING STUDY
SKILLS USING WIKIs

Why Use Wikis?

One important part of language arts is to teach students study skills, and one of the skills is to take effective notes for later review. This skill, with its various formats, helps students engage in their reading and supports their comprehension of texts. Note taking is thus also a powerful learning and reading strategy. You might have used different graphic organizers as structures for students to take effective notes; for example, column notes and responses such as double-entry journals, split-page note taking, and text structures. You might also have used mapping (concept maps, mind maps, or story maps), charting (I-charts, relationship charts, etc.), and outlining (story outline, sequence outline, power notes, etc.). Another example of note taking is SQ3R (Robinson, 1946/1970). SQ3R has been very effective for many adolescents with its five-step process: survey, question, read, recite, and review.

How can we enhance this note taking study skill through technologies that adolescents use every day so that they will feel more engaged in the process? Some teachers choose free Web software programs that enable students to write, edit, organize, and search their notes efficiently while collaborating with other students on the knowledge construction. One example is the wiki technology, which offers an easy-to-learn, minimally structured format within which all users can access and edit the pages on an ongoing basis (Luce-Kapler & Dobson, 2005). Wikipedia (*en.wikipedia.org/wiki/Main_page*) might be the most visible example of this technology.

Wiki is a Hawaiian term meaning "quick," which captures one of its unique characteristics: Users can create their notes, search notes, or organize their notes within minutes. A wiki is a website that includes a collection of webpages designed to enable anyone who accesses it to contribute or modify content. Each page in the wiki can contain links to several other pages, and these pages in turn contain more links to different pages (see, e.g., Farabaugh, 2007; Wax, 2007, available at *dwax. wikidot.com/pem-davidson-buck-constructing-race-creating-white-privilege.*)

Wax (2007) listed some of the benefits that wikis offer to students: legibility, durability, searching, links, collaboration, and affordability. Wiki notes are legible and save time when trying to organize messy and scattered thoughts. Unlike regular school notes, wiki notes are durable and can be developed over the entire process of a student's education; indeed notes taken years earlier can be accessed quickly simply by clicking some links. Using its search function, wiki notes can be accessed immediately across the entire collection of pages. Besides links to other pages within their wikis, students can link to other sites on the Web and thus bring new sources of information together in one place. The ability to link topics and ideas creates a very effective learning and review tool. Another unique feature of wikis is that they allow several people to collaborate on the same wiki through the adding function. More important, this collaboration is free from distance or time constraints. School time is limited, and wiki notes provide a platform for both teacher and students to communicate with each other outside of the schoolday schedule; this in turn allows more ideas and opinions to be shared. Finally, wikis are affordable; in fact, many wiki programs and services are free.

Wikis are especially effective and efficient for group work; students benefit from the strengths of their classmates by reading and editing each others' notes while still being able to access their original writing. After a topic is divided into parts and students are working on their individual subtopics, they can link to their group members' pages, and vice versa. As new material is covered, they can go back to each others' pages to edit or correct factual errors. Wikis are incredibly flexible, which makes this tool even more exciting to adolescents who love new technologies. Now let's look at how Andrew, an eleventh grader, used wiki with his classmates. The essay they are reading is *The Death of My Father* (2002) by Steve Martin.

Steps for Creating a Wiki

1. *Set up a wiki account.* Before starting to read the essay, Andrew's teacher demonstrated how they could set up a wiki account. Andrew and his classmates went to the Wiki Dot site *www.wikidot.com/,* one of the most popular wikis used by students. After entering, they created their accounts by clicking on "Create Account" at the top right and then followed the procedure.

2. *Read the text and put notes on the wiki website.* Once their wiki was set up, the teacher showed them how to create webpages. Andrew and his classmates then began to add their notes. Figure 6.2 shows one example of Andrew's wiki notes.

3. *Edit page and create links.* After adding their notes, Andrew and his classmates started to edit the page and create links. Their teacher also illustrated how to change the appearance of their texts through a simple set of text cues explained on the website. Like most wikis, Wiki Dot has an "Edit Page" button placed prominently on the page. When they clicked the button, a text box appeared in which to make their changes. Wikis such as Wiki Dot have a command bar at the top or bottom of the text box for formatting and manipulating text. Some wikis use a special set of text cues called *markup* (e.g., // this// makes the text *italic*); the markup can be found when clicking on "Help Tips."

At the same time, Andrew and his classmates started to create links to other pages, including each others' on the website where they might see connections. For instance, Andrew wanted to link the text about love to other pages, so he put that part in triple brackets, [[[like this]]]. If the text was the same as the title of a page already created, it was automatically linked to that page. Otherwise, a new page was created by click-

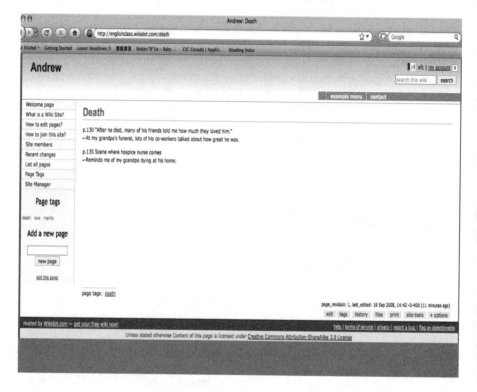

FIGURE 6.2. Example of Andrew's wiki notes.

ing on the link, and this led to the next step, tag pages. So as students worked, they could link to other pages.

4. *Tag pages.* Andrew's teacher modeled how to tag pages with keywords describing the content. Simply clicking the "Page Tags" bar on the Wiki Dot enabled Andrew and other students to type keywords of the text and quickly see related pages, even readings.

5. *Collaborate with others.* When Andrew and his classmates accessed, edited, or corrected each others' notes, they could always track changes and revert to earlier versions. Plus, they could always check new thoughts or missed notes on others' pages simply by clicking the links. These features of wiki, together with its powerful searching function, made the review of what they have covered easy and quick.

From the example in Andrew's class, you might be able to see what a powerful tool wikis can be for enhancing adolescents' note-taking study skills. They enable students to get highly engaged in their reading and note taking and can make learning more efficient and effective. If your school has limited technology and/or access to wiki websites, you might use a wiki template, such as that included in Appendix 6.2, to motivate and engage students in their reading and collaboration and to maximize their learning.

ENHANCING CRITICAL THINKING SKILLS THROUGH TECHNOLOGY AND MULTIPLE TEXTS

Adolescent students today face a flood of information from multiple texts both print and electronic. Therefore, it is more important than ever for us to tap into a form of reading that adolescents often find engaging, while supporting students in their ability to read information critically. Language arts classrooms must reflect and tune into the literacies of our adolescent students outside of school while also providing them with the skills to think critically about the information. The IRA/NCTE Standards for the English Language Arts (2002) emphasize that in today's classrooms, more than ever before, students need explicit instruction in reading electronic text.

In this section, we provide a strategy to scaffold students' reading of the Internet through a reading guide. Also, we provide examples of diverse texts to integrate into the language arts classroom, again to engage adolescents and to foster critical reading skills.

Thinking Critically about Internet Text

The IRA/NCTE Standards for the English Language Arts (2002) state that the profusion and complexity of Internet texts "require new levels of sophistication in search techniques and an expanded ability to choose, assess, and synthesize materials " (p. 29). To help students think critically about the decisions they make when searching on the Internet, we developed the Internet Reading Guide (see Figure 6.3), based on the Internet research skills suggested by Leu, Kinzer, Coiror, & Cammack, 2004):

1. Identifying important questions.
2. Locating information.
3. Critically evaluating the usefulness of information.
4. Synthesizing information to answer questions.
5. Communicating answers to others.

We adapted the strategies of a reading road map (Wood, 1988) and a selective reading guide (Cunningham & Shablak, 1975) to reflect the

Setting your purpose:

What is my purpose for this search?

What do I hope to learn?

Searching:

Once you enter key terms, how do you decide which link to select?

Do you need to refine your key terms?

Evaluate and analyze:

Once you select your link, how will you decide if this is a reliable site?

Synthesize:

How will you read so as to acquire the important information you need?

Evaluate and analyze:
You may have clicked on a hyperlink in the site that is not helpful. Will you go back to the original page or go to a new site?

Write down key questions and key terms:

_____
_____
_____

Hint: It's tempting to just select the first link!
– Look at the URL: Is this a .gov, .com, .edu, .net, or .org? Which one would help answer your questions?
– Look for your key terms in the description.

Stop and look:
Who is the author? (Look on home page, "About Us," at the bottom of the page, "Contact Us," etc.)
Who is the audience for the site?
What is the purpose of this site?

If you can't find the answer to these questions on the site, do you think it will be reliable? If not, try a new site!

Skim and scan:
Consider:
– Text boxes, subtitles, important terms in bold or colored font

Write down new information learned:

_____
_____
_____

Refocus:
Look back at your original question(s) and key terms.
Has this site been helpful, or do you need to go to a new site?
Do you need to refocus?

Going to a new site? Remember to think about your reading!

FIGURE 6.3. Internet Reading Guide.

unique reading demands of reading material on the Internet. This guide allows students to create a purpose for their search, to make decisions about sites they encounter, and to refocus if a selected site does not help them answer their questions.

As with any strategy, successful implementation of the Internet Reading Guide depends on explicit modeling. Students must be shown how to stop and think about their thinking while searching. Using the think-aloud strategy, teachers can project a preselected website and show students how they use the guide to ask themselves questions about the site. For instance, some students may not know how to find the author of a webpage. You can model this process by thinking aloud:

"I sometimes look at the bottom of the page for an author, but on this site, I see that they also have a link titled 'About Us.' I think I will click on this and see. No, this just gives information about the publisher. I will go back to the original page and look for more clues about the author. Wait. See this link titled 'Credits'? This looks promising. Look at what I found—a list of all the experts consulted for this site. Did you notice how I had to look in several places to find the author? Sometimes the author's name will be clearly stated on the webpage; however, you still have to think about whether the author is a credible source."

Through this think-aloud model, students observe a reader in action thinking about the information and making critical reading decisions. Once students have seen the Internet Reading Guide modeled, they can practice the strategy, ideally with a partner so that they can check each other's thinking as they search. Let's take a look at two students at work using the Internet Reading Guide as they research topics in Valarie's classroom.

Louis, a seventh grader, wants to know more about the civil rights movement while reading *The Watsons go to Birmingham—1963* by Christopher Paul Curtis (2000). After typing in "civil rights history" in the yahoo.com search box, he notices that the first link is promising: "This one looks okay. You can see the two words right there [in the description] so it will be good." When it comes time for Louis to locate the author, he immediately clicks on the hyperlink "About Us." He notices that it gives information about the publisher, not the author. When he goes back to the home page, he remarks, "Well, look at these cool graphics. They must know what they are talking about." Valarie reminds him to look at the guide. He then locates the "Credits" link. "This means who made it. Look. They all have PhDs in history," he says as he scrolls down the list of over 10 names.

When he searches for his next question, "Why is there prejudice?", some of the links he encounters are related to clearly biased sites. Louis decides immediately that one link would not be good, laughing, "It says 'ignorant idiots.' That won't be good." Later, he finds a reputable site with a stated author, but he decides against it: "I'm not the audience. He uses really tough words."

Joshua, a tenth grader, is researching information about the Trojan War during his reading of *The Odyssey*. Specifically, he wants to know if the war was real, and if so, how long it lasted and how many died. Joshua likes to use Google.com and always types his searches as a question. The first four sites he receives use "wiki" in the description. He reads the "Hint" section on the guide again and says, "It is not always truthful. People post their own things on wiki." Joshua scrolls down and finds an .edu link and opens it. Valarie reminds him to look for an author. At the bottom of the page, he clicks on the hyperlink "Click Here for Syllabus" and locates the name of the professor and the university. When asked about the purpose of the site, Joshua observes, "He is basically giving background for reading *The Odyssey* and mentions that the war lasted 10 years."

Joshua then types in "Was the Trojan War real?" Again, he scrolls through many wiki sites, until he comes to an Encarta MSN site. "Is this the same as Wikipedia?" He finds out that the site is an online encyclopedia. Joshua skims and scans the document and notices that the first paragraph gives historical background while the rest of the paragraphs deal with the legend.

From examining the conversations of these two students, we can learn several important teaching points. First, both students needed direction in how to use effective search terms in their initial search. Simply typing in the question as a search often leads to community postings. Also, both students had a clear purpose for the search and were able to stay focused on their task, questioning information they read and searching for better information. Some students will need to be reminded of the importance of considering their purpose so as not to go offtrack in their search. In addition, Joshua particularly needed help with the skimming portion of the search. He was inclined to skim too quickly and miss important information. As with his reading in textbooks, Joshua needs strategies for using helpful external text features such as headings, bold font, and transition word clues to identify important and unimportant information in his search. Finally, while both students recognize the importance of asking critical questions about the reliability of the site and making inferences about the information they find on the site, they both were inclined to hurry through this step and needed coaching from Valarie to look back at the guide for direction. After practicing with the Internet Reading Guide, Louis realized that the author and purpose for the site are important to consider. "They don't seem important, but you don't want to waste your time. It could all be wrong information." Pairing students when they first use the guide can be helpful; they can check each other to make sure that they are asking and answering the critical questions.

The ultimate goal is for students to be able to internalize a new strategy and, in this case, to also internalize the critical thinking skills needed to make sense of Internet information. As classroom teachers, we need to create multiple opportunities for students to think critically about information so that they can practice these skills. Another strategy for enhancing critical thinking is to provide opportunities for students to compare multiple texts.

Thinking Critically through Multiple Texts

Now more than ever, it is imperative that we use multiple texts in our classrooms, expanding our definition of what counts as reading and as a result, motivating our adolescent readers (Moje, 2002; Vacca, 1998). We must tune in to our students' reading interests and seize the opportunity to integrate some of these texts into the language arts curriculum. In this section we suggest many texts to be used to promote critical literacy and engagement.

From our experiences, we know that students often benefit from the pairing of a classic text with a young adult novel; this strategy provides entrance into the more difficult language of the classic text and thus aids comprehension. In Table 6.1 we provide examples of contemporary texts and websites that can be used to build interest, support comprehension, and provide background context for students' reading of classics. Many of the examples represent the kind of texts our adolescents read for enjoyment. For instance, we might pair Edgar Allan Poe stories with the retelling of his tales in graphic novel format from Dan Whitehead's (2008) collection titled *Nevermore*. The graphic novel enhances our students' comprehension through the visual representations in the text, and as a result, increases their engagement. We also suggest the use of interactive websites for building interest, but also for providing students with important historical context and/or author background before they read a difficult text. For example, before reading Arthur Miller's *The Crucible* (1952/2003), students can navigate the National Geographic website focused on the Salem witch hunts, which provides the historical background of witch hunts while also offering a virtual experience of living in Salem. In short, pairing a classic text with a text from our students' experiences often facilitates better understanding of the classic text.

Another benefit in using multiple texts is the opportunity for students to use critical literacy skills. Reading texts critically allows students to use analysis and evaluation to examine an author's purpose. For example, students can participate in a pairing of the Jean Fritz's (1987) young adult historical novel *The Double Life of Pocahontas* with John Smith's (2006) *General Historie of Virginia,* focusing on the dramatic scene where John Smith nearly meets an untimely death at the hand of

TABLE 6.1. Multiple Texts: Providing Background Information and Piquing Interest

Classics	Young adult/contemporary	Media/other
Edgar Allen Poe's short stories	*Nevermore* graphic short stories edited by Dan Whitehead	Maryland Public Television interactive website: View an interactive time line of Poe's life: *knowingpoe. thinkport.org/default_ flash.asp.*
Romeo and Juliet by William Shakespeare	*Romiette and Julio* by Sharon M. Draper (black girl, Hispanic boy) *If You Come Softly* by Jacqueline Woodson (Jewish girl, black boy)	National Geographic Society: Article about two 5,000-year-old skeletons found in an embrace near Verona: *news. nationalgeographic.com/ news/2007/02/070213- bones-photo.html.*
The Grapes of Wrath by John Steinbeck	*Out of the Dust* by Karen Hesse *Worst Hard Time* by Timothy Egan *Esperanza Rising* by Pam Munoz Ryan	WebQuest project: *The Grapes of Wrath: www. umsl.edu/~ryanga/amer. studies/amst.grapesproject. html.*
The Crucible by Arthur Miller	*The Witch Child* by Celia Rees	National Geographic Society interactive website: *www.nationalgeographic. com/salem/.*
Adventures of Huckleberry Finn by Mark Twain	*The Day They Came to Arrest the Book* by Nat Hentoff	WHYY interactive scrapbook of Twain's life: *www.pbs.org/marktwain/ scrapbook/index.html.*

the Algonquian chief Powhatan. Students are instructed to look carefully at the word choice as Smith talks about the "barbarians" and how Pocahontas begged her father to spare Smith, eventually laying her body over Smith's to save his life. From the Fritz novel, however, students see a young Algonquian girl calmly preparing to approach Smith and adopt him as kin, a common practice for the tribe. We can then teach students how to ask essential critical reading questions about the two texts:

- Who tells the story?
- Whose perspective do we hear?
- How does that person's perspective shape the narrative?
- What might be the author's motive for telling the story?

- What similarities and differences can we find in the two renditions of the same event?

Behrman (2006) emphasizes the importance of using multiple texts: "By experiencing different treatments of the same topic or event, students begin to recognize that text is not 'true' in any absolute sense but a rendering as portrayed by an author" (p. 492).

Otis (1996) offers another example of critical literacy through paired texts. By reading excerpts from Paul Fleischman's (1996) book *Dateline Troy* and excerpts of the same account in Homer's *The Iliad* (Lombardo edition, 1999), students can also think critically about the decisions Fleischman made as the author:

- What material did Fleischman choose to omit?
- What would the inclusion of the material have done to the book's effect?

In Table 6.2, we provide examples of diverse text pairs that share a common theme, historical period, and/or genre. By pairing a classic memoir such as Elie Wiesel's *Night* (1999) with the graphic novel *Maus I* and *Maus II* by Art Speigelman (1986, 1992), or *Red Scarf Girl* by Ji-Li Jiang (2008) with *Persepolis* by Marjane Satrapi (2004), we are also able to teach students to think critically about the decisions a graphic novelist makes in relation to choice of words and the relationship of the illustrations and graphics:

- How does the author's choice of graphics support the meaning of the text?

TABLE 6.2. Pairing Texts with Similar Theme, Genre, or Time Period

Fiction	Nonfiction
Fever, 1793 by Laurie Halse Anderson	*An American Plague: The True and Terrifying Story of the Yellow Fever Epidemic of 1793* by Jim Murphy
Out of the Dust by Karen Hesse	*The Worst Hard Time* by Timothy Egan
Hatchet by Gary Paulsen	*Into Thin Air* by Jon Krakauer
Memoir	Graphic novel
Night by Elie Weisel	*Maus I* and *Maus II* by Art Spiegelman
Red Scarf Girl: A Memoir of Cultural Revolution by Ji-Li Jiang	*Persepolis: The Story of a Childhood* by Marjane Satrapi

- Find a similar event in each text. What differences do you notice in the authors'choice of description? Similarities?

Requiring all students to read a single text in language arts classes ignores the diverse reading interests our students bring into our classrooms. Using multiple, diverse texts allows for increased interest in the language arts curriculum and more opportunities for students to think critically about the author's purpose and bias. We must always be on the lookout for new, engaging texts to read with our students to meet them both at their comprehension and their interest levels.

CONCLUDING REMARKS

As teachers, we must continue to explore effective formats and strategies for helping our students read challenging materials and for motivating them to want to read. Often, this means we need to go outside of the texts of school to tap into the texts and technology of our students' out-of-school experiences. We hope that through reading this chapter, you have learned how to take familiar texts and familiar strategies and update them to reflect your adolescent students' reading comprehension needs and diverse interests. With effort, we can avoid the trap of Mrs. Frazier's classroom and show our students that comprehending text can be a meaningful experience, embedded in the contexts of their lives.

NOTE

1.   Conversation between Xiufang Chen with Mrs. Vicki Sellers, July 2, 2008.

SUGGESTED RESOURCES
Drama and Moviemaking

Barchers, S., & Kroll, J. (2002). *Classic Readers Theatre for young adults*. Portsmouth, NH: Teacher Ideas Press.

Kelner, L. B. (1993). *The creative classroom: A guide for using creative drama in the classroom, pre k–6*. Portsmouth, NH: Heinemann.

Kelner, L. B., & Flynn, R. M. (2006). *A dramatic approach to reading comprehension: Strategies and activities for classroom teachers*. Portsmouth, NH: Heinemann.

Latrobe, K., & Laughlin, M. (1989). *Readers Theatre for young adults: Scripts and script development*. Portsmouth, NH: Teacher Ideas Press.

Free Play Scripts for Adolescents in Schools or Community Groups:

www.shadowhousepits.com.au/play%20scripts%20for%20teen-aged%20performers.htm

Using Windows Movie Maker to Create Movies step by step:
center.uoregon.edu/ISTE/uploads/NECC2006/KEY_13349523/Her-zog_MovieMakerTutorial.pdf

Digital Storytelling, Student Movies, Consulting, Presentations, etc.:
homepage.mac.com/torres21/

Tutorial for Digital Storytelling:
www.techsoup.org/learningcenter/training/page5897.cfm

How to Create a Digital Story with Examples:
www.umass.edu/wmwp/DigitalStorytelling/How%20to%20Create%20a%20digital%20story.htm

Promoting Videos to a Wider Audience:
www.techsoup.org/learningcenter/internet/page5876.cfm

RAFT

Reading Strategies: Scaffolding Students' Interactions with Text:
www.greece.k12.ny.us/instruction/ela/6-12/Reading/Reading%20Strat-egies/RAFT.htm (including a ninth-grade example of a RAFT assignment for John Steinbeck's *The Pearl*.)

Instructional Strategies Online:
olc.spsd.sk.ca/DE/PD/instr/strats/raft/ (including many graphic organiz-ers, examples, instructions, and handouts)

Wikis

Wax, D. (2007, February). *Advice for students: Use a Wiki for better note-taking.* Retrieved June 17th, 2008, from *www.lifehack.org/articles/tech-nology/advice-for-students-use-a-wiki-for-better-note-taking.html.*

Parallel Note Taking:
www.greece.k12.ny.us/instruction/ela/6-12/Reading/Reading%20Strat-egies/parallelnotetaking.htm

Note Taking:
edutechwiki.unige.ch/en/Note_taking
en.wikipedia.org/wiki/Notetaking

Multiple Texts

Herz, S. K., & Gallo, D. R. (2005). *From Hinton to Hamlet: Building bridges between young adult literature and the classics.* Westport, CT: Greenwood.
Richison, J. D., Hernandez, A., & Carter, M. (2002). Blending multiple genres in theme baskets. *English Journal, 92*(2).

REFERENCES

Allen, J. (2000). *Yellow brick roads: Shared and guided paths to independent reading 4–12.* Portland, ME: Stenhouse.

Alvermann, D. E. (2001). *Effective literacy instruction for adolescents.* Executive summary and paper commissioned by the National Reading Conference. Chicago: National Reading Conference.

Alverman, D. E., Phelps, S. F., & Ridgeway, V. G. (2007). *Content area reading and literacy: Succeeding in today's diverse classrooms* (5th ed.) Boston: Allyn & Bacon.

Behrman, E. H. (2006). Teaching about language, power, and text: A review of classroom practices that support critical literacy. *Journal of Adolescent and Adult Literacy, 49*(6), 490–498.

Chambers, A. (1996). *Tell me: Children, reading and talk.* York, ME: Stenhouse.

Cunningham, R., & Shablak, S. (1975). Selective reading guide-o-rama: The content teacher's best friend. *Journal of Reading, 18,* 380–382.

Farabaugh, R. (2007). "The isle is full of noise": Using wiki software to establish a discourse community in a Shakespeare classroom. *Language Awareness, 16*(1), 41–56.

Hinchman, K. A., Alvermann, K., Boyd, F. B., Brozo, W. G., & Vacca, R. T. (2003). Supporting older students' in- and out-of-school literacies. *Journal of Adolescent and Adult Literacy, 47*(4), 304–310.

International Reading Association National Council of Teachers. (2002). *Standards for the English language arts.* Retrieved September 2, 2008, from *www.ncte.org/library/files/Store/Books/Sample/46767Chap01.pdf.*

Kamil, M. L., Borman, G. D., Dole, J., Kral, C. C., Salinger, T., & Torgesen, J. (2008). *Improving adolescent literacy: Effective classroom and intervention practices—IES practice guide.* Washington, DC: National Center for Education Evaluation and Regional Assistance.

Leu, D. J., Jr., Kinzer, C. K., Coiro, J., & Cammack, D. W. (2004). Toward a theory of new literacies emerging from the Internet and other communication technologies. In R. Ruddell & N. Unrau (Eds.), *Theoretical models and processes of reading* (5th ed., pp. 1570–1613). Newark, DE: International Reading Association.

Luce-Kapler, R., & Dobson, T. (2005, May/June). In search of a story: Reading and writing e-literature. *Reading Online, 8*(6). Available at *www.readingonline.org/articles/art_index.asp?HREF=luce-kapler/index.html.*

Mitchell, D. (2003). *Children's literature: An invitation to the world.* Boston: Allyn & Bacon.

Moje, E. B. (2002). Re-framing adolescent literacy research for new times: Studying youth as a resource. *Reading Research and Instruction, 41*(3), 211–238.

Otis, R. (1996). *Carol Hurst's children's literature site.* Available at *http://www.carolhurst.com.*

Peterson, C. L., Caverly, D. C., Nicholson, S. A., O'Neal, S., & Cusenbary, S.

(2000). *Building reading proficiency at the secondary school level: A guide to resources*. San Marcos, TX: Southwest Texas State University and the Southwest Educational Development Laboratory.

Robinson, F. P. (1970). *Effective study*. New York: Harper & Row. (Original work published 1946)

Santa, C. (1988). *Content reading including study systems*. Dubuque, IA: Kendall/Hunt.

Shanahan, T. (2004). Overcoming the dominance of communication: Writing to think and learn. In Jetton & Dole (Eds.), *Adolescent literacy research and practice* (pp. 59–74). New York: Guilford Press.

Vacca, R. (1998). Foreword. In D. E. Alvermann, K. A. Hinchman, D. W. Moore, S. F. Phelps, & D. R. Waff (Eds.), *Reconceptualizing the literacies in adolescents' lives* (pp. xv–xvi). Mahwah, NJ: Erlbaum.

Wax, D. (February, 2007). *Advice for students: Use a wiki for better note-taking*. Retrieved June 17th, 2008, from *www.lifehack.org/articles/technology/advice-for-students-use-a-wiki-for-better-note-taking.html*.

Wood, K. D. (1988). A guide to subject matter material. *Middle School Journal, 19*, 24–26.

TRADE BOOK REFERENCES
Nonfiction

Egan, T. (2006). *The worst hard time*. New York: Houghton Mifflin.

Jiang, J.-L. (2008). *Red scarf girl: A Memoir of a Cultural Revolution*. HarperTeen.

Krakauer, J. (1999). *Into Thin Air*. Anchor.

Martin, S. (2002, June 17). "The death of my father." *The New Yorker*, p. 84.

Murphy, J. (2003). *An American plague: The true and terrifying story of the yellow fever epidemic of 1793*. New York: Houghton Mifflin.

Satrapi, M. (2004). *Persepolis: The story of a childhood*. Pantheon.

Smith, J. (2006). *General historie of Virginia*. Carlisle, MA: Applewood Books.

Spiegelman, A. (1986). *Maus I*. New York: Pantheon.

Spiegelman, A. (1992). *Maus II*. New York: Pantheon.

Wiesel, E. (1999). *Night*. Holt, Rinehart & Winston.

FICTION

Anderson, L. H. (2000). *Fever 1793*. New York: Aladdin Paperbacks.

Curtis, C. P. (2000). *The Watsons go to Birmingham—1963*. New York: Laurel Leaf.

Draper, S. (2001). *Romiette and Julio*. Simon Pulse.

Fleischman, P. (1996). *Dateline Troy*. Somerville, MA: Candlewick.

Fritz, J. (1987). *The double life of Pocahontas*. New York: Penguin Putnam Books.

Hentoff, N. (1983). *The day they came to arrest the book.* Laurel Leaf.
Hesse, K. (1997). *Out of the dust.* New York: Scholastic Press.
Miller, A. (2003). *The crucible.* London: Penguin. (Original work published 1953)
Munoz Ryan, P. (2002). *Esperanza rising.* Blue Sky Press.
Paulson, G. (2006). *Hatchet.* New York: Aladdin.
Poe, E. A. (2007). *The great tales and poems of Edgar Allan Poe.* Enriched Edition. New York: Simon & Schuster.
Rees, C. (2002). *The witch child.* Somerville, MA: Candlewick.
Shelley, M. (1981). *Frankenstein.* New York: Bantam. (Original work published 1818)
Steinbeck, J. (1939, 2002). *The grapes of wrath.* London: Penguin Classics.
Twain, M. (1881, 2008). *The adventures of Huckleberry Finn.* London: Puffin.
Whitehead, D. (2008). *Nevermore: A graphic adaptation of Edgar Allan Poe's short stories.* New York: Sterling.
Woodson, J. (2006). *If you come softly.* London: Puffin.

WEBSITE REFERENCES

Chamberlein, T. (February 13, 2007). Photo in the news: Skeleton "valentines" won't be parted. *National Geographic News Online.* Retrieved August 10, 2008, from *news.nationalgeographic.com/news/2007/02/070213-bones-photo.html.*
EduTech Wiki. (n.d.). *Note taking.* Retrieved April 21, 2009, from *edutechwiki.unige.ch/en/Note_taking.*
Greece Central School District. (n.d.). *Parallel note-taking.* Retrieved April 21, 2009, from *www.greece.k12.ny.us/instruction/ela/6-12/Reading/Reading%20Strategies/parallelnotetaking.htm.*
Herzog, J. (Nyco Fuentes and Outlier Solutions, Inc.) (July, 2006). *Using Windows Movie Maker to create movies.* National Educational Computing Conference. Retrieved April 20, 2009, from *center.uoregon.edu/ISTE/uploads/NECC2006/KEY_13349523/Herzog_MovieMakerTutorial.pdf.*
Instructional strategies online. (2008). *Saskatoon Public Schools.* Retrieved April 21, 2009, from *olc.spsd.sk.ca/DE/PD/instr/strats/raft/.*
Knowing Poe: The literature, life and times of Edgar Allan Poe in Maryland and beyond. (2002). Maryland Public Television. Retrieved July 20, 2008, from *knowingpoe.thinkport.org/default_flash.asp.*
Lasica, J. (October 2, 2006). *Digital storytelling: A tutorial in 10 easy steps.* Retrieved April 21, 2009, from *www.techsoup.org/learningcenter/training/page5897.cfm.*
Mark Twain: The scrapbook. *PBS Online: WHYY Interactive Website.* Retrieved August 20, 2008, from *www.pbs.org/marktwain/scrapbook/index.html.*
Reading strategies: Scaffolding students' interactions with text: RAFT. *Greece*

Central School District. Retrieved April 21, 2009, from *www.greece. k12.ny.us/instruction/ela/6-12/Reading/Reading%20Strategies/RAFT. htm.*

Salem: Witchcraft hysteria. (1996). *National Geographic Online.* Retrieved July 1, 2008, from *www.nationalgeographic.com/salem/.*

Satterfield, B. (September 28, 2006). *Share your nonprofit's videos with the world. Promote your organization's work using free online services.* Retrieved April 20, 2009, from *www.techsoup.org/learningcenter/internet/page5876.cfm.*

Shadow House PITS. (n.d.). *Free play scripts with some real bite for talented teenaged performers in schools or community groups?* Retrieved April 20, 2009, from *www.shadowhousepits.com.au/play%20scripts%20for%20 teenaged%20performers.htm.*

Torres, M. (n.d.). *Digital storytelling, student movies, etc.* Retrieved April 20, 2009, from *homepage.mac.com/torres21/.*

Web quest project: *Grapes of Wrath. CBC American Studies.* Retrieved August 12, 2008, from *www.umsl.edu/~ryanga/amer.studies/amst.grapesproject. html.*

Western Massachusetts Writing Project. (May 10, 2005). *Digital storytelling: Using technology to tell stories.* Retrieved April 21, 2009, from *www. umass.edu/wmwp/DigitalStorytelling/Digital%20Storytelling%20 Main%20Page.htm.*

Wikipedia. (n.d.). *Notetaking.* Retrieved April 21, 2009, from *en.wikipedia. org/wiki/Notetaking.*

The reproducibles in this chapter are also provided in a large-size format on Guilford's website (www.guilford.com/p/ganske4) for book buyers to download and use in their professional practice.

APPENDIX 6.1. Student "Webpage" Template

Hello!

Here's What's New!

What I did this weekend:

Who I most admire:

Three objects you'd find in my room:

My Contacts

Blogs

What you need to know about:

What you need to know about:

What I am listening to:

APPENDIX 6.2. Wiki Notes Template

My notes:
My friends' notes:
New understandings:

7

Thinking and Comprehending in the Mathematics Classroom

Douglas Fisher
Nancy Frey
Heather Anderson

Literacy—reading, writing, speaking, and listening—is a critical foundational skill that provides individuals access to information in all other disciplines and domains. As teachers and researchers, we know that literacy impacts every aspect of a person's life, from success in school and work to living a productive life. As Shanahan (2007) noted in his International Reading Association keynote, low levels of literacy put people at risk in all kinds of ways, from being taken advantage of by scam artists to not understanding health information.

Literacy involves more than learning how to read. Breaking the code and developing fluency are important aspects in the development of a literate life. But that's not our focus in this chapter. We're interested in how literacy, broadly defined to include thinking in words and images, impacts content learning and achievement. This book has examples of successful content literacy initiatives in every subject area. Our focus in this chapter is mathematics and the ways in which literacy and numeracy can be integrated such that students learn more content.

MATHEMATICS KNOWLEDGE IS CRITICAL

Failing a year of mathematics is highly correlated with failures in future years of school and difficulty in finding gainful employment (Nichols, 2003; Thompson & Lewis, 2005). Math, specifically algebra, is a gatekeeper course. Haycock (2003) says: "Just as we educators have learned that courses like Algebra II are the gatekeepers to higher education, we must now come to understand that they are gatekeepers to well-paying jobs, as well."

Failure in mathematics is also a common cause of college dropouts (Heck & Van Gastel, 2006). Colleges spend significant resources remediating students in mathematics, most commonly college-level algebra. The largest higher educational system in the world, the California State University (CSU), has established goals to reduce the number of students who require remedial instruction upon entering college. As part of the CSU effort, an Early Assessment Program (EAP) was developed. This is an optional assessment given to 11th graders that provides students and their families with feedback about readiness for college algebra, the first in a sequence of required mathematics courses for undergraduates. Of 141,648 students who took the math test in 2007, only 77,870 (55%) demonstrated proficiency. Remember that these are the students who chose to take the exam thinking that they were ready for college. Data from the ACT is even worse. Of the 1.2 million students tested, just 40% were ready for their first course in college algebra (ACT, 2004).

Although it can be argued that students are doing better today than they have in the past, there is a clear and immediate need to continue to raise mathematics achievement. Thankfully, there is evidence for how to do this. Before we explore three ideas for using literacy to improve understanding in mathematics, let's recall how many students experience math class. The following comes from Doug's experience in a ninth-grade algebra class.

A COMMON EXPERIENCE IN MATH CLASS

"The day starts like every other so far this semester. As we enter the room, our teacher calls off odd numbers. By now, we know that when we're called on like this, we have to solve the assigned homework problem on the board. Our teacher watches the group of students assigned to complete the problems and offers periodic criticisms and compliments. When everyone is finished and the answers are correctly posted on the board, we check our homework and then pass it forward to the teacher (of course, we've all checked our homework on the bus to make sure we've all got the same answers because homework counts for 25% of the grade).

"With the homework review complete, now 15 minutes into the period, our teacher rolls out the overhead projector. It's the kind with rollers on both sides so that the transparency paper slides across as he finishes writing. He solves algebra problems for us for about 15 minutes. It's the last period of the day and his hands have blue stains from the number of times he's spit on them to erase.

"Our task during this time is to take notes exactly as he presents them. Our notebooks must have specific page numbers that match his and are worth 25% of our grade. He provides us with a table of contents for our notes during the first week of school, and we are to keep the page numbers current. For example, as noted in Figure 7.1, page 13 focuses on "inverse of functions." If we want to take notes on examples, we are told to add pages such as 13a, 13b, etc., so that we do not make mistakes with the numbering system. We do not summarize our notes or organize them in any systematic way; we copy them exactly as they are presented in class.

"When he finishes the lecture and note-taking component of the class, we have the remainder of the period available to start our odd-numbered problem set for the day. If we do not finish the problems in class, we are to take them home and complete the rest. If we talk during class, our teacher will call out an even-numbered problem for which there is no answer in the back of the book. As punishment for talking, we have to go to the board and attempt to demonstrate our prowess in front of our peers. Obviously, we quickly learned to be quiet in this class! We also learned to talk with one another outside of the class to check answers and get help.

"Every fourth week, we have a test. The tests comprise the remaining 50% of our grade and include long lists of problems to solve, selecting from the correct multiple-choice answer. We never had to explain our thinking, either orally or in writing. We just needed to select the correct answer from the choices provided. As our teacher said many times during the year, 'This is what you'll have to do on the standards test, so you might as well get used to it now.'"

You're probably asking yourself, "How will anyone learn anything in this class?" Yet our experiences, and probably yours, bear out the fact that this type of instruction is very common in mathematics classrooms. To analyze the scenario a bit further, it is clear that the teacher values practice—he provides his students with lots of opportunities to engage in independent learning. He also values students having correct informa-

(13)

Inverse of Functions

Let $f = \{(1,2), (2,6), (3,5)\}$
Suppose we want a function that
will take us back to the domain
of f. Consider
$g = \{(2,1), (6,2), (5,3)\}$
Consider the following:
$f \circ g = \{(2,2), (6,8), (5,5)\}$ $g \circ f = \{(1,1),(2,2),(3,3)\}$
Both $f \circ g$ and $g \circ f$ are the
IDENTITY FUNCTION

Definition: If f and g are two functions
such that $f(g(x)) = g(f(x)) = x$, then f and g
are *inverse* of each other.

Notation. $f^{-1}(x)$ is the inverse of $f(x)$.
$f(g(2)) = f(1) = 2$
$f(g(6)) = f(2) = 6$

Procedure to find Inverse when given
Equation
1) Interchange x and y
2) Solve new equation for y.

Example 1: Let $f(x) = 2x-5$ find Inverse. Is the Inverse
a function
$f(x) = 2x-5$ to prove
$y = 2x-5$
$x = 2y-5$ $f(f^{-1}(10)) = 10$
$2y-5 = x$ $f(15/2) = 2(15/2)-5$
$2y = x+5$ $= 15-5$
$y = x/2 + 5/2$ $\boxed{= 10}$

$f^{-1}(x) = \frac{x+5}{2}$ (yes)

Example 2: Let $g(x) = x^2$ find
Inverse? Is it a function?
$g(x) = x^2$ $g^{-1}(x) = \pm\sqrt{x}$
$y = x^2$ $x = 4$
$x = y^2$ $\pm 4 = \pm 2$
$y = \pm\sqrt{x}$ NO/ 2 answers (not funct.)

Example 3: Let $f: x \to \frac{x+1}{x-1}$ find Inverse
$f(x) = \frac{x+1}{x-1}$
$y = \frac{x+1}{x-1}$
$(1/y) x = \frac{y+1}{y-1} (\frac{y-1}{})$
$x(y-1) = y+1$
$xy-x = y+1$
$xy = y+x+1$
$xy-y = x+1$
$y(x-1) = x+1$
$y = \frac{x+1}{x-1}$ Same function
                          are their
                          own Inverse

FIGURE 7.1. Sample note page.

tion and right answers. He wants their notes to be exact, and he wants students to practice testing formats. Unfortunately, this teacher has no way of understanding his students' thinking and the types of errors they make. Although he explains information, he doesn't let his students in on his thinking—the thinking of an expert.

With a few adjustments to the structure of the classroom, students would likely develop a deeper understanding of mathematics and begin to see the relevance of this content in their lives. The remainder of this chapter focuses on three areas that we know to be effective ways to engage students in thinking about mathematics (e.g., Fisher & Frey, 2007): modeling, vocabulary development, and productive group work.

ENGAGING STUDENTS IN THINKING ABOUT MATHEMATICS

Modeling

There exist decades of evidence that teacher modeling positively impacts student performance and achievement (Afflerbach & Johnston, 1984; Duffy, 2003; Olson & Land, 2007). Modeling provides students with examples of the thinking required, as well as the language demands, of the task at hand. In essence, the student gets to peer inside the mind of an expert to see how that person thinks about, processes, and solves a problem.

Unfortunately, there is significant confusion between modeling and explaining. Think of a lecture you've attended. It was probably full of explanations. And explanations aren't all bad. We all need things explained to us sometimes. But we also need modeling, which personalizes the experience for the learner as the teacher uses "I" statements to share his or her thinking. Modeling also provides information about the cognitive process that went on in the mind of the expert; it's the *why* that we're after here. But as Duffy (2003) pointed out, "The only way to model thinking is to talk about how to do it. That is, we provide a verbal description of the thinking one does or, more accurately, an *approximation* of the thinking involved" (p. 11).

Accordingly, mathematics teachers must model their thinking by talking and thinking aloud for their students. Some of the common areas of thought that math teachers model include:

- Background knowledge (e.g.., "When I see a triangle, I remember that the angles have to add up to 180°.
- Relevant versus irrelevant information (e.g., "I've read this prob-

lem twice, and I know that there is information included that I don't need.").

- Selecting a function (e.g., "The problem says 'increased by,' so I know that I'll have to add.").
- Setting up the problem (e.g., "The first thing that I will do is ... because ... ").
- Estimating answers (e.g., "I predict that the product will be about 150 because I see that there are 10 times the number.").
- Determining reasonableness of an answer (e.g., "I'm not done yet as I have to check to see if my answer makes sense.").

Let's listen in on Heather's modeling of her thinking relative to the algebra problem: The sum of one-fifth p and 38 is as much as twice p. In her words:

> "Okay, I've read the problem twice, and I have a sense of what they're asking me. I see the term *sum*, so I know that I'm going to be adding. I know this because *sum* is one of the signal words that are used in math problems [for a list of signal words, see Figure 7.2]. I also know that when terms are combined, like *one-fifth p*, they are related because they make a phrase 'one-fifth of p' so I'll write that $1/5p$. The next part says *and 38*, so I know that I'll be adding 38 to the equation. Now my equation reads $1/5p + 38$. But I know that's not really an equation. I know from my experience that there has to be an equal sign someplace to make it an equation. Oh, they say *as much as,* which is just a fancier way of saying *equal to*. So, I'll add the equal sign to my equation: $1/5p + 38 =$. And the last part is *twice p*. And there it is again, one of those combined phrases like *one-fifth p*, but this time *twice p*. So I'll put that on the other side of the equation: $1/5p + 38 = 2p$. That's all they're asking me to do. For this item, I just need to set up the equation. But I know that I can solve for p, and I like solutions. I know that you can solve for p as well. Can you do so on your dry erase boards?"

Heather clearly understands the task and expectations. But more importantly, she understands her own thinking on the subject. To be effective modelers, teachers have to move beyond their expert blind spots. Gladwell (2005) notes that even brilliant experts have biases and blind spots that prevent them from seeing the problem as it really is. Expert blind spots prevent teachers from recognizing content that would be helpful to students. Too often teachers are unaware that much of their subject matter knowledge, while second nature to them, is very difficult for their students to learn. Nathan and Petrosino (2003) noted in their

Function	Sample terms	Examples
Words that signal addition	and, made larger, more than, in addition, sum, in excess, added to, plus, add, greater, increased by, raised by	Forty-five and twenty-two are what? Translation: $45 + 22 =$
Words that signal subtraction	decreased by, subtract, difference, from, made smaller by, diminished by, reduce, less than, minus, take away	If you take away 3 from 29, what do you have left? Translation: $29 - 3 =$
Words that signal multiplication	product, multiplied by, times as much, of, times, doubled, tripled, etc., percent of interest on	What is the product of fourteen and sixteen? Translation: $14 \times 16 =$
Words that signal division	per, quotient, go(es) into, how many, divided by, contained in	How many times can 5 go into 100? Translation: $100 / 5 =$

FIGURE 7.2. Math signal words.

study of new secondary math teachers that this blind spot was prevalent because they lacked the experience to recall how a new concept is acquired by a novice.

Our experience suggests that there is a good reason for these expert blind spots. The goal of instruction is for students to reach automaticity such that they no longer have to pay conscious attention to every aspect of the problem at hand. As students develop their understanding of mathematics, components become automatic. For example, by mid-elementary school, multiplication facts should have moved from conscious thought to automatic execution. This process frees up working memory such that the brain can work on other parts of the problem. Many math teachers have reached automaticity with mathematics in general and, as a result, have lost the awareness of their cognitive problem-solving processes. The key is to slow down thinking such that the process once again becomes clear. When you know what you think, it's easier to model for students. And simply said, students desperately need to witness experts in action.

Vocabulary Development

Returning to the modeling provided by Heather in the example above, it's hard not to notice the vocabulary that she used. In every academic endeavor, words matter. We use words to communicate with one another, and our selection of specific words is intended to convey specific information. The problem is that students often don't know what the words mean, especially in a mathematical context.

In response to this problem, teachers often identify words for students to learn. Of course, learning words requires much more than a list. It is also more than providing definitions for students to memorize, such as, "A polygon is a simple closed figure comprised of line segments." Although definitional meaning is an aspect of learning a word, when it comes too early in the process it can confound rather than clarify. Consider the vocabulary embedded in that definition—you need to understand what a *closed figure* is, be able to identify a *line segment*, and know the meaning of *comprised*. Students have to engage with the words multiple times to get a sense of their meaning and usage. A number of instructional routines are useful in mathematics word learning (e.g., Fisher & Frey, 2008b), including the following:

- *Word walls,* on which teachers post 5–10 words on a wall space that is easily visible from anywhere in the room. The purpose of the word wall is to remind teachers to look for ways to bring words they want students to own back into the conversation so that students get many and varied experiences with those words (Ganske, 2006, 2008).
- *Word cards,* in which students analyze a word for its meaning, what it doesn't mean, and create a visual reminder. A sample card for the word *rhombus* can be seen in Figure 7.3.
- *Word sorts,* in which students arrange a list of words by their features. Word sorts can be open (students are not provided with categories) or closed (students are given categories in which to sort). An example of a word sort in which words could be used more than once can be found in Figure 7.4.
- *Word games,* in which students play with words and their meanings. For example, this might involve a bingo game of sorts (Pat Cunningham calls it *Wordo*), wherein students write words from the class in various squares and then the teacher randomly draws definitions until someone gets bingo. We also like games such as Jeopardy, Who Wants to Be a Millionaire, or $25,000 Pyramid because they allow students to review words while having a bit of fun. A great website that provides information about vocabulary games is *jc-schools.net/tutorials/vocab/ppt-vocab.html.*

These instructional routines are useful, especially for technical words, that is, those words that are specific to a discipline or content area. In mathematics, it's important that students learn the accepted

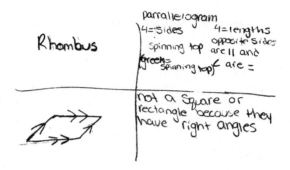

FIGURE 7.3. Sample word card.

meanings of words and phrases such as *square root, polygon, linear equation* and *Fibonacci sequence*. Of course, those aren't the only words students need to know. In addition to technical words, students in mathematics classrooms must learn the intended mathematical meanings of common words. These are known as the specialized vocabulary terms as they tend to change their meaning in different contexts. For example, the word *prime* has a common meaning related to the best in quality, as in *prime beef*. However, in mathematics the term takes on a specialized meaning: a number that is only divisible by itself and 1. Our experience suggests that students need these differences made explicit to them, especially English language learners who may know one meaning of a term, but a meaning that does not help them understand the mathematics. For example, one of our students understood the term *expression,* having heard it in her English language development (ELD) class. That teacher talked about facial expressions and reading social clues through expressions. The newcomers in the ELD class developed an appreciation of the term *expression* and were able to read nonverbal clues in their

Circle	Square	Triangle
Radius	Area	Angle
Diameter	Perimeter	Area
Circumference	Quadrilateral	Altitude
Area	Angles	Sides
	Sides	
	Length	
	Height	

FIGURE 7.4. Sample word sort.

new environment. However, when this student enrolled in algebra, the knowledge she had about the term failed her. She had no idea what the teacher meant when he said, "Let's write an expression for the information we have" or "Evaluate the expression $5 \times z + 12$ when $z = 3$."

The best way we've found to teach and reinforce specialized vocabulary is through a mathematics journal such as the one in Figure 7.5. Of course this requires that teachers notice the specialized vocabulary in their speaking and in the texts they use. It also requires that teachers take the time to provide instruction on the difference between the common meaning of the word and the math-specific definition or usage. But as the student who did not understand the mathematical use of *expression* taught us, focusing on specialized vocabulary terms is time well spent.

The first two areas that we've presented have focused a lot on the teacher: The teacher provides expert modeling, the teacher determines which words are worthy of instruction, and then the teacher provides time for students to engage effectively with the words. The final area of attention focuses on the role of students. To significantly raise achievement in mathematics, students have to have opportunities to interact with one another in regard to content.

Productive Group Work

Unlike the classroom scenario that we used to start this chapter, classrooms that work well are filled with student talk, student interaction, and meaningful work. Simply listening to math instruction and then doing math problems will not result in learners who understand and use mathematical concepts in their daily lives, much less in their college

Word	Common Meaning	Math Meaning	Where I Found It
Prime	Best or high quality	A number that can only be divided by 1 or itself	Math book, page 34
Expression	Something someone says or the feelings on a person's face	A group of symbols that make a mathematical statement	Wikipedia
Set	To put something someplace	A collection of specific numbers	Afterschool tutor

FIGURE 7.5. Sample mathematics journal.

classrooms. As noted in the opening scenario, students want, and need, to talk about the content. Our experience suggests that the productive group-work phase of instruction allows students to consolidate their thinking about the content. In that respect, it's a critical aspect of learning. Importantly, we have evidence that students use the information modeled by the teachers when they are working with their peers. And even more importantly, independent work is of higher quality when students have first had an opportunity to collaborate with others. In fact, this aspect is so important that it is one of the foundational principals of *Working on the Work* (Schlechty, 2002), a reform effort with the aim of improving student achievement by focusing on the tasks students are asked to complete.

The following five features should be considered in any productive group-work task (Fisher & Frey, 2008a; Johnson, Johnson, & Smith, 1991).

1. *Positive interdependence.* Members must see how their efforts contribute to the overall success of the group. The task cannot be one that individuals could have completed independently. Rather, the task has to have at least an aspect of interdependence such that students need each other to complete their work successfully.

2. *Face-to-face interaction.* As part of the task, group members must have time to interact live. While they can also interact in virtual and electronic worlds, our experience suggests that the opportunity to interact on the physical level encourages accountability, feedback, and support.

3. *Individual and group accountability.* As we have noted, productive group work is not simply a matter of having a group of students complete a task in parallel with peers that they could have done alone. Having said that, we also know that the risk of productive group work lies in participation. In nearly every group, there are likely members who would allow their peers to complete the required tasks. To address this issue, each member of the group must be accountable for some aspect of the task. Of course, this is a perfect opportunity to differentiate based on students' needs and strengths. In addition to the individual accountability, the group must be accountable for the overall product. This also ensures that overly involved students will not monopolize the conversations during productive group work.

4. *Interpersonal and small-group skills.* One of the opportunities presented during productive group work is social skill development. Wise teachers are clear about their expectations related to interpersonal skills and communicate these to students. For example, during a group brainstorming session about ways to represent the concept of slope,

Heather reminds her students that "put-downs for ideas are not allowed, especially during a brainstorming session."

5. *Group processing.* As part of the learning associated with productive group work, students need to learn how to think about, and discuss, their experiences. The goal of the discussion is for students to consider ways in which they can improve their productivity and working relationships.

Following her modeling in which she thinks aloud about a problem and its solution, Heather provides groups of three students (triads) with a problem. Each triad has the same problem as one other triad, and the two triads with the same problem will discuss their results at the end of the class session. Before doing so, students in each triad must solve the problem with words, numbers, and pictures. They are working on reasonableness of their answers. One of the groups received the problem: If Esme cuts an apple into 8 equal pieces and gives Kaila 1 piece, how much of the apple is left? Is it reasonable to suggest that there is more than 50% of the apple left?

The group members go into action, first talking about the problem. Andrew asks how Esme got the pieces to be equal. Maria responds, "That's extraneous to the problem. We can ask that as a follow-up, but first we have to solve the problem." Their individual accountability is widened by their separate ability to explain the solution to their teacher and another group. The group accountability includes a presentation of the solution in words, numbers, and a picture. This group decides that each member will take one of the required representations and work alone for a minute before sharing the results with the team.

Maria takes writing, Jamal takes numbers, and Andrew takes the picture, and they begin to work. As they finish, they trade papers for a quick review and an opportunity to ask clarifying questions. Jamal suggests that Maria add a sentence about subtracting fractions with common denominators. Andrew asks Jamal if the answer is reasonable, "You have the problem worked out, but I think you forgot the second part. Is it reasonable to suggest that there is more than 50% of the apple left?"

The students then discuss the answer and the various ways that they solved the problem. Using a timer, they each get 60 seconds to explain their thinking. When the 3 minutes are up, triads with the same problem meet. They each explain their thinking and their solutions to the members of the other triad that solved the same problem while Heather listens in on the conversations. Naturally, there are a number of ways that students solved their assignment problems and they're having a chance to hear about alternatives.

Returning to their triads, the students talk about what they learned from the experience. Heather reminds them to "Talk about what you learned about problem solving and also what you can do to make your triad more effective." Maria talks about adding numbers to her writing like Sophia did. Andrew talks about how all six of them got the answer right, but in different ways. He says, "I like Michael's picture better than mine, but we got the same answer." In response to increasing the productivity of the group, Jamal suggests that next time they each solve the problem two different ways (writing, numbers, or pictures) and then compare all of the different ways, "so that we'll know more ways to figure out what we have to do."

The amount of student talk and student engagement in Heather's class is significant. Students know what is expected of them from the models she provides. They also learn a lot of words and have opportunities to use those words in context with their interactions with peers. And students in Heather's class collaborate on productive tasks that allow them to consolidate their understanding of mathematics. It's no wonder that Heather's students do so well on state assessments—they know the content very well because of the structures in place in the classroom.

CONCLUSION

Importantly, we are not suggesting that mathematics instructors become reading teachers any more than we are suggesting that reading specialists become math educators. However, we do recognize the value that modeling, vocabulary, and productive group work play in learning mathematics content, regardless of the level of mathematics being taught. Mathematics instructors, K–12, can improve student achievement through the use of key "literacy" instructional routines. We put the word literacy in quotations because the ideas presented in this chapter are not owned by reading teachers; they are ways to get students to think about and understand the content. And that's the goal of every teacher—to ensure that comprehension occurs.

REFERENCES

ACT, Inc. (2004). *ACT national data release*. Iowa City, IA: Author.
Afflerbach, P., & Johnston, P. (1984). On the use of verbal reports in reading research. *Journal of Reading Behavior, 16,* 307–322.
Duffy, G. G. (2003). *Explaining reading: A resource for teaching concepts, skills, and strategies.* New York: Guilford Press.
Fisher, D., & Frey, N. (2007). A tale of two middle schools: The role of structure and instruction. *Journal of Adolescent and Adult Literacy, 51,* 204–211.

Fisher, D., & Frey, N. (2008a). *Better learning through structured teaching: A framework for the gradual release of responsibility.* Alexandria, VA: Association for Supervision and Curriculum Development.

Fisher, D., & Frey, N. (2008b). *Word wise and content rich: Five essential steps to teaching academic vocabulary.* Portsmouth, NH: Heinemann.

Ganske, K. (2006). *Word sorts and more: Sound, pattern and meaning explorations K–3.* New York: Guilford Press.

Ganske, K. (2008). *Mindful of words: Spelling and vocabulary explorations 4–8.* New York: Guilford Press.

Gladwell, M. (2005). *Blink: The power of thinking without thinking.* New York, Little Brown.

Haycock, K. (2003). Foreword. In A. P. Carnevale & D. M. Desrochers, *Standards for what? The economic roots of K–16 reform.* Princeton, NJ: Educational Testing Service.

Heck, A., & Van Gastel, L. (2006). Mathematics on the threshold. *International Journal of Mathematical Education in Science and Technology, 37*(8), 925–945.

Johnson, D. W., Johnson, R. T., & Smith, K. (1991). *Active learning: Cooperation in the college classroom.* Edina, MN: Interaction Book.

Nathan, M. J., & Petrosino, A. (2003). Expert blind spot among preservice teachers. *American Educational Research Journal, 40,* 905–928.

Nichols, J. D. (2003). Prediction indicators for students failing the state of Indiana high school graduation exam. *Preventing School Failure, 47*(3), 112–120.

Olson, C. B., & Land, R. (2007). A cognitive strategies approach to reading and writing instruction for English language learners in secondary school. *Research in the Teaching of English, 41*(3), 269–303.

Schlechty, P. C. (2002). *Working on the work: An action plan for teachers, principals, and superintendents.* San Francisco, CA: Jossey-Bass.

Shanahan, T. (2007, May 15). Presidential address for International Reading Association, Toronto, Canada.

Thompson, L. R., & Lewis, B. F. (2005). Shooting for the stars: A case study of the mathematics achievement and career attainment of an African American male high school student. *High School Journal, 88*(4), 6–18.

8

Comprehension in Social Studies

Donna Ogle

WHY SOCIAL STUDIES?

What better way to develop comprehension than by using social studies content and materials as the basis for comprehension instruction? The content is rich, interesting, and more practical than in other curricular areas. It is important knowledge for our students, our future voting citizens, to possess, something that has not been respected recently in the testing-driven curriculums that focus narrowly on mathematics and reading. The range of materials used in social studies highlight the need to look for multiple perspectives and points of view (e.g., letters, documents, reports, essays). This range also points to the need for students to adjust their reading to meet the demands of the text and their purposes.

Social studies provides teachers with clear contexts with which to help students learn to use informational texts, with their varied organizational patterns and dense presentation of information. Students must coordinate a linear, chronological sense with a spatial framework (location) to begin making sense of what they read. They also need to look for expository organizational patterns that can guide understanding, as for example, patterns that move from identification of causes to their effects and from identifying problems to explaining the solutions attempted or achieved (Ogle, 2007). Not only can students learn to use informational text through social studies, but the more students read particular genres, the more likely they will learn to construct their own, for instance, persuasive essay—the classic writing assignment given to secondary students. Social studies provides one of the few places where good persuasive writing is introduced in the study of content.

The diverse range of social studies materials also makes it easy for teachers to connect with students' prior knowledge and their engagement with the world around them. As a group, students usually possess personal experiences, have seen movies and videos, or have read about the content they are asked to study. They can be guided to make connections through their own personal experiences, their reading of fictional literature, informational magazines, primary sources, textbooks, news sources, and their increasingly regular engagements with visual and electronic media. Some schools help students to make strong connections with service learning projects to build bridges between school "studies" and life beyond—by working in political campaigns; helping with refugee settlements; addressing local issues; and taking part in model "city government" and national and international United Nations (UN) events.

Linking comprehension instruction with social studies helps students broaden their concept of what counts as "reading." In some schools the concept of "reading" has taken on an overly narrow definition, or courses in reading and literature have been so limited to reading fiction that many active readers don't see themselves as readers. Reading needs to be conceived in a much broader way than just in terms of reading novels and stories. Although basal reading programs are now including a much larger proportion of informational pieces, often teachers skip these and teach from a "novels" or "children's author" framework. The positive aspect of the current instruction is that teachers love novels and storybooks, and there are thousands of new books published each year that tempt elementary teachers to stay with the fiction they love. However, the reality of the world, the students' future needs as readers, and in many cases students' own interests are such that informational reading dominates. And there is now a wide variety of materials available for students, from historical fiction, biography, and autobiography to visual media and online historical documents such as the rich collection at the Library of Congress. Students deserve a better basis for reading informational texts of all kinds.

Although the wide variety of text types used in social studies makes it an ideal setting for the focus on comprehension, so, too, does the fact that the meaning and significance of the texts are central. Social studies materials aren't read to practice reading; they are read to gain information and broaden knowledge and concepts that are important to life in the 21st century. Teachers regularly check for comprehension of key ideas and important details. They also focus on important concepts often represented by particular vocabulary. Even the kinds of projects students are generally asked to complete put a premium on understanding, synthesizing, and connecting information from varied sources.

Reading in social studies is also important for teachers who use fictional literature regularly. For students to comprehend fiction, they need a good understanding of history and culture, geography, and movements of people. Students miss a great deal of the meaning of historical and contemporary fiction if they lack knowledge of the period, the geography, and the social and political contexts of the literature. For example, when middle grade students read *My Brother Sam Is Dead* (Collier & Collier, 1974), they need to have a clear sensitivity to the conditions of America in the 1860s. To empathize with Koly in *Homeless Bird* (Whelan, 2005), Hasim in *The Kite Runner* (Hosseini, 2004), or Shabanu in *Shabanu: Daughter of the Wind* (Staples, 2000), students need some understanding of India, Afghanistan, and Pakistan, the impact of poverty, and the traditional low regard for women in those Asian societies. Even to understand the importance and impact of news reports of the "I Have a Dream Speech" 45 years ago by Martin Luther King or the fear and tragedy surrounding the Birmingham bombings (*The Watsons Go to Birmingham—1963*, Christopher Paul Curtis, 1995), more historical knowledge is needed than many of our current students seem to possess. My argument is that deeply understanding and comprehending fiction requires a grounding that social studies provides. Integrating instruction by combining studies of literature and social studies creates purpose, provides enough context for comprehension, and increases motivation for learning in both areas.

Integrating instruction is also helpful as students develop their research and writing abilities. Many teachers complain that students who are asked to write reports for school projects don't know how to evaluate materials they locate, especially those on the World Wide Web. Students accept all sources as equal and need to learn how to use the unedited Internet by checking sources and identifying and locating authoritative materials. A teacher recently reported to me that her own son did all of his research for an eighth-grade American history project online. In reporting later on his decisions for which sources to use, he explained that he chose those that were most colorful and visually attractive; unfortunately, he didn't check the sources of these websites, and they were all Klan sponsored! His report began, "One of the most patriotic and important organizations ... ,"—not quite what his mother was expecting. Just recently one of my colleagues was asked to work with teachers in a Southern community because the students had downloaded and used information from a website of a university professor who denies the Holocaust; a group had used his site as the basis of its report, which concluded that the Jewish Holocaust in World War II hadn't actually happened. Clearly these students need to learn strategies for evaluating sites and checking them against other textbooks and edited materials.

In the past few years I have been privileged to work on projects designed to help students engage more fully in learning social studies: the Creating a Community of Scholars project (Evanston Township High School) and the American Memory Project funded by the Library of Congress (a statewide effort in Illinois to introduce teachers to the rich resources available for teaching with Library of Congress online resources). Both experiences have raised to a high level my interest in convincing teachers of the import and value of social studies as a foundation for developing comprehension. They underscore for me the flexibility required of students in reading a wide range of documents and visual texts (Ogle, Klemp, & McBride, 2007). A major effort in the teaching of social studies involves having students read primary-source documents and then answer document-based questions as part of their assessments. Yet, little instruction is given to students in how to approach these texts and make sense of them. All too often it is assumed that students can read demographic tables, personal letters, newspaper articles and editorials, as well as published essays and reports. As an example of the range of materials and documents required of students, middle and high school social studies and history teachers in our Transitional Adolescent Literacy Leaders project identified some of the kinds of texts they expect their students to read. The list included:

Primary sources
Secondary sources, including news reports
Biographies
Textbooks
Editorials and essays
Letters
Poetry
Political cartoons
Media literacy (video and still)
Online reports and websites

With students expected to comprehend information through such varied materials, social studies seems a natural place to continue reading comprehension instruction. And, it can prepare students to develop a realistic understanding of "reading" as a complex activity that varies considerably with the purpose and materials used.

HOW CAN TEACHERS USE THE CONTEXT OF SOCIAL STUDIES TO DEVELOP COMPREHENSION?

Types of Texts

Students deserve instruction in reading a wide variety of text types. One that merits particular guidance in the elementary grades is the social studies textbook. With the interest in hands-on and inquiry-based units, some teachers have ignored teaching students how to use textbooks. The intermediate grades is a good time to provide direction in how textbooks are set up, the supports authors and editors provide to help students learn with these resources, and to teach some active strategies for engaging with these dense texts. Because textbook authors generally are good about alerting students to key vocabulary, it is helpful for teachers to focus students on the ways the books identify these—through boldface type, italics, marginal definitions, and glossaries. Because the texts include so much information, elementary students also need to learn how the books provide guidance for them through headings and subheadings and pre and post questions that highlight the main ideas. Some books even include a list of main ideas within sections of the text. The shift from reading stories and novels to reading textbooks is a substantial one; the more children can use the aids to comprehension provided in the textbooks, the more easily they will make sense of the information.

During the elementary years teachers should receive some news magazine or children's social studies magazine and be guided in how to use the short articles they contain. Usually the headlines are coupled with a strong picture or photograph that communicates the main idea of the article. The articles often have authors so children can look for the authors/editors who write the periodical. Some magazines come in a large format, too, so teachers can point out the way the articles are arranged, the use of headings and subheadings, and guide their young readers to scan the printed text and then look carefully at the graphics and the captions that indicate what is important and how the information connects with the article. In the news magazines for primary grades through the upper grades ideas are communicated through a combination of verbal and visual information. The visual elements make the texts more appealing, but the task for readers is much more sophisticated. As Hegarty, Just, and Carpenter (1991) made clear, when a text is accompanied by a visual component, the comprehension process is more challenging because the reader has to integrate material presented in two different media. Students need help in learning how to synthesize such diverse types of information.

In the middle grades, if not earlier, teachers focus more on using online resources and combining visual and narrative information. Students learn to look for authorship of articles and websites and are taught to interpret photographs and cartoons. Many teachers find that they can help students become more critical thinkers by having them interpret pictures. They begin by asking students to make a list of what they "see" in a photograph. They may follow this by asking what the students think the photographer was trying to communicate—what was the reason for this photograph? They may also ask students to think about what was not shown: What if the lens had been wider? What if the shot had been closer up? Having students create captions for photographs can also be a good activity to build comprehension (Ogle & Beers, 2009; Newman, Spirou, & Danzer, 2007).

Combining information from maps and tables with narrative text is important and yet may not become part of students' reading without teacher guidance and regular reminders to combine these different types of information in building a meaning for a text or texts. In high school more attention is paid to reading primary sources and to students' engagement with multiple sources to understand varied points of view before building one's own argument. Developing a sense of how history and the other social sciences involve ongoing interpretive endeavors using evidence and reports from others is important. Students deserve the opportunity to compare essays, editorials, and even textbooks from different eras to see clearly how interpretations and focus change. Students need to read different published interpretations and also participate in their own interpretive quest for meaning with primary-source documents and document-based questions coming from teachers and programs (Brady & Radin, 2002). They also can learn to argue their own point of view after building a knowledge base around issues being studied (McBride, 2008).

Variety of Text Structures

One of the least taught strategies for students to use when trying to comprehend informational texts is to identify the text structure or frame the authors have employed to organize the information. It is not difficult to help students preview articles and textbook chapters to identify their central structure: chronological, compare–contrast, problem–solution, or a simple description of varied components. Yet few teachers take the time to do so. When students can begin by looking at the way the authors have put together the information, they gain more control over what is important and can figure out how to prioritize the ideas.

Powerful strategies are available in the literature that help students with this task. In fact, a foundation of Buehl's *Classroom Strategies for Interactive Learning* (2009) is based on the understanding that students need to identify structure as a key to learning and memory. Buehl and others in the state of Wisconsin drew on the work of Jones, Palinc- sar, Ogle, and Carr (1987) in creating the framework they used with instructional strategies teachers can use to guide students in learning. When students think about the overarching structure content specialists use, they have an entry point for creating categories and mapping the content. Students can begin by surveying the structure of the text using the headings and subheadings and the other visual information pro- vided. Caverly, Mandaville, and Nicholson (1995) developed another powerful prereading strategy called PLAN (Preview, Locate, Add, and Note). Students learn to preview the structure of a chapter or article and create a graphic overview with the title in the center and the major headings around it. Students then reference the key visual information by the headings to which they belong and note highlighted vocabu- lary (Radcliffe, Caverly, Hand, & Franke, 2008). See Figure 8.1 for an example of a middle-grade student's PLAN for reading a chapter section on Ancient Greece.

Another way to highlight the text organization has come from spe- cial education educators. They noted that students don't seem to notice the connections among sections of the textbook materials that they are assigned to read. To help students read across pages of text, these teach-

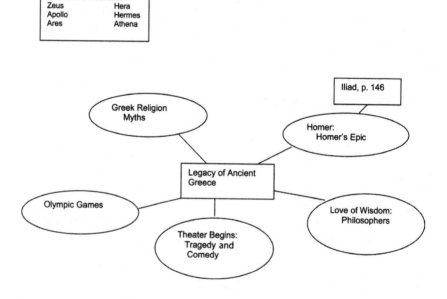

FIGURE 8.1. PLAN: Preview guide to text section.

ers make a single horizontal copy of all the pages in the section of text, tape them together, and post them on the wall. They ask students to outline each section with colored magic markers. This helps students see how text content follows from one column to another and across page boundaries. Even the traditional outlining and Cornell notes can be used to help students identify major headings in texts. Looking for structure and organization is a key to good comprehension; students deserve guidance in starting their reading of informational text at this level.

This habit can begin early in elementary grades when teachers have students continue the idea of a "picture walk" with an expanded "content and graphics walk" through informational texts and articles. In one project at the elementary level we used the attractive news magazines to which most schools subscribe to help students identify structure. Using just the titles of the articles, we asked students to predict how each text would be structured: "Gray Wolves at Home"; "Wolves and Their Relatives"; "The Life Cycle"; and "Hated Predator?" Having had practice thinking about how authors organize information, they were quite adept at identifying description, compare–contrast, sequence/chronology, and problem–solution as likely organizing frames. Teachers can also ask students to compare the tables of contents of possible selections to identify their structure (Blachowicz & Ogle, 2008). This habit of looking for organization and structure is an important starting point to help students understand that informational texts are organized in predictable frames and that using these frames can enhance students' engagement with authors. These are the same frames that they will use when they write, too.

When I developed the K-W-L (What We Know, What We Want to Learn, and What We Learned) and the K-W-L+ frameworks many years ago, a key component was that students would not only brainstorm what they thought they knew about a topic but would also list what they thought would be major *categories* of information they would encounter. It is the second part of the brainstorming that has been lost by many teachers, yet, to me it is the most powerful. When teachers complain that students don't know anything about a topic being initiated, my response is that it is essential for teachers to *guide* students in finding the underlying structure or major divisions of the content, starting with what is known. For example, if students are going to begin learning about a new continent (Africa or Asia) and have little familiarity with it, the starting place could be: What would we want to write about North America? What do we know about our own part of the world that would be important chapters in a book or article we might write? This type of question can lead to students' identification of countries, regions, land forms, transportation, etc. Then teachers can guide students to thinking about which of these categories might be important as the class initiates their study of another part of the world. By connecting what students already know at a high level of concepts, it is possible to lead them to good questions about a new area. They must know something and have anchors they can use if any study involving new information is going to be memorable.

Varied Points of View

Social studies also provides a natural setting for students to learn to question the authorship of the texts they read. Most social studies teachers use a textbook as part of their instructional materials but extend that considerably by having students regularly read and discuss news articles, engage in individual research, use primary-source documents, and include reading materials such as the Hakim personalized history books (Hakim, 2005). By providing opportunities for students to read pieces on many topics and from a wide range of perspectives, teachers can instill in students the habit of "questioning the author," to use the label Beck and her colleagues (Beck, McKeown, Hamilton, & Kucan, 1997) have given to a powerful approach to facilitating engaged content-area reading. In questioning the author (QtA) approach, students work in small groups with a teacher guiding their discussion of text segments. Their stance is one of trying to interpret the author's intent and success in communicating with them as readers. They learn to ask questions such as these: "Why do you think the author wrote this? What do you think he or she really meant? How else could it have been explained? What would you want to add or modify?" By taking the stance of an active participant in a dialogue about texts, students begin to look at printed texts in a new way and build their confidence as readers.

In my own work, I have frequently suggested that every student deserves to read, hear, or see multiple points of view. No single text should stand alone, given the rich resources that are available to us from libraries, online resources, museums, and primary sources (Ogle et al., 2007). There are ample materials from which to choose. Publishers have also produced a wide range of supplemental text materials and collections of documents and artifacts to make learning accessible to students with varied interests and levels of sophistication, and some of these are multimodal. In contrast to the use of long novels where point of view emerges over extensive text, it is easy to provide short texts on the same topic that clearly illustrate how differently people can interpret the same event, context, or movement.

It is even interesting for students to compare textbooks from different publishers or even the same publisher to see how priorities shift over time. For example, only in the last decade has there been much of an interest in the life of the common people among historians who write syntheses of history; before the fixation was on politics, and often history was organized by wars. Some social studies textbooks have different versions depending on the state or region of the United States for which they are designed to be used. I first encountered the term "war of Northern aggression" when I looked at the U.S. history textbook used in Virginia schools. Being from Minnesota, this term and concept were new to me. Though regional interpretations can influence the way content is presented, even in textbooks, more often it is changing priorities within disciplines that determine shifts in content emphasis. These changes can be interesting for students and can help them understand why it is important to look for several points of view before coming to their own conclusion.

The use of the Internet has made it even more imperative that students learn to ask questions about authorship (Burniski, 2007). As previously noted, students need to be taught how to question the sites they visit and how to identify the most authoritative ones. Identifying the guide to the source is a starting place. Then checking out the sponsors to determine their biases is a second step. For students who are unsure about the point of view represented, it is good to refer back to a textbook or edited encyclopedia, not a Wikipedia, to see if the perspective in an online site is similar to those edited sources. Learning how to "fact check" and ask for credentials can be a valuable lifelong skill. New resources are available for learning the skills needed to read effectively online. One engaging site, *www.allaboutexplorers.com,* has been developed by a teacher and librarian who teach students informational literacy skills as they learn about explorers. Embedded in the texts are pieces of misinformation that challenge students to read and think critically. The site is an excellent example of how social studies, literacy, and library informational literacy can be combined to the benefit of all students.

Several good teaching activities are available to help students learn to question the authority of the texts they read and to read to find the author's points of view, even when the authority is sound. The job of historians is to analyze and reinterpret history, so there is no dearth of materials from which to choose. Most students love looking at the headline stories from international newspapers and online sources; just seeing how different the press interpretations are can be an eye-opening catalyst for critical or evaluative thinking. Buhle includes the point of view guide in his resources; Woods, Lapp, Flood, and Taylor (2008) and Ogle et al. (2007) also have several teaching strategies that help students develop an awareness of, and ability to articulate, positions or points of view. Students who learn that ideas and events have multiple explanations or interpretations are more likely to take time to think about their own interpretation—to interpret critically what they read and see.

This can lead to their writing from multiple points of view, too. A favorite writing activity, RAFT (role, audience, format, and topic) provides a great framework for students to play with ideas they are studying by sharing them in different formats from different perspectives (Santa, 1988). Students in one Chicago class studying the women's suffrage movement of the late 1800s used RAFT to synthesize what they were learning. Figure 8.2 shows the different roles, audiences, formats, and themes they decided to use in their projects. One group had read an international journalist's editorial about the conflict in the United States and so chose that point of view for its piece. Another group created a poster advertising an upcoming rally of the suffragettes. Another group was upset by the conservative men's perspectives and wrote a somewhat satirical song from the feminists' perspective; part of the song is shown in Figure 8.3. All groups were able to demonstrate a deep understanding of the issues through their different perspectives and products.

Students deepen their comprehension when they can see ideas and issues from multiple perspectives and understand some of the foundation for those differences. Alvermann's (1991) discussion web and McBride's (2008) guide to using debate in classrooms both help students take this identification of perspective to a shared community level. Listening to others and engaging in debate over issues with backing from evidence in the information that has been studied is a strong way to deepen students' comprehension. One of my doctoral students, a reading teacher, worked

Role	Audience	Format	Theme
Musician of the time	Cabaret or community gathering	Song	Supporting women's suffrage movement
Advertiser at the turn of the century	General public	Poster	Opponent of women's rights
African American woman	Ilinois newspaper readers	Editorial to the paper	Personal point of view supporting women's rights; women do much of the work
Foreign journalist	To native countrymen	News article	Women's suffrage supporter; surprised at opposition

FIGURE 8.2. RAFT on women's suffrage movement.

Women's Suffrage Rallying Song
Sung to the Tune of Jimmy Crack Corn

Verse 1: I can do more than cook and clean.
I'm not just a beauty queen. I have a son of 21.
That through his voice MY life he runs.
Chorus: Get up the vote, don't despair.
              Get up the vote, don't despair.
              Get up the vote, don't despair –
              Our voices will be heard!

FIGURE 8.3. Portion of a song written as part of a RAFT activity.

with the social studies teacher in their urban middle school to help students learn to identify evidence for different points of view using discussion web. They downloaded the form from the *readwritethink* website and used short articles on global warming and pollution to help students identify evidence. In small groups students read about and responded to the question: Is the world going to run out of resources? See Figures 8.4 and 8.5 for samples of student work. Their conclusions were written on the back of the think sheets.

Finally, in addition to analyzing points of views and arguments, students need to learn to establish credibility with their own voices, especially as they communicate online. Burniske (2007) provides many engaging projects that involve distance communities where students can learn to express ideas and explore deeper understanding with peers in very different situations from their own. In the 21st century students love to use the Internet for personal communication and connecting. There is no reason teachers can't tap into this powerful tool to connect students around the world to learn from each other. I have been amazed at the depth of online conversations students from Chicago have had with counterparts in Bulgarian schools as a result of the International Reading Association (IRA)-sponsored Reading–Writing Critical Thinking Project. When students have authentic purposes and partners in dialogue, they can make tremendous gains in understanding others and their worlds.

CONCLUSION

I began this article explaining why it is so essential that literacy be developed as a foundation for students' learning in social studies. Whether in reading traditional texts, biographies and literary essays,

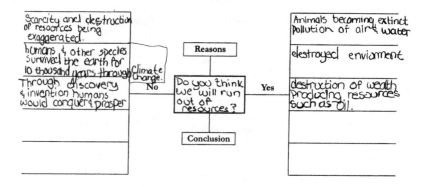

1. After reading a selection, form groups of three to five students each.
2. Discuss the focus question with your group and come up with evidence to support both a yes position and a no position.
3. Analyze the question and record information and the group's responses. Jot down only key words and phrases and try to use an equal number of reasons for pros and cons.
4. Work together to come to a consensus by stating your conclusion and reason(s) for your conclusion.
5. Finally, choose a spokesperson to share your group's point of view with the entire class.

FIGURE 8.4. Discussion web. Form from Alvermann (1991). Copyright 1991 by the International Reading Association. Reprinted by permission.

(a) We concluded that *Yes* we soon will run out of resources because one animals are going extinct and are air is being polluted second people and new technology is destroying are enviornment and third there is destruction of wealth producing resources such as oil/minerals.

example
Polar bears

(b) no, because we humans always comes up with good solutions.

We concluded that no because we have been surviving for a long time

FIGURE 8.5. Two sample conclusions from the student discussion webs.

magazines and newspapers, or when using Internet sites, the demands of social studies require that students read and think critically. By using important questions and themes to guide their inquiry in the powerful learning opportunities we provide, students can be fully engaged as learners. The work they produce and the depth of their thinking provide the proof that students CAN. It also shows that teachers CAN. Yes, together we CAN.

REFERENCES

Alvermann, D. (1991). The discussion web: A graphic aid for learning across the curriculum. *Reading Teacher, 45,* 92–99.

Beck, I., McKeown, M., Hamilton, R., & Kucan, L. (1997). *Questioning the author.* Newark, DE: International Reading Association.

Blachowicz, C., & Ogle, D. (2008). *Reading comprehension: Strategies for independent learners.* New York: Guilford Press.

Brady, C., & Roden, P. (2002). *The DBQ project.* Evanston, IL: Authors.

Buehl, D. (2009). *Classroom strategies for interactive learning* (3rd ed.) Newark, DE: International Reading Association.

Burniske, R. B. (2008). *Literacy in the digital age* (2nd ed.) Thousand Oaks, CA: Corwin Press.

Caverly, D., Mandeville, T., & Nicholson, S. (1995). PLAN: A study–reading strategy for informational text. *Journal of Adolescent and Adult Literacy, 39,* 190–199.

Collier, J. L., & Collier, L. (1974). *My brother Sam is dead.* New York: Scholastic.

Curtis, C. P. (1995). *The Watsons go to Birmingham—1963.* New York: Delacorte.

Hakim, J. (2005). *A history of us.* New York: Oxford University Press.

Hegarty, M., Carpenter, P., & Just, M. (1991). Diagrams in the comprehension of scientific texts. In R. Barr, M. Kamil, P. Mosenthal, & P. D. Pearson (Eds.) *Handbook of reading research* (vol. II, p. 652). White Plains, NY: Longman.

Hosseini, K. (2004). *The kite runner.* New York: Penguin.

Jones, B. F., Palincsar, A. M., Ogle, D., & Carr, E. (1987). *Strategic teaching and learning: Cognitive instruction in the content areas.* Alexandria, VA: Association for Supervision and Curriculum Development.

McBride, W. (2008). *If they can argue well, they can write well.* Nashville, TN: Incentive Publications.

Newman, M., Spirou, C., & Danzer, G. (2007). *Chicago stories: 1830–World War I—visual images for classroom instruction.* Chicago: National-Louis University.

Ogle, D. (2007). Best practices in adolescent literacy instruction. In L. B. Gambrell, L. M. Morrow, & M. Pressley (Eds.) *Best practices in literacy instruction* (3rd ed., pp. 127–158). New York: Guilford Press.

Ogle, D., & Beers, J. (2009). *Engaging in the language arts: Exploring the power of language.* Boston: Pearson.

Ogle, D., Klemp, R., & McBride, W. (2007). *Building literacy in social studies.* Alexandria, VA: Association for Supervision and Curriculum Development.

Radcliffe, R., Caverly, D., Hand, J., & Franke, D. (2008). Improving reading in a middle school science classroom. *Journal of Adolescent and Adult Literacy, 51*(5), 398–408.

Santa, C. (1988). *Content reading including study systems.* Dubuque, IA: Kendall/Hunt.

Staples, S. F. (2000). *Shabanu: Daughter of the wind.* New York: Dell Laurel Leaf.

Whelan, G. (2005). *Homeless bird.* New York: HarperCollins.

Wood, K. D., Lapp, D., Flood, J., & Taylor, D. B. (2008). *Guiding readers through text: Strategy guides for new times.* Newark, DE: International Reading Association.

9

Comprehension Connections to Science

Maria Grant

Those who are able to successfully understand science reading material must participate in a whole series of comprehension activities, including the interpretation of new and challenging vocabulary words, the generation of new ideas built on a foundation of existing background knowledge, and the construction of questions based on learned science content. While this may sound like a daunting task for anyone, it is especially challenging for a young person who lacks either science background knowledge or word deciphering skills.

Consider ninth-grade earth science student Ahn Nguyen. Ahn was born of immigrant parents 14 years ago. While English is her first language, at home Ahn's parents speak mostly Vietnamese. Ahn enjoys science, but has arrived at the classroom door of her ninth-grade earth science course with gaps in her background knowledge and vocabulary. As a matter of fact, at least 60% of Ahn's classmates are in the same boat. What has created this regretful, yet common, state of the science classroom? Many will point the finger at Ahn's previous teachers—perhaps one might blame the seventh- and eighth-grade science teachers who taught science vocabulary by issuing 50-word lists followed by the edict *define each term*. That task never made sense to Ahn.

Or maybe it's because there was never an opportunity for Ahn to read books such as *Weather Words and What They Mean* (Gibbons, 1992), and trips to the local science museum were not commonplace in Ahn's life. In actuality, there are any number of reasons that students may not be able to truly and independently comprehend science material by the time they reach high school. Many of them are beyond the control of the individual learner. That certainly does not mean that we should throw in the towel or relegate the student to remedial or repeat courses. What it does mean is that teachers need to find ways to help students build background knowledge, decode new vocabulary terms independently, and construct meaning by asking and answering questions when encountering new science material.

Is it truly possible for an earth science teacher to confidently face a classroom full of students like Ahn, knowing that he or she is able to help students think about, write about, and discuss science content? The answer is an emphatic *yes!* All it takes is an ability to diagnose what each student needs in terms of background knowledge and word building skills and the aptitude to implement needed strategies.

THE IMPORTANCE OF BACKGROUND KNOWLEDGE

Determining Background Knowledge Is an Appropriate First Step to Diagnosing Student Needs

Let's first examine how a teacher might determine what students know and don't know in a science class. In Ahn's class her earth science teacher might decide to focus student interest and tap into background knowledge by developing and using an anticipation guide (Figure 9.1). An anticipation guide can be strategically created to determine what students know and what they need to be taught; it can also be used to motivate students to learn more. The latter factor—motivation—is imperative to the process of entry-level assessment. Specifically, if students are disinterested in a subject or in the curriculum, they will not expend the energy needed to accurately determine their degree, or lack of, background knowledge. It is therefore incumbent on the teacher to both motivate students and assess prior knowledge simultaneously.

To develop an anticipation guide, the teacher creates 5–10 content-related questions and places these into a framework or template that allows a student to quickly respond by agreeing or disagreeing or by indicating whether or not each statement is true or false. Such an activity not only focuses students on the upcoming content but also fosters retrieval of personal knowledge that has been acquired but perhaps has been "tucked away" for a while. In some cases, background knowledge does not exist for a student. In such instances, the anticipation guide serves as a way to prepare students for new learning by fostering their anticipation to discover whether the responses they chose were correct or not. After teachers have helped them learn the targeted content, they

Before Agree/Disagree		After Agree/Disagree
	1. Earth is the only planet in the solar system with water.	
	2. Stars, like the sun, have a life cycle.	
	3. Mercury has the largest volcano in the solar system.	
	4. Black holes release gravity when objects expand.	
	5. The solar system is nearly 5 billion years old.	

FIGURE 9.1. An earth science anticipation guide.

can ask students to revisit the anticipation guide to assess their learning. Additionally, when students revise their responses to an anticipation guide after instruction, they become aware of what they have learned. It's motivating for students to realize that they have grown in terms of content knowledge and understanding.

If it becomes clear to a teacher, such as Ahn's teacher, that a majority of the students lack the background knowledge necessary for making connections and growth in terms of new content, then the teacher must take action. How can a teacher help students build needed background knowledge? Marzano (2004) suggests several direct approaches that increase the array and depth of out-of-class experiences and include field trips to museums, galleries, and other off-site learning centers. In addition to these experiences, establishing mentoring relationships with caring adults can also help create environments that foster the construction of academic background knowledge. To help students on a daily basis, a teacher may need to draw on other, more easily accessible means, such as reading aloud magazine articles or excerpts from books, showing and discussing relevant pictures or photographs, and using demonstrations and artifacts.

Marzano (2004) suggests that any program that intends to help students build background knowledge must include the following three aspects of learning so that students can process the information in a way that will enable it to become part of their permanent memory: First, the new information must be encountered by the learners multiple times. Second, the information must be considered in detail and in depth. Third, the new ideas must be connected, by association, to other information.

In short, teachers must present new learning multiple times, in multiple ways, with opportunities for students to connect new understandings to what they already know. Let's take a closer look at what this might look like in science.

Wide Reading Can Help Students Build Background Knowledge

Wide reading offers students the opportunity to experience content in different ways that can motivate them by extending reading material beyond textbooks to genres that may be more accessible to them in terms of reading level, concept load, and general engagement. To encourage wide reading in a content area, such as science, teachers provide students with lots of texts that touch on science content from a variety of perspectives. With guidance, students can examine a topic in detail from multiple perspectives and genres, as, for example, magazine or newspaper articles, picture books, essays, science-based fiction, biographies, popular "how to" books, or other informational texts. When students have a choice of genres from which to read, they are more likely to be able to make personal connections that will assist them in building background knowledge. Consider Ahn's earth science class. Midsemester, when Ahn's teacher broached the standards-based topic of climate change and global warming, he loaded up her classroom bookshelf with a wide range of reading materials on the topic, including the following books:

- *An Inconvenient Truth: The Crisis of Global Warming* (Gore, 2007)
- *The Greenhouse Effect: Warming the Planet (Exploring Science)* (Stille, 2006)
- *Global Warming and Climate Change Demystified* (Silver, 2008)
- *Six Degrees: Our Future on a Hotter Planet* (Lynas, 2008)
- *Boiling Point: How Politicians, Big Oil and Coal, Journalists, and Activists Have Fueled a Climate Crisis—And What We Can Do to Avert Disaster* (Gelbspan, 2005).

She even included books that present alternative perspectives to the global warming issue, just to guide students to understand the nature of debate, discussion, and scientific review. To introduce students to the idea of wide reading, Ahn's teacher begins with an excerpt from *The North Pole Was Here: Puzzles and Perils at the Top of the World* (Revkin, 2006), a book that moves from an examination of North Pole explorers of the past onto the adventures of the scientists who today are attempting to understand global climate change. She reads aloud to the class:

> For nearly two hours I have been staring out a small window on a droning propeller-driven airplane. The low, unsetting sun casts the plane's shadow off to the side, where it slides over what looks like an endless crinkled white landscape. But there is no land below us. There is only an ocean—a frozen one. We are flying out across a cap of floating, drifting ice that's the size of the United States. As far as the eye can see, colliding plates of ice raise jumbled miles-long ridges, some as high as houses. Here and there, the ice is split by cracks that expose the black depths of the Arctic Ocean underneath. (p. 9)

Thus begins Ahn's acquaintance with the idea that the earth is heating up, polar ice is melting, and life on earth, as we know it, may be changing. Ahn's teacher allows students to check out her books and other materials for extended lengths of time. She also encourages wide reading by providing time to explore the materials in class and to discuss, question, clarify, and reflect on the reading as a whole class and in small groups. To become scientifically literate, students need the kind of opportunities Ahn and her classmates are being afforded. They need to read many and varied texts on a topic, to deepen their understanding through reflections and peer/teacher interactions, and they need to develop strategies for learning from these texts (Zmach et al., 2006) through activities such as shared reading with think-aloud modeling, which as we will see, is a mainstay for learning in Mr. Watson's chemistry class.

Shared Readings Can Deepen Background Knowledge

In Darnell Watson's third-period science classroom, his students often struggle with reading the chemistry book chosen by the school district during the last textbook adoption. The vocabulary is challenging, the text is dense, and assumptions are made that students have extensive background knowledge when it comes to the foundations of atomic structure, including the basics of chemical bonding. Despite this obstacle for all those students without this background knowledge, Mr. Watson has found a way to help his students approach this text so that they can derive meaning, make connections to their personal lives, and delve deeper in their knowledge of chemistry concepts. To do this, Mr. Watson has incorporated shared readings into his curriculum. Shared readings are conducted by the teacher while students simultaneously view the text. When a teacher wants to show students how to maneuver through difficult texts, shared reading is an effective strategy (Hicks & Wadlington, 1994).

When it was time for students to read about covalent bonds, Mr. Watson drew upon his ability to offer a shared reading, augmented by a think-aloud, which serves as a model for students about to embark on a challenging reading assignment, such as reading a science text. In essence, a think-aloud is a verbal articulation of what's going on in a reader's mind while he or she reads. The teacher doing the think-aloud reveals his or her thinking for the students to hear. If no one ever shows students how to think about a piece of text while reading, they may never know. A well-conducted think-aloud can inform and demonstrate for students how to approach complicated science information.

In preparation for a think-aloud, it is best for the teacher to record notes on his or her own copy of the reading. These notes indicate where to pause and introduce the following activities:

- Predicting upcoming content based on the meaning of a heading or italicized title.
- Deciphering word meaning using prefixes, suffixes, and/or root words.
- Identifying common science text structures, including compare–contrast, problem–solution, cause–effect, description, and sequence.
- Determining text meaning by drawing on background knowledge.
- Making text-to-text and text-to-self connections to the reading.
- Utilizing graphics, including charts, diagrams, figures, and photos, to predict and interpret the meaning of the text.
- Modeling how to make connections between a figure's caption and the content of the figure.

A think-aloud must be strategically developed with the intent of focusing on typical problem spots, followed by a modeling of how to tackle the identified challenging areas in a way that shows that good readers persevere when they read (Lapp, Fisher, & Grant, 2008). This does not necessarily mean that they "get" everything they read. Instead, it implies that good readers persist in their reading. They use comprehension skills, and they don't give up, even in the face of an arduous challenge. Below is an example of Mr. Watson's chemistry think-aloud for a section of the textbook entitled *physical changes*. He presented this segment as a shared reading. The *italicized print* indicates Mr. Watson's articulated thoughts:

> *As I look over this page of text, I see photos of ice, water, and fog rolling in over a coastline. The bold print says "physical changes."*

I wonder if this is going to be about how materials like water go through changes to become different. I know that if I put water in the freezer, it becomes ice. I'm not sure what the picture of fog means, but I'm sure I'll find out if I read. "Sometimes a substance undergoes changes that result in a very different appearance. Despite this, the composition of the substance remains the same." *I guess water, whether frozen or in a liquid form, is still H_2O.* "For example, when you take a long piece of wire and coil it up, it may have a different shape, but it is still made of the same material— copper." *Last night after I made dinner, I wrapped up the leftovers with a piece of foil. Before I used the foil, it was in the shape of a large square. Then I crumpled it up. Regardless of the shape, it was still made up of the same material—aluminum. I think this is the same as the copper example. Notice that I just made a text-to-self connection!* "Clearly, the state of matter is dependent on the temperature and pressure surrounding a material. This is true for all physical properties." *I remember when we read about physical properties a couple of days ago. They are characteristics that can be observed. Here I'm making a text-to-text connection.* "When temperature and/or pressure change, substances can undergo physical changes or changes from one state to another." *I know that the word "state" can mean many things, but in this case, I think it refers to whether or not the material is a solid, liquid, or gas. Here I'm trying to determine word meaning for a term that has multiple meanings. I'm using context—or the ideas and words surrounding the term—to figure out the specific meaning of "state" in this case.* "At atmospheric pressure and at temperatures below 0°C, water is found in a solid state better known as ice." *I can see I was right about the meaning of "state."* "When heat is added to ice, it melts and changes to a liquid known as water. Even though water and ice appear to be different, the composition of the two is the same. Both are made up of H_2O—two hydrogen atoms for every oxygen atom. This is a physical change. If the temperature of the water increases to 100°C, the water boils and is converted to steam." *I don't know what "converted" means, but I think it might mean "changed to" because the text is talking about changes of state. Again, I'm predicting word meaning from context.* "Melting and evaporating are both physical changes and phase changes." *I know that substances can be in different phases—solid, liquid, or gas.* "The figure below shows condensation, another phase change." *I'm going to look at this figure to see if I can determine what "condensation" means. I see that there is a glass of ice water with mist on the sides. Then there's also a picture of fog rolling over the top of a container. The* *caption says, "The dry ice forms fog, which is actually drops of water formed by condensation as the surrounding air comes in contact with the cold dry ice." I think that condensation must be little drops of water formed from a gas, like air. It must have something to do with the contact of the air and cold materials.*

By drawing on background knowledge, text-to-text connections, text-to-self connections, context clues, figures, captions, and knowledge of word parts, Mr. Watson modeled how to read a challenging chemistry-related text. Clearly, the selection of a text is critical. A text should be chosen purposefully. According to Fisher, Frey, and Lapp (2008), expert teachers will dot their shared reading texts with sticky notes and pencil marks that indicate where to pause, what to say, and how to say it. A shared reading must be planned, rehearsed, and transparent to the students—intended purpose must be made clear.

Following his think-aloud, Mr. Watson asked his students to partner with one another to read the next two paragraphs entitled *chemical changes*. As each person shared his or her version of a think-aloud for one paragraph of the text, Mr. Watson walked around and monitors progress and understanding.

The next day, as a follow-up to this initial reading, Mr. Watson asked his students to work in teams of four to produce a poster that displayed their discovered learnings. Additionally, students were encouraged to add to their knowledge by accessing designated websites found on nearby classroom computers. All this activity was part of a strategic plan put forth by Mr. Watson to encourage students to persevere in their reading, even when presented with what seems like a mountain of a task. "You can climb that mountain. I'm helping you acquire the tools to do it." That's one of Mr. Watson's favorite sayings. Clearly his students are being offered the tools needed to persist when reading about chemical changes, the periodic table, or even ionic bonding—a future topic for this class.

INTEGRATING AN INSTRUCTIONAL ROUTINE INTO YOUR CURRICULUM TAKES A CONCERTED EFFORT

According to Fisher and Frey's instructional protocol (2008), which is based on the gradual-release-of-responsibility model (Pearson & Gallagher, 1983), students need to experience learning in various ways before they can personally call upon an appropriate strategy to help mitigate the challenges of reading. This instructional model consists of four parts: focus lessons, guided instruction, collaborative learning, and independent work.

Focus lessons are intended to prime the students for learning. When Ahn's teacher read from *The North Pole Was Here: Puzzles and Perils at the Top of the World,* she was building background knowledge, promoting student interest, and previewing upcoming content—all intentional goals of a focus lesson. Similarly, Mr. Watson conducted a shared reading with a think-aloud for the purpose of showing his students how to approach a text in science. In essence, Mr. Watson modeled what proficient readers do when they are confronted with a reading challenge. Focus lessons set the stage for further learning; students are prepared, motivated, and bolstered with the skills needed to tackle an upcoming task.

As a next step, Mr. Watson asked his students to work with a partner to practice conducting a think-aloud. As students began to try out this strategy, Mr. Watson walked around the classroom monitoring progress, occasionally jumping in to mediate learning when he noticed that students needed help. For example, when chemistry student Jaime Lopez stumbled over the word *combustion,* he hesitated. Mr. Watson asked Jaime to look at the root part of the word. Jaime responded, "I think the root word is *combust* and I know that has something to do with burning. Maybe *combustion* means that something is burned and heat is given off." Mr. Watson commended Jaime on his skillful deciphering methodology, "That's exactly how you figure out what new words mean. Use what knowledge you have and make an educated guess." Jaime and his partner proceeded with the reading—obviously confident that they were on the right track in terms of implementing this new strategy. What Mr. Watson did was allow his students to engage in *guided practice,* another component of the Fisher and Frey protocol. Guided practice is an opportunity for students to carry out and rehearse a new strategy— in this case students were involved in predicting and clarifying meaning when reading and were provided with expert support from their teacher as they practiced.

To further proceed with this protocol, the next time students met, Mr. Watson asked them to collaboratively create a poster that illustrated the main points they discovered in the reading the previous day. Mr. Watson allowed students to augment the information with ideas from a couple of bookmarked websites that could be accessed from five computers located in various spots around the room. Jaime, Marcus, Cassidy, and Elizabeth spent 10 minutes deciding what to include as a *discovered* idea. Ultimately they decided to focus on presenting examples of physical properties by including the phase changes of water, along with extended information provided from a website that included the concepts of density and solubility. This *collaborative learning* was yet another step in the protocol presented by Mr. Watson. Students were required to reread the text they had previously used within the context of a group effort. They had to discuss the content meaning and were allowed the opportunity to seek out additional related material to augment their understanding of the text. Students further negotiated meaning with the support of each other—a critical step in learning how to process difficult science material.

As an end result, Mr. Watson clearly wants his students to be able to independently tackle the challenges of new vocabulary, gaps in background knowledge, and difficult phrasing when reading. After allowing his students numerous opportunities to hear how good readers approach science text, to work with the guidance of a teacher, and to determine meaning with a collaborative team, Mr. Watson intends to ask his students to use what they have learned to read on their own in an effort of *independent practice*. Through use of repeated independent practice, students will acquire the skills needed to attack academic reading with the confidence and skill that, in the end, yield success.

Different students clearly will need adjustments to this protocol, but that is best determined by the teacher, Mr. Watson in this case, their expert teacher. It is clearly the teacher who, through progress monitoring, will determine how to proceed in order to create the best learning environment for his or her students. Occasionally, a teacher will begin with a collaborative task, as there are times when he or she may want students to muddle through a reading or other strategy before being given the opportunity to see a modeled presentation of the task. How and when to implement focus lessons, guided instruction, collaborative learning, and independent work is best determined by the teacher, who always has the end goal of learning the content in mind.

VOCABULARY KNOWLEDGE
CAN BOOST COMPREHENSION

An individual's knowledge of word meanings correlates with his or her ability to comprehend text (Stahl & Nagy, 2006). Think back to a challenging text that you were required or asked to read. Were you able to tackle it? If so, you were most likely familiar with much of the vocabulary that was part of the text. If not, you perhaps were confronted with an overabundance of new terms. Certainly the latter situation would leave you struggling to comprehend the meaning of the text as you spent time stumbling over words you simply didn't know. In sum, word knowledge is powerful. Along with background knowledge, word knowledge significantly contributes to reading comprehension (Stahl, 1999). Given this, you might ask the question: Can a science teacher empower students with the ability to learn new words independently? The answer is, once again, an emphatic *yes*.

Juanita Perez teaches eighth-grade life science. When beginning a unit about the structure of matter, Mrs. Perez uses several strategies to help students learn the many new vocabulary terms they will encounter. At the start of a unit, she asks her students to think about content-related words by having them complete a vocabulary self-awareness chart (Figure 9.2). To complete this chart, students must indicate whether they can provide a definition and/or an example for each term. A vocabulary self-awareness chart allows teachers to assess what they will need to teach based on an understanding of what students know at the beginning of a lesson. Additionally, students are provided with advance knowledge of what to expect in terms of new vocabulary. As a bonus, students are made aware that vocabulary understanding goes beyond merely copying a definition from a glossary. In fact, most technical vocabulary terms

Vocabulary Word	I can define it.	I can provide an example.	I can do both.	Definition	Example
Volume		√		A glass of water has volume.	
Mass			√	how much matter is in a substance	A book has mass.
Matter					
Solid					
Liquid					
Gas					
Plasma					
Thermal energy					
Kinetic energy					

FIGURE 9.2. A vocabulary self-awareness chart, which can guide students to tap into prior knowledge while also directing them to focus on new terms.

have intricate meanings that are best acquired by connecting new terms to existing semantic networks. Simply speaking, each word is connected to other words, concepts, facts, and memories (Fisher & Frey, 2008; Stahl & Nagy, 2006). By completing a vocabulary self-awareness chart, Mrs. Perez's students are prompted to think about not only definitions, but also about possible examples related to the lesson vocabulary. They learn to think about vocabulary in ways that go beyond the dictionary definition.

To further support vocabulary acquisition, Mrs. Perez asks her students to make Frayer models on index cards (Frayer, Frederick, & Klausmeier, 1969). Frayer models are intended to help students organize their understanding of specific words through the identification of examples and nonexamples (Figure 9.3).

There are several steps to follow when creating a Frayer model. Below is a synopsis of the content for each of the four quadrants that students could create as a Frayer model.

1. Define the new terms by including key characteristics. When defining *kinetic energy* in a chemistry or physics class, for example, students would need to identify that kinetic energy involves *motion*.

2. Distinguish between the new concept and similar concepts. The intent of this step is to dispel misconceptions and to clarify confusing ideas. A student might distinguish *kinetic energy* from the associated term *potential energy*. Although both words describe a type of energy, kinetic energy involves *motion* and potential energy is *stored energy*.

3. Give an example of the term. For kinetic energy, students could mention any object or material that is moving. Physics students might list a car being driven or a book being pushed. In a chemistry course, students could discuss molecules moving as they are being heated.

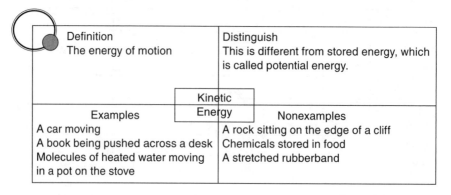

FIGURE 9.3. Frayer models require that students understand what a term is and what it is not.

4. Finally, provide a nonexample. It's important for students to be able to provide examples to show that they know what a term means; it's equally important to understand what a term is *not*. For the term *kinetic energy*, students can clarify their understanding by listing nonexamples that demonstrate the unmoving nature of an object that does not have kinetic energy. For this term, students might mention a rock poised on a cliff, a stretched rubberband, or chemicals stored in food.

If the Frayer models are created on index cards, sketches depicting aspects of the target term can be drawn on the back. It's convenient and useful for students to assemble a unit's worth of cards that they can secure with a notebook ring or a simple brad. In this way, cards may be easily shuffled through for studying and/or referencing in some other manner.

As aforementioned, word meanings are stored in semantic networks—connected webs of ideas, terms, and concepts (Stahl & Nagy, 2006). Given this, it's logical to assume that guiding students to create visual representations of the semantic networks that are stored in their brains would help them with vocabulary development and, as an extended result, with reading comprehension. Consider the term *conservation*. In a science sense, it literally means *preservation* or *prevention of injury, decay, waste, or loss*. However, there is so much more to the development of an understanding of *conservation* than the recollection of a mere definition. A biologist knows that *conservation* involves actions, awareness, and collaborative efforts. It's also dependent on the type of resource being considered. When referring to *water conservation*, a topic that is at the forefront of discussion in many communities, students might need to understand the role of the water authority, public service campaigns, and grass-roots or individual efforts. When reading about or discussing *conservation biology*, a student might find him- or herself engrossed in learning about wildlife populations and endangered species—related, yet different concepts. In essence, if vocabulary is a foundational aspect of reading comprehension and if vocabulary development involves complex understandings, then it is well worth an effort on the teacher's part to help students learn about words and related concepts. One effective way to do this is to have students create semantic word maps. If the term *conservation* was explained through the reading, then the semantic word map could be created during or after the reading. If, however, the term is referred to but not clarified in the reading, then vocabulary instruction would have to take place prior to reading the text. One way to prepare students for reading about a concept is to present ideas related to a key term in the format of an interactive lecture. Students can then capture main ideas via a brainstorm session and insert these ideas into a semantic map.

In Rose Wang's middle school science class, students studied El Niño, plate tectonics, and other related earth science phenomena. When it was time to review for the summative state assessment, Ms. Wang presented this information in the form of an interactive lecture, meaning that she incorporated audio clips from science newscasts, YouTube videos, demonstrations, and partner talk into what would otherwise be a traditional lecture format. As students listened and participated in the lecture, they generated notes, using a double-entry format to which they could refer when they created their semantic maps during a subsequent class meeting (Figure 9.4). To scaffold the note taking, Ms. Wang developed a template that followed the format of her lecture. The left side of the template prompted students with questions and general statements. The right side was left blank for students to respond with answers, sketches, and their own ideas. From this, students were able to create a semantic map that recorded their own thoughts about how plate tectonic concepts are related (Figure 9.5). To build their maps, students were asked to focus on main ideas that they would turn into a web of related concepts. The specific way in which the student webs were generated was left open-ended, for the students to decide.

Because Ms. Wang's students had a clear and deep understanding of *plate tectonics*—both from a vocabulary standpoint and from a position of background knowledge—as a next step, she was able to have students delve into a more challenging text. In this particular case, students were able to go beyond the features produced as a result of plate tectonics (mountains, island arcs, etc.) and approach more complex content. Specifically, Ms. Wang's students were able to read about heat flow measurements, magma composition, viscosity, and flow rates—very technical content.

Clearly, such a reading assignment would have been beyond most students were it not for Ms. Wang's focus on building background knowledge and augmenting vocabulary instruction. The ultimate goal for Ms Wang, and for most teachers, is to be able to present challenging and complex texts to students, but only after they are prepared to meet the challenges of reading.

COMPREHENSION CAN BE ENHANCED BY ENCOURAGING STUDENTS TO ASK QUESTIONS WHEN READING

At the start of every school year, sixth-grade science teacher Anthony Reed asks his students, "What do good readers do when they read?" Most students shrug their shoulders in uncertainty as a response. To get

Name:

Date: 7-28-08   Hour of Lab Class:

Questions, Main Ideas	Details, Comments, Sketches
What's the difference between El Niño and La Niña?	• above average tempuratures in central Pacific for El Nino • Below average for La Niña
What happens when an El Niño occurs every 2-7 years?	Winds get weaker, warm water goes back east & upwelling lessons
List the three types of boundaries.	Convergent Divergent sliding
Describe a divergent boundary.	Plates move apart
What drives plates to diverge?	Convection Currents.
Describe a convergent boundary.	Plates move towards eachother
Listen to the explanation of the various types of convergent boundaries–sketch or describe important points: Continental vs. oceanic	Continental Oceanic
Oceanic vs. oceanic	Newer older
Continental vs. continental	
What's a transform boundary? Asthenosphere – melted mantle	It is a boundary in which 2 plates move past eachother
Describe the structure of an earthquake. hypocenter – location below surface were it starts epicenter – on surface,	2 blocks of rock suddenly move past each other

FIGURE 9.4. Notes produced by a student participating in an interactive lecture.

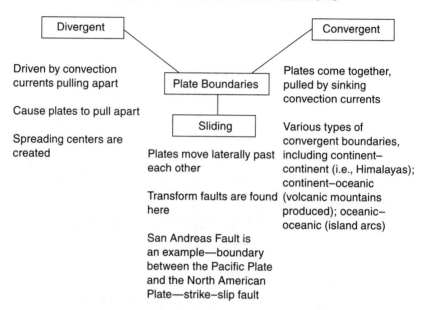

FIGURE 9.5. Semantic map centered on the vocabulary term *plate boundaries,* created from an interactive lecture.

his students to understand what a proficient reader must do, Mr. Reed integrates questioning strategies into his science curriculum.

ReQuest (Manzo, 1969) is a routine that encourages *thinking* during the reading process and requires that students participate in a question–answer conversation about a given text. As a result, students not only read but also *reread,* focusing on key ideas and foundational concepts. In essence, they do what good readers do when they read a text—they read, think, reread, question, and answer questions. To scaffold this strategy, Mr. Reed provides students with cue cards (Figure 9.6). One student plays the role of the *questioner* while his or her partner acts as the *respondent.* Students are asked to chunk the text by reading one paragraph at a time. All students simultaneously read a paragraph silently. The questioner thinks of one or two questions to ask his or her partner about the chunked text, while the respondent thinks about what he or she might be asked. Following the silent reading, the questions are asked and answered. If the respondent needs help in answering the question, his or her partner may offer a hint and may even direct the respondent to a section of the text. Following this, a new chunk of text is read and roles are switched. The process of questioning and answering continues until the assigned text is read.

When Simone Matthews wants her twelfth-grade physics students to

Questioner	Respondent
1. Read a chunk of text silently and think of two or three questions to ask your partner.	1. Read a chunk of text silently and think of two or three questions that your partner might ask you.
2. With the text in front of you, ask your partner to answer each of your questions.	2. Cover the text and try to answer each of your partner's questions.
3. If your partner needs a *hint,* you may provide one.	3. If you need a *hint,* you may ask your partner for one.
4. If your partner needs more help, you may show him or her where the answer can be found in the text.	4. If you need more help, you may ask your partner to show you where the answer can be found in the text.

FIGURE 9.6. Cue cards can aid students as they follow the proocol of ReQuest.

tackle a challenging text, she employs questioning strategies that require reading in partner or small-group arrangements. Miss Matthews realizes that not all students are at the same reading level, and whereas some struggle with decoding text, others are highly proficient. To tackle this common classroom challenge, Miss Matthews uses grouping in a variety of ways. Sometimes she'll group students that are at the same proficiency level in reading. In one instance, she used ReQuest and provided her struggling readers with a text that had a lower reading level, but still tackled the deeper aspects of the content. More proficient readers were given a text with similar content, presented at an appropriate reading level for them. On other occasions, Miss Matthews will group students in a heterogeneous manner—English learners, struggling readers, and proficient readers all in one group, for example—as she implements the strategy *reciprocal teaching.* For this, she directs students to think about four aspects of reading:

1. *Predicting.* Using cues from bold print, headings, graphics, and captions, students anticipate and forecast what will happen next.
2. *Clarifying.* When students encounter a word or phrase that is confusing or unclear, they use context clues, knowledge of root words and word parts, and help from others in the group to decipher meaning. Occasionally, students simply acknowledge the need for more clarification and must continue with the reading until future opportunities to clarify are presented.
3. *Questioning.* Students read a chunk of text, then develop ques-

tions that connect with the reading. They answer their own
questions as they read.
4. *Summarizing.* Students summarize content as they read by noting main ideas and general themes.

This instructional routine allows students to discuss and clarify
content while they construct knowledge for themselves. They also get
practice with four cognitive strategies readers use to understand texts.
Confusing points are laid out for discussion, ideas are presented, and
connections to previous learnings are made. Reciprocal teaching allows
students to struggle with content, share thoughts, and question. These
are founding elements in the processes of thinking creatively and critically. To aid her students as they go through the collaborative steps of
reciprocal teaching, Miss Matthews supplies cue cards with tasks for
easy reference (Figure 9.7). Reciprocal teaching is a way for students to
negotiate reading in a collaborative, supportive manner—one that often
encourages students to think beyond the text.

CONCLUSION: READING IN SCIENCE

| **Predict** |
| I think this will be about ... |
| I expect _____ will |
| happen next. |
| I wonder if this will occur ... |

| **Clarify** |
| I think this word means ... |
| This phrase is confusing but |
| maybe ... |
| I wonder if this means ... |

| **Question** |
| Who did ... ? |
| What happened ... ? |
| Why did ... ? |
| Where does ... ? |
| When did ... ? |
| How does ... ? |

| **Summarize** |
| The main ideas are ... |
| This reading discusses ... |
| After reading this, I know |
| that ... |

FIGURE 9.7. Cue cards help scaffold the reciprocal teaching conversations so
that students integrate predicting, clarifying, questioning, and summarizing
into their conversations about text..

TAKES PREPARATION AND ATTENTION
TO PREREADING ACTIVITIES

Although it may be tempting for a teacher to start a new unit by simply giving an assignment such as "Read pages 234–262 and answer the questions on page 263," care must be taken first to ensure that students are prepared for the reading. This sometimes requires an entry-level assessment to determine if background and prior knowledge are sufficient for the particular reading. If gaps in either of these two areas are identified, it's incumbent on the teacher to offer opportunities for students to develop needed vocabulary and augment background knowledge. Readalouds, shared readings with think-alouds, Frayer models, lectures with note taking, semantic mapping, ReQuest, and reciprocal teaching are all ways to support students as they develop the skills necessary to successfully read and comprehend science texts. It is the hope of any biology, chemistry, earth science, or physics teacher that students will be able to read any science text independently. That hope has the chance of becoming reality when students learn how to acquire vocabulary and build background knowledge for themselves.

REFERENCES

Fisher, D., & Frey, N. (2008). *Better learning through structured teaching: A framework for the gradual release of responsibility.* Alexandria, VA: Association for Supervision and Curriculum Development.

Fisher, D., Frey, N., & Lapp, D. (2008). Shared readings: Modeling comprehension, vocabulary, text structures, and text features for older readers. *Reading Teacher, 61,* 548–556.

Frayer, D., Frederick, W. C., & Klausmeier, H. J. (1969). *A schema for testing the level of cognitive mastery.* Madison, WI: Center for Education Research.

Gelbspan, R. (2005). *Boiling point: How politicians, big oil and coal, journalists, and activists have fueled a climate crisis—and what we can do to avert disaster.* New York: Basic Books.

Gibbons, G. (1992). *Weather words and what they mean.* New York: Holiday House.

Gore, A. (2007). *An inconvenient truth: The crisis of global warming.* New York: Viking Juvenile.

Hicks, K., & Wadlington, B. (1994, March). *The efficacy of shared reading with teens.* Paper presented the Association for Childhood Educational International Study Conference, New Orleans, LA.

Lapp, D., Fisher, D., & Grant, M. (2008). "You can read this text—I'll show you how": Interactive comprehension instruction. *Journal of Adolescent and Adult Literacy, 51,* 372–382.

Lynas, M. (2008). *Six degrees: Our future on a hotter planet*. Washington, DC: National Geographic.

Manzo, A. V. (1969). ReQuest procedure. *Journal of Reading, 13,* 123–126.

Marzano, R. J. (2004). *Building background knowledge for academic achievement*. Alexandria, VA: Association for Supervision and Curriculum Development.

Pearson, P. D., & Gallagher, G. (1983). The instruction of reading comprehension. *Contemporary Educational Psychology, 8,* 112–123.

Revkin, A. (2006). *The North Pole was here: Puzzles and perils at the top of the world*. London: Kingfisher.

Silver, J. (2008). *Global warming and climate change demystified*. New York: McGraw-Hill.

Stahl, S. A. (1999). *Vocabulary development*. Cambridge, MA: Brookline Books.

Stahl, S. A., & Nagy, W. E. (2006). *Teaching word meanings*. Mahwah, NJ: Erlbaum.

Stille, D. (2006). *The greenhouse effect: Warming the planet*. Mankato, MN: Compass Point Books.

Zmach, C., Sanders, J., Patrick, J., Dedeoglu, H., Charbonnet, S., Henkel, M., et al. (2006). Infusing reading into science learning. *Educational Leadership, 64*(4), 62–67.

10

Comprehension Instruction

Using Remix as a Tool
for Meaning Making

Diane Lapp
Jesse Gainer

"Get your mouth ready."
"Does that sound right?"
"Does that look right?"

These three statements are often said by teachers when attempting to teach a child to read or to at least sound out and recognize words. The effectiveness of similar instruction appears to have been quite successful for at least 22,000 children whose reading performances were repeatedly assessed during their kindergarten through third-grade years as part of a Childhood Longitudinal Study (National Center for Education Statistics, 2004). The data collected suggest that the majority experienced large gains in sight-word recognition, decoding, and using context to recognize the meanings of words but were unable to proficiently interpret or comprehend written text. Further evidence of the latter finding can be seen in recent results from the National Assessment of Educational Progress (NAEP; 2005), which indicate that more than half of all American students scored below a level of proficiency in reading.

Perplexed as to why a disconnect seems to exist between word-level processing and comprehension skills of many students, we must ask how much time is being spent teaching comprehension, and also what type of comprehension instruction is occurring in classrooms across the nation. This is not the first time these questions have been asked.

Findings from a seminal study that addressed the question of time spent on comprehension instruction as well as the type of instruction that was occurring, reveal that instruction designed to teach children to comprehend narrative text occurred for approximately 20 minutes per day (Durkin, 1978–1979). After approximately 4,500 hours of observation Durkin also noted that few comprehension strategies were being taught; instead children were merely being questioned about what they had read. These findings were supported by the earlier work of Guszak (1967), who had noted that 70% of the questions asked by teachers could be answered with literal-level responses.

For several decades following Guszak's and Durkin's studies much attention was focused on how best to foster comprehension development. Results highlighted the need for reading instruction to develop students' thinking skills and knowledge of strategies to support their ability to interpret, visualize, self-question, summarize, and reason while reading (Anderson & Pearson, 1984; Applebee, Langer, & Mullis, 1987; Myers, 1991; Pearson & Dole, 1987; Pressley, 2000; Pressley & Wharton-McDonald, 1997; Riely, 1992). Yet 20 years after Durkin's study, students in at least some fourth- and fifth-grade classrooms were still answering questions rather than being taught how to read for comprehension (Pressley, Wharton-McDonald, Hampson, & Echevarria, 1998), and in some first-grade classrooms children were being taught to read informational texts for only 3.6 minutes per day (Duke, 2000).

Today a plethora of information exists regarding the teaching of comprehension strategies through a wider array of materials (Burniske, 2000; Lambert & Carpenter, 2005; English, 2007; Leu et al., 2007; Frey & Fisher, 2007; Blachowicz & Ogle, 2008; Coiro, Knobel, Lankshear, & Leu, 2008; Fisher, Frey, & Lapp, 2009). Like these and other educators, we believe that a key component to reading with comprehension is a personal, intrinsic desire to read (e.g., Guthrie et al., 1996; Gambrell, 2001) and that instruction has the potential to support the development of this desire or motivation to read (Anderson, Wilson, & Fielding, 1988; Taylor, Frye, & Maruyama, 1990; Block & Pressley, 2001; Flood, Lapp, & Fisher, 2003). Motivation fuels students' interest in reading and that in turn leads to increased vocabulary knowledge and comprehension (Stanovich, 1986; Cunningham & Stanovich, 2003). Realizing this, we wondered how we could design motivating instruction that would support increased comprehension. The purpose of this chapter is to "broaden the lens" (Flood & Lapp, 1995) regarding the possibilities of comprehension instruction, while being sensitive to the need to teach more than a set of strategies that are disconnected from the text and reader (Baumann & Ivey, 1997; Ivey, 2008).

CHANGING DEMANDS OF LITERACY

The 21st century has brought many changes in the way we live and think. One of the greatest and most rapid changes has occurred in the area of technology. New technologies related to computers and the Internet seriously alter the ways in which we do business, communicate, and live life. Increased access to computers with high-speed Internet connections, as well as access to other tools for digital communication, means that shifts are happening for increasingly diverse populations worldwide. In short, the rise of interconnectivity made possible by new technologies has caused major shifts in the ways in which people communicate and relate to one another.

The term *Web 2.0* is often equated with changing mindsets that accompany the rise in digital technologies. Although the term sounds like a new version of the World Wide Web, it merely refers to new ways in which the Web is used—blogs, social networking, wikis, and so on. Included in discussions of Web 2.0 are ways in which technologies have positioned regular people as "designers" rather than mere "consumers" of information. As a simple way to think about this shift, we can consider the rise of interactive websites such as *Wikipedia, Flickr,* and *Google,* just to name a few. Each of these examples allows users not only to access desired information, but also to have a hand in the creation, maintenance, and sharing of new information. The emphasis on sharing rather than consuming leads to a change in mindsets about authority and authoring that is less hierarchical; that is distributed rather than centered on "experts" (Lankshear & Knobel, 2006).

The heightened interconnectivity among diverse peoples along with new tools that expand the ways in which we are able to communicate lead to new forms of meaning making. Increasingly, researchers and teachers view literacy as more than simply decoding alphabetic-print text. More and more people involved in the area of literacy education are adopting sociocultural perspectives on literacy learning that broaden definitions of what counts as text and what it means to be literate. Such definitions take into account the importance of social, cultural, and historical contexts of meaning making as well as the increasingly broad ways in which humans use symbols to communicate. We find the concept of "multiliteracies" (New London Group, 2000) useful for framing the broadened notion of what it means to be literate in today's world, because it includes the interactions of increasingly diverse communities as well as the increasingly multimodal forms of meaning making. We believe that Lankshear and Knobel (2003) make a compelling case that new literacies offer us a new way to broaden our instructional lens about literacy; a new way to think about how to navigate the world; and in some cases, a new way to think about approaches to problems and situations.

A PEDAGOGY OF MULTILITERACIES: DESIGN AND REDESIGN

Although schools do not always have access to the most up-to-date advances in technology, teachers increasingly recognize the importance of integrating technology throughout the curriculum. Broadened concepts of what it means to be literate in today's digital world have implications for classrooms. The New London Group (2000) identifies "design" as a key concept in relation to developing a pedagogy of multiliteracies. Very much related to the interactive mindset of Web 2.0, the New London Group discusses design "in which we are both inheritors of patterns and conventions of meaning while at the same time active designers of meaning. And, as designers of meaning, we are designers of social futures—workplace futures, public futures, and community futures" (p. 7). This concept of design attributes an active role to the reader/writer. While it recognizes the importance of social interaction, existing text and context, design also puts the onus of shaping meaning on the reader and therefore positions reading as an active and creative process. Through the meaning-making process that happens when a reader transacts with a text (an "available design"), a new text, a "redesigned" text, is formed. We draw on this active model of literacy as "redesign" to "broaden the lens" (Flood & Lapp, 1995) of reading comprehension instruction as a form of "remix."

COMPREHENSION AS REMIX

The idea of remix has often been associated with music. Wikipedia, the online encyclopedia, defines remix in the following way:

> A *remix* is an alternative version of a song, different from the original version. A remixer uses audio mixing to compose an alternate master recording of a song, adding or subtracting elements, or simply changing the equalization, dynamics, pitch, tempo, playing time, or almost any other aspect of the various musical components.

This for m of manipulating preexisting textual materials of music for the creation of new musical texts is mostly attributed to hip hop (Mahiri, 2004). Although some critics have dismissed such practice as lacking in creativity, proponents of remixing highlight the creative processes necessary to transform "stray technological parts intended for cultural and industrial trash heaps into sources of pleasure and power" (Rose, 1994, p. 22). In other words, remixing is akin to recycling and the end results are very creative because they make new use of old materials.

Not only is remix a creative process, the act of creating something new out of used parts requires analysis on the part of the creator and therefore is a learning process. Hip-hop artist Daddy-O discusses how one type of remix, the practice of sampling—namely, taking a portion of one recorded song and using it in another—relates to learning (Rose, 1994). He states, "We learn a lot from sampling, it's like school for us. When we sample a portion of a song and repeat it over and over we can better understand the matrix of the song" (Rose, 1994, p. 79). When creating a new text from preexisting ones, the "writer" must strategically select specific parts and incorporate them into the new material to fulfill specific purposes.

Researchers of literacy and education have conceptualized the ideas of remix in a broadened definition of literacy. Lankshear and Knobel (2006) refer to remix as "a practice of taking cultural artifacts and combining and manipulating them into a new kind of creative blend" (p. 106). This definition is not limited to musical text; in fact, it can be argued that all meaning making involves remix. Similar to the way the New London Group (2000) discussed notions of design, Lessig (cited in Lankshear & Knobel, 2006) likened writing done by students to remix in that they draw on the texts of multiple authors to inform their own writing. This occurs as "learners take words that are presented as text in one place or another and they use these words and texts and the tools of pen and pencil to make new texts, or to remix text" (Lankshear & Knoble, 2006, pp. 106–107). Young people are increasingly engaging in such literacy practices both in and out of school, especially with increased access to digital tools for the creation of multimodal texts that involve mixing images, texts, and sounds.

LESSON EXAMPLES

Some people may argue that complex practices of multiliteracies defy simplistic attempts to create teacher-oriented lesson plans. We agree. Although we do not wish to co-opt out-of-school literacies students may find pleasurable for the teacher-centered goals of schooling, we do draw on concepts of design (New London Group, 2000) and literacy as remix (Lankshear & Knobel, 2006) in efforts to broaden pedagogical practice in reading comprehension. It is our hope that the following examples using remix for reading comprehension are open-ended and student-centered enough that students will find them purposeful, meaningful, and engaging—not simply a "fun" way to do more of the same old teacher-directed reading activities often found in traditional practice. First, we would like to make the caveat that our examples are meant to serve as ideas to provoke thinking and should not be interpreted as "best practices" or even "expert knowledge." We encourage teachers to collaborate with their students—the true experts of their own experiences—to redesign our lesson ideas, to remix them, to fit their own classroom contexts and reading/writing interests and needs. The following examples address four types of remixing: sampling, fan fiction, mash-ups, and bubbling.

Activity 1: Sampling, with Example Using "I'll Be Missing You" by P. Diddy and Faith Evans

What Is Sampling?

Sampling is a term that is used in popular music when a portion of one sound recording is used in another. Many examples of songs use the technique of sampling. P. Diddy is one artist well known for employing this technique—many of his songs contain "samples" from other songs. Popular examples of sampling include remixing sounds and/or voice recordings to create a new "text." When students select one, or more, text sources from which to sample, they must analyze messages found in the texts, determine which portions best communicate their intended message, and add new text around the selected sample in order to construct the "redesigned" text.

Step by Step

1. Students explore sampling in music by analyzing a song that employs the technique.
2. Students individually select and read lyrics to one or more favorite (or popular) songs and reflect on *why* the songs are meaningful to them.
3. Students select "samples"—words or short passages from the songs.
4. Students write a new text incorporating words and or melodies from the original songs.

Literacy Foci

Oral Language—conversation, presentation; *Reading*—synthesizing, evaluating, parsing, studying words and phrases in context; *Writing*—free write; *Listening*—comparison, evaluation; *New Literacies*—sampling

Building Background

Begin by discussing and sharing the concept of *sampling*.

1. Sampling is a technique used in some music and refers to the practice of borrowing portions of other songs, or other audio material, to use in the creation of a new song. Many songs incorporate sampling.

2. What songs can you think of that use sampling? *Teacher's note:* An Internet search using the term *sampling* will provide further information and many examples of songs that incorporate the technique. If students are not familiar with any songs that use sampling, tell them that they are about to listen to an example. In our example we use Puff Daddy (a.k.a. P. Diddy) and Faith Evans's song "I'll Be Missing You." This song incorporates samples from The Police's "Every Breath You Take." In addition, the song samples a melody from the American spiritual "I'll Fly Away," and if you select to use the extended version of the song, the introduction samples from "Adagio for Strings" by Samuel Barber (source: Wikipedia).

3. Why do you think artists might use this technique? Do you think it is creative or do you think it is simply copying? *Teacher's note:* There are no correct answers to this question. The idea here is to get students discussing and thinking critically about the issues. If you would like further information about differing arguments on the creativity involved when using sampling, you can find information by searching the topic on the Internet.

Collaborative Conversations: Let's Do It Together

1. First, let's listen to the song "I'll Fly Away." *Teacher's note:* There are many recordings of this popular American spiritual. The song can be downloaded for a small fee from iTunes or played free on YouTube.com. If you elect to use YouTube, we suggest you play only the audio and do not show the video because the goal is to get the students to interpret the words and melody of the song. Printer-friendly versions of lyrics to this song, as well as other songs, can be found by searching the Internet using the song title and the key word *lyrics*.

- Play the song for the class and have students read along on lyric printouts as they listen.
- Ask students to fill out the graphic organizer for songs (see Appendix 10.1; for additional graphic organizer ideas, see Wood, Lapp, Flood, & Taylor, 2008).
- Invite students to share their interpretations of the song.

2. Repeat the same listening/discussing exercise with "Every Breath You Take" by The Police.

3. Now listen to the song "I'll Be Missing You" by Puff Daddy and Faith Evans.

- Before playing the song, tell students to pay attention for examples of sampling.
- Ask students to read along on lyrics as they listen.
- In table groups discuss the following questions:
- How are the sample songs incorporated into the text of this song?
- Why do you think the artists chose to sample the particular songs they did?
- What emotions are conveyed in the text?

Teacher's note: There are no correct answers to these questions. The questions are designed to get the students thinking about how the song was made and why artists might employ this technique to aid in their meaning-making efforts. The use of the term *text* for the song should be interpreted broadly to include the lyrics as well as the melodies because all of these contribute to the overall meaning that is conveyed in the song.

On Your Own: Supported Practice

Now the students will have a chance to create their own sampling. Invite them to select one or more songs, which may include segments of audio from television shows, movies, newscasts, or other sources. They will need to bring printed lyrics for at least one of the songs they have chosen. Students might also choose portions of text from their favorite books, poems, comics, or other sources. The important point is that students select a text that holds meaning for them. Tell students:

1. Read and reread your selected text and circle key phrases and words that communicate special meaning to you.

2. Write each phrase or word that you have circled on top of a blank sheet of paper and free-write underneath. When you free-write, think

about the words you have selected as your sample and what thoughts, memories, feelings, and images they evoke in you. For example:

Source: "The Star Spangled Banner" by Francis Scott Key
Sample: Then conquer we must, when our cause it is just
Free Write: I stand on the side of the field, soft grass beneath my cleats and helmet in my hand. The game is about to begin. The familiar music is all that I hear. I clear my mind and get ready for the game. I know football is not the same as war, but in my head at that time, I just think of "conquer" and "triumph." Later, after the game, I can think of other stuff.

3. Reread your samples and free writing. Try to draft a new text that incorporates your samples. Use ideas you have generated in your free writing to guide you as you draft your new piece.

Performance: Independence

Students do not necessarily take all their work in the writing process to publication. However, we encourage students to share from their working and/or final drafts so that we collectively engage in reading and writing and building a community in our classroom that treasures meaning making and literacy. To that end we reserve time and space in the curriculum for students to share and discuss works such as those created using the technique of sampling. Generally, the sharing is reserved for finished pieces and is a celebratory time when students read and their classmates ask questions and offer compliments. In the case of the sampling activities, students' questions and comments often make explicit why authors selected the samples they did. When students share drafts that are still in progress, they usually seek suggestions from peers on how to address particular issues. With the sampling activities, it would be common for the presenter to ask classmates to comment on whether or not the sampled pieces are effective and if they flow well with the other writing. *Teacher's note:* It is important for students to understand that they are not required to sing when they share their work. In fact, the use of sampling in this lesson plan does not even require that students create a song as their written piece. The intent is for students to draw on other text sources in their own writing, and this can be done in many forms and different genres.

Reflective Evaluation

As is the case with other types of writing, and especially readers' response activities, the sampling activity can be evaluated by examining work samples. The graphic organizers, the free-writing sheets, and the writing drafts provide evidence of students' thinking and demonstrate their comprehension. In addition, the comments made by students when they are sharing their pieces and answering questions about them provide further insights into their thinking process. Teachers can keep records of these activities, using anecdotal notes and portfolio assessment. Some teachers may wish to include a written prompt that asks students to reflect on their own thinking process. The following are some possible scaffolded questions that could be used:

> What song, or text, did you sample?
> Why did you select this text as your sample?
> How does your sample fit into your new piece and help communicate your message?

The students' answers to the questions can be included with the work samples in their portfolios.

Activity 2: Fan Fiction, with Example Using *Scooby Doo*

What Is Fan Fiction?

Fan fiction refers to a body of writing that is created by fans of popular culture texts such as television shows, movies, books, and sequential art texts such as graphic novels, anime, manga, and books. Fan fiction writers employ a wide variety of styles when springboarding off of their favorite texts. To see examples go to *fanfiction.net.*

In some cases devotees create new episodes of the original media texts building on narratives and characters that are already developed in the original versions. In other cases writers place themselves directly into the narrative of a popular media text, often as a hybrid between their real-life self and an actual character from the original text. In such examples, as well as other forms of fan fiction, writers remix narratives of popular media and other texts to create new texts. In order to create a successful new text based on one from popular media, the fan-fiction writer must have deep understandings of the narrative structure, common themes, and character histories from the original.

In our example we use the popular television cartoon *Scooby Doo.* We invite you to try our lesson, but we encourage you to take the framework of the lesson and adapt it to the interests and out-of-school literacies of your students. Ultimately, the lesson will be most powerful when the students themselves determine the popular media texts from which they will draw.

Step by Step

1. Students analyze typical plot structure and character attributes from *Scooby Doo* cartoons.
2. Students determine the style they wish to use when creating new text based on the original.
3. Students use a story map to outline characters, setting, important events, problems, and resolutions.
4. Students write a new text incorporating elements (concrete and/or stylistic) from the original.

Literacy Foci

Oral Language—conversation, presentation; *Reading*—character analysis, story structure, summarizing; *Writing*—prewriting, organizing ideas, drafting; *New Literacies*—fan fiction.

Building Background

Today we are going to explore a type of writing called fan fiction. *Fan fiction* refers to a body of writing that is created by fans of popular culture texts such as television shows, movies, books, and other sources. You can see many examples at *fanfiction.net*. People use many different styles when they create fan fiction. Here are just a few:

1. Sometimes writers build on narratives and characters already developed in the original texts—like writing a new episode of a show and staying true to the style.
2. Sometimes writers place themselves in the text by creating a character that is a sort of cross between him- or herself and a character in the original text. An example of this could be making yourself take the place of Hannah Montana and writing a new episode where you are actually a teen rockstar with an alter ego.
3. Sometimes writers mix scenes and characters from two or more texts. An example of this could include the story of what would happen if Babe the gallant pig visited Wilbur from *Charlotte's Web*.

Collaborative Conversations: Let's Do It Together

1. Most of you are familiar with the popular cartoon *Scooby Doo*. By watching, you become familiar with the characters, things they typically say and do, and you become familiar with the typical plot structure

of each episode. Today we will take a closer look at *Scooby Doo* as a *text* and then use what we learn to write something new.

2. In small groups (three or four students) watch one episode of *Scooby Doo*. *Teacher's note:* Complete episodes can be viewed online at *www.video.aol.com,* or they can be rented at most local video stores or from Netflix. This activity will be optimized if there are at least three different groups, and each watches a different episode of the show.

3. In groups, create "open-mind portraits" (Tompkins, 2006) for each of the main characters (Scooby, Shaggy, Fred, Daphne, and Velma). This step helps us get to know the characters better by thinking deeply about each character's personality, interests, and viewpoints.

- First, make a portrait of the head of the character.
- Next, add blank pages behind the portrait and trace around the character's head. Cut the pages to the shape of the portrait and staple them into a "book."
- The pages behind the portrait are the "mind" pages. On these, write details about what the character does and thinks during important points from the episode you watched. Also, write any phrases that the character typically says and note any other details that are characteristic of him or her. For example, Velma loses her glasses a lot and Shaggy starts most sentences with the word *like.*
- Share portraits with other students in the class and discuss what each of you chose to put into the "mind" pages (see Figures 10.1 and 10.2 for an example of an open-mind portrait).

4. Next, in small groups create a story map (with beginning, middle, end) for the episode you watched (see Appendix 10.2 for a story map template).

5. Each group discusses the episode they viewed using their story map as a guide for their retelling. *Teacher's note:* As each group shares, record important points on an enlarged comparison chart (see Appendix 10.3 for a comparison chart template).

6. Look at the comparison chart and think about the elements from the different episodes you viewed. What common threads seem to appear in each episode of this show?

7. Let's identify the plot "formula" for an episode of *Scooby Doo:*

- Gang bumps into an evil ghost/monster that has been terrorizing a place.
- Gang offers to solve the mystery.
- They look for clues. Usually Shaggy and Scooby run into the monster and a chase ensues.

FIGURE 10.1. Example of an open-mind portrait: Shaggy from *Scooby Doo*.

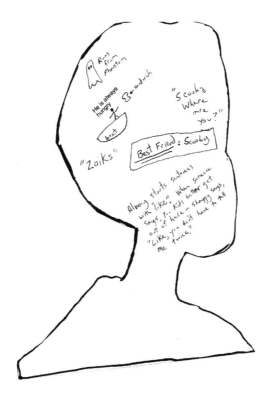

FIGURE 10.2. Example of an open-mind portrait: Shaggy from *Scooby Doo*.

- The gang analyzes clues and figure out it is a hoax.
- They capture the monster and bring it to the police.
- They reveal the true identity of the villain—usually someone they met earlier in the show.
- They explain how the villain used disguises and/or special effects to create terror to distract attention away from the true crime.
- In the end the villain shakes his or her fist in the air and says something like "And I would have gotten away with it if it wasn't for those nosey kids!"

Teacher's note: We like to have this formula prepared in advance on chart paper. After students discuss common elements, we post the formula to help students synthesize elements during the group discussion.

On Your Own: Supported Practice

Now students take what they have learned about the typical plot structures and other characteristics of *Scooby Doo* and apply them when creating a fan fiction. This can be done individually, but we like to have students continue the small-group work for this portion of the lesson.

1. Now you will use the typical plot formula of *Scooby Doo* to create a new episode. You might try using one of the styles of fan fiction that we mentioned earlier, or you may come up with your own idea. Here are some possibilities to get you started in your thinking:

- Make yourselves one of the main characters and tell the story of a new mystery adventure with the gang.
- Write a new episode of the show and use the same characters from the original.
- Write a new episode and have the setting take place in the world of another popular media text and have the gang interact with characters from the other text.

2. After deciding on some general ideas for your new episode, use the writing guide (see Appendix 10.4 for a template) to help you organize and plan your piece.

3. Write a draft of your new episode.

Performance: Independence

We like to have students write their final drafts as stories, Readers' Theaters, or screenplays. When students draft stories, we have them create the final drafts as books that can be added to the classroom library and enjoyed by all students during free reading times. The Readers' Theaters and screenplays can also be placed in the classroom libraries but are usually performed by students first.

Reflective Evaluation

Students' work provides an excellent source of evidence for evaluation. Students' comprehension, based on their viewing of the episode of the show, is documented in their story maps and the open-mind portraits they create for each main character. Their oral commentary during the comparison chart activity provides evidence of their abilities to make connections between texts and further demonstrates their skills in literary analysis. Finally, the new episodes they write documents their abilities to draw on plot structures and character analysis, synthesize information, and extend information to create new material.

Activity 3: Mash-Ups with Example Using *Where the Wild Things Are* versus "Wild Thing"

What Are Mash-Ups?

Wikipedia defines a mash-up as "a digital media file containing any or all of text, graphics, audio, video, and animation, which recombines and modifies existing digital works to create a derivative work." A search of YouTube.com using the term "mash-up" yields over 70,000 examples of music videos, movie promos, and other creations that blend visuals (still and moving) with audio from various different sources to produce new texts. The creators of mash-ups often go to great lengths to painstakingly sync lips and other movements to the newly imported audio track(s). Like other forms of remix, creators of mash-ups need to analyze content of the various text sources in order to create a coherent and meaningful new text. In classroom practice we do not limit the technique of mash-up to digital texts only. In fact, students can use any text types to create a unique amalgamation.

Step by Step

1. Explore the elements of mash-up by analyzing examples.
2. Select two or more text sources (can be from one or more media such as music, video, written, etc).
3. Make a plan on how to integrate the various sources.
4. Use tools (digital or other) to blend the text sources into a new creation.

Literacy Foci

Oral Language—conversation; *Reading*—synthesizing, making connections; *Writing*—organizing information, drafting with digital tools, multimodal writing with audio and visual texts; *New Literacies*—mash-ups.

Building Background

1. Today we will create new texts by combining elements from two or more sources. These texts are called mash-ups. Let's look at a couple of examples of video mash-ups on YouTube.

- *Happy Feet versus Walk It Out (www.youtube.com/watch?v=g-LRuhmFSBU)*
- *Hey Ya! Charlie Brown Style (www.youtube.com/watch?v=KGnYw-OuCnI)*

Both of these examples sync video footage from popular animations with audio from popular music. The first example blended a scene from the movie *Happy Feet* with a song from the rapper Unk. The second was a scene from *A Charlie Brown Christmas* with music from the group Outkast.

2. As a class discuss the following questions:

- Why do you think the authors of the mash-up videos chose the particular video footage with the particular song in each example?
- Do you think it would be difficult to make a mash-up? Why or why not?

Teacher's note: There are no correct answers for these questions. The main point for having this conversation is to encourage students to begin to think about how mash-up videos combine elements of different texts by synching audio and video tracks. The result is an often entertaining "new" text that incorporates elements of each original.

Collaborative Conversations: Let's Do It Together

Together we will create a digital mash-up using the book *Where the Wild Things Are* by Maurice Sendak (1963) and the song "Wild Thing" by The Troggs.

1. We will begin by revisiting the book and song.

- First, let's review the book and carefully analyze the pictures. *Teacher's note:* As you read the text, stop and discuss each of the pictures. Ask students how Sendak's illustrations communicate the wildness of the beastlike creations and the main character, Max. Also, use the illustrations to discuss what the mother is feeling toward her son throughout the course of the story.
- Now let's listen to the song "Wild Thing." Read along from the printed lyrics as you listen. *Teacher's note:* The song can be purchased on iTunes for a small fee or can be heard on *YouTube.com* (as we noted previously, we suggest using the audio track and not sharing the video for this activity). Printable versions of the lyrics can be downloaded using an Internet search of the song title along with the keyword *lyrics*.
- Even though this song is not really related to the story we just read, do you think there are some similarities? Which character from *Where the Wild Things Are* might sing this song? To whom would he or she sing it? Why do you think that? *Teacher's note:* There are no correct answers to these questions. The activity is simply an exercise to stimulate students to make connections and defend their thinking by drawing on examples from the text sources.

2. We will plan our mash-up using a storyboard to organize how we want the book pictures to match up with the song lyrics (see Appendix 10.5 for a storyboard template).

- In each square, we will sketch the illustration we want to use in our mash-up. Here we can also record the page number where the picture can be found in the original text.
- Then on the lines under the picture, we will write the lyrics from the song that we wish to match with the picture. It is important that we pay attention that the words and the pictures relate to one another, similar to the way we see pictures that support the words in the picture books we read and enjoy.

3. Next, we will create digital images of the selected illustrations. *Teacher's note:* You can either scan the illustrations onto your computer or simply take digital photographs of the illustrations with a digital camera and download them onto a computer. If you use a digital camera, we recommend that you turn off the flash so it does not reflect off of the page and show up in the picture.

4. Upload the digital images and audio track onto a computer with moviemaking software. We use iMovie with a Mac or Photostory for the personal computer.

5. Using the moviemaking software on the computer, place the pictures on the video track and the song on the audio track. You can sync the two tracks by adjusting the length of each still picture so that it coincides with the lyrics in the way you planned on the storyboard. *Teacher's note:* Depending on the age and technology experience of the students, you may need to provide a great deal of support during this step. If you do not know how to do this procedure, there are step-by-step tutorials included with the moviemaking software on the computer.

6. Watch the mash-up video with the class.

Teacher's note: Allowing students freedom to choose topics and means of expression can lead to exciting possibilities. For example, one of our students created a mash-up of a mock interview with singer Michael Jackson. She used *claymation* to create a character of herself and one of Michael Jackson. On the audio track she alternated between questions recorded in her voice and excerpts from a variety of songs that served as the answers from the interviewee. The end result was a comical movie that demonstrated technical skills as well as multiple intertextual connections made by the student.

On Your Own: Supported Practice

Create a center in the room where students can use storyboards to design and make their own mash-up stories. If access to technology is an issue, remember that mash-ups do not have to be done digitally, and any text sources can be utilized. Allow students to be creative with medium and mode! The more opportunities students have to explore the medium and the tools for this type of writing, the more skilled they will become at creating meaningful texts.

Performance: Independence

The student-generated mash-ups can be viewed and discussed by the whole class. In addition, the students' work can be saved on classroom computers and viewed by individual students during center time. Allowing students multiple opportunities to view and discuss each others' work is important because it can motivate and inspire the creation of new material.

Reflective Evaluation

Students' comprehension will be evidenced in their discussions of the texts as well as in the work samples that result from the planning and creation of their own mash-up texts. The evidence can be documented using anecdotal notes recording students' comments and actions. In addition, electronic portfolios can be utilized to save examples of students' digital texts.

Activity 4: Bubbling with Example Using Popular Magazines Geared toward Youth

What Is Bubbling?

Bubbling is a way for students to "talk back" to media text sources using speech bubbles like those found in cartoons. The idea is an adaptation of the work of guerilla artist Ji Lee (see *thebubbleproject.com* for examples of his work) who places blank speech bubbles on billboards and other public advertisements. The blank speech bubbles are filled in by anonymous people and later photographed and posted on the Web by Lee. In our classroom application, we provide students with opportunities to analyze ads and other images from popular culture magazines and then use speech bubbles to "talk back" to the images. In this "redesign" activity students create new meanings by extending, critiquing, and sometimes poking fun at the mainstream media messages.

Step by Step

1. Class discusses mainstream messages in media. Consider why some people might critique certain messages sent in advertising and popular culture about topics such as beauty, consumption, gender roles, etc.
2. Teacher introduces background on the Bubble Project (see *thebubbleproject.com* for information).
3. Students view and discuss actual examples from the Bubble Project website. Teacher should be sure to preview site and preselect examples that are appropriate for given classroom context (some have mature themes).
4. Do a few practice examples with the class using images from popular media and premade blank speech bubbles.
5. Students create their own speech bubbles responding to media texts from magazines targeting their age groups.
6. Class does a "gallery walk" to view and discuss each others' work.

Literacy Foci

Oral Language—conversation, presentation; *Reading*—synthesizing, evaluating; *Writing*—dialogue; *New Literacies*—critical media literacy, visual literacy

Building Background

1. Let's think about how the text of advertisements such as seen on billboards, television commercials, and magazine ads act on us, the readers. We will start by watching and discussing a video that critiques some forms of advertising. We will watch the video *Dove Evolution,* created by the Dove Campaign for Real Beauty (accessed at: *www. youtube.com/watch?v=iYbCn0jf46U*). As a group let's discuss the following:

- Why are the makers of this video critical of the way beauty (especially that of women) is often portrayed in mainstream media?
- Can you think of other examples of advertising that reflect certain values that some people may find objectionable?
- Who has the power to create advertisements? Whose voice is not heard in advertising?

Teacher's note: There are no correct answers to these questions. The purpose of the discussion is to introduce students to ideas of critical media literacy—specifically, how mass media contributes to societal notions of ideas such as beauty. Students should explore the problematic nature of such representations that are often based in sexist and racist subtext.

2. A guerilla artist in New York by the name of Ji Lee has created a concept he calls the "Bubble Project." He posts blank speech bubbles, like the kinds found in comic strips, on public ads. Later, random people fill them in. Lee claims that this allows average people to "talk back" to the ads that are all around us.

Collaborative Conversations: Let's Do It Together

1. Let's view some examples from the Bubble Project website: *thebubbleproject.com. Teacher's note:* You will want to visit the website in advance and select the examples of "street bubbles" that you feel are appropriate for your students. Some of the examples on the website contain adult themes.

2. As we look at the examples, let's discuss:

- What is being advertised?
- What is the underlying value (or message) that is conveyed by the media example?
- What is the critique of the media that is offered in the speech bubble?

3. Now let's practice together by viewing some ads with blank speech bubbles and thinking about what we would put in them. *Teacher's note:* Although you can find blank bubbles at *thebubbleproject.com,* we find it powerful to also include examples of advertising from billboards and other sources that exist in the community around the school. You can create these by taking digital photos of billboards and uploading them on a computer for viewing.

On Your Own: Supported Practice

1. Now that you have seen some examples from the Bubble Project, and we have discussed ways in which advertising subtly communicates values, you will have a chance to create your own speech bubbles to "talk back" to ads, and other images, found in texts marketed to young people your age. *Teacher's note:* You will need to provide students with popular magazines that are marketed to young people or ask students to bring in magazines. Students will also need blank speech bubbles, pens or pencils, and glue.

2. Take some time to look through the magazines. Think about the images you see in the advertisements and the other parts of the magazine. Select and cut out advertisements and other images that market style (e.g., photos of pop stars). Create speech bubbles for the images you have selected, providing commentary on the underlying, and often unstated, messages of the mainstream media source.

Performance: Independence

Students position their completed work around the room for the gallery walk. Classmates walk around the room to observe and discuss the work samples. This is a good opportunity for the teacher to guide discussions and push students' thinking about critical readings of mainstream media texts.

Reflective Evaluation

Evidence of students' critical thinking and comprehension can be documented using anecdotal notes taken on their comments during group

FIGURE 10.3. Bubbling example.

discussions. Another source of such documentation is in the work samples generated by the students. Each sample, along with students' commentary about the significance of their selected media text and their efforts to "talk back" to the source using bubbling, can be saved in student portfolios.

CONCLUSIONS: COMPREHENSION AS REMIX

Given the changing face of communication, due in a large part to developments in technology as well as shifts in what it means to be literate in today's society, educators must consider new ways to address reading comprehension pedagogy that take into consideration multimodal texts. Traditional print-based reading and writing are still important, but they are not sufficient in today's digitized world. In order to prepare 21st-century citizens, schools must broaden the lens when considering what should count as text and what comprehension instruction should look like.

The notion of remix fits well with current social constructivist conceptualizations of literacy learning. In this view, readers are active meaning makers who must fit new material into existing prior knowledge based on past experiences. Therefore, each learner must "remix" the new material and old material to create new understandings.

The lessons we have designed are merely meant to illustrate a variety of possibilities when teaching comprehension as remix. We have tried to design lessons that provide clear guidance to teachers but are also sufficiently open-ended and promote higher-order thinking. We hope readers will find our ideas thought provoking, and we encourage those interested to experiment with our lesson ideas and remix them to meet your literacy teaching needs.

REFERENCES

Anderson, R. C., & Pearson, P. D. (1984). A schema-theoretic view of basic processes in reading. In P. D. Pearson (Ed.), *Handbook of reading research* (pp. 255–291). New York: Longman.

Anderson, R. C., Wilson, P. T., & Fielding, L. G. (1988). Growth in reading and how children spend their time outside of school. *Reading Research Quarterly, 23,* 285–303.

Applebee, A., Langer, J., & Mullis, I. V. (1987). *Learning to be literate in America: Reading, writing, and reasoning.* National Assessment of Educational Progress. Princeton, NJ: Educational Testing Service.

Baumann, J. F., & Ivey, G. (1997). Delicate balances: Striving for curricular and instructional equilibrium in a second-grade, literature/strategy-based classroom. *Reading Research Quarterly, 32*(3), 244–275.

Blachowicz, C., & Ogle, D. (2008). *Reading comprehension: Strategies for independent learners* (2nd ed.). New York: Guilford Press.

Block, C. C., & Pressley, M. (2001). *Comprehension instruction: Research-based best practices.* New York: Guilford Press.

Burniske, R. W. (2000). *Literacy in the cyberage: Composing ourselves online.* Arlington Heights, IL: Skylight Professional Development.

Coiro, J., Knobel, M., Lankshear, C., & Leu, D. J. (Eds). (2008). *Handbook of research on new literacies.* Mahwah, NJ: Erlbaum.

Cunningham, A., & Stanovich, K. E. (2003). Reading matters: How reading engagement influences cognition. In J. Flood, D. Lapp, J. R. Squire, & J. M. Jensen (Eds.), *Handbook of research on teaching the English arts* (2nd ed., pp. 666–675). Mahwah, NJ: Erlbaum.

Duke, N. K. (2000). 3.6 minutes per day: The scarcity of informational texts in first grade. *Reading Research Quarterly, 35,* 202–224.

Durkin, D. (1978–1979). What classroom observations reveal about comprehension instruction. *Reading Research Quarterly, 15,* 481–533.

English, C. (2007). Finding voice in a threaded discussion group: Talking about literature online. *English Journal, 97*(1), 56–61.

Fisher, D., Frey, N., & Lapp, D. (2009). *In a reading state of mind.* Newark, DE: International Reading Association.

Flood, J., & Lapp, D. (1995). Broadening the lens: Towards an expanded conceptualization of literacy. In K. Hinchman, D. Leu, & C. Kinzer (Eds.),

Perspectives on literacy research and practice (pp. 1–6). Chicago: 44th Yearbook of the National Reading Conference.

Flood, J., Lapp, D., & Fisher, D. (2003). Reading comprehension instruction. In J. Flood, D. Lapp, J. R. Squire, & J. M. Jensen (Eds.), *Handbook of research on teaching the English language arts* (2nd ed., pp. 931–941). Mahwah, NJ: Erlbaum.

Frey, N., & Fisher, D. (2007). *Reading for information in elementary school: Content literacy strategies to build comprehension.* Upper Saddle River, NJ: Merrill Prentice-Hall.

Gambrell, L. B. (2001). What we know about motivation to read. In R. F. Flippo (Ed.), *Reading researchers in search of common ground* (pp. 129–143) Newark, DE: International Reading Association.

Guszak, F. J. (1967). *Reading comprehension development as viewed from the stand point of teacher questioning strategies.* ERIC Document Reproduction Service No. ED 010984.

Guthrie, J. T., Van Meter, P., McCann, A. D., Wigfield, A., Bennett, L., Poundstone, C. C., et al. (1996). Growth in literacy engagement: Changes in motivation and strategies during concept-oriented reading instruction. *Reading Research Quarterly, 31,* 306–332.

Ivey, G. (2008). The content teacher's instructional role: Moving students toward strategic independent reading. In D. Lapp, J. Flood, & N. Farnan (Eds.), *Content area reading and learning: Instructional strategies* (3rd ed., pp. 175–186). Mahwah, NJ: Erlbaum.

Lambert, M., & Carpenter, M. (2005). Visual learning: Using images to focus attention, evoke emotions, and enrich learning. *Multimedia and Internet@ Schools, 12*(5), 20–25.

Lankshear, C., & Knobel, M. (2003). *New literacies: Changing knowledge and classroom learning.* Maidenhead, Berkshire, UK: Open University Press.

Lankshear, C., & Knobel, M. (2006). *New literacies: Everyday practices and classroom learning.* New York: Open University Press.

Leu, D. J., Zawilinski, L., Castek, J., Banerjee, M., Housand, B., Liu, Y., et al. (2007). What is new about the new literacies of online reading comprehension? In L. Rush, J. Eakle, & A. Berger (Eds.), *Secondary school literacy: What research reveals for classroom practices* (pp. 37–68). Urbana, IL: National Council of Teachers of English.

Mahiri, J. (2004). *What they don't learn in school: Literacy in the lives of urban youth.* New York: Lang.

Myers, S. S. (1991). Performance reading comprehension: Product or process? *Educational Review, 43*(3), 257–273.

National Assessment of Educational Progress. *Assessment of reading instruction.* Retrieved June 15, 2008, from *nces.ed.gov/nationsreportcard/.*

National Center for Education Statistics. (2004). *From kindergarten through third grade: Children's beginning school experiences.* Institute for Educational Sciences, U.S. Department of Education, Washington, DC.

New London Group. (2000). A pedagogy of multiliteracies: Designing social futures. In B. Cope & M. Kalantzis (Eds.), *Multiliteracies: Literacy learning and the design of social futures* (pp. 9–38). New York: Routledge.

Pearson, P. D., & Dole, J. A. (1987). Explicit comprehension instruction: A review of research and a new conceptualization of instruction. *Elementary School Journal, 88,* 151–165.

Pressley, M. (2000). What should comprehension instruction be the instruction of? In M. Kamil, P. Mosentahal, P. D. Pearson, & R. Barr (Eds.), *Handbook of reading research* (Vol. 3., pp. 545–562). Mahwah, NJ: Erlbaum.

Pressley, M., & Wharton-McDonald, R. (1997). Skilled comprehension and its development through instruction. *School Psychology Review, 26*(3), 448–467.

Pressley, M., Wharton-McDonald, R., Hampson, J. M., & Echevarria, M. (1998). The nature of literacy instruction in ten grade 4/5 classrooms in upstate New York. *Scientific Studies of Reading, 2,* 159–194.

Riely, J. D. (1992). Using the proficient reader protocol to evaluate middle school reading behaviors. *Clearing House, 66*(1), 41–44.

Rose, T. (1994). *Black noise: Rap music and black culture in contemporary America.* Hanover, NH: Wesleyan University Press.

Sendak, M. (1963). *Where the wild things are.* New York: Harper & Row.

Stanovich, K. E. (1986). Matthew effects in reading: Some consequences of individual differences in the acquisition of literacy. *Reading Research Quarterly, 21,* 360–407.

Taylor, B. M., Frye, B. J., & Maruyama, G. M. (1990). Time spent reading and reading growth. *American Educational Research Journal, 27,* 351–362.

Tompkins, G. (2006). *Literacy for the 21st century: A balanced approach* (4th ed.). Upper Saddle River, NJ: Merrill Prentice-Hall.

U.S. Department of Education. (2005). *The nation's report card: Reading 2005.* National Center for Education Statistics, Washington, DC.

Wikipedia. (2007). *Remix.* Retrieved June 14, 2008, from *en.wikipedia.org/wiki/Remix.*

Wood, K., Lapp, D., Flood, J., & Taylor, B. (2008). *Guiding readers through text: Strategy guides for new times.* Newark, DE: International Reading Association.

The reproducibles in this chapter are also provided in a large-size format on Guilford's website (www.guilford.com/p/ganske4) for book buyers to download and use in their professional practice.

APPENDIX 10.1. Graphic Organizer for Songs

Song title: Artist:
What is the message of this song?
What emotions are evoked by the lyrics?
How does the music/melody contribute to the meaning of the song?
Why is the song meaningful?
Who does this song target as audience?

APPENDIX 10.2. Story Map
for *Scooby Doo* Episode

Title of Episode:
Beginning:
Middle:
End:
Extra Information (such as common phrases and recurring themes):

APPENDIX 10.3. Comparison Chart
for *Scooby Doo* Episodes

Episode Title	Opening Scene	Setting	Supernatural Element	How Supernatural Is Explained	True Identity of Villain	Attempted Crime	Final Words of Villain

From *Comprehension Across the Curriculum: Perspectives and Practices K–12*, edited by Kathy Ganske and Douglas Fisher. Copyright 2010 by The Guilford Press. Permission to photocopy this appendix is granted to purchasers of this book for personal use only (see copyright page for details).

APPENDIX 10.4. Writing Guide for *Scooby Doo* Fan Fiction

Title:
Setting:
Characters:
"Supernatural" (monster/ghost/etc.):
True Crime (and how supernatural hoax will be explained):
Beginning:
Middle:
End:

APPENDIX 10.5. Storyboard Planning Guide

Storyboard for: _____
                        (Title of Your Project)

A mash-up of these sources: _____

Page number for picture: _____

_____
_____
_____

Page number for picture: _____

_____
_____
_____

Page number for picture: _____

_____
_____
_____

Page number for picture: _____

_____
_____
_____

11

Developing Comprehension in English Language Learners

Research and Promising Practices

Diane August
Jennifer Letcher Gray

This chapter focuses on the development of comprehension in English language learners (ELLs). These students are growing in numbers, comprise a large percentage of the U.S. student population, and are at risk for poor educational outcomes because of their poor reading performance. In the 10 years between 1996 and 2006, the nation's K–12 ELL population rose by over 60%, while the size of the overall student population remained essentially unchanged. As a result, the proportion of school children who are English learners has grown markedly—from 6.8% of the total K–12 school population in 1995–1996 to 10.3% in 2005–2006 (Batalova, Fix, & Murray, 2006). On the National Assessment of Educational Progress (NAEP) in 2005 (National Center for Education Statistics, 2006), only 7% of fourth-grade ELLs scored at or above the proficiency level in reading English compared with 32% of English speakers. Only 4% of eighth-grade ELLs scored at or above the proficiency level in reading, compared with 30% of English speakers.

Research that examines the development of reading comprehension in English monolinguals has provided insight into its prerequi-

225

sites, including the ability to read words accurately and rapidly, good language skills, and well-developed stores of world knowledge (RAND Reading Study Group, 2002). A review of the research on developing literacy in second-language learners (Lesaux, Koda, Siegel, & Shanahan, 2006) found these prerequisites to be important for ELLs as well.

Although the same factors related to reading comprehension are prerequisites for both ELLs and English monolinguals, ELLs need more support in some areas than others. Whereas ELLs with appropriate instruction generally perform at levels commensurate with monolingual English speakers in English word reading (Lesaux & Geva, 2006), this is not the case for English language proficiency, where their performance is significantly worse (Cobo-Lewis, Pearson, Eilers, & Umbel, 2002; Proctor, Carlo, August, & Snow, 2005). Thus, to build comprehension in ELLs, it is important to develop their language proficiency in English. One key component of English language proficiency is vocabulary. Researchers have identified a number of methods to develop students' English vocabulary, regardless of language background, including providing rich and varied language experiences, teaching words, and teaching word-learning strategies (August & Shanahan, 2006; Ellis, 2008; Graves, 2006; Nagy & Stahl, 2006).

Researchers working with English monolinguals have also identified instructional methods aimed directly at improving reading comprehension in children, including comprehension monitoring, cooperative learning, use of graphic and semantic organizers, question answering, question generation, and summarization (National Institute of Child Health and Human Development, 2000).

In some cases these methods have been used with ELLs but have been modified to meet the unique needs of students reading in a second language (Shanahan & Beck, 2006). The modifications include more of a focus on building background knowledge, scaffolding, and reinforcement, as well as capitalizing on first language strengths, and are all intended to ensure that ELLs understand oral and written English as well as to further develop their text comprehension.

In the remainder of this chapter we describe methods that have been successful in building comprehension in second language learners. We first focus on methods to build vocabulary and next turn to methods focused directly on developing comprehension. For each method, we review the research briefly and then illustrate the method with examples of curriculum from our research studies. Figure 11.1 illustrates the model of comprehension development that guides our curriculum.

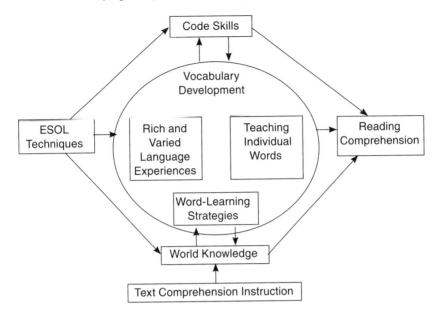

FIGURE 11.1. Model of reading comprehension.

METHODS TO DEVELOP VOCABULARY

As children progress through school and attempt to comprehend more challenging text, vocabulary becomes increasingly important (Lesaux & Siegel, 2003). This section describes three techniques that have been used to build vocabulary: providing rich and varied language experiences, instruction of individual words, and instruction in word-learning strategies.

Providing Rich and Varied Language Experiences

Vocabulary is primarily acquired incidentally, through listening, talking, and reading (Graves, 2006). Thus, to the extent possible, teachers need to immerse students in a rich language environment that provides them with opportunities to acquire vocabulary.

Listening and Talking

One method that has been used frequently and successfully to provide rich and varied language experiences is interactive shared reading. This method exposes students to language not often heard in classrooms and not encountered by young children or struggling readers in the texts that they are able to read. It also offers teachers meaningful contexts in which to discuss new words and provide students with opportunities to engage in conversational interactions (Beck, McKeown, & Kucan, 2002; Coyne, Kame'enui, & Simmons, 2004).

Research with monolingual speakers indicates that interactive shared reading has a large impact on vocabulary, as well as composite measures of oral language that include grammar and listening comprehension (Wasik & Bond, 2001; Zevenbergen, Whitehurst, & Zevenbergen, 2003). Although many studies have been conducted with young children, there is some evidence that this technique can be effective with older learners as well (Brabham & Lynch-Brown, 2002).

Dialogic reading, one common method of interactive shared reading, is based on three broad principles: "Encourage the child to participate, provide feedback to the child, and adapt your reading style to the child's growing linguistic abilities" (Hargrave & Sénéchal, 2000, p. 76). The adult reader asks the child evocative questions about the story or the pictures in the book and provides feedback in the form of repetitions, expansions, and modeling of answers. As children become more proficient, the reader tailors the interactive reading to match the students' proficiency levels.

Interactive shared reading has also been used with ELLs and has been successful in building students' vocabulary and comprehension (Saunders & Goldenberg, 1999; Carlo et al, 2004; Roberts & Neal, 2004; Liang, Peterson, & Graves, 2005; Biemiller & Boote, 2006; Silverman, 2007a). The interactive reading methods, which build on first language research, have generally been modified for ELLs. For example, English for speakers of other languages (ESOL) techniques such as building background knowledge, scaffolding, and providing reinforcement are used to help ensure students' understanding of the text (Saunders & Goldenberg, 1999). Additionally, reading materials relevant to ELLs' experience or culture are selected, and students' first languages may be strategically used to make text more comprehensible (Carlo et al., 2004).

Although our approach builds on first language interactive shared reading methods, it has been adapted to meet the needs of ELLs. For example, whereas methods developed for first language learners introduce a new book with an uninterrupted read-through followed by an interactive reading, we present the book interactively first and then read the book through for reinforcement and enjoyment. As with first language methods, we ask carefully selected literal, inferential, and critical questions at strategically selected intervals during the read-aloud, but we ask more questions than is generally the case in methods used with first language learners. The frequent questions enable teachers to focus students' attention on key ideas or details, as well as to help students make inferences that are essential to their understanding of the text and to make connections between the text and their own lives, experiences, and ideas. Partner talk is used to give students more opportunity to engage in oral language development. During partner talk, student pairs, consisting of a more proficient ELL student and weaker ELL student, are given the opportunity to talk among themselves in response to the teacher's questions. Subsequently, several pairs of students respond to the teacher.

Other techniques cited above that maximize ELL language development are demonstrated in Figures 11.2 and 11.3. In the first example (Figure 11.2) the teacher applies these techniques to four passages in the story *Chrysanthemum* by Kevin Henkes (1991). The techniques include (1) building background knowledge, including *previewing* material prior to questioning students; (2) scaffolding, including exploiting information carried by accompanying text *pictures* to help convey meaning; incorporating *gestures* and *body language* by both teachers and students to demonstrate meaning and enhance retention of words and content; and (3) providing reinforcement, including the use of *choral repetition* of selected words and phrases, *repeated exposures* to words and concepts, and a brief *summary* after reading pages that present challenging content.

The second example (see Figure 11.3) features interactive reading that supports ELLs' understanding of expository text. This example is taken from a third-grade science lesson about electricity. Prior to the interactive reading demonstrated in Figure 11.3, students have engaged in a hands-on experiment that familiarizes them with science concepts that are presented in the text; in this case the concepts include atoms, electrons, protons, and neutrons. With the aid of visual images specially created for the lesson, they have reviewed the meanings of general and discipline-specific vocabulary and engaged in a picture walk of the text to be covered during the interactive reading. Then, during the interactive reading, teachers pause at regular intervals to ask carefully crafted literal, inferential, and critical questions. These questions focus students' attention on key ideas or details, help them make inferences that are essential to their understanding of the text, and make connections between the text and their own lives, experiences, and ideas. This questioning method provides *scaffolded support* for students' comprehension. After the interactive read-aloud is complete, the students' language development is further reinforced through a number of *extension activities* that

Passage 1:

Look at Chrysanthemum's miserable face (*point to Chrysanthemum*).

Let's make a face like that. (*Gesture*)

How do we feel? We feel miserable! [Previewing prior to open-ended questioning, below.]

Let's say that together: We feel miserable! We feel miserable! [Choral repetition]

Why does Chrysanthemum feel so miserable? [Anticipated response: Because the children, especially Victoria, keep making fun of her name.] [Knowledge structure development: causes]

Passage 2:

Here is the new baby (*point to Chrysanthemum*).

Her parents are so happy. They said she was perfect, absolutely perfect.

Let's say that together: Absolutely perfect! [Choral repetition] The little baby is perfect; that means she is just right. She is as good as she could be. [Repeated exposure to pretaught word *perfect*]

Chrysanthemum's parents loved their new baby. She was absolutely perfect. [Summary]

Passage 3:

See (*point to the picture in the upper left hand corner*), here Chrysanthemum is a little baby, with her rattle and blanky.

Now look at this picture (*point to the bottom right picture*). Is Chrysanthemum still a baby? No! Here she is saying, "I love my name!" [Previewing prior to open-ended questioning, below]

Say that with me: I love my name! [Choral repetition]

Look at all of these pictures and think of one thing that Chrysanthemum learned to do from the time she was a baby (*point again to the first picture*), to the time she was a little girl saying "I love my name!" (*point again to the last picture*). Tell your neighbor your idea. [Knowledge structure development: how something changes]

Chrysanthemum grew from a baby into a big girl. She loved her name. [Summary]

Passage 4:

Poor Chrysanthemum wilted again. Wilted is what a flower does when it needs water.

It droops like this (*demonstrate wilting*).

Show me what you would look like if you were wilting. (*Gesture*)

FIGURE 11.2. Interactive shared reading, narrative text. In this example of interactive reading, narrative text is used with a kindergarten class. After reading each passage (one page of text) from the book *Chrysanthemum* while showing children the pictures, teachers engage children in the kinds of interactions you see in the figure.

Passage 1:
To understand what an atom is, imagine you had a pure gold coin (*hold up a picture of a gold coin*). If you cut it in half, each half is still gold. If you keep cutting, you will get very tiny pieces that are still gold. Eventually, if you had special tools and microscopes, you would get to the tiniest piece that was still gold. That piece would be called an atom.

Q: Why would you need a special microscope to see an atom? [Inferential question—anticipated response: Because atoms are very, very small, and microscopes are special tools that are used to help people see things that are very, very small.]

If you could look inside the atom, you would see tiny particles that are not gold by themselves. They are called electrons, protons, and neutrons. Electrons are said to have a "negative charge" and protons are said to have a "positive charge."

Q: How are electrons different from protons? [Inferential question—anticipated response: They have different types of charges: electrons have a negative charge and protons have a positive charge.] How are electrons and protons alike? [Inferential question—anticipated response: Electrons and protons are both types of tiny particles that are found inside atoms.]

Passage 2:
Static electricity happens when objects have an electric charge, or unequal number of protons and electrons. Static means "stationary" or not moving. In static electricity, the charge is not moving. Static electricity is sometimes seen as a spark after objects rub against each other. If your body is one of the objects, you might feel the static electricity as a "shock." Static electricity can also make things stick to one another.

Q: Partner talk: Have you ever felt a "shock" when you touched something or someone? Have you ever seen clothes sticking together when they were taken out of the dryer? Tell your partner. [Critical question, tapping into students' background knowledge—anticipated response: open. What caused the "shock"? What made the clothes stick together? [Literal question, used to reinforce key ideas and concepts—anticipated response: static electricity.]

FIGURE 11.3. Interactive shared reading, expository text. In this example of interactive reading, expository text is used with a third-grade science class.

provide additional opportunities for them to interact with both the text and the target words selected for each lesson.

Reading

Students also acquire new vocabulary through texts that they read on their own. Prior research indicates that "book floods," in which a large number of new and engaging reading materials is added to classroom libraries, has led to increases in second language learners' independent reading and improvements in comprehension and oral language development (Elley, 1991; Tudor & Hafiz, 1989). In giving students books to read on their own, it is important to ensure that the texts are at their independent reading level, that is, at the highest grade equivalent at which they can read with high accuracy and good comprehension. Additionally, research indicates that independent reading along with structured support for ELLs' reading comprehension and language development facilitates their language development to a greater degree than reading that is not accompanied by these tasks (Laufer, 2003).

Our curriculum uses a number of different methods to engage students in activities that support their comprehension and language development while they are reading independently. Figure 11.4 illustrates an example of one such activity. In this take-home reading activity, second-grade students first read a short selection to their parents or older siblings to build more fluent reading, and then answer a series of questions related to the text. The questions are formatted to familiarize students with the type of questions that appear on state reading assessments. The teacher reviews their responses the following day. These questions require students to interpret vocabulary within the context of the reading selection, and to answer questions related to the selections' content.

Figure 11.5 displays a partial list of questions associated with another method we use to support comprehension during independent reading. In this case, students first listen to a story as a read-aloud and then have the opportunity to read the selection with a partner and answer a variety of questions about it.

Teaching Individual Words

A second method of developing vocabulary is through teaching individual words. Commonly accepted general guidelines for teaching individuals words call for "including both definitional and contextual information, involving students in active and deep processing of the words, providing students with multiple exposures to the word, reviewing, rehearsing, and reminding students about the word in various contexts over time, involving students in discussions of the word's meaning, and spending a significant amount of time on the word" (Graves, 2006, pp. 69–70).

One well-researched method to teach individual words is in the context of read-alouds. Research indicates that children with poor expressive vocabulary skills who were engaged in interactive shared reading made significantly greater gains in vocabulary introduced in the books, as well as gains on a standardized expressive vocabulary test, than did children in a regular book-reading situation in which vocabulary was not taught explicitly (Hargrave & Sénéchal, 2000).

Ben's Celebration

Ben could not wait for his birthday party to begin. He was anxious to celebrate with his family! Ben's Aunt Sandra was the first to arrive. Next, Ben's grandparents came to the front door. They brought an enormous chocolate cake. Ben said hello to his family, and then hurried to the kitchen to help prepare his birthday dinner—pizza! Ben made the pizza sauce all by himself. Ben's family sat down to eat dinner. They all said that the pizza was delicious.

After dinner, Aunt Sandra and Mama told stories of their childhood. Then Mama went up to the attic and brought down a box filled with photographs of Ben and his family. Everyone looked at the photographs together. After they finished looking at the photographs they sang Happy Birthday and ate cake and ice cream.

1. In this story, the word *anxious* means—
   o worried
   o nervous
   • eager
   o scared

2. Which of these happened first in the story?
   o Aunt Sandra and Mama told stories.
   o Everyone ate cake and ice cream.
   o Mama brought down the box of photos.
   • Aunt Sandra arrived.

3. In this story, which of these is a FACT?
   o Ben loved to make pizza.
   • Ben made the pizza sauce.
   o Aunt Sandra was proud of Ben.
   o Ben was taller than Aunt Sandra.

4. What did the family do after looking at the photographs?
   o Played board games
   o Ate dinner
   • Ate cake and ice cream
   o Watched television

5. When Ben's family said that the pizza was delicious, he probably felt
   • proud
   o scared
   o sad
   o tired

FIGURE 11.4. Independent reading with structured support.

Several methods have been used to teach individual words in the context of shared interactive reading. In one method that has generally been successful, teachers provide embedded explanations of target words when they are encountered during the story reading. In one study that used embedded explanations with kindergarten, first- and second-grade children, some of whom were ELLs, during the second reading of

The Patchwork Quilt

1. Why did Grandma say that her patchwork quilt will be better than a quilt you can buy at the store? [page 327]

2. What did Grandma do with Jim's blue corduroy pants? [page 328]
   a. She threw them away.
   b. She cut out a patch to put in the quilt.
   c. She gave them to another child.
   d. She kept them in a box.

3. In this story, Tanya worked on the quilt because she knew it was important to Grandma. Think of a time when you did something for someone in your family because you knew that it was important to him or her. What did you do? Who did you do it for? Why was it important?

FIGURE 11.5. Independent reading with structured support.

the book teachers repeated the sentence in which the target word was found, asked students to define the word, and, if no one could, provided a brief explanation. In an example described by the authors in which the target word was *solution,* the teacher might offer the following explanation: "A *solution* is the answer to a problem" (Biemiller & Boote, 2006, p. 49).

Several researchers have provided extended vocabulary instruction rather than simple embedded explanations within the context of read-alouds with good results (Coyne, McCoach, & Kapp, 2007; Silverman, 2007a). Extended vocabulary instruction is characterized by "explicit teaching that includes both contextual and definitional information, multiple exposures to target words in varied contexts, and experiences that promote deep processing of word meanings" (Coyne et al., 2007, p. 74). For example, in one study that used extended vocabulary instruction (Silverman, 2007b), students were exposed to three different extension methods: discussion-based, in which teachers lead children to discuss words in relation to the story they are reading or their personal experience (contextual), active word-meaning analysis activities such as comparing and contrasting words (analytical), and letter–sound activities calling attention to the written and spoken forms of words (anchored). Findings indicate that combining all three methods was more powerful than any one method; moreover, the overall method was equally beneficial for ELLs and educationally disadvantaged first language learners.

To increase ELLs' oral vocabulary, our approach builds on this research. We use both embedded explanations, in which we define words as they appear in the text, as well as the extended vocabulary instructional method described above. Additionally, we use scaffolding techniques known to be effective with ELLs, such as the use of visual aids, drama, and repeated pronunciation of the target words. In the case of words that represent something concretely, the visuals provide images of the target word (e.g., *empty*); for words representing more abstract concepts, the visuals create a scenario that provides a mini-context for introducing the meaning of the word. In selecting words that appear in narrative text, we choose high-frequency academic words that are important for understanding the text. In the case of read-alouds used to reinforce discipline-specific knowledge, we choose both high-frequency academic and discipline-specific words.

Figure 11.6 is an example of extended vocabulary instruction of a general academic word that appears in a storybook being read to kindergartners or first graders. We provide a simple definition of the word, show a picture that demonstrates the word's meaning, explain how the picture demonstrates the word's meaning, and engage students in an activity that reinforces the word's meaning. We then pose questions that require students to discuss words in relation to the story they are reading or their personal experience (contextual), ask questions that require students to actively analyze words (analytical), and engage students in letter–sound activities that call attention to the written and spoken forms of words (anchored).

Figure 11.7 is an example of extended vocabulary instruction of a discipline-specific word that appears in a third-grade math lesson. Note that both the general and discipline-specific meanings of the word are taught and we provide a definition in Spanish as scaffolding to students whose first language is Spanish. After students learn the word *multiple* through preteaching, they participate in a math lesson where they learn to recognize multiples and count by multiples of 2, 5, and 10.

Glossaries are used to reinforce word meanings after preteaching and exposure to these words during classroom interactive reading or after "hands-on" activities such as science experiments. In Figure 11.8, the words *graph* and *label* are from a math lesson. In Figure 11.9, the word *ceremony* is from a social studies lesson. Note that these are just examples. Students receive a glossary each week that includes all the target words taught during the week. Note that the glossaries not only define the target vocabulary for students but require them to apply the meaning in a new context.

Teaching Word-Learning Strategies

A third method of building vocabulary is to teach word-learning strategies. Well researched word-learning strategies used with first language

Preteaching the word PERFECT

The word we are going to learn is *perfect*. *Perfect* means *just right*. If something is perfect, it is as good as it could be.

Let's look at a picture of something perfect. (*Show picture.*)

This is a perfect day to go to the beach. You can see it is sunny and warm outside.

It's a perfect day. Let's pretend that we are collecting shells on the beach. (*Have children pretend to collect shells.*)

And some of the shells we find are perfect also. They are not broken, and they are very shiny.

Can you name something you think is perfect? Why do you think it is perfect? [Contextual instruction]

If you had a toy that was broken, would that toy be perfect? Why or why not? [Analytic instruction]

Say *perfect* with me three times—perfect, perfect, perfect.

Point to the letter *p* in the word *perfect*. What sound does the word *perfect* start with? What is the letter name? [Anchored instruction]

As we read, I want you to listen for the word *perfect*. If you hear it, touch your nose! [Contextual instruction]

Reinforcing the word's meaning during the read-aloud

During the read-aloud children are asked: If Chrysanthemum's name is dreadful or awful, is it perfect? Why not? [Anticipated response: No, it's not perfect, because if something is perfect, it's just right. It's as good as it could be. *Dreadful* and *awful* mean *very bad*.]

FIGURE 11.6. Preteaching: General academic words.

Multiple

5   10   15   20

Teacher Talk

1. Multiple
2. In English, *multiple* means more than one, or many.
3. *En español,* multiple *significa* múltiple. *Quiere decir más que uno o mucho.*
4. These pictures demonstrate the word *multiple.* In the first picture, there are multiple, or many, people on a sled. In math, multiples are also the numbers you say as you are skip counting. When you are skip counting by 5s, you will say 10, 15, and 20. Ten, 15, and 20 are multiples of 5.

Call on One
Child

5. Tell about a time you went somewhere with multiple friends. [Anticipated response: responses will vary.]

Partner Talk

6. With your partner, skip count by 2. Then name some multiples of 2.
7. Ask one or two pairs for their response. [Anticipated response: Responses will vary.]

Teacher Talk

8. What is the focus word? Say it with me three times: *multiple, multiple, multiple.*

Partner Talk

9. What does *multiple* mean? Tell your partner.
10. Ask one or two pairs for their response. [Anticipated response: Responses will vary.]

FIGURE 11.7. Preteaching: Discipline-specific words.

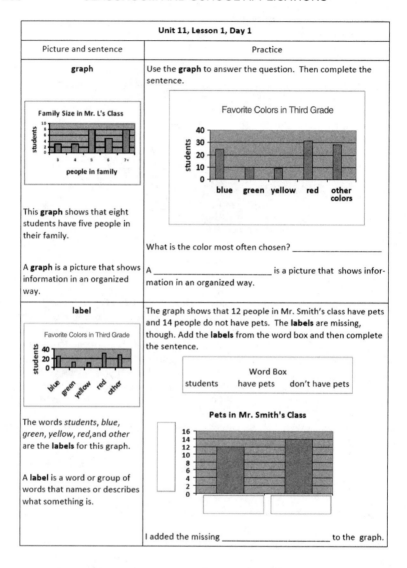

FIGURE 11.8. Vocabulary reinforcement: Math.

learners include using context clues, using word parts, and using dictionaries (Graves, 2006). The second language research literature has used these methods as well as methods particular to second language learners, such as using cognate knowledge to uncover word meanings in a second language (in cases where two language share cognates)

ceremony	A ceremony is an activity with special actions, words, and often music that marks an important occasion. When two people get married, they have a wedding ceremony. **Your sentence:** _____ _____

FIGURE 11.9. Vocabulary reinforcement: Social studies.

(Shanahan & Beck, 2006). For example, in one study (Carlo et al., 2004), students were taught to use cognate knowledge by working in linguistically heterogeneous (Spanish–English) groups where they searched for Spanish–English cognates in a series of specially designed passages, discussed the meanings of the Spanish–English cognates with one another, and determined whether the words were true or false cognates.

There is a substantial body of first language research that supports two approaches to teaching word-learning strategies (Graves, 2006, pp. 90–93). In the first, direct explanation of strategies, teachers first explain the strategy, note its importance, model its use, and then gradually give students responsibility for employing it. In the second, transactional strategies instruction, there is some direct explanation as part of the initial instruction; however, this tends to be brief and less structured than direct explanation and carried out as part of the ongoing reading activities of the classroom when the occasion arises for students to use a particular strategy.

Figure 11.10 provides an example of a word-learning strategy using first language knowledge to infer the meanings of second language words that are cognates. Besides providing direct explanations of the strategy, we also point out to students or ask them to point out to us, cognates that they encounter when listening to or reading text.

TEXT COMPREHENSION INSTRUCTION

There are also well-researched methods of text comprehension instruction intended to improve comprehension by teaching students to use particular cognitive strategies to reason, including comprehension monitor-

In this figure, the teacher provides and discusses two cognates that were taken from the third-grade science text that students were about to read, and one false cognate. The chart provides examples of different types of Spanish–English cognate pairs: a pair in which the word is spelled the same way in both languages and carries a similar meaning, and a pair in which the word is spelled in a similar way in both languages and carries a similar meaning, The third example is a false cognate—the English and Spanish words are spelled the same way but carry different meanings. After discussing these examples, the teacher and students locate other Spanish–English cognate pairs in the text and discuss their similarities and differences with respect to meaning, phonology, and orthography.

Cognates

English Word	English Meaning	Spanish Word	Spanish Meaning
Normal	Usual or regular	Normal	Usual or regular
Electricity	A form of energy caused by the motion of electrons and protons.	Electricidad	A form of energy caused by the motion of electrons and protons.
Pie	A type of pastry	Pie	Foot

FIGURE 11.10. Word-learning strategies.

ing, question generation, summarization, using graphic organizers, and answering questions (National Institute of Child Health and Human Development, 2000, pp. 4–42). Additionally, multiple strategies, in which several methods are combined and used flexibly, are effective. Typically, instruction consists of "developing an awareness and understanding of the reader's own cognitive processes that are amenable to instruction and learning; guiding the reader or modeling for the reader the actions that the reader can take to enhance comprehension processes used during reading; and giving the reader practice in the strategies until they are internalized" (National Institute of Child Health and Human Development, pp. 4–40).

In the review of studies focused on ELLs, several of these methods were also apparent. For example, in a literature program for upper-elementary students (Saunders & Goldenberg, 1999), they were taught to monitor their comprehension through pausing occasionally and summarizing what they had read, and formulating and answering questions about the text. Having students practice summarization in their first (non-English) language in cooperative homogeneous language groups (Calderón, Hertz-Lazarowitz, & Slavin, 1998) or having them practice inferring meaning from context in mixed groups of ELLs and monolingual English speakers (Carlo et al., 2004) has also been used to improve reading comprehension.

Our curriculum model includes a variety of opportunities for students to use the methods cited above to support reading comprehension. In Figure 11.11 we present an example from work with third-grade ELLs in language arts. Here the teacher explicitly models making inferences and then gives students practice applying this strategy as they read text selections. The teacher leads students through an explicit step-by-step explanation of how to make a specific inference while reading the story *The Patchwork Quilt* (Flurinov, 1952) and then asks students to practice as a group. It is important to note that students work with this strategy only after they have been helped to understand the meaning of the text they have read. We use the same techniques to teach students other text comprehension methods such as summarization and prediction (where there is some basis in the text for making educated predictions).

SUMMARY AND CONCLUSIONS

Second-language text-level skills such as English reading comprehension are a significant weakness for ELLs, and they rarely approach the levels achieved by English-proficient students (Lesaux et al., 2006). For this reason, sustained efforts, beginning in preschool are crucial.

Throughout this chapter we have described a variety of methods borrowed from the first language and literacy research, including creating language rich environments, directly teaching words, teaching word-learning strategies, and text comprehension instruction. Because ELLs are learning in a second language, adjustments have been made to the methods used with first language learners, notably a greater emphasis on building background knowledge, scaffolding, and reinforcement. Additionally, we have demonstrated how to capitalize on students' first language strengths. We have provided the reader with examples for each of these methods, which we hope will make the methods come alive and will encourage their use in classrooms with ELLs.

Students practice "inferencing," after reading Flurinov's (1952) *The Patchwork Quilt.* In the example from Day 1 of the lesson, the students have just read that Grandma is sitting in a chair in the living room, surrounded by many scraps of fabric. She tells Tanya (her granddaughter) that she will use this fabric to make a quilt. Mama (Tanya's mother) comes into the room and is upset by the "mess" that Grandma has made with the fabric scraps. Mama tells Grandma that she will buy her a quilt at the store. Using this information, students are asked to make an inference. Other examples of inferencing occur on Day 1 as well as Day 2 of the week's lesson.

Teacher: Now we are going to make an inference: Does Mama think that Grandma should make the patchwork quilt? [Anticipated response: No, Mama does not think that she should make it.] What evidence from the story supports this inference? [Anticipated response: Mama thinks that Grandma is making a mess, and she tells her that she will get her a quilt, that she does not need the scraps.] Write this information on your chart.

SKILL CHART: Inferencing

As we read the story, think about what inferences you can make, based on evidence that you find in the story. Write the evidence you find and your inferences on the chart. Note that this is a correctly completed chart.

Inference	Evidence from the story
Day 1: Pages 324 and 325: Mama does not think that Grandma should make the quilt.	Mama says Grandma is making a mess. Says she will get Grandma a quilt.
Day 1: Pages 326 and 327: Grandma's quilt will be better than a department store quilt.	It will last longer. It will be a masterpiece. Grandma needs time to do it right.
Day 1: Pages 330 and 331: Tanya understands why the quilt is important to Grandma.	Tanya knows that Grandma is not lonely if she is working on her quilt.
Day 2: Pages 332 and 333: Mama thinks that the quilt is important now.	Mama talked to Grandma about the quilt. Mama is helping Grandma make the quilt.
Day 2: Page 337: Tanya has decided to work on the quilt.	Tanya thinks about how to cut the scraps. Mama says that she will stitch the squares together.

FIGURE 11.11. Text comprehension instruction.

CHILDREN'S BOOKS

Flurinov, V. (1952). *The patchwork quilt*. New York: Penguin Books.
Henkes, K. (1991). *Chrysanthemum*. New York: Harper Collins.
King-Mitchell, M. (2006). *Grandaddy's gift*. New York: Scholastic.

REFERENCES

Batalova, J., Fix, M., & Murray, J. (2006). *Measures of change: The demography and literacy of adolescent English language learners*. Washington, DC: Migration Policy Institute.

Beck, I., McKeown, M., & Kucan, L. (2002). *Bringing words to life: Robust vocabulary instruction*. New York. Guilford Press.

Biemiller, A., & Boote, C. (2006). An effective method for building vocabulary in primary grades. *Journal of Educational Psychology, 98*(1), 44–62.

Brabham, E. G., & Lynch-Brown, C. (2002). Effects of teachers' reading aloud styles on vocabulary acquisition and comprehension of students in the early elementary grades. *Journal of Educational Psychology, 94*, 465–473.

Calderón, M., Hertz-Lazarowitz, R., & Slavin, R. E. (1998). Effects of bilingual cooperative integrated reading and composition on students making the transition from Spanish to English reading. *Elementary School Journal, 99*(2), 153–165.

Carlo, M. S., August, D., McLaughlin, B., Snow, C. E., Dressler, C., Lippman, D., et al. (2004). Closing the gap: Addressing the vocabulary needs of English language learners in bilingual and mainstream classrooms. *Reading Research Quarterly, 39*(2), 188–215.

Cobo-Lewis, A. B., Pearson, B. Z., Eilers, R. E., & Umbel, V. C. (2002). Effects of bilingualism and bilingual education on oral and written Spanish skills: A multifactor study of standardized test outcomes. In D. K. Oller & R. E. Eilers (Eds.), *Language and literacy in bilingual children* (pp. 3–21). Clevedon, UK: Multilingual Matters.

Coyne, M. D., McCoach, B., & Kapp, S. (2007). Vocabulary intervention for kindergarten students: Comparing extended instruction to embedded instruction and incidental exposure. *Learning Disability Quarterly, 30*, 74–88.

Coyne, M. D., Kame'enui, E. J., & Simmons, D. C. (2004). Improving beginning reading instruction and intervention for students with LD: Reconciling "all" with "each." *Journal of Learning Disabilities, 37*, 231–239.

Elley, W. B. (1991). Acquiring literacy in a second language: The effect of book-based programs. *Language Learning, 41*(3), 375–411.

Ellis, R. (2008). *Principles of instructed second language acquisition*. CAL Digests, Washington, DC: Center for Applied Linguistics. Retrieved September 26, 2009, from *www.cal.org/resources/digest/digest_pdfs/ Instructed 2ndLangFinalWeb.pdf*.

Fung, I. Y. Y., Wilkinson, I. A. G., & Moore, D. W. (2003). L1-assisted reciprocal teaching to improve ESL students' comprehension of English expository text. *Learning and Instruction, 13,* 1–31.

Graves, M. F. (2006). *The vocabulary book.* New York: Teacher's College
Press.

Hargrave, A. C., & Sénéchal, M. (2000). Book reading interventions with lan-
guage-delayed preschool children: The benefits of regular reading and dialogic reading. *Early Childhood Research Quarterly, 15,* 75–90.

Laufer, B. (2003). Vocabulary acquisition in a second language: Do learners
really acquire most vocabulary by reading? Some empirical evidence.
Canadian Modern Language Review, 59(4), 567–587.

Lesaux, N. K., & Geva, E. (2006). Development of literacy in language-minority students. In D. August & T. Shanahan (Eds.) *Developing literacy in
second-language learners: Report of the National Literacy Panel on language minority children and youth* (pp. 27–61). Mahwah, NJ: Erlbaum.

Lesaux, N. K., Koda, K., Siegel, L. S., & Shanahan, T. (2006). Development
of literacy. In D. L. August & T. Shanahan (Eds.), *Developing literacy in
a second language: Report of the National Literacy Panel* (pp. 75–122).
Mahwah, NJ: Erlbaum.

Lesaux, N. K., & Siegel, L. S. (2003). The development of reading in children
who speak English as a second language (ESL). *Developmental Psychology, 39*(6), 1005–1019.

Liang, L. A., Peterson, C., & Graves, M. F. (2005). Investigating two approaches
to fostering children's comprehension of literature. *Reading Psychology,
26,* 387–400.

Nagy, W. E., & Stahl, S. A. (2006). *Teaching word meanings.* Mahwah, NJ:
Erlbaum.

National Center for Education Statistics. (2006). *National assessment of educational progress reading assessments.* Washington, DC: U.S. Department
of Education.

National Institute of Child Health and Human Development. (2000). *Report of
the National Reading Panel. Teaching children to read: An evidence-based
assessment of the scientific research literature on reading and its implications for reading instruction* (NIH Publication No. 00-4769). Washington,
DC: U.S. Department of Health and Human Services.

Proctor, C. P., Carlo, M., August, D., & Snow, C. (2005). Native Spanish-
speaking children reading in English: Toward a model of comprehension.
Journal of Educational Psychology, 97(2), 246–256.

RAND Reading Study Group. (2002). *Reading for understanding: Toward an
R&D program in reading comprehension.* Washington, DC: RAND Education.

Roberts, T., & Neal, H. (2004). Relationships among preschool English learners, oral proficiency in English, instructional experience, and literacy
development. *Contemporary Educational Psychology, 29,* 283–311.

Saunders, W. M., & Goldenberg, C. (1999). Effects of instructional conversations and literature logs on limited- and fluent-English proficient students'

story comprehension and thematic understanding. *Elementary School Journal, 99*(4), 277–301.

Shanahan, T., & Beck, I. L. (2006). Effective literacy teaching for English-language learners. In D. L. August & T. Shanahan (Eds.), *Developing literacy in a second language: Report of the National Literacy Panel* (pp. 415–488). Mahwah, NJ: Erlbaum.

Silverman, R. (2007a). Vocabulary development of English-language and English-only learners in kindergarten. *Elementary School Journal, 107*(4), 365–383.

Silverman, R. (2007b). A comparison of three methods of vocabulary instruction during read-alouds in kindergarten. *Elementary School Journal 108*(2), 97–113.

Tudor, I., & Hafiz, F. (1989). Extensive reading as a means of input to L2 learning. *Journal of Research in Reading, 12*(2), 164–178.

Wasik, B. A., & Bond, M. A. (2001). Beyond the pages of a book: Interactive book reading and language development in preschool classrooms. *Journal of Educational Psychology, 93*(2), 243–250.

Zevenbergen, A. A., Whitehurst, G. J., & Zevenbergen, J. A. (2003). Effects of a shared-reading intervention on the inclusion of evaluative devices in narratives of children from low income families. *Journal of Applied Developmental Psychology, 24,* 1–15.

12

Selecting and Using Nonfiction in Grades K–12

Social Studies and Science

Donna L. Knoell

All that mankind has done, thought or been, is lying in the magic preservation in the pages of books.
—THOMAS CARLYLE

There is a rich and diverse array of nonfiction, including trade books, informational magazines, reference materials, and other informational resources, available for providing and enhancing social studies and science instruction. In fact, it is difficult to think of a topic that has not been the subject of a book or magazine article. Themes have included everything from the history of toilets and the history of underwear, to gains in women's rights; and from Einstein's special theory of relativity to an up-close study of the rainforest. This chapter explores the selection and use of nonfiction trade books (including biography) and other informational resources, to engage readers, develop their background knowledge, and teach essential and accurate concepts in social studies and science. It includes extensive listings of social studies and science informational books for use with grades K–2, 3–5, and middle school and high school students.

WHY NONFICTION?

Before delving into why nonfiction trade books should be used in K–12 classrooms, let's define the terminology. *Nonfiction trade books* are any nonfiction books other than reference books and textbooks. They are the type of books you expect to find at a bookstore. There is often confusion regarding whether to refer to factual trade books as *nonfiction* or whether they should be classified as *informational* books. Primary teachers historically referred to these books as informational books, whereas intermediate and secondary teachers usually referred to them as nonfiction (Olness, 2007). The trend today, and in this chapter, is to use the terms *nonfiction* and *informational* interchangeably.

The importance of nonfiction in our lives is evident in the fact that most of what adults read is informational text, and students are required to read for information in school. Students of all ages need to be exposed to this type of text and learn how to read and access information from it, not only because these skills are needed for formal schooling and lifelong reading, but also because students of all ages enjoy reading nonfiction, love information, and are innately curious and inquisitive about natural phenomena and real-life events. They need opportunities to pursue their interests, to read, and to find answers to satisfy and further stimulate their curiosity in ways that may lead to a lifetime of continued reading and inquiry. Increased use of nonfiction trade books can also help students to master the "challenging subject matter" that continues to be a long-term goal at both state and national levels (Marzano, 2004). Finally, informational texts provide interesting, engaging content, within formats, writing styles, and vocabulary that are accessible to readers of varying abilities.

Although all readers can benefit from reading nonfiction, informational texts may be especially important for building background knowledge and motivating reluctant or struggling readers. Readers' interest can be sparked by the chance to read books or other sources on self-selected topics of interest. Also, with fiction, students have to read an entire story or an entire book to grasp the action and important ideas. But with nonfiction, students can find answers to their questions by reading a very short portion of a book or a magazine article. Teachers can capitalize on interests expressed by students, as does the fifth grade teacher in the following vignette:

"John, you seemed extremely interested in science today when we talked about ocean life and examined the seashells and seaweed specimens that Angie brought back from her trip. I think you might really enjoy reading this book (shows John the Delta Science Reader titled *Ocean*, from their classroom shelf) or parts of this other book, *Oceans* by Beverly McMillan and John Musick. I have some *Odyssey* magazines from our school library, and you might also like to read an article in one of the issues. The magazine articles are short and packed with interesting information. If you'd like my help in finding the ocean article, just let me know."

PROVIDING AND USING ADEQUATE RESOURCES

Because students' interests and instructional needs differ, it is essential that classroom and school libraries include abundant supplies of interesting books on a wide range of topics, reading levels, and genres, including nonfiction. The International Reading Association (IRA) recommends a minimum of seven titles per student in each elementary classroom, and the American Library Association (ALA) recommends a minimum of 20 titles per student for school libraries. Of these, at least half should be informational, or nonfiction books. Despite the wealth of nonfiction that exists, size recommendations for classroom and school libraries, and learners' interests in seeking information, students still do not always have adequate access to nonfiction texts. Typically, a notable imbalance of genres has existed at the primary level, with a scarcity of informational text for young readers.

Imbalance has also been evident in instruction. Though children's literature has always been a valuable component of elementary reading programs, most of it has been narrative fiction. In secondary language arts programs, nonfiction as a genre is typically not included or taught but instead is relegated to the domain of content-area teachers, and more often than not textbooks, rather than trade books, have been the mainstay. If we are to get more broad-based content into the hearts and minds of students, a much larger percentage of nonfiction will need to be made available and utilized in all classrooms and at all levels.

UNDERSTANDING NONFICTION: GENRES AND FORMATS

Using a variety of nonfiction trade books for instruction can have big benefits for students' learning. Certainly trade books provide more in-depth reading, learning, and a potentially deeper understanding of concepts than a single textbook, which typically presents minimal coverage of topics because the range of subjects is much greater. Reading from multiple sources with interesting and varied formats can also pique students' interests about a broad range of related topics and enhance reading engagement. Reading multiple books on a particular topic by different authors may also provide multiple perspectives. Because trade books on a particular topic are available with varied reading levels, they are also often much more accessible to students than textbooks. Many trade books can be used in more than one subject area, providing teachers with a wider use of resources. For example, a book on habitats might be used in social studies, as students learn about geographic regions; the same resource on habitats might fit well in the science curriculum, as students learn about animals or plants. Students can also learn about a topic by reading books of various genres. For instance, when studying the ocean, as in the fifth-grade vignette previously presented, students might read a factual book or magazine article on the ocean, but they might also increase their understanding by reading poetry, a picture book, an alphabet book, or a biography of Jacques Cousteau. Each lens affords a unique perspective on the topic and helps students build a complex understanding of oceans.

The Structure of Nonfiction

Although informational books can be written in either narrative or expository format, most nonfiction is written in expository format with one or more of the following text structures: compare and contrast; cause and effect; question and answer format; sequential order; problem–solution format; and the enumeration of facts. (Notable exceptions are biography and much history, which are typically written in narrative.) The structure of expository text, as well as the vocabulary used, tends to be more complex than either the structure or language in narrative fiction. This greater complexity can make it hard for teachers to match students to texts they are able to read and understand using typical measures of readability. The yardstick of readability, which often relies on word and sentence length and sentence structure to determine text difficulty, does not take into account the complexity of the text structure or the vocabulary of nonfiction. Teachers who know their students, however, factor other characteristics into their text selections for instruction, recognizing that students' motivation, background knowledge, or experience can sometimes compensate for the greater complexities of informational text (Wolpow & Tonjes, 2005).

Nonfiction Picture Books

Picture books were once viewed as exclusively for very young children. This limited and inaccurate perspective is beginning to change, however.

Picture books, with their shorter and usually easier texts and compelling illustrations, are resources that can be used to introduce abstract concepts to readers of all ages—they quite literally paint a clear picture for readers of any age. Students who might need to read and reread lengthy text about a topic can easily experience a profound "ahha" moment from reading a nonfiction picture book. Picture books maximize the value of stimulating illustrations by immersing readers in a powerful text–illustration synergy. Because of the universal power of illustrations and photographs to communicate, informational picture books can also have a profound and positive impact in helping English Language Learners gain understanding. The illustrations of many picture books help readers to comprehend abstract concepts and new vocabulary, and they make it easier for students to develop background knowledge that can be used to bridge understanding for textbook readings. Finally, picture books are ideal read-alouds for all levels of readers. They provide opportunities to introduce concepts and to follow up with discussion and clarification; they afford teachers with opportunities to model fluent reading and to teach students about text structures and other important reading and writing understandings; and they have the added advantage of being relatively short.

Alphabet Books

Like picture books, alphabet books were once thought to be appropriate only for primary-grade readers. Fortunately, however, many educators now realize the potential of alphabet books to communicate important information in an appealing and accessible format. Typically, the text is limited, with key words for each alphabet letter bolded or highlighted in some way, and appealing illustrations are used to extend or enhance students' understanding.

The greatest advances in alphabet books are the amazing ones being published by Sleeping Bear Press. In addition to delightful verse, perfect for read-alouds and independent reading at the elementary level, there are sidebars for each letter that are packed with compelling information that will inform even secondary students and adults. This company has published an alphabet book for each of the 50 United States and one for every province in Canada. Additional alphabet book titles focus on important science and social studies topics, as well as on other interesting sports and recreational subjects. These books are rich with accurate information and packed with instructional opportunities. Some of the more popular Sleeping Bear Press titles include *D Is for Democracy: A Citizen's Alphabet*; *P Is for Passport: A World Alphabet*; and *W Is for Wind: A Weather Alphabet*. Three newer titles are also perfect for curriculum demands: *W Is for Waves: An Ocean Alphabet*; *D Is for Drum: A Native American Alphabet*; and *D Is for Drinking Gourd: An African American Alphabet*. The joy, however, is that these books are not only filled with information, but they are also engaging and fun to read.

Biographies and Autobiographies

Using outstanding biographies within science and social studies instruction gives teachers the opportunity to present the stories of real people to students, increasing reading engagement and extending background knowledge at the same time. For students who may be particularly interested in reading about the particular eccentricities or idiosyncrasies of an individual, Kathleen Krull's collective biographies are especially engaging. She seems to find the most amazing idiosyncrasies about which readers marvel, as in *Lives of the Presidents, Lives of Athletes,* and *Lives of Extraordinary Women* (Houghton–Mifflin–Harcourt Trade).

David Adler's extensive Picture Biography series (Holiday House) offers very accessible reading for elementary children. Yet, these books present information that will engage even older students or adults, and because there are so many titles about so many varied individuals, there are certain to be titles to interest even the most reluctant reader.

Differentiated Text Resources

A relatively new format of informational trade books includes a group of books that features differentiated text. Heinemann–Raintree, Delta Education, and National Geographic have introduced titles in this format, and they have great potential for meeting the reading needs of all students. With differentiated texts, two books (or magazines) with the same title and topic are written. To the casual observer, the books look identical. But in reality, they are very different treatments of the same subject. Key technical vocabulary terms remain and typically appear in boldface type. But other word choices and sentence structures change to simplify the text for students who have reading difficulties. The shorter, less complex sentences and the selection of more familiar, descriptive words make the text easier to comprehend than its more complex counterpart. In the cited examples above (Heinemann's *Free Style* and *Free Style Express*, Delta Education's *Science Content Readers*, and National Geographic's *Theme Sets*), the photographs and graphics are identical. So to struggling readers who are required to read and understand complex topics, these differentiated texts are extremely helpful while not making the less proficient readers feel that their books are at a lower level. (Examples of these books appear in the bibliography at the end of this chapter.)

Nonfiction Periodical Literature

There are many excellent nonfiction magazines for students to enjoy, and some of these even offer differentiated editions, such as *National Geographic Explorer's Pathfinder* and *Pioneer* magazines. Magazine topics often involve subject matter that coordinates with classroom curricula, and students enjoy the short, easy-to-read format of magazines. In addition to the weekly magazines to which teachers often subscribe for use in the classroom, such as *Scholastic News* and *Time for Kids,* there are many monthly publications that extend both reading and curricular connections to the content areas. As is true for nonfiction books, the demand for accuracy in these publications should never waiver. Also worth noting is that the practice of receiving a regular subscription in the mail as a child can start a reading habit that will likely extend throughout life. (Titles of recommended magazines appear in the selected bibliography at the end of this chapter, for school use and for recommendations to parents for home delivery.)

Reference Resources and Newspapers

Most students are familiar with encyclopedias. In fact, many young children think that writing a report means going to their favorite encyclopedia and copying two paragraphs as their report. Unfortunately, that all too frequent scenario has given encyclopedias some undue censure.

The encyclopedia can actually be a good starting point for students who have no background knowledge about a topic for which they need to seek information. It can give some essential information that will then guide students to appropriate keywords in the indices of trade books, leading them to important information. Otherwise, students with limited or no background knowledge would be clueless as to which keywords or topics to locate in the index. As a caution, however, students must be guided to encyclopedias whose reading levels enable them to read and construct meaning.

Atlases are another reference resource that can be helpful instructionally for students. Atlases with clear, detailed maps can help students of all ages identify important information regarding locations and encourage them to make mental connections among time, place, and a variety of geographic and socioeconomic factors. Also, because the visual nature of maps transcends language barriers, atlases can provide an easy means for English language learners to access information.

Although almanacs seem to be used less and less frequently in class-rooms, they are an excellent source for providing and checking the accuracy of many facts and much statistical information. An additional plus for almanacs: Many students simply love "facts." They love lists and love accumulating a storehouse of detailed and unique information. And for these students, the almanac can be engaging as well as informative.

Students and teachers alike need to watch for important newspaper articles about both science and social studies topics because these can provide invaluable, up-to-date information for both subject areas. These articles appear in every major city's newspaper. Likewise, another valuable source for science information is the *Science Times,* a special weekly section of the *New York Times* that appears every Tuesday. This could be read by students in middle and high school, and it could also serve as a valuable teacher resource at all grade levels. (*Science Times* can be accessed online, via subscription, or with home and school delivery in all major cities of the United States.)

Informational videos and CDs are also valuable sources of information for students. The obvious advantage of these multimedia resources is that students can glean information through both auditory and visual means, an approach especially helpful for struggling readers and those with limited English.

For secondary students, diaries, government documents, letters, and other primary sources can serve to inform in a powerful and meaningful way. Archival photographs are also fascinating for students and communicate important information; they speak with compelling voices, usually more powerfully than any group of words an author can find.

CRITERIA FOR SELECTING INFORMATIONAL TEXTS

What does a good nonfiction text look like? Given the large numbers of books that are published, and to avoid wasting time or money on the many inaccurate or poorly written ones, it is crucial to adhere to the standards of excellence and criteria for appropriately evaluating trade books. Guidelines for selecting nonfiction books, periodicals, and electronic resources follow, as does a discussion of visual learning enhancements that are often part of nonfiction texts.

Selection Guidelines for Books

1. Is the information accurate? This is the most important consideration in the selection of nonfiction! There simply is no place for inaccuracy, whether in facts, concepts, theories, or illustrations.

2. Is the information well organized: clear and logical with topics arranged in a well-ordered manner? This order places information where it can be linked to other topics, enhances student understanding, and enables students to make connections to what they already know and understand.

3. Does the book design and appearance contribute to understanding and engagement? The size of the print needs to be appropriate for the reader's age. Illustrations need to be accurate in color, size, and proportion, and there needs to be a balance of "white space" on the page to avoid clutter and distraction. Illustrations or photographs need to match and support adjoining text, and when appropriate, captions and labels need to be clearly written, accurately describing and extending understanding. Also important is whether there are maps, charts, and graphs to visually communicate salient information.

4. Are the words and concepts in the book age-appropriate? Clearly, the choice of words and the extent of informational concepts vary from primary to intermediate grades and from middle school to high school.

5. Does the book have good reference aids (table of contents, glossary, index)? Are sections labeled with clear headings? Is there an author's note, and if so, does it provide helpful or important background information that promotes understanding?

6. What is the authority of the author? Is the author knowledgeable? Has the author established a reputation for outstanding research and unbiased, balanced treatment of subjects?

7. Does the writing demonstrate literary quality? Are words well chosen and sentences well written? Does the writing flow, giving the reader an accessible, smooth reading experience?

8. Is the information up to date? Where relevant, are new theories, discoveries, and ideas presented?

9. If the topic is controversial, does the writing avoid bias and stereotyping? Are multiple perspectives included?

10. If animals are the subject, does the book avoid anthropomorphism (giving human characteristics to non-human subjects)?

Visual Learning Enhancements

Some especially engaging, informational books show cutaway views of buildings or other structures, allowing readers literally to look inside and through the structure. Sometimes the images are also enhanced with transparent pages that allow readers to turn the page and literally remove the outside covering of a structure, as they look inside. And certainly giving a reader this inside look is a real plus both for promoting engagement and also for helping readers understand with greater clarity and depth. For some readers, seeing with their own eyes is much more informative than reading any number of words.

Some informational books make good use of sidebars and "fact boxes," where additional information is included and singled out for the reader. This graphic aid helps readers recognize interesting ideas and details and focus on what authors identified as important. The visual enhancements may be features for which some readers will need explicit instruction to navigate: Is it better to read the sidebars and fact boxes before or after reading other matter on the page? What about reading just the sidebars or fact boxes?

Likewise, as indicated in the criteria listing, visuals such as graphs, charts, and tables enhance informational books by presenting quantities of information in a visually clear format, showing relationships and comparative data. And the use of photographs and illustrations in informational books offers a great advantage, especially to English language learners, since illustrations, photographs, and other graphics communicate clearly across all languages.

Guidelines for Periodical and Electronic Resources

The same criteria for accuracy, organization, and literary quality apply to magazine articles as they do for books, and certainly, accuracy in news articles and websites should be demanded. The Internet actually poses serious concerns regarding accuracy of information, as well as presenting a great opportunity to teach students about reliability and validity of information. One suggestion would be to show students age 10 and above an accurate website alongside a very unprofessional or inaccurate website. Looking at them together can demonstrate first-hand why readers must select carefully, to assure accuracy and unbiased presentations. Students should also develop the habit of questioning the author or source: Who maintains the website? What are the interests or possible biases of the person or organization?

PUTTING THEORY INTO PRACTICE

Activity 1: Comparing Information and Checking for Accuracy

This activity is an effective way for middle and high school students to compare the accuracy and reliability of information in various books. It can be done in small groups, and it fosters collaboration on research.

The activity might also be adapted to accommodate an investigation of websites.

1. Collect several nonfiction books about the same subject or topic.
2. Place students, or allow them to self-select, into groups of three or four.
3. Ask each student to read each of the books in the collection (alternatively, each student can read one of the books and then the group can collaborate on completing the chart after all the books have been read).
4. Ask each student to divide a sheet of paper into columns (one column for each book).
5. As students read, they note important facts or concepts that are included in the book, under the column for that book.
6. After reading and noting important information for each book (or compiling the group's notes, if each person read one title), students star or check any facts or ideas that are inconsistent across the books.
7. Students research to validate or invalidate the facts that are in disagreement. Potential resources for the validation process include the Internet, encyclopedias, periodical literature, textbooks, other trade books, or known experts from the community.
8. Each group determines which facts are credible and valid and reports its conclusions and the resources that were consulted.

Activity 2: Analyzing Advantages and Disadvantages of Science Trade Books and Textbooks

Students can also compare the positive and negative features of information found in textbooks with those in trade books. This activity is especially effective in focusing students' attention on particular features of each print format (e.g., number and quality of the visuals, writing style and format, length and clarity of sentences, purposes, as well as students' personal preferences for a variety of features, formats, and writing styles).

1. Students select a topic in their science textbook that either interests or confuses them.
2. Then students each select an informational picture book or other trade book about the same topic or issue.

3. Students read the textbook selection and the trade book.
4. Using a T-diagram or double-entry draft (created by folding a notebook page in half, vertically), students identify the positive and negative features of each selection using these column headings: *Textbook Information and Features* and *Tradebook Information and Features*. Students should "read" and note the clarity and quantity of the visuals as well as the information that is communicated, their personal preferences for style and format, and any additional thoughts they have about the resources. Purpose, potential limitations, and any inaccuracies should also be noted.

AWARDS AND REVIEWS TO GUIDE BOOK SELECTION

Professional publications are an excellent source for reviews and recommendations of informational books. The American Library Association (ALA) regularly reviews both fiction and nonfiction. The National Science Teachers' Association (NSTA) also reviews books in each of their professional journals, as does the National Council for the Social Studies (NCSS). Each of these organizations also grants highly respected awards and honors to the books that meet their criteria and are considered to be the very best of the year.

Awards by Professional Organizations

The IRA gives book awards annually to authors whose first or second published work for children is deemed exceptional. The IRA awards for nonfiction are awarded in three categories, by age of the intended reader. The 2008 nonfiction recipients were: primary nonfiction: *Louis Sockalexis: Native American Baseball Pioneer* by Bill Wise (Lee & Low); intermediate nonfiction: *Tracking Trash: Flotsam, Jetsam, and the Science of Ocean Motion* by Loree Griffin Burns (Houghton Mifflin); and young adult nonfiction: *Tasting the Sky: A Palestinian Childhood* by Ibtisam Barakat (Farrar, Straus & Giroux).

The Orbis Pictus Award is presented by the National Council of Teachers of English (NCTE) for the one book considered by the selection committee to be the most outstanding nonfiction book created in the preceding year. The committee can also name up to five Honor Books each year. The criteria for selection include accuracy, organization of content, book design, and style. Award winners are expected to be not only excellent for reading, but also useful for classroom teaching in grades K–8. The committee also lists "Recommended Titles," which are additional books the committee recommends for instructional use. The 2008 Orbis Pictus Award winner was *MLK: The Journey of a King*, by Tonya Bolden (Abrams Books for Young Readers).

The Robert F. Sibert Informational Book Award was established in 2001 by ALA and is awarded annually to the author(s) and illustrator(s) of the "most distinguished informational book printed in English during the preceding year" (ALA). The award is named for Robert F. Sibert, long-time president of the Bound to Stay Bound Publishing Company, and it is supported by the company in his honor. The 2008 Sibert Medal was awarded to *The Wall: Growing Up Behind the Iron Curtain* by Peter Sis (Farrar/Frances Foster).

Notable Social Studies Trade Books for Young People K–12 is a list of outstanding trade books and represents a joint effort between NCSS and the Children's Book Council (CBC) in New York City. The annotated list has been published annually since 1972, and it is organized by broad subject categories within the social sciences. The list also identifies which thematic social science strand each book reflects, as described within the NCSS curriculum document, *Expectations of Excellence: Curriculum Standards for Social Science*. This annotated list includes both nonfiction and fiction titles in which rich social studies themes are developed and explored.

Outstanding Science Trade Books for Students K–12 is a list of the best science trade books published during the preceding year. The list is a joint endeavor between NSTA and the CBC and has been published every year since 1973. Rigorous standards are considered as the review committee selects the books deemed to be of the highest quality, both for accuracy and presentation. Reviewers also seek books that are engaging for readers, hoping to capture the interest and curiosity of readers. The list is then organized by subject category, so that educators can select books for instruction that match curricular needs. The annotated list also notes the National Science Content Standards that each book addresses and the recommended reader age/grade.

Professional Publication Reviews

Booklist is a review journal of ALA. Both in-house editors and contributing writers review more than 7,500 books per year, including children's fiction, nonfiction, reference books, and media. Librarians rely heavily on *Booklist* reviews before purchasing books, and other media. Classroom teachers can also make good use of these reviews to guide their instructional selections.

Book Links is another ALA publication that regularly reviews the latest recommended children's books. This publication differs from *Booklist* by providing articles tied to national standards and giving suggestions for ways to use trade books to engage young readers. *Book Links* articles also give suggestions for ways to use and link new titles with "tried and tested" favorites.

The *Horn Book Magazine* regularly reviews children's and young adult literature. Its companion, *The Horn Book Guide,* is published twice per year and reviews over 2,000 titles in each volume. The guide has five indices, including a subject index, which is indispensable for planning instruction and identifying recommended titles to gather for classroom use, so that students can select outstanding titles that interest them.

School Library Journal (SLJ) also regularly publishes reviews of children's and young adult literature. SLJ divides their reviews in age groupings: Preschool to grade 4; grade 5 to 8; high school and adult; and multimedia reviews. It is noteworthy that although SLJ groups reviews of high school titles with adult book reviews, there are many high school students and middle school students who will learn from and enjoy titles that fall within the "grade 5 and up" category.

SUMMARY

Printed language is a very special way of saving ideas! Teachers would be wise to harness the motivational and instructional power of engaging, informative nonfiction books, periodical literature, and other nonfiction resources. These amazing resources communicate compelling information, help readers consider and analyze varying perspectives of the real world, and give teachers the opportunity to teach reading strategies while students absorb immeasurable quantities of important information via accessible formats. Teachers can share their passion for these amazing resources as they include them in their instruction and encourage their use for enjoyable, independent reading.

RECOMMENDED ADDITIONAL READING

Kane, S. (2007). *Literacy and learning in the content areas* (2nd ed.). Scottsdale, AZ: Holcomb Hathaway.

Kane, S. (2008) *Integrated literature in the Content areas: Enhancing adolescent learning and literacy.* Scottsdale, AZ: Holcomb Hathaway.

REFERENCES

Marzano, R. J. (2004). *Building background knowledge for academic achievement*. Alexandria, VA: Association for Supervision and Curriculum Development.

Olness, R. (2007). *Using literature to enhance content area instruction: A guide for K–5 teachers*. Newark, DE: International Reading Association.

Wolpow, R., & Tonjes, M. (2005). *Integrated content literacy*. Dubuque, IA: Kendall/Hunt Publishing.

APPENDIX 12.1. Selected Bibliography of Nonfiction Books and Periodicals for Children and Youth

Instructional Materials with Strong Nonfiction Content

Delta Science Content Readers (differentiated text). Nashua, NH: Delta Education, 2008.

Delta Science Dictionary (grades 1–3; grades 3–5; grades 5–8). Nashua, NH: Delta Education, 2003.

Einstein's Who, What, and Where. Cambridge, MA: Educators Publishing Service, 2002.

Ervin, Jane. *Reading Comprehension in Varied Subject Matter.* Cambridge, MA: Educators Publishing Service, 2003.

Kovalevs, Kay & Alison Dewsbury. *Making Connections: Reading Comprehension Skills and Strategies.* Cambridge, MA: Educators Publishing Service, 2006.

National Geographic Explorer Series. Washington DC: National Geographic Society, 2007.

National Geographic Reading Expeditions. Washington, DC: National Geographic Society, 2005.

National Geographic Theme Sets (differentiated text). Washington, DC: National Geographic Society, 2005.

Seeds of Science, Roots of Reading. Nashua, NH: Delta Education, 2007.

Student Periodicals for Science and Social Studies

Cobblestone Publications, Peterborough, NH:
  Appleseeds (history and cultures for ages 7–10).
  Ask (arts and science: inventors, scientists, thinkers, and great ideas for ages 7–10).
  Caliope (world history for ages 9–14).
  Click (primary science for ages 4–7).
  Cobblestone (events, places, and people who have shaped U.S. history for ages 9+).
  Dig (archeology for ages 9–14).
  Faces (people, places, and world cultures for ages 9–14).

Footsteps (African American history and culture for ages 9–14).

Odyssey (science topics and hands-on experiments for ages 9+).

Kids Discover (science and social studies for ages 6+).

Owl (Canadian; features interesting facts and the science that explains how things work).

National Geographic for Kids (ages 10+).

National Geographic for Kids (ages 7–12).

National Wildlife Magazine (science, nature, and the environment for ages 12+).

New York Times (*Science Times*—special section, every Tuesday, ages 12+).

Ranger Rick (science and nature), published by National Wildlife Foundation for ages 7+).

Science News (biweekly); a Science Service Publication, Washington, DC (for ages 12+).

Science World (a Scholastic Publication, New York).

Your Big Backyard (science and nature), published by National Wildlife Foundation (for ages 3–7).

Selected Nonfiction Science Trade Books

Grades K–2

Aston, Dianna Hutts. *An Egg Is Quiet*. San Francisco: Chronicle Books, 2006.

Aston, Dianna Hutts. *A Seed Is Sleepy*. San Francisco: Chronicle Books, 2007.

Bishop, Nic. *Frogs*. New York: Scholastic Nonfiction, 2007.

Bishop, Nic. *Spiders*. New York: Scholastic Nonfiction, 2007.

Brooke, Samantha. *Coral Reefs in Danger*. New York: Penguin Group, 2008.

Bryant, Megan E. *Fireflies*. New York: Penguin Group, 2008.

Chancellor, Deborah. *The Kingfisher First Animal Picture Atlas*. Boston: Kingfisher, 2006.

Chrustowski, Rick *Turtle Crossing*. New York: Henry Holt & Company, 2006.

Clarke, Ginjer L. *Cheetah Cubs*. New York: Penguin Group, 2007.

Collard, Sneed B. *Teeth*. Watertown, MA: Charlesbridge, 2008.

Collard, Sneed B. *Wings*. Watertown, MA: Charlesbridge, 2008.

Davies, Nicola. *Ice Bear: In the Steps of the Polar Bear*. Cambridge, MA: Candlewick Press, 2008.

Davies, Nicola. *Surprising Sharks*. Cambridge, MA: Candlewick Press, 2008. Other titles include *Big Blue Whale* (2008) and *One Tiny Turtle* (2008).

Delta Science Readers Series. Nashua, NH: Delta Education, 2004. K–2 titles include *Butterflies and Moths, Classroom Plants, Force and Motion, From Seed to Plant, Properties, Sink or Float?,* and *Weather Watching.*

Dowson, Nick. *Tracks of a Panda*. Cambridge, MA: Candlewick Press, 2007.

Dunphy, Madeleine. *Here Is the Tropical Rain Forest*. Berkeley, CA: Web of Life Children's Books, 2006.

Dunphy, Madeleine. *Here Is the Wetland*. Berkeley, CA: Web of Life Children's Books, 2007.

Foss Science Stories for Grades K–2 Series. Nashua, NH: Delta Education, 2003. *Air and Weather, Animals Two by Two, Insects, Pebbles, Sand and Silt, Solids and Liquids,* and *Trees.*

French, Vivian. *Growing Frogs*. Cambridge, MA: Candlewick Press, 2008.

Ganer, Anita. *From Seed to Sunflower*. Chicago: Heinemann Library, 2006.

Ganer, Anita. *From Tadpole to Frog*. Chicago: Heinemann Library, 2006.

Gibbons, Gail. *Dinosaurs!* New York: Holiday House, 2008.

Gibbons, Gail. *The Planets*. New York: Holiday House, 2008.

Guiberson, Brenda Z. *Ice Bears*. New York: Henry Holt & Company, 2008.

Guibert, Francoise de. *Sing, Nightingale Sing! A Book and CD for Discovering the Birds of the World*. La Jolla, CA: Kane/Miller Book Publishers, 2006.

Haldane, Elizabeth. *Desert: Around the Clock with the Animals of the Desert*. New York: DK Publishing, 2006.

Hatkoff, Isabella, Craig Hatkoff, & Paula Kahumbu. *Owen & Mzee: The Language of Friendship*. New York: Scholastic Press, 2007.

Havard, Christian. *The Wolf: Night Howler*. Watertown, MA: Charlesbridge Publishing, 2006.

Jenkins, Martin. *Ape*. Cambridge, MA: Candlewick Press, 2007.

Malone, Peter. *Close to the Wind: The Beaufort Scale*. New York: Penguin Young Readers Group, 2007.

O'Brien, Patrick. *Sabertooth*. New York: Henry Holt & Company, 2008.

O'Neill, Michael Patrick. *Let's Explore Sea Turtles*. Palm Beach Gardens, FL: Batfish Books, 2005.

Posada, Mia. *Guess What Is Growing Inside This Egg*. Minneapolis: Lerner Publishing Group, 2007.

Sidman, Joyce. *Butterfly Eyes and Other Secrets of the Meadow*. Boston: Houghton Mifflin, 2006.

Sill, Cathryn. *About Habitats: Deserts*. Atlanta, GA: Peachtree Publishers, 2007.

Souza, Dorothy M. *Look What Tails Can Do*. Minneapolis: Lerner Publications, 2007. Other titles include *Look What Feet Can Do* and *Look What Mouths Can Do*.

Stewart, Melissa. *A Place for Butterflies*. Atlanta, GA: Peachtree Publishers, 2006.

Grades 3–5

Animals: A Visual Encyclopedia. New York: DK Publishing, 2008.

Arnold, Caroline. *Super Swimmers: Whales, Dolphins, and Other Mammals of the Sea*. Watertown, MA: Charlesbridge, 2006.

Arnold, Nick & Tony De Saulles. *The Stunning Science of Everything: Science with the Squishy Bits Left In!* New York: Scholastic, 2005.

Bingham, Caroline. *First Space Encyclopedia*. New York: DK Publishing, 2008.

Bradley, Timothy J. *Paleo Sharks: Survival of the Strangest*. San Francisco: Chronicle Books, 2007.

Campbell, Janis & Cathy Collison. *G is for Galaxy: An Out of This World Alphabet*. Chelsea, MI: Sleeping Bear Press, 2005.

Cherry, Lynne & Gary Braasch. *How We Know What We Know about Our Changing Climate: Scientists and Kids Explore Global Warming*. Nevada City, CA: Dawn Publications, 2008.

Collins, Andrew. *Violent Weather: Thunderstorms, Tornadoes, and Hurricanes*. Washington, DC: National Geographic Society, 2006.

Costain, Meredith. *Into the Earth: The Story of Caves.* Washington, DC: National Geographic Society, 2006.

Delta Science Readers Series. Nashua, NH: Delta Education, 2004. Titles include *Astronomy, Electrical Circuits, Electromagnetism, Food Chains and Webs, Matter and Change, Oceans, Plant and Animal Life Cycles, Rocks and Minerals, Simple Machines, Sound, Water Cycle, Weather Forecasting,* and *Weather Instruments.*

Demarest, Chris L. *Hurricane Hunters! Riders on the Storm.* New York: Simon & Schuster Children's Publishing, 2006.

DK Encyclopedia of Science. New York: DK Publishing, 2006.

Dorling Kindersley Animal Encyclopedia. New York: DK Publishing, 2005.

Ehrlich, Amy. *Rachel: The Story of Rachel Carson.* Orlando, FL: Harcourt, 2008.

Fortey, Jacqueline. *Great Scientists: Eyewitness Books.* New York: DK Publishing, 2007.

Foss Science Stories for Grades 3–6 Series. Nashua, NH: Delta Education, 2003. Titles include *Levers and Pulleys, Magnetism and Electricity, Measurement, Mixtures and Solutions, Variables,* and *Water.*

Fradin, Dennis Brindell. *With a Little Luck: Surprising Stories of Amazing Discoveries.* New York: Dutton Children's Books, 2006.

Fradin, Judy & Dennis. *Hurricanes: Witness to Disaster.* Washington, DC: National Geographic Society, 2007.

Glover, David. *Levers.* Chicago: Heinemann Library, 2006. Other titles include *Screws; Springs; Wheels and Cranks;* and *Levers.*

Goldish, Meish. *Deadly Praying Mantises.* New York: Bearport Publishing, 2008.

Gunzi, Christianne. *The Best Book of Snakes.* Boston: Kingfisher Books, 2006.

Halpern, Monica. *All about Light.* Washington, DC: National Geographic Society, 2006.

Halpern, Monica. *All about Tide Pools.* Washington, DC: National Geographic Society, 2007. Other titles include *Rivers of Fire: The Story of Volcanoes* and *Venus Flytraps, Bladderworts, and Other Amazing Plants.*

Hammond, Richard. *Can You Feel the Force?* New York: DK Publishing, 2006.

Hannemann, Monika, Patricia Hulse, Brian Johnson, Barbara Kurland, & Tracey Patterson. *Gardening with Children.* Brooklyn, NY: Brooklyn Botanic Garden, 2007.

Harris, Caroline. *I Wonder Why Whales Sing and Other Questions about Sea Life.* Boston: Kingfisher, 2006.

Hilliard, Richard. *Lucky 13: Survival in Space.* Honesdale, PA: Boyds Mills Press, 2008.

Hillman, Ben. *How Big Is It?: A Big Book All about Bigness.* New York: Scholastic Nonfiction, 2007.

Hirschi, Ron. *Lions, Tigers, and Bears: Why Are Big Predators So Rare?* Honesdale, PA: Boyds Mills Press, 2007.

Hirschi, Ron. *Our Three Bears.* Honesdale, PA: Boyds Mills Press, 2008.

Hynes, Margaret. *Rocks and Fossils.* Boston: Kingfisher, 2006.

Inskipp, Carol. *Killer Whale.* Chicago: Heinemann Library, 2005.

Johnson, Delores. *Onward: A Photobiography of African American Polar Explorer*

Matthew Henson. Washington, DC: National Geographic Children's Books, 2006.

Johnson, Jinny. *Rain Forest*. Boston: Kingfisher, 2006.

Kelly, Irene. *It's a Butterfly's Life*. New York: Holiday House, 2007.

Koscielniak, Bruce. *Looking at Glass through the Ages*. Boston: Houghton Mifflin, 2006.

Krull, Kathleen. *Isaac Newton* (Giants of Science Series). New York: Viking Books, 2006.

Krull, Kathleen. *Marie Curie* (Giants of Science Series). New York: Penguin Young Readers Group, 2007. Other titles include *Leonardo Da Vinci* and *Sigmund Freud*.

Laidlaw, Rob. *Wild Animals in Captivity*. Brighton, MA: Fitzhenry & Whiteside, 2007.

Lang, Aubrey. *Nature Babies Series*. Brighton, MA.: Fitzhenry & Whiteside, 2004–2008. Titles include *Baby Elephant, Baby Fox, Baby Grizzly, Baby Ground Squirrel, Baby Koala, Baby Lion, Baby Mountain Sheep, Baby Owl, Baby Penguin, Baby Porcupine, Baby Sea Turtle, Baby Seal, Baby Sloth*, and *The Adventures of Baby Bear*.

Leedy, Loreen & Andrew Schuerger. *Messages from Mars*. New York: Holiday House, 2006.

Mack, Lorrie. *Arctic and Antarctic*. New York: DK Publishing, 2006.

Macken, JoAnn Early. *Flip, Float, Fly: Seeds on the Move*. New York: Holiday House, 2008.

Malam, John & John Woodward. *Dinosaur Atlas: An Amazing Journey through a Lost World*. New York: DK Publishing, 2006.

Mallory, Kenneth. *Diving to a Deep-Sea Volcano*. Boston: Houghton Mifflin, 2006.

Manning, Mick & Brita Granstrom. *Under Your Skin: Your Amazing Body*. Morton Grove, IL: Albert Whitman & Company, 2007.

Markle, Sandra. *Great White Sharks* (Animal Predators Series). Minneapolis: Lerner Publications, 2004.

Markle, Sandra. *Killer Whales* (Animal Predators Series). Minneapolis: Lerner Publications, 2004. Other titles include *Lions; Octopuses; Owls; Polar Bears; Slippery, Slimy Baby Frogs; Tough, Toothy Baby Sharks*; and *Wolverines*.

Martin, Sam. *The Curious Boy's Book of Exploration*. New York: Razorbill (Penguin), 2007.

Mason, Adrienne. *Skunks*. Tonawanda, NY: Kids Can Press, 2006.

Mason, Paul. *Creature Camouflage*. Chicago: Heinemann-Raintree, 2008. Other titles include *Animal Spies; Nature's Armor and Defenses;* and *Nature's Tricks*.

McMillan, Beverly & John A. Musick. *Oceans*. New York: Simon & Schuster Books for Young Readers, 2007.

Michaels, Pat. *W Is for Wind: A Weather Alphabet*. Chelsea, MI: Sleeping Bear Press, 2005.

Miller, Edward. *The Monster Health Book: A Guide to Eating Healthy, Being Active and Feeling Great for Monsters and Kids*. New York: Holiday House, 2006.

Morrison, Marianne. *Mysteries of the Sea: How Divers Explore the Ocean Depths.* Washington, DC: National Geographic Society, 2006.

Murawski, Darlyne A. *Face to Face with Caterpillars.* Washington, DC: National Geographic Society, 2007.

Murrie, Steve & Matthew Murrie. *Every Minute on Earth: Fun Facts That Happen Every 60 Seconds.* New York: Scholastic Reference, 2007.

My Food Pyramid. New York: DK Publishing, 2007.

Nagda, Ann Whitehead. *Panda Math: Learning about Subtraction from Hua Mei and Mei Shing.* New York: Henry Holt & Company, 2005. Other titles include *Chimp Math: Learning about Time from a Baby Chimpanzee; Polar Bear Math: Learning about Fractions from Klondike and Snow;* and *Tiger Math: Learning to Graph from a Baby Tiger.*

Nagda, Ann Whitehead. *Cheetah Math: Learning about Division from Baby Cheetahs.* New York: Henry Holt & Company, 2007.

Nicklin, Flip & Linda Nicklin. *Face to Face with Dolphins.* Washington, DC: National Geographic Society, 2007.

O'Sullivan, Robyn. *Your 206 Bones, 32 Teeth, and Other Body Math.* Washington, DC: National Geographic Society, 2006.

Parker, Steve. *The Science of Forces.* Chicago: Heinemann Library, 2005. Other titles include *Microlife That Lives in Soil; Microlife That Makes Us Ill; Microlife That Rots Things; The Science of Air; The Science of Electricity and Magnetism; The Science of Light; The Science of Sound;* and *The Science of Water.*

Parker, Steve. *Microlife That Helps Us* (The Amazing World of Microlife Series). Chicago: Raintree, 2006.

Platt, Richard. *Moon Landing.* Cambridge, MA: Candlewick Press, 2008.

Pratt-Serafini, Kristin Joy & Rachel Crandell. *The Forever Forest: Kids Save a Tropical Treasure.* Nevada City, CA: Dawn Publications, 2008.

Rosing, Norbert & Elizabeth Carney. *Face to Face with Polar Bears.* Washington, DC: National Geographic Society, 2007.

Rushby, Pamela. *Discovering SuperCroc.* Washington, DC: National Geographic Society, 2007.

Schwartz, David M., & Yael Schy. *Where in the Wild?: Camouflaged Creatures Concealed ... and Revealed.* Berkeley, CA: Tricycle Press, 2007.

Schwarz, Renee. *Wind Chimes and Whirligigs.* Tonawanda, NY: Kids Can Press, 2007.

Science Detectives: How Scientists Solved Six Real Life Mysteries. Tonawanda, NY: Kids Can Press, 2006.

Sereno, Paul & Natalie Lunis. *SuperCroc: Paul Sereno's Dinosaur Eater.* New York: Bearport Publishing, 2007.

Sheldon, David. *Barnum Brown: Dinosaur Hunter.* New York: Walker Books, 2006.

Simon, Seymour. *Giant Snakes.* San Francisco: Chronicle Books, 2006.

Simon, Seymour. *Penguins.* New York: HarperCollins, 2007. Other titles include *Horses* and *Lungs: Your Respiratory System.*

Singer, Marilyn. *Eggs.* New York: Holiday House, 2008.

Siy, Alexandra. *Sneeze.* Watertown, MA: Charlesbridge, 2007.

Smith, Marie & Roland. *W Is for Waves: An Ocean Alphabet.* Chelsea, MI: Sleeping Bear Press, 2008.

Smith, Penny & Lorrie Mack. *See How It's Made.* New York: DK Publishing, 2007.

Sobol, Richard. *Breakfast in the Rain Forest: A Visit with Mountain Gorillas.* Cambridge, MA: Candlewick Press, 2008.

Spilsbury, Richard. *Great White Shark.* Chicago: Heinemann Library, 2004.

Star, Fleur. *Rain Forest: Around the Clock with the Animals of the Jungle.* New York: DK Publishing, 2006.

Stone, Lynn M. *Box Turtles.* Minneapolis, MN: Lerner Publishing Group, 2007.

Strauss, Rochelle. *One Well: The Story of Water on Earth.* Tonawanda, NY: Kids Can Press, 2007.

Swinburne, Stephen R. *Saving Manatees.* Honesdale, PA: Boyds Mills Press, 2006.

Thimmesh, Catherine. *Team Moon: How 400,000 People Landed Apollo 11 on the Moon.* New York: Houghton Mifflin, 2006.

Todd, Traci N. *A is for Astronaut: Exploring Space from A to Z.* San Francisco: Chronicle Books, 2006.

Walker, Richard. *Nature Ranger.* New York: DK Publishing, 2006.

Weaver, Jeanne. *Wetlands Journey.* Washington, DC: National Geographic Society, 2006.

Weber, Belinda. *The Best Book of Nightime Animals.* Boston: Kingfisher, 2006.

Whiting, Sue. *All about Ants.* Washington, DC: National Geographic Society, 2006.

Williams, Judith. *The Discovery and Mystery of a Dinosaur Named Jane.* Berkeley Heights, NJ: Enslow Publishers, 2007.

Winston, Robert. *It's Elementary! How Chemistry Rocks Our World.* New York: DK Publishing, 2007.

Woodward, John. *Weather Watcher.* New York: DK Publishing, 2006.

Wyckoff, Edwin Brit. *The Teen Who Invented Television: Philo T. Farnsworth and His Awesome Invention.* Berkeley Heights, NJ: Enslow Publishers, 2007.

Middle School and High School

Arnold, Caroline. *Giant Sea Reptiles of the Dinosaur Age.* New York: Clarion Books, 2007.

Baldwin, Carol. *Chemical Reactions.* Chicago: Heinemann-Raintree (FreeStyle in 2004 and FreeStyle Express in 2006).

Baldwin, Carol. *States of Matter.* Chicago: Heinemann-Raintree (FreeStyle in 2004 and FreeStyle Express in 2006). Other titles include *Metals, Mixtures, Compounds and Solutions,* and *Nonmetals.*

Burnie, David. *e.guides: Plant.* New York: DK Publishing, 2006.

Collier, Michael. *Over the Mountains: An Aerial View of Geology.* New York: Mikaya Press, 2007.

Denega, Danielle. *Gut-Eating Bugs: Maggots Reveal the Time of Death!* New York: Franklin Watts, 2007.

Dingus, Lowell, Rodolfo Coria, & Luis M. Chiappe. *Dinosaur Eggs Discovered! Unscrambling the Clues.* Minneapolis: Lerner Publishing Group, 2007.

Faulkner, Rebbecca. *Fossils* (Geology Rocks! Series). Chicago: Heinemann-Raintree (FreeStyle in 2007 and FreeStyle Express in 2008).

Faulkner, Rebbecca. *Metamorphic Rock* (Geology Rocks! Series). Chicago: Heine-mann-Raintree (FreeStyle in 2007 and FreeStyle Express in 2008). Other titles include *Crystals; Igneous Rock; Minerals; Sedimentary Rock;* and *Soil.*

Fleisher, Paul. *Parasites: Latching On to a Free Lunch.* Minneapolis: Lerner Publishing, 2006.

Glass, Susan. *Analyze This!: Understanding the Scientific Method* (How to Be a Scientist Series). Chicago: Heinemann Library, 2007. Other titles include *Prove It: The Scientific Method in Action* and *Watch Out: Science Tools and Safety.*

Goldsmith, Connie. *Influenza: The Next Pandemic?* Minneapolis: Lerner Publishing Group, 2006.

Goldsmith, Connie. *Superbugs Strike Back: When Antibiotics Fail.* Minneapolis: Lerner Publishing Group, 2007.

Gordon, Sherri Mabry. *Peanut Butter, Milk, and Other Deadly Threats: What You Should Know about Food Allergies.* Berkeley Heights, NJ: Enslow Publishers, 2006.

Grady, Denise. *Deadly Invaders: Virus Outbreaks around the World, From Marburg Fever to Avian Flue.* New York: Kingfisher Books, 2006.

Hakim, Joy. *Einstein Adds a New Dimension.* Washington, DC: Smithsonian Books, 2007.

Holtz, Thomas R. *Dinosaurs: The Most Complete, Up-to-Date Encyclopedia for Dinosaur Lovers of All Ages.* New York: Random House Books for Young Readers, 2007.

Jerome, Kate Boehm. *Atomic Universe: The Quest to Discover Radioactivity.* Washington, DC: National Geographic Children's Books, 2006.

Map: Satellite. New York: DK Publishing, 2007.

McClafferty, Carla Killough. *Something Out of Nothing: Marie Curie and Radium.* New York: Farrar, Straus & Giroux Books for Young Readers, 2006.

Miller, Ron. *Rockets.* Minneapolis: Twenty-First Century Books (Lerner), 2007.

Montgomery, Sy. *Quest for the Tree Kangaroo: An Expedition to the Cloud Forest of New Guinea.* Boston: Houghton Mifflin, 2006.

Nardo, Don. *Tycho Brahe: Pioneer of Astronomy.* Minneapolis: Compass Point Books, 2007.

Oxlade, Chris. *Storm Warning: Tornadoes.* Chicago: Heinemann-Raintree (Free-Style in 2004 and FreeStyle Express in 2006). Other titles include *Violent Skies: Hurricanes.*

Phelan, Glen. *Double Helix: The Quest to Uncover the Structure of DNA.* Washington, DC: National Geographic Children's Books, 2006.

Phelan, Glen. *Killing Germs, Saving Lives: The Quest for the First Vaccines.* Washington, DC: National Geographic Children's Books, 2006.

Revkin, Andrew C. *The North Pole Was Here: Puzzles and Perils at the Top of the World.* New York: Kingfisher Books, 2006.

Roberts, David & Jeremy Leslie. *Pick Me Up: Stuff You Need to Know.* New York: DK Publishing, 2006.

Saunders, Nigel & Steven Chapman. *Fossil Fuel.* Chicago: Heinemann-Raintree (FreeStyle in 2004 and FreeStyle Express in 2006).

Saunders, Nigel & Steven Chapman. *Renewable Energy.* Chicago: Heinemann-Raintree (FreeStyle in 2004 and FreeStyle Express in 2006).

Silverstein, Alvin, Virginia Silverstein, & Laura Silverstein Nunn. *The Breast Cancer Update*. Berkeley Heights, NJ: Enslow Publishers, 2007.

Silverstein, Alvin, Virginia Silverstein, & Laura Silverstein Nunn. *Adaptation*. Minneapolis: Lerner Publishing Group, 2007.

Sloan, Christopher. *How Dinosaurs Took Flight: The Fossils, the Science, What We Think We Know, and Mysteries Yet Unsolved*. Washington, DC: National Geographic Children's Books, 2005.

Solway, Andrew. *Poison Frogs and Other Amphibians*. Chicago: Heinemann Library, 2007.

Solway, Andrew. *Sharks and Other Fish* (Adapted for Success Series). Chicago: Heinemann Library, 2007. Other titles include *Eagles and Other Birds; Lions and Other Mammals; Snakes and Other Reptiles;* and *Spiders and Other Invertebrates*.

Steele, Philip. *Isaac Newton: The Scientist Who Changed Everything*. Washington, DC: National Geographic Society, 2007.

Steele, Philip. *Marie Curie: The Woman Who Changed the Course of Science*. Washington, DC: National Geographic Children's Books, 2006.

Stefoff, Rebecca. *Great Inventions: Microscopes and Telescopes*. Tarrytown, NY: Marshall Cavendish Benchmark, 2007.

Stott, Carole. *The World of Astronomy*. Boston: Kingfisher, 2006.

Sullivan, Edward T. *The Ultimate Weapon: The Race to Develop the Atomic Bomb*. New York: Holiday House, 2007.

Tilden, Thomasine E. Lewis. *Belly-Busting Worm Invasions! Parasites That Love Your Insides*. New York: Franklin Watts, 2007.

Townsend, John. *Incredible Amphibians*. Chicago: Raintree, 2006.

Townsend, John. *Pox, Pus + Plague: A History of Disease and Infection* (A Painful History of Medicine Series). Chicago: Heinemann-Raintree, 2006. Other titles include *Bedpans, Blood + Bandages; Incredible Arachnids; Incredible Birds; Incredible Fish; Incredible Insects; Incredible Mammals; Incredible Mollusks; Incredible Reptiles; Pills, Powders + Potions;* and *Scalpels, Stitches + Scars*.

Walker, Richard. *How the Incredible Human Body Works by the Brainwaves*. New York: DK Publishing, 2007.

Winner, Cherie. *Circulating Life: Blood Transfusion from Ancient Superstition to Modern Medicine*. Minneapolis: Lerner Publishing Group, 2007.

Zoehfeld, Kathleen Weidner. *Wildlives: 100 Years of the People and Animals of the Bronx Zoo*. New York: Knopf, 2006.

Selected Nonfiction Social Studies Trade Books

Grades K–2

Crowther, Robert. *Ships: A Pop-Up Book*. Cambridge, MA: Candlewick Press, 2008.

Giovanni, Nikki. *Rosa*. New York: Henry Holt & Company, 2005.

Our World: A Child's First Picture Atlas. Washington, DC: National Geographic Society, 2006.

Rotner, Shelley & Anne Love Woodhul. *Every Season*. New Milford, CT: Roaring Brook Press, 2006.

Stauffacher, Sue. *Nothing But Trouble: The Story of Althea Gibson*. New York: Random House Children's Books, 2008.

Grades 3–5

Adler, David A. *Enemies of Slavery*. New York: Holiday House, 2004. Other titles include *Heroes of the Revolution; Hero of the Holocaust: The Story of Janusz Korczak and His Children;* Dr. Martin Luther King, Jr., and B. Franklin, Printer.

Adler, David A. *Heroes for Civil Rights*. New York: Holiday House, 2007.

Arnold, Caroline & Madeleine Comora. *Taj Mahal*. Minneapolis: Carolrhoda, 2007.

Aronson, Marc & John W. Glenn. *The World Made New: Why the Age of Exploration Happened and How It Changed the World*. Washington, DC: National Geographic Society, 2008.

Barretta, Gene. *Now and Ben: The Modern Inventions of Benjamin Franklin*. New York: Henry Holt & Company, 2006.

Bausum, Ann. *Freedom Riders: John Lewis and Jim Zwerg on the Front Lines of the Civil Rights Movement*. Washington, DC: National Geographic Children's Books, 2006.

Bausum, Ann. *Our Country's First Ladies*. Washington, DC: National Geographic Society, 2008. Other titles include *With Courage and Cloth: Winning the Fight for a Woman's Right to Vote*.

Buckley, Susan & Elspeth Leacock. *Journeys for Freedom: A New Look at America's Story*. Boston: Houghton Mifflin, 2006.

Buckley, Susan & Elspeth Leacock. *Kids Make History: A New Look at America's Story*. Boston: Houghton Mifflin, 2006.

Buller, Laura. *A Faith Like Mine: A Celebration of the World's Religions—Seen through the Eyes of Children*. New York: DK Publishing, 2005.

Chin-Lee, Cynthia. *Amelia to Zora: Twenty-Six Women Who Changed the World*. Watertown, MA: Charlesbridge Publishing, 2005.

Chin-Lee, Cynthia. *Akira to Zoltan: Twenty-Six Men Who Changed the World*. Watertown, MA: Charlesbridge Publishing, 2006.

Cline-Ransome, Lesa. *Helen Keller: The World in Her Heart*. New York: Harper-Collins Publishers, 2008.

Cooper, Michael L. *Hero of the High Seas: John Paul Jones and the American Revolution*. Washington, DC: National Geographic Society, 2006.

Crane, Carol. *D Is for Dancing Dragon: A China Alphabet*. Chelsea, MI: Sleeping Bear Press, 2006.

Delano, Marfe Ferguson. *American Heroes*. Washington, DC: National Geographic Society, 2005.

Delano, Marfe Ferguson. *Genius: A Photobiography of Albert Einstein*. Washington, DC: National Geographic Society, 2005.

Demi. *Mother Teresa*. New York: Simon & Schuster Children's Publishing, 2005.

Denenberg, Dennis. *50 American Heroes Every Kid Should Meet*. Minneapolis: First Avenue Editions, 2006.

Dillon, Leo & Diane. *Jazz on a Saturday Night*. New York: Blue Sky Press, 2007.

Edelman, Marian Wright. *I Can Make a Difference: A Treasury to Inspire Our Children*. New York: HarperCollins Publishers, 2005.

Fleming, Candace. *Our Eleanor: A Scrapbook Look at Eleanor Roosevelt's Remarkable Life*. New York: Atheneum Books for Young Readers, 2005.

Fleming, Thomas. *Everybody's Revolution: A New Look at the People Who Won America's Freedom*. New York: Scholastic, 2006.

Freedman, Russell. *Children of the Great Depression*. New York: Clarion Books, 2005.

Freedman, Russell. *Washington at Valley Forge*. New York: Holiday House, 2008. Other titles include *Give Me Liberty: The Story of the Declaration of Independence* and *In Defense of Liberty: The Story of America's Bill of Rights*.

Gill, Shelley. *Alaska*. Watertown, MA: Charlesbridge Publishing, 2007.

Greenwood, Marie. *Explorer*. New York: DK Publishing, 2006.

Grodin, Elissa. *D Is for Democracy: A Citizen's Alphabet*. Chelsea, MI: Sleeping Bear Press, 2004.

Grodin, Elissa. *Everyone Counts: A Citizen's Number Book*. Chelsea, MI: Sleeping Bear Press, 2006.

Gruber, Beth. *Mexico*. Washington, DC: National Geographic Society, 2006.

Harness, Cheryl. *The Adventurous Life of Myles Standish and the Amazing-But-True Survival Story of Plymouth Colony*. Washington, DC: National Geographic Society, 2006.

Heiligman, Deborah. *Holidays around the World Series*. Washington, DC: National Geographic Children's Books, 2006. Other titles include *Celebrate Diwali with Sweets, Lights, and Fireworks; Celebrate Hanukkah with Light, Latkes, and Dreidels; Celebrate Ramadan and Eid Al-Fitr with Praying, Fasting, and Charity*; and *Celebrate Thanksgiving with Turkey, Family, and Counting Blessings*.

Heuer, Karsten. *Being Caribou: Five Months on Foot with a Caribou Herd*. New York: Bloomsbury/Walker, 2007.

Johnson, Tony. *P Is for Piñata: A Mexico Alphabet*. Chelsea, MI: Sleeping Bear Press, 2008.

Knox, Barbara. *Forbidden City: China's Imperial Palace*. New York: Bearport Publishing, 2006.

Krull, Kathleen. *Houdini: World's Greatest Mystery Man and Escape King*. New York: Walker & Company, 2005. Other titles include *Lives of the Athletes* and *Lives of Extraordinary Women*.

Layne, Steven L. *Over Land and Sea: A Story of International Adoption*. Gretna, LA: Pelican Publishing, 2004.

Lourie, Peter. *Hidden World of the Aztec*. Honesdale, PA: Boyds Mills Press, 2006.

Maestro, Betsy. *Liberty or Death: The American Revolution 1763–1783.* New York: HarperCollins Publishers, 2005.

Marrin, Albert. *Saving the Buffalo.* New York: Scholastic, 2006.

Miller, Debbie S. *Big Alaska: Journey across America's Most Amazing State.* New York: Walker Books for Young Readers, 2006.

Miller, Lee. *Roanoke: The Mystery of the Lost Colony.* New York: Scholastic, 2007.

Miller, Millie. *Our World: A Country-by-Country Guide.* New York: Scholastic, 2006.

Minor, Wendell. *The Spirit of 1776 from A to Z.* New York: G. P. Putnam's & Sons, 2006.

National Children's Book and Literacy Alliance. *Our White House: Looking In, Looking Out.* Cambridge, MA: Candlewick Press, 2008.

Ray, Deborah Kogan. *Down the Colorado: John Wesley Powell, the One-Armed Explorer.* New York: Farrar, Straus & Giroux, 2008.

Robertson, James I. *Robert E. Lee: Virginian Soldier, American Citizen.* New York: Atheneum Books for Young Readers, 2005.

Ruurs, Margaret. *My Librarian Is a Camel: How Books Are Brought to Children around the World.* Honesdale, PA: Honesdale Press, 2005.

Sanders, Nancy I. *D Is for Drinking Gourd: An African American Alphabet.* Chelsea, MI: Sleeping Bear Press, 2007.

Schonberg, Marcia. *I Is for Idea: An Inventions Alphabet.* Chelsea, MI: Sleeping Bear Press, 2005.

Scillian, Devin. *P Is for Passport: A World Alphabet.* Chelsea, MI: Sleeping Bear Press, 2003.

Scillian, Devin. *H Is for Honor: A Military Family Alphabet.* Chelsea, MI: Sleeping Bear Press, 2006.

Shapiro, William E. *The Student Encyclopedia of the United States.* Boston: Kingfisher, 2005.

Shoulders, Debbie & Michael. *D Is for Drum: A Native American Alphabet.* Chelsea, MI: Sleeping Bear Press, 2006.

Shoveller, Herb. *Ryan and Jimmy: And the Well in Africa that Brought Them Together.* Tonawanda, NY: Kids Can Press, 2006.

Smith, Marie & Roland Smith. *N Is for Our Nation's Capital: A Washington, DC Alphabet.* Chelsea, MI: Sleeping Bear Press, 2005.

Smith, Penny & Zahavit Shalev. *A School Like Mine: A Unique Celebration of Schools around the World.* New York: DK Publishing and UNICEF, 2008.

St. George, Judith. *Take the Lead, George Washington.* New York: Philomel, 2005.

Streissguth, Tom. *Jesse Owens.* Minneapolis: Lerner Publications, 2005.

Sutcliffe, Jane. *John F. Kennedy.* Minneapolis: Lerner Publications, 2005.

Talbott, Hudson. *United Tweets of America.* New York: G. P. Putnam's & Sons, 2008.

The Nystrom Desk Atlas. Chicago: Nystrom, 2005.

Thompson, Gare. *Serengeti Journey: On Safari in Africa.* Washington, DC: National Geographic Society, 2006.

Time for Kids Biographies Series. New York: HarperCollins Publishers, 2005. Titles include *Benjamin Franklin: A Man of Many Talents*; *George Washington*; *Jimmy Doolittle: American Hero*; and *Thomas Edison: A Brilliant Inventor.*

Vieira, Linda. *The Mighty Mississippi: The Life and Times of America's Greatest River.* New York: Walker & Company, 2005.

Waryncia, Lou & Ken Sheldon. *If I Were a Kid in Ancient China.* Peterborough, NH: Cricket Books, 2006.

Waryncia, Lou & Sarah Elder Hale. '*Young Heroes of the North and South.* Peterborough, NH: Cobblestone Publishing, 2005.

Weatherford, Carole Boston. *A Negro League Scrapbook.* Honesdale, PA: Boyds Mills Press, 2005.

Wilkinson, Philip. *Gandhi: The Young Protester Who Founded a Nation.* Washington, DC: National Geographic Society, 2005.

Wilkinson, Philip. *The World of Exploration.* Boston: Kingfisher, 2006.

Williams, Marcia. *Archie's War: My Scrapbook of the First World War, 1914–1918.* Somerville, MA: Candlewick Press, 2008.

Yoo, Paula. *Sixteen Years in Sixteen Seconds: The Sammy Lee Story.* New York: Lee & Low Books, 2005.

Zalben, Jane Breskin. *Paths to Peace: People Who Changed the World.* New York: Penguin Books for Young Readers, 2006.

Middle School and High School

Adams, Simon. *The Kingfisher Atlas of the Ancient World.* Boston: Kingfisher, 2006.

Adler, David A. *President George Washington.* New York: Holiday House, 2005.

Aronson, Marc. *The Real Revolution: The Global Story of American Independence.* New York: Clarion Books, 2005.

Aronson, Marc. *Race: A History Beyond Black and White.* New York: Atheneum Books for Young Children, 2007.

Barnes, Trevor. World Faiths Series. Boston: Kingfisher, 2005. Titles include *Christianity; Hinduism and Other Eastern Religions; Islam;* and *Judaism.*

Beller, Susan Provost. *Battling in the Pacific: Soldiering in World War II.* Minneapolis: Twenty-First Century Books, 2008.

Blair, Margaret Whitman. *The Roaring 20: The First Cross-Country Air Race for Women.* Washington, DC: National Geographic Society, 2006.

Brown, Laaren & Lenny Hort. *Nelson Mandela: A Photographic Story of a Life* (DK Biography Series). New York: DK Publishing, 2006.

Bruchac, Joseph. *Jim Thorpe: Original All-American.* New York: Dial Books, 2006.

Caputo, Philip. *10,000 Days of Thunder: A History of the Vietnam War.* New York: Atheneum Books for Young Readers, 2005.

Colman, Penny. *Adventurous Women: Eight True Stories about Women Who Made a Difference.* New York: Henry Holt Books for Young Readers, 2006.

Crow, Joseph Medicine. *Counting Coup: Becoming a Crow Chief on the Reserva-*

tion and Beyond. Washington, DC: National Geographic Children's Books, 2006.

DeSaix, Deborah Durland & Karen Gray Ruelle. *Hidden on the Mountain: Stories of Children Sheltered from the Nazis in Le Chambon*. New York: Holiday House, 2007.

Fradin, Dennis Brindell. *The Founders: The 39 Stories Behind the U.S. Constitution*. New York: Walker & Company, 2005.

Fradin, Dennis Brindell & Judith Bloom Fradin. *Jane Addams: Champion of Democracy*. New York: Clarion Books, 2006. Other titles include *Let It Begin Here: Lexington and Concord*.

Freedman, Russell. *Freedom Walkers: The Story of the Montgomery Bus Boycott*. New York: Clarion Books, 2006.

Freedman, Russell. *Who Was First? Discovering the Americas*. New York: Clarion Books, 2008. Other titles include *The Adventures of Marco Polo* and *The Voice That Challenged a Nation*.

Giblin, James Cross. *Good Brother Bad Brother: The Story of Edwin Booth and John Wilkes Booth*. New York: Clarion Books, 2005.

Giovanni, Nikki. *On My Journey Now: Looking at African American History through the Spirituals*. Cambride, MA: Candlewick Press, 2007.

Gourley, Catherine. *War, Women, and the News: How Female Journalists Won the Battle to Cover World War II*. New York: Atheneum Books for Young Readers, 2007.

Greenwood, Barbara. *Factory Girl*. Tonawanda, NY: Kids Can Press, 2007.

Halpern, Monica. *Moving North: African Americans and the Great Migration, 1915–1930*. Washington, DC: National Geographic Children's Books, 2006.

Harness, Cheryl. *Tragic Tale of Narcissa Whitman and a Faithful History of the Oregon Trail*. Washington, DC: National Geographic Society, 2006.

Harness, Cheryl. *The Remarkable Rough-Riding Life of Theodore Roosevelt and the Rise of Empire America*. Washington, DC: National Geographic Society, 2007.

Kaywell, Joan F. *Dear Author: Letters of Hope*. New York: Philomel Books, 2008.

Kimmel, Elizabeth Cody. *Ladies First: 40 Daring American Women Who Were Second to None*. Washington, DC: National Geographic Children's Books, 2006.

Knoell, Donna L. *France*. Mankato, MN: Bridgestone Books, 2002.

Kramer, Ann. *Mandela: The Rebel Who Led His Nation to Freedom*. Washington, DC: National Geographic Society, 2005.

Kuhn, Betsy. *The Race for Space: The United States and the Soviet Union Compete for the New Frontier*. Minneapolis: Twenty First Century Books, 2006.

Levine, Ellen. *Up Close: Rachel Carson*. New York: Penguin Young Readers Group, 2008.

Lewis, J. Patrick. *The Brothers' War: Civil War Voices in Verse*. Washington, DC: National Geographic Society, 2008.

Meltzer, Milton. *Tough Times*. New York: Clarion Books, 2007.

Morris-Libsman, Arlene. *Presidential Races: The Battle for Power in the United States*. Minneapolis: Twenty-First Century Books, 2008.

Murphy, Jim. *The Real Benedict Arnold*. New York: Clarion Books, 2008.

Myers, Walter Dean. *Blues Journey.* New York: Holiday House, 2007.

Nicholson, Dorinda Makanaonalani. *Remember WWII: Kids Who Survived Tell Their Stories.* Washington, DC: National Geographic Society, 2005.

O'Connell, Kim A. *Primary Source Accounts of the Vietnam War.* Berkeley Heights, NJ: Enslow Publishers, 2006.

Revkin, Andrew C. *The North Pole Was Here: Puzzles and Perils at the Top of the World.* Boston: Houghton Mifflin, 2006.

Ritchie, Donald A. *Our Constitution.* New York: Oxford University Press, 2006.

Roberts, David & Jeremy Leslie. *Pick Me Up: Stuff You Need to Know.* New York: DK Publishing, 2006.

Rosen, Daniel. *New Beginnings: Jamestown and the Virginia Colony 1607–1699.* Washington, DC: National Geographic Society, 2005.

Rossi, Ann. *Bright Ideas: The Age of Invention in America 1870–1910.* Washington, DC: National Geographic Society, 2005. Other titles include *Created Equal: Women Campaign for the Right to Vote 1840–1920.*

Rubin, Susan Goldman & Ela Weissberger. *The Cat with the Yellow Star: Coming of Age in Terezin.* New York: Holiday House, 2006.

Sandler, Martin W. *Lincoln through the Lens: How Photography Revealed and Shaped an Extraordinary Life.* New York: Walker Publications, 2008.

Schlosser, Eric & Charles Wilson. *Chew on This: Everything You Don't Want to Know about Fast Food.* Boston: Houghton Mifflin, 2006.

Sis, Peter. *The Wall: Growing Up Behind the Iron Curtain.* New York: Farrar, Straus & Giroux, 2008.

Sommer, Shelley. *John F. Kennedy: His Life and Legacy.* New York: HarperCollins Publishers, 2005.

Sullivan, George. *Berenice Abbott, Photographer: An Independent Vision.* New York: Clarion Books, 2006.

Walker, Paul Robert. *Remember Little Bighorn: Indians, Soldiers, and Scouts Tell Their Stories.* Washington, DC: National Geographic Children's Books, 2006.

Walker, Richard. *Epidemics and Plagues.* Boston: Kingfisher, 2006.

Walker, Sally M. *Secrets of a Civil War Submarine: Solving the Mysteries of the H. L. Hunley.* Minneapolis: Carolrhoda Books, 2005.

Williams, Marcia. *Archie's War: My Scrapbook of the First World War, 1914–1918.* Somerville, MA: Candlewick Press, 2008.

Yero, Judith Lloyd. American Documents Series. Washington, DC: National Geographic Society Children's Books, 2006. Other titles include *The Bill of Rights; The Constitution; The Declaration of Independence; The Emancipation Proclamation;* and *The Mayflower Compact.*

PART III

HISTORICAL PERSPECTIVES

13

The Roots of Reading
Comprehension Instruction

P. David Pearson

Even though reading comprehension has been a serious topic of study for psychologists for over 100 years and a goal of reading instruction for centuries, it was not until the 1980s that it really started to take hold as a fact of everyday classroom instruction informed by theory and research. And then suddenly, after 15 years of prominence in conversations of theory, research, and practice—and for a host of reasons, many having to do with curricular politics (Pearson, 2004, 2007)–reading comprehension was placed on a back burner from the mid-1990s to the mid-2000s. It is time it returned to a central role in discussions of reading pedagogy. To assure its return, we will have to give it our rapt and collective attention. And this volume will help to promote just the attention it requires.

Reading comprehension, both its instruction and its assessment, is arguably the most important outcome of reform movements designed to improve reading curriculum and instruction—or at least it ought to be. The trends over the past 5 or 6 years are encouraging (e.g., Israel & Duffy, 2009; Snow, 2003). The emphasis on comprehension has been reinforced by attention to the plight of older readers, for whom compre-

This chapter adapted from S. E. Israel and G. G. Duffy (Eds.), *Handbook of Research on Reading Comprehension*. London: Routledge. Copyright 2009 by Taylor & Francis Group. Adapted by permission. Many of the concepts in this chapter first appeared in other works, such as Pearson and Stephens (1993), Pearson (2000), or Pearson (2004).

hension is both the central goal and the barrier (Biancarosa & Snow, 2006). The time is right to undertake a new initiative in the area of reading comprehension, and this volume marks our professional commitment to do so. By taking stock of our past and present, we pave the way for future lines of inquiry, curriculum, and professional development to make sure we will all keep comprehension in clear professional focus.

The process of text comprehension has always provoked exasperated but nonetheless enthusiastic inquiry within the research community. Comprehension, or "understanding," by its very nature, is a phenomenon that can only be observed *indirectly* (Pearson & Johnson, 1978; Johnston, 1984). We talk about the "click" of comprehension that propels a reader through a text, yet we never see it directly. We can only rely on indirect symptoms and artifacts of its occurrence. People tell us that they understood, or were puzzled by, or enjoyed, or were upset by a text. Or, more commonly, we quiz them on "the text" in some way— requiring them to recall its gist or its major details, asking specific questions about its content and purpose, or insisting on an interpretation and critique of its message. All of these tasks, however challenging or engaging they might be, are little more than the residue of the comprehension process itself. Like it or not, it is precisely this residue that scholars of comprehension and comprehension assessment must work with in order to improve our understanding of the construct. The transparency of the act of comprehension is not much better for instruction than assessment. We talk about activities that foster reading comprehension and those that allow students to monitor their comprehension (Palincsar & Brown, 1984), we teach skills and strategies explicitly (Afflerbach, Pearson, & Paris, 2008), and we engage in rich talk about text (Nystrand, Gamoran, Kachur, & Prendergast, 1997; Nystrand, Wu, Garnoran, Zeiser, & Long, 2003), but we are seldom privy to the "aha!" that occurs when there is a "meeting of the minds" between author and reader (King, 2000).

Most of this chapter is history—a history that attempts to weave together threads from research, theory, and curricular practice for the expressed purpose of understanding what we do inside schools and classrooms to support and promote reading comprehension. But in such a chapter, all I can do is to highlight themes, trends, and insights with the broadest of brush strokes. The real stuff of comprehension, enlivened by all of the excruciating detail of research studies and practices, can be found in the other chapters of this volume. In the pages that follow, I try to provide a systematic unpacking of those themes, trends, and insights. My goal is to provide sufficient detail to bring you to the brink of the current era, roughly, the latest turn of the century, as a way of providing a historical perspective for what appears in the rest of the volume. I have divided the world of reading comprehension instruction into three periods with decidedly and admittedly overlapping boundaries; the one observation I am sure of is that any divisions made in the historical timeline are doomed to misrepresentation. Ideas and practices come with ancestors and precedents, even when they appear to emerge suddenly, and they persist long after their theoretical and research foundations appear to have been overturned. But some rough divisions are helpful, even if they obscure some of the truth. The first period tracks the evolution of reading comprehension instruction before the beginning of the revolution in cognitive psychology that led to a paradigm shift in how we think about comprehension and its instruction—roughly the first 75 years of the 20th century. The second period is a short 15 years, from 1975 to the early 1990s; it examines the theoretical and research bases of the instructional activities and routines spawned by the cognitive revolution. The last period is even shorter, from the early 1990s, but with strong roots in the 1980s and even the 1970s, to the end of the century, spilling over into the early years of the 21st century.

READING COMPREHENSION
INSTRUCTION BEFORE 1975

Reading comprehension has been a part of classrooms as long as there have been schools, texts, students who desire (or are required) to read them, and teachers wanting to both promote and assess their understanding. Throughout the history of reading instruction, every assignment given by a teacher, every book report or chapter summary, and every conversation about a book, story, article, or chapter has provided an opportunity promoting comprehension. However, it was not until well into the 20th century that comprehension arrived as a modal index of reading competence and performance. There are two plausible explanations for the relatively late arrival of comprehension as an indicator of reading accomplishment. First, the default indicator of reading prowess in the 17th to 19th centuries was definitely oral capacity, indexed either by accuracy or by expressive fluency, in the tradition of declamation and oratory (see Smith & Miller, 1966, or Mathews, 1966, for accounts of this emphasis). Second, within ecclesiastical circles, comprehension, at least in the sense of personal understanding, was not truly valued; if it mattered, it mattered largely as a stepping stone to the more valued commodity of text memorization.

An Indirect Look Inside Classrooms

To get a handle on how reading comprehension was "taught" in class-rooms in the early half of the 20th century, one can examine what is asked of students in their reading anthologies, which date back to the 1840s, by the way, and what is suggested to teachers in training manuals and textbooks. Given the emphasis on accuracy and expressive fluency, the answer, "not much," is not surprising. But there were some consistent threads. Dating back to late 1890s, basal authors included right in the student books (at the end of each selection) several types of "study aids" for students: words to study, phrases to study, and questions to use in preparing for a discussion and/or quiz (Elson & Keck, 1911; Gates & Ayer, 1933). As early as 1912, Longmans Green & Co. published a separate book of *Daily Lesson Plans* with suggested vocabulary and comprehension probes to use in introducing and discussing selections. Scott, Foresman, the publisher of the Elson Readers from 1909 through the 1930s, also published teachers' manuals with answers to the questions in the student books. They added William S. Gray, who made his mark in the field with one of the earliest standardized tests, the Gray Oral Reading Test (Thorndike, 1914), to the roster in the 1920s. The Gray–Elson collaboration resulted in the *Curriculum Foundation Series* (Elson & Gray, 1936)—most famous, of course, for Dick and Jane (who were actually Elson's creation, nor Gray's), but even more influential in shaping the course of reading instruction over four decades from the early 1930s through the late 1960s. By the 1940s (Gray, Arbuthnot, et al., 1940–1948; Gray, Arbuthnot, Artley, Monroe, et al., 1951–1958), after Elson's death, Gray became the driving force in this influential series. An examination of the manuals (e.g., 1946–47) during this period is instructive because it is clear that the implicit theory behind promoting comprehension (as well as response to literature) was to have the teacher use a range of questions to guide students in conversation during page-by-page guided reading and in a postreading discussion.

Testing as a Catalyst for Comprehension

The scientific movement and the changing demographic patterns of schooling in the United States conspired, albeit inadvertently, to bring reading comprehension into instructional focus in the first third of the 20th century. Schools had to accommodate rapid increases in enrollment due to waves of immigration, a rapidly industrializing society, the prohibition of child labor, and mandatory school attendance laws. The spike in school enrollment, coupled with a population of students with dubious literacy skills, dramatically increased the need for a cheap, efficient screening device to determine students' levels of literacy. During this same period, psychology struggled to gain the status of a "science" by employing the methods that governed physical sciences and research. In the United States, the behaviorist schools of thought, with their focus on measurable outcomes, strongly influenced the field of psychology (Johnston, 1984; Resnick, 1982; Pearson, 2000); quantification and objectivity were the two hallmarks to which educational "science" aspired. Thus, when psychologists with their newfound scientific lenses were put to work creating cheap and efficient tests for beleaguered schools, the course of reading assessment was set. More efficient, group-administered, multiple-choice, standardized tests would be the inevitable result. And while there were curricular forces campaigning for a shift away from skills, phonics, and oral reading, the need for efficiency certainly served as a catalyst for accelerating the move to more silent reading in our classrooms. Unlike oral reading, which had to be tested individually and required that teachers judge the quality of responses, silent reading comprehension (and rate) could be tested in group settings and scored without recourse to professional judgment; only stop watches and multiple-choice questions were needed. In modern parlance, we would say that they moved from a "high-inference" assessment tool (oral reading and retelling) to a "low-inference" tool (multiple-choice tests or timed readings). Thus, it fit the demands for efficiency (spawned by the move toward more universal education for all students) and objectivity (part of the emerging scientism of the period). The practice proved remarkably persistent for at least another 50 or 60 years. And, of course, just like in today's world, if a phenomenon can be assessed, then curriculum and pedagogy to teach it will soon follow.

Early Forays into Theorizing Comprehension

Both Edmund Burke Huey (1908) and Edward Thorndike (1917) undertook early efforts to understand the comprehension process. Huey, a theorist, researcher, and practitioner, anticipated constructivist views of reading development (the reader creates the meaning from the traces left on the page by the author) but regarded comprehension as a somewhat mysterious, unapproachable phenomenon, suggesting (1908, p. 163) that

> the consciousness of meaning itself belongs in the main to that group of mental states, the feelings, which I regard with Wundt as unanalyzables, or at lest as having a large unanalyzable core or body.

Huey also foreshadowed the constructivist turn in psychology, literary theory, and pedagogy that would come in the 1970s and 1980s, arguing for a model of sense making rather than accurate rendition as the hallmark of expert reading:

> And even if the child substitutes words of his own for some that are on the page, provided that these express the meaning, it is an encouraging sign that the reading has been real, and recognition of details will come as it is needed. (Huey, 1908, p. 349)

Huey went on to argue that teachers need to rid themselves of the false ideal that had taken over reading pedagogy: "that to read is to say just what is upon the page, instead of to think, each in his own way, the meaning that the page suggests" (Huey, 1908, p. 349).

Thorndike was probably the first educational psychologist to try to launch inquiry into the complex thought processes associated with comprehension. He regarded reading "as reasoning," suggesting there are many factors that comprise it: "elements in a sentence, their organization ... proper relations, selection of certain connotations and the rejection of others, and the cooperation of many forces" (Thorndike, 1917, p. 323). He proposed ideas about what should occur during "correct reading," claiming that a great many misreadings of questions and passages are produced because of under- or over-potency of individual words, thus violating his "correct-weighting" principle:

> Understanding a paragraph is like solving a problem in mathematics. It consists in selecting the right elements in the situation and putting them together in the right relations, and also with the right amount of weight or influence or force of each" (Thorndike, 1917, p. 329)

Of course, Thorndike assumed that there are such things as "correct" readings. He argued further that in the act of reading, the mind must organize and analyze ideas from the text. "The vice of the poor reader is to say the words to himself without actively making judgments concerning what they reveal" (Thorndike, 1917, p. 332). Clearly, for Thorndike, reading was an active and complex cognitive process. Thorndike's account of reading as meaning making, like Huey's epic treatment of all aspects of reading (1908), is best viewed as an interesting and curious anomaly. It did not become dominant in this early period, either for the field or for Thorndike, but it certainly anticipated, as did Huey's account, the highly active view of the reader that would become prominent during the cognitive revolution of the 1970s.[1]

Text Difficulty and Readability

Text difficulty, codified as readability, emerged as an important research area and curricular concept in the first half of the 20th century. Unlike the developments in testing, which were grounded in the scientific movement in psychology, readability was grounded in child-centered views of pedagogy dating back to theorists such as Pestalozzi, Froebel, and Herbart and championed by the developmental psychology emerging in the 1920s and 1930s.[2] The motive in developing readability formulas was to screen texts to match students' interests and developmental capacities rather than to baffle students with abridged versions of adult texts. The first readability formula, created to gauge the grade placement of texts, appeared in 1923 (Lively & Pressey), and it was followed by some 80 additional formulas over the next 40 years until the enterprise drew to at least a temporary close in the late 1960s.[3] Irrespective of particular twists in individual formulas, each more or less boiled down to a sentence difficulty factor, typically instantiated as average sentence length, and a word factor, typically codified as word frequency. These formulas were critical in the production of commercial reading materials from the 1920s through the 1980s. For reasons that will become apparent later in this chapter, readability formulas did not survive the cognitive revolution in reading instruction in the 1970s and 1980s, although there are signs of their recovery in the last decade.[4]

Reading Skills

The most influential construct influencing the comprehension curriculum of schools in this period was the "reading skill"—that discrete unit of the curriculum that ought to be learned by students and taught by teachers. It is hard to fix the precise genesis of the "reading skill," but it is clearly and hopelessly confounded with the testing movement. Tests had to measure something, and the something they measured looked a lot like skills that were a part of the basal reading programs for elementary and secondary schools of the period. As an example of this relationship, consider the groundbreaking psychometric work of Frederick Davis (1944) to establish an infrastructure of reading comprehension skills (see Leslie & Caldwell, 2009, for a more extensive treatment of Davis's work). He was able to develop test items for nine separate categories, which, when he examined the degree of interrelatedness among them, reduced to two—a word factor (something like vocabulary) and a reasoning factor (something like drawing inferences between the text and knowledge). But the key question is, Where did those nine candidate skills come from? The answer is straightforward: Davis reviewed the literature describing reading comprehension as a construct and commonly used elementary and high school curricula of the times. He found literally hundreds of labels to name the skills, but they all reduced to these nine conceptual categories (see Table 13.1), which he felt constituted conceptually distinct groups; from these, as I indicated, he deduced two independent factors—word knowledge and reasoning.

While we cannot be sure where the skills came from, for either instruction or assessment, it is clear that both domains were using the same infrastructure of tasks; clearly, what happened in either domain influenced the other. These tasks/labels—finding main ideas, noting important details, determining sequence of events, cause–effect relations, comparing and contrasting, and drawing conclusions—are noteworthy for their persistence for they are all a part of current curricula and assessments in the early part of the 21st century.

An important related construct was the notion of a scope and sequence of skills, a linear outline of skills that if taught properly ought to lead to skilled reading. While skills have always been a part of reading instruction (witness all the bits and pieces of letter sounds and syllables in the alphabetic approach), the skill as a fundamental unit of curriculum and the scope-and-sequence chart as a way of organizing skills that extend across the elementary grades are 20th-century phenomena.

The basal experience with skills led quite directly to two additional curriculum mainstays—the teachers manual and the workbook.[5] Throughout the 19th century and at least up through the first three decades of the 20th century, basal programs consisted almost entirely of a set of student books. Teachers relied on experience, or perhaps normal school education, to supply the pedagogy used to teach lessons with the materials. Occasionally, for students who had progressed beyond the primer to one of the more advanced readers, questions were provided to test understanding of the stories in the readers. In the early 1900s, publishers of basals began to include supplementary teaching suggestions, typically a separate section at the front or back of each book with a page or two of suggestions to accompany each selection. In one common practice of the period, publishers provided a model lesson plan for two

TABLE 13.1. Davis's Nine Potential Factors

1. Word meanings	6. Text-based questions with paraphrase
2. Word meanings in context	7. Draw inferences about content
3. Follow passage organization	8. Literary devices
4. Main thought	9. Author's purpose
5. Answer specific text-based questions	

or three stories; for later stories, they referred the teacher back to one of the models with the suggestion that they adapt it for the new story. By the 1930s, the teachers' manuals had expanded to several pages per selection.[6] The other significant development in the 1930s was the workbook, often marketed with titles like *My Think and Do Book* or *Work Play Books*.[7]

Both of these developments were symptomatic of the expansion of scope-and-sequence efforts: the more skills included, the more complicated the instructional routines and the greater the need for explicit directives to teachers and opportunities for students to practice the skills. From the 1930s until at least the 1980s, this approach to skills development increased in intensity and scope. It was gradually extended beyond phonics to include comprehension, vocabulary, and study skills.[8] As I indicated earlier, the comprehension skills that made their way into basal workbooks and scope-and-sequence charts were virtually identical to those used to create comprehension tests. The trend toward heftier and more complex manuals and workbooks for teachers has continued virtually unchecked since it began in the 1930s until today, when the manual for each grade consists of a small library rather than a single book.

Theory and professional thinking were not divorced from this expansion of the skills in basals and on tests. The practice in each succeeding generation is mirrored by research-based accounts of reading curricula in influential yearbooks published by the National Society for Studies in Education (NSSE); in this series, reading research and curriculum is synthesized every decade or so. So, for example, in the 24th Yearbook of the Society (1925), William S. Gray's chapter on objectives for teaching reading included both simple and complex "interpretation habits." Among the simple were:

- Concentrating attention on the content.
- Associating meanings with symbols.
- Anticipating the sequence of ideas.
- Associating ideas together accurately.
- Recalling related experiences.
- Recognizing the important elements of meaning.
- Deriving meanings from the context and from pictures (Gray, 1925, p. 14).

Among the more complex were these:

- Analyzing or selecting meanings;
  - To select important points and supporting details
  - To find answers to questions

- Associating and organizing meanings; for example,
  - To grasp the author's organization
  - To associate what is read with previous experience
  - To prepare an organization of what has been read
- Evaluating meanings; for example,
  - To appraise the value or significance of statements
  - To compare facts read with items of information from other sources
  - To weigh evidence presented
  - To interpret critically
- Retaining meanings; for example,
  - To reproduce for others
  - To use in specific ways (Gray, 1925, pp. 14–15)

Durrell (1949), writing the first chapter devoted exclusively to comprehension in any NSSE Yearbook (by that time, 10 yearbooks had been partially or exclusively devoted to reading), provided a perspective that focused on skills but acknowledged that reader knowledge, motivation, and attention would exert strong influences on comprehension. He outlined the following general characteristics of a skills program in reading comprehension:

- Selection of essential skills to be observed and taught.
- Analysis of difficulties of those skills.
- Intensive teaching of those skills through graded exercises in suitable material.
- A motivation program which shows the child the importance of those skills and enables him to see his progress in them (Durrell, 1949, p. 200).

Durrell never outlined the specific skills with the detail and precision provided in the 1920s by Gray, but it is clear that an approach that decomposed comprehension into a set of teachable skills was assumed in his general approach. As close as he comes to defining skills (pp. 200–202) is in discussing the difficulties in text at the word (vocabulary and word meaning), sentence (overcoming the barriers of complex syntax by careful analysis), and paragraph and passage (discovering the often implicit organization of ideas) levels that teachers must attend to in diagnosing and remediating students' problems in comprehension. He also pointed to the importance of a solid program in decoding and fluency as a firm basis for comprehending, implying, of course, that he believed, at least in part, in the simple view of reading—that decoding words to an auditory code would enable oral language competence to enact text comprehension (i.e., that reading comprehension is the product of decoding and listening comprehension).

McKee (1949) in the chapter on reading in grades 4–8 for the same 48th Yearbook, also mentioned "comprehension" fostering activities, although he used the word *comprehension* only once in his 20-page chapter. In discussing what students needed to become independent readers who could cope with difficulty on their own, he mentioned knowing lots of word meanings (including navigating multiple meanings), using context to infer word meanings, figurative language, using syntax to relate ideas to one another in a sentence, linking ideas across sentences, and distinguishing emotive from informative expressions (p. 135). He also acknowledged—and this is the first mention of it I can find in any of the NSSE volumes up until that time—the role of text discussion as contributing to understanding; interestingly, he pled for open rather than closed conversations about text:

> The discussion which follows the reading of a given selection should be, not a quizzing activity in which the teacher tests the pupil's retention of what has been read, but rather an informal conversation ·in which pupils make comments and raise queries about the selection, just as an individual and his friends discuss a book they have read or a movie they have seen.

In 1968, just on the cusp of the cognitive revolution in psychology that would spawn a paradigm shift in our views of comprehension, the NSSE Yearbook on reading would have a different character. What is most striking in the chapter most clearly related to comprehension (Clymer, 1968) is how much the development of theory over the 1950s and 1960s had altered the views of comprehension presented. Clymer cited the empirical theories of scholars such as Holmes (substrata factor theory), the emerging cognitive work in Project Literacy at Cornell, and the instructional framework of Barrett to ponder the question What is reading? In privileging the emerging work of Barrett, he placed comprehension at the center of the answer to that question. He also provided some indirect evidence that Gray was moving toward a more comprehension-centric view of reading processes.

The centerpiece of Clymer's chapter is Barrett's taxonomy, which is loosely coupled to Bloom's (1956) Taxonomy of Educational Objectives. Essentially, he borrowed liberally, whenever there was a comfortable fit, from Bloom's constructs of knowledge, comprehension, application, analysis, synthesis, and evaluation, as well as from the key descriptors Bloom used to "enact" those basic constructs—words like *recall, recognize, infer,* and *summarize.* Perhaps even more important, he used the taxonomic frame established by Bloom to unpack his infrastructure for reading comprehension. According to Clymer (1968), "The type of comprehension demanded and the difficulty of the task is a product of (a) the selection, (b) the questions, and (c) the reader's background" (p. 19). Barrett then embedded some familiar terms into his taxonomy—popular standards such as main idea, sequence, comparison, cause–effect relationships, and character traits. While he did not choose a tabular format for presenting, three of the major categories certainly invite a matrix presentation, as depicted in Table 13.2.

His other categories—Reorganization, Judgment, Evaluation, and Appreciation—are idiosyncratic in nature. But Barrett's taxonomy and Clymer's treatment of it and other conceptions of reading are notable not so much for their particular content as for serving as harbingers of things to come a half decade later with the onset of the cognitive revolution and a major paradigm shift in comprehension.

A Portent of Things to Come: Psycholinguistics

Beginning in the late 1950s, and marked most vividly by the publication of Chomsky's groundbreaking work in linguistics (1957) and critique of behaviorist views of language, psycholinguistics had tremendous appeal for three reasons. Part of its appeal stemmed from the feeling that it would constitute a paradigm shift. Based upon studies like that of Gough (1965), there was a genuine feeling that behavioristic views of language development and processing would have to be supplanted with views that were both nativistic (people are born with a genetic capability to learn language) and cognitive (something really does go on inside that black box) in orientation. Furthermore, these research studies seemed to suggest that the transformational–generative grammar created by Chomsky (1957, 1965) might actually serve as a model of human language processing. Thus, there was a ready-made theory

TABLE 13.2. A Tabular Account of a Part of Barrett's Taxonomy

	Literal comprehension		
	Recognition	Recall	Inferential comprehension
Main ideas	√	√	√
Supporting details	√	√	√
Sequence	√	√	√
Comparison	√	√	√
Cause–effect	√	√	√
Character traits	√	√	√

waiting to be applied to reading comprehension. Psycholinguistics was also appealing to educational scholars because it commanded academic respectability. There was something appealing about standing on the shoulders of the new psychology, working within a paradigm for which there was a model that made fairly precise predictions and thus had testable hypotheses.

Hence it was that beginning in the late 1960s and extending into the mid-1970s, considerable empirical and theoretical work was completed within the psycholinguistic tradition. The influence of psycholinguistics on reading is nowhere better demonstrated than in the work of Kenneth Goodman (1965) and Frank Smith (1971). For both Goodman and Smith, looking at reading from a psycholinguistic perspective meant looking at reading in its natural state, as an application of a person's general cognitive and linguistic competence. It seems odd even to mention their names in discussing the influence of psycholinguistics on comprehension research, because neither Goodman nor Smith distinguishes between reading and reading comprehension. Their failure to make the distinction is deliberate, for they would argue that reading is comprehending (or that reading without comprehending is not reading). A distinction between word identification and comprehension would seem arbitrary to them. For others, the influence of the psycholinguistic tradition (particularly the use of transformational–generative grammar as a psychological model) on views of reading comprehension was quite direct. The work of Bormuth (1966), Bormuth, Manning, Carr, and Pearson (1971), Fagan (1971), and Pearson (1974–1975) reveals a rather direct use of psycholinguistic notions in studying reading comprehension. Such was the scene in the early 1970s. The conventional modes of research, while still strong, were being challenged by a new interloper from the world of linguistic research—psycholinguistics.

Several points about the teaching and learning of reading comprehension during the first 75 years of the century seem warranted from the perspectives presented thus far:

1. Whatever theorizing about reading comprehension might have been done by a few early scholars and by psycholinguistics very late in the period, the bulk of the writing and activity focus on comprehension focus comprehension skills as a way of organizing curriculum (what gets taught) and assessment (what gets tested).

2. Most scholars thought that comprehension skill resulted from practicing separable skills within a balanced scope and sequence. The most common criterion for sequencing comprehension skill was from literal to inferential to some beyond-the-text activity, such as creative, aesthetic, or critical.

3. Curriculum and assessment were tightly bound together, so much so that they present a classic chicken-and-egg problem.

4. Notably absent in discussions of curriculum was any advice about pedagogy supporting the development of these skills.[9]

5. The role of discussion and questions about text were not well represented in the professional literature on comprehension, but questions and talk about text were ubiquitous in the materials throughout this period. Thus an implicit theory, evident in practice, is that the ability to answer questions was considered to be the most basic piece of evidence that students could comprehend, and asking them to practice answering lots of questions was thought by many to be the best path to nurturing comprehension.

6. Implicit in much of the presentation of comprehension (save Huey's account) was an assumption that the simple view of reading (RC = Dec * LC) is accurate, so that if we can get those lower-order skills in place and provide students with lots of opportunity to practice skills in text discussions and workbooks, reading comprehension will take care of itself.

READING COMPREHENSION INSTRUCTION AFTER THE COGNITIVE REVOLUTION: 1975–1990

The Cognitive Turn in Psychology

In comparison to what happened in the space of 5 years from roughly 1975 to 1980, the sum total of developments in the first 75 years of the 20th century pale. Rooted, as suggested, in the Chomskian revolution in linguistics (Chomsky, 1957, 1959, 1965) and experiencing a trial run in the young field of psycholingustics in the late 1960s, the cognitive perspective allowed psychologists to reembrace[10] and extend constructs such as human purpose, intention, and motivation to a greater range of psychological phenomena, including perception, attention, comprehension, learning, memory, and executive control or "metacognition" of all cognitive process. All of these would have important consequences in reading pedagogy.

The most notable change within psychology was that it became fashionable for psychologists, for the first time since the early part of the century, to study complex phenomena such as language and reading.[11] And in the decade of the 1970s, works by psychologists flooded the literature on basic processes in reading. One group focused on characteristics of the text and a second on the nature of the knowledge students bought to the reading task. Those who privileged text comprehension tried to explain how readers come to understand the underlying structure of texts. They offered story grammars—structural accounts of the nature of narratives, complete with predictions about how those structures impede and enhance story understanding and memory (Rumelhart, 1977; Stein & Glenn, 1977). Others chose to focus on the expository tradition in text (e.g., Kintsch, 1974; Meyer, 1975). Like their colleagues interested in story comprehension, they believed that structural accounts of the nature of expository (informational) texts would provide valid and useful models for human text comprehension. And in a sense, both of these efforts worked. Story grammars did provide explanations for story comprehension. Analyses of the structural relations among ideas in an informational piece also provided explanations for expository text comprehension (see Pearson & Camparell, 1981). But neither text-analysis tradition really tackled the relationship between the knowledge of the world that readers bring to text and comprehension of those texts. In other words, by focusing on structural rather than the ideational, or content, characteristics of texts, they failed to get to the heart of comprehension. That task, as it turned out, fell to one of the most popular and influential movements of the 1970s, schema theory.

The Emergence of Schema Theory

The most prevalent metaphor to emerge from this revolutionary period was the "reader as builder"—an active meaning constructor (Anderson, 1977; Collins, Brown, & Larkin, 1980), an aggressive processor of language and information who filters the raw materials of reading (the clues left by the author on the printed page) through his or her vast reservoir of knowledge to continuously revise a dynamic, ever-emerging model of text meaning. The reader assumed greater importance in the period, and the text assumed less: the builder became more important than the materials used to do the building. This is not to say that text was neither appreciated nor studied during this period; what occurred is better characterized as a shift in emphasis from the dominance of text variables in the reading models leading into 1970s.

Schema theory (see Anderson & Pearson, 1984; Rumelhart, 1981) is not a theory of reading comprehension but rather a theory about the structure of human knowledge as it is represented in memory. In our memory, schemas are like little containers into which we deposit the particular traces of particular experiences as well as the "ideas" that derive from those experiences. So, if we see a chair, we store that visual experience in our "chair schema." If we go to a restaurant, we store that experience in our "restaurant schema," if we attend a party, our "party schema," and so on.

Even so, schema theory was readily appropriated to provide a credible account of reading comprehension, which probably, more than any of its other features, accounted for its popularity within the reading field in the 1970s and 1980s. Schema theory struck a sympathetic note with researchers as well as practitioners. It provided a rich and detailed theoretical account of the everyday intuition that we understand and learn what is new in terms of what we already know. It also accounted for the everyday phenomenon of disagreements in interpreting stories, movies, and news events—we disagree with one another because we approach the phenomenon with very different background experiences and knowledge. Anderson (1984) provided us with the most elaborate account of the uses that we, as readers, can make of schemas:

1. Schemas provide ideational scaffolding for assimilating text information. Schemas have slots that readers expect to be filled with information in a text. Information that fills those slots is easily learned and remembered.
2. Schemas facilitate the selective allocation of attention. Put simply, schemas guide our search for what is important in a text, allowing us to separate the wheat from the chaff.
3. Schemas enable inferential elaboration. No text is ever fully explicit. Schemas allow us to make educated guesses about how certain slots must have been filled.
4. Schemas allow for orderly searches of memory. For example, suppose a person is asked to remember what he did at a recent cocktail party. He can use his cocktail party schema, a specification of what usually happens at cocktail parties, to recall what he ate, what he drank, whom he talked to, and so on.
5. Schemas facilitate editing and summarizing. By definition, any schema possesses its own criteria of what is important. These can be used to create summaries of text that focus on important information.
6. Schemas permit inferential reconstruction. If readers have a gap in their memory, they can use a schema, in conjunction with the information recalled, to generate hypotheses about missing information. If they can recall, for example, that the entree was beef, they can infer that the beverage was likely to have been red wine.

So powerful was the influence of prior knowledge on comprehension that Johnston and Pearson (1982; see also Johnston, 1984) found that prior knowledge of topic was a better predictor of comprehension than either an intelligence test score or a reading achievement test score.

With respect to reading comprehension, schema theory did not ignore text. Instead, it encouraged educators to examine texts from the perspective of the knowledge and cultural backgrounds of students in order to evaluate the likely connections that they would be able to make between ideas inscribed[12] in the text and the schema that they would bring to the reading task. Schema theory also promoted a constructivist view of comprehension; all readers, at every moment in the reading process, construct the most coherent model of meaning for the texts they read.[13] Perhaps the most important legacy of this constructivist perspective was that it introduced ambiguity about the question of where meaning resides. Does it reside in the text? In the author's mind as he or she sets pen to paper? In the mind of each reader as he or she builds a model of meaning unique to his or her experience and reading? In the interaction between reader and text? Schema theory raised, but did not settle these questions. But it did privilege the interaction metaphor in suggesting that comprehension occurs at the intersection of reader, text, and context (see Figure 13.1).

Metacognition

Nearly as popular as the builder was the metaphor of the "fixer"—the problem solver who can repair virtually any comprehension failure with her toolbox of strategies.[14] Most commonly referred to as the *strategic reader* (Paris, Lipson, & Wixson, 1983), he or she is a paragon of adaptability and flexibility, immediately sizing up the potential influence of relevant factors in the reading environment (particular attributes of the text; the situation, which can be construed to include other learners; and the self) and then selecting, from among a healthy repertoire of strategies that enable and repair comprehension, exactly that strategy or set of strategies that will maximize comprehension of the text at hand.

Sometime during the late 1970s, this new interloper burst onto the research stage, bearing the cumbersome but intellectually appealing label of *metacognition*. It seemed a logical extension of the rapidly

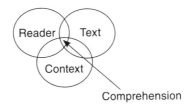

FIGURE 13.1. Comprehension occurs at the intersection of reader, text, and context.

developing work on both schema theory and text analysis. These latter two traditions emphasized declarative knowledge, knowing that X or Y or Z is true, but were scant on specifying procedural knowledge, knowing how to engage a strategy for comprehension or memory. This is precisely the kind of knowledge that metacognitive research has emphasized. The key phrases associated with metacognition reveal its emphasis: "awareness," "monitoring," "control," and "evaluation." Two parallel strands of research dominated the early work in metacognition. The first, metamemory research, is most typically associated with Flavell and his associates at Stanford. They discovered that along with the capacity to remember more information, human beings develop tacit and explicit strategies for remembering. The second line of research, metacomprehension, was more typically associated with Brown and Campione and their colleagues at Illinois, and with Paris at Michigan. It emphasized the strategies that readers use online in monitoring, evaluating and repairing their comprehension of written text (see Paris et al., 1983; also Baker & Beall, 2009).

The metacognitive turn helped us understand that reading involves many different kinds of knowledge (Paris et al., 1983). First, declarative knowledge, knowing *that*, includes our knowledge of the world at large and our knowledge of the world of text (prototypical structures and authorial devices). Procedural knowledge, knowing *how*, includes all of the strategies we use to become aware of, monitor, evaluate, and repair our comprehension. To these more transparent sources of knowledge, Paris and colleagues (1983; also Paris & Hamilton, 2009) argued convincingly that we should add conditional knowledge, knowing *when* and *why* we would call up a particular strategy (in preference to others), to aid our comprehension. The real contribution was helping us understand that we cannot characterize comprehension or comprehension instruction without including all of these kinds of knowledge.

From Process to Pedagogy: The Impact of Cognitive Research on Reading Comprehension Instruction

Research on reading comprehension instruction in the 15 years following the onset of the revolution tended to fall into one of two categories (see Pearson & Gallagher, 1983)—descriptions and interventions. Some studies attempted to describe what is going on in the name of reading comprehension, either in our schools or our textbooks. Other studies attempted to try out different ways of teaching or allowing students to practice reading comprehension strategies or activities. They represent what we might call pedagogical experiments; their goal was (and is) to evaluate competing practices over relatively short but intensive treatment periods (1–10 weeks). A few, very few, of these experiments had more of a program evaluation flavor and examined a practice or set of practices embedded into a larger curriculum and usually for a longer period of time.

Descriptions

The descriptions in this period taught us more about what is not being done than what is. The landmark study in the period was Durkin's (1978–1979) documentation of the paucity of instruction inside classrooms and a follow-up (1981) examination of the comprehension instruction pedagogy recommended in teachers' manuals. In short, she found very little direct instruction of comprehension in intermediate-grade classrooms (1978–1979) or suggested in teachers' manuals (1981). Instead of offering students advice about how to employ reading skills, teachers and manuals tend to assess comprehension by asking or suggesting many questions about the selections students read and by providing enormous quantities of practice materials in the form of worksheets and workbooks. Sometimes, teachers or manuals "mention" or say just enough about the skill so that students understand the formal requirements of the task. Rarely do teachers or manuals require application of the skill to reading real texts. Even more rarely do they discuss the kind of conditional knowledge suggested by Paris et al. (1983). Durkin (1981) found that teachers rarely use that section of the teachers' manual suggesting background knowledge activities but rarely skip the story questions or skillsheet activities.

Beck and her colleagues at Pittsburgh (Beck, McKeown, McCaslin, & Burkes, 1979) have found several features of commercial reading programs that may adversely affect comprehension. Among them are the use of indirect language (using high-frequency words such as *this* or *him* instead of lower-frequency but more image-evoking words like *garbage can* or *Mr. Gonzalez*), elaborate but misleading pictures, inappropriate story divisions, misleading prior knowledge and vocabulary instruction, and questions that focus on unimportant aspects of the stories students read.

Other descriptive studies of the era concentrated more on pupil texts than on teacher manuals or classroom instruction. For example, Davison and Kantor (1982) studied the kinds of adaptations publishers make when they rewrite an adult article for students in order to meet readability guidelines. They found a number of examples of practices that may actually make passages harder rather than easier to understand: (1) reducing sentence length by destroying interclausally explicit connectives, (2) selecting simpler but less descriptive vocabulary, (3) altering the flow of topic and comment relations in paragraphs, and (4) eliminating qualifying statements that specify the conditions under which generalizations are thought to hold. Anderson and Armbruster (Armbruster & Anderson, 1981, 1982, 1984; Anderson, Armbruster, & Kantor, 1980) examined a number of dimensions of student text material in social studies and science that may cause unintentional difficulty. Among their observations are that content-area texts often (1) fail to structure the information within a predictable and recurrent frame (like a schema for text); (2) use subheadings that do not reveal the macrostructure of the topic; (3) avoid using visual displays of information, particularly to summarize information presented textually; (4) use obscure pronoun references; and (5) fail to use obvious connectives, such as *because, since, before, after,* etc., when they clearly fit. To make the picture even drearier, Bruce (1984) compared basal stories to those found in trade books and concluded that basal stories avoid features commonly found in stories, such as inside view, internal conflict, and embedded narratorship. An apt summary of the descriptive research of this period is pretty dismal: texts with counterproductive features; teacher manuals with scant, misleading, or unhelpful suggestions; teachers who do not teach comprehension skills and strategies in any explicit way.

Experiments

The experimental work was more encouraging (see Pearson & Fielding, 1991, or Tierney & Cunningham, 1991, for elaborate summaries of this work). More comprehension instruction research was conducted between 1980 and 1990 than in all of the previous history of reading research. Examined in the broadest strokes, this body of work was strongly supportive of instructional applications of schema theory and the new work on metacognitive development.

1. Whether it comes packaged as a set of questions, a text summary, a story line, or a visual display of key ideas, students of all ages and abilities benefit from conscious attempts by teachers to focus attention either on the structure of the text to be read or the structure of the knowledge domain to which the text is related (see Pearson & Camparell, 1981).
2. Students' disposition to draw inferences or make predictions improves when they and their teachers make a conscious effort to draw relationships between text content and background knowledge (Hansen, 1981; Hansen & Pearson, 1983).
3. When students learn how to monitor their reading to make sure it makes sense to them, their comprehension skill improves (Pal-

incsar & Brown, 1984; Paris, Cross, & Lipson, 1984). This third generalization is predictable from the first two because the only criterion readers can use to evaluate the "sense" of the model of meaning they are building is their own knowledge.

4. When strategies are taught in explicit, transparent ways, students can learn to apply them in ways that improve both their comprehension of the texts in which they are embedded and texts they have yet to encounter.

Taken together, these general findings supported instruction that is based upon the driving metaphors of the new comprehension paradigm—the reader as builder and the reader as fixer; these findings support a "generative" view of comprehension and learning (Wittrock, 1992), in which comprehension is facilitated by the transformation of ideas from one form into another. It may be in this transformation process that what began as the author's ideas become the reader's ideas (Pearson & Fielding, 1991).

Another outcome of these early pedagogical experiments was the evolution of an instructional model that has persisted from the early 1980s. The model, which defines the dynamic role of the teacher as

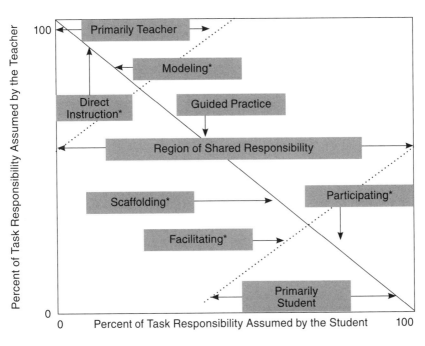

FIGURE 13.2. Updated gradual release of responsibility model.

instruction ensues, was implicit in virtually all of the research evaluating the explicit teaching of strategies, but was first made explicit by Pearson and Gallagher (1983)[15] as a tool for explaining commonalities across a range of research efforts from the late 1970s and early 1980s. Dubbed the "gradual release of responsibility model," the idea is that as teachers move from the teacher roles of modeling and direct instruction to scaffolding and guided practice and onto facilitation and participation, they release more and more responsibility to students for completing key tasks. An updated version reprinted here (Figure 13.2) is an adaptation of the original Pearson and Gallagher graphic from Duke and Pearson (2002).

FROM REVOLUTION TO RECONTEXTUALIZATION AND REVISIONISM: THE 1990s

The impact of schema theory and metacognition on pedagogy continued into at least the middle 1990s. But it did begin to lose its hold as the dominant theory of comprehension processing. It was not as though schema theory died, but it is probably best to regard the decade from of the 1990s as the era in which reading, including schema theory, was recontextualized as a process that is intimately related to its sibling linguistic processes of writing, listening, and speaking and to the social and cultural contexts underlying.[16] In fact, it became increasingly common for scholars to refer to *literacy* research rather than either reading or writing research. A telling example of this change in perspective occurred in the latter part of the decade when the National Reading Conference (NRC) changed the name of its journal from the *Journal of Reading Behavior* to *JRB: A Journal of Literacy.*[17] Conferences and edited volumes of the period also revealed these trends toward contextualizing reading. We moved from conferences about reading or writing to conferences about the dynamics of language learning, the contexts of school-based literacy, and multidisciplinary perspectives on literacy research. In the 1980s, we were arguing for integration; in the 1990s, we were assuming it.

Advances in Research on Comprehension Processes

Cognitive Shifts

If schema theory (see Anderson & Pearson, 1984), with its twin emphases on the importance of knowledge in determining comprehension and the central role of inference in helping to build complete models of text meaning, was the conventional wisdom leading us into this post-paradigm shift period, beginning in the mid-1980s, then the rest of the decade, and indeed most of the following decade, is best viewed as a series of attempts to account for weaknesses attributed to schema-theoretic accounts of reading comprehension. In fact, the theme of this period might be labeled, "moving beyond schema theory."

The more general notion of building mental models (see McNamara, Miller, & Bransford, 1991, for a summary of this work) has characterized basic research on comprehension processes completed by the cognitive science community in the latter part of the decade. Mental models, which appear to be more spatial, episodic, and almost cinematic in character, as least when compared to abstract, semantically based schemas, provide readers with alternatives to propositional and schema models for representing emerging models of text meaning. The purported advantage (Johnson-Laird, 1983) of mental models over schema models is that they can handle both heavily scripted events like going to a restaurant or a movie, which schema models also handle quite well, and unique, unscripted activities, which schema models can accommodate only with great strain. The comprehension research evaluating the efficacy of mental models (see McNamara et al., 1991) suggests that they are quite useful in accounting for the dynamic course of comprehension during reading. For example, the mental models approach is quite sensitive to subtle shifts in comprehension focus (e.g., when a reader shifts from an hypothesis that character A rather than character B is the likely candidate for protagonist). This work on mental models reached its zenith in the middle 1990s in the work of Kintsch, fully summarized in his 1998 book on comprehension and featuring his highly influential constructs of the text base and the situation model. The text base is a largely veridical map of the key ideas in the text that is hammered out with deliberate bottom-up processes that involve decoding in a central way. The situation model is akin to the model of meaning put forward in the early 1980s by that ever evolving, always elusive model built at the intersection of prior knowledge and the text base and providing the momentarily best account.

Another attempt to accommodate for problems with schema theory came from the work of Spiro and his colleagues (Spiro, Vispoel, Schmitz, Smarapungavan, & Boerger, 1987). Operating out of a Wittgensteinian perspective, Spiro argued that the schema model of comprehension so dominant in prior periods runs the risk of seducing us into oversimplified notions of comprehension and learning by implying that schemas have a fixed, static character. According to Spiro's cognitive flexibility theory, we need to expand schema theory to account for the dynamic nature of comprehension and learning, especially in domains of knowledge that have an ill-structured character, where the category distinctions are fuzzy and the operational rules have numerous exceptions. We need to view the development of these fundamental cognitive processes from multiple perspectives. It is not enough to facilitate the understanding of a text, for example, by helping readers adopt the most appropriate schema for understanding it. Instead, we must encourage learners to approach the comprehension of a text and the learning of a new domain of knowledge by examining each from as many perspectives as possible. Spiro is wary of the process of schema selection, or activation. Consistent with his preference for multiple perspectives, Spiro prefers to talk about *assembling* schemas to fully comprehend a specific text, topic, or situation rather than *selecting* a particular schema to do the job.

Working simultaneously in a wide range of domains of knowledge, Spiro and his colleagues were able to demonstrate the constricting, oversimplifying, and conceptually misleading effects of singular perspectives, including simplifying analogies, when students try to understand or learn information in a complex, ill-structured domain of inquiry. In arguing for multiperspectival approaches to learning and comprehension, Spiro takes a "case-well-studied" approach. To that end, he uses the Wittgensteinian metaphor of criss-crossing a landscape from many directions in order to achieve an understanding and appreciation of it. For example, in examining the ways in which medical students acquire (or fail to acquire) knowledge about the heart and what causes heart attacks, Spiro and his colleagues have found that students develop misconceptions whenever they cling to a single concept, analogy, or model. In order to overcome misconceptions, students must confront multiple models and analogies, even though they may sometimes logically contradict one another. In learning about heart muscles, part of the truth is captured by the "crew analogy"—a bunch of rowers all pulling and relaxing in unison—while part of the truth is captured by the "turnbuckle" analogy—tension from within creates external stretching. And to counteract the unison and synchrony implied by the crew analogy, a Roman galley ship analogy—with more emphasis on the voluntary, and hence asynchronous (maybe even chaotic), actions of individual oars—must be provided. According to Spiro and his colleagues, it is only when a single, complex construct is informed by these multiple, sometimes contradictory, perspectives that adequate comprehension and learning can occur.

A third initiative, dubbed "situated cognition," with strong roots in the Vygotskian tradition of learning theory (see Gavelek & Bresnahan, 2009) emerged from the work of Brown, Collins, and Duguid (1989). They argued that our approaches to nurturing cognitive development are so abstract and divorced from the "authentic activity" that they are designed to nurture, that they cannot and do not promote adequate comprehension of either a particular text or the more general topic exemplified by a particular text. Even an inherently abstract domain such as mathematics has a specific context of application and "practice." In our zeal to develop context-free, transferable concepts and skills, we have inadvertently and inappropriately focused upon the teaching and learning of explicit but abstract rules and conceptual features. What we need, they argued, is a "situated" view of cognition and epistemology. If cognition, including comprehension and learning, is regarded as a situated phenomenon, then we will accept and take advantage of the fact that most events and concepts derive most of what we regard as meaning from the contexts in which we encounter them. Meaning is as much "indexical" (i.e., contextually bound) as it is conceptual. Notice that while the rationale for moving beyond schema theory is different from that proposed by Spiro and his colleagues, the final recommendation for "teaching" is quite similar: in order to help learners develop useful models of meaning for text or experience, teachers need to design work that situates students in the specific rather than the abstract. In the end, both of these positions argue, we are faced with the paradox that in order to learn what is abstract, general, and context free, we have to behave as though understanding phenomena as they exist within their natural context is all that mattered.

The Social Turn

Perhaps the most important development in this period was the increased prominence of a range of social perspectives on reading and learning more general; they came with a range of hyphenated names, such as socio-cultural, social-historical, and even socio-psycho-linguistic. These scholars (e.g., Harste, Burke, & Woodward, 1984) provided more socially oriented critiques, with constructs like the social construction of reality imported from sociology. They also provided new research methodologies that emphasized the social and cultural and even political contexts of teaching, learning, and understanding (see Pearson & Stephens, 1993), but that most interesting and controversial topic is beyond the scope of this analysis. Suffice it to say that the shift in methods used by doctoral students and presented at national conferences in this era revealed a marked trend toward understanding in its highly contextualize, situated, and particular aspect.

The rediscovery of the Russian psychologist Vygotsky (1978) alluded to earlier and the Russian literary theorist Bakhtin (1981) provided even more ammunition for socially based views of cognition, learning, and development. From Vygotsky (see Gavelek & Besnahan, 2009) reading researchers fixed their attention on the social nature of learning and the key role that teachers and peers play in facilitating individual learning. Vygotsky's "zone of proximal development," that range defined by the difference between the learning a child can accomplish on his or her own and what he or she can accomplish with the assistance of someone else (a teacher, a mentor, a parent, or a knowledgeable peer), may be the most popular learning construct of the 1980s. From Bakhtin's dialogical perspective, scholars forged a preview of coming attractions in what is destined to become a classic perspective of the future—an intertextual view of reading comprehension and the basic premise that we under-stand each new "text"—be it written, oral, or experiential—in relation to all the previous "texts" we have experienced (see Hartman, 1995). While some observers have questioned whether these more socially driven views of cognition represent a substantial departure from schema theory, they nonetheless shifted the attention of reading researchers from the individual and the text to the situational context surrounding the act of reading.

But one cannot understand the changes in pedagogy that occurred in the late 1980s and early 1990s without understanding the impact of literary theory, particularly reader response theory. From literary the-ory came the reincarnation of Rosenblatt's (1978) Deweyian-inspired transactional view of the relationship between reader and writer and Bleich's (1988) concept of the intersubjective negotiation of meaning; these constructs were eagerly and readily repositioned in pedagogical language and activity (e.g., Langer, 1990). In our secondary schools, the various traditions of literary criticism have always had a voice in the curriculum, especially in guiding discussions of classic literary works. Until the middle 1980s, the "new criticism" (Richards, 1929) that began its ascendancy in the Depression era dominated the interpretation of text for several decades. It had sent teachers and students on a search for the one "true" meaning in each text they encountered.[18] With the emergence (some would argue the reemergence) of reader response theo-ries, all of which gave as much authority to the reader as to either the text or the author, theoretical perspectives, along with classroom prac-tices, changed dramatically. The basals that had been so skill oriented in the 1970s and so comprehension oriented in the 1980s, became decid-edly literature based in the late 1980s and early 1990s. Comprehension gave way to readers' response to literature. Reader response emphasized affect and feeling that can either augment or replace cognitive responses to the content. To use the terminology of the most influential figure in the period, Louise Rosenblatt (1978), the field moved from efferent to aesthetic response to literature. And a "transactive model" replaced the "interactive model" of reading championed by the cognitive views of the 1980s. According to Rosenblatt, meaning is created in the transaction between reader and text. This meaning, which she refers to as the "poem," is a new entity that resides above the reader–text interaction. Meaning is therefore neither subject nor object nor the interaction of the two. Instead, it is transaction, something new and different from any of its inputs and influences.[19]

In the most fully articulated version of this perspective, Smagorinsky (2001) borrowed heavily from the reader response theory of Rosenblatt (1978) and the activity theories emanating from the Vygotskian tradition (e.g., Wertsch, 1993) to create what he called a cultural model of reading, in which he argued that the meaning in understanding resides not within the text or within the reader but within that transactional zone (borrowing from Rosenblatt) in which reader, text, and context meet and become something more than their sums or products. The fundamental argument in Smagorinsky's model is that readers quite literally compose new texts in response to texts they read; their recompositions are based upon the evocations (links to prior texts and experiences) that occur during the act of reading within a context that also shapes the type and manner of interpretations they make. These evocations hearken back to both Bakhtin's notion of intertextuality (for they are, even in a literal sense, connections to other texts), the cultural practices notions of writers such as Wertsch (1993) and Gee (1992), and the reading as writing models of the middle 1980s (e.g., Tierney & Pearson, 1983).

Developments in Comprehension Instruction

A New Generation of Strategy Instruction Research

Gathering momentum from landmark studies (e.g., Palincsar & Brown, 1984; Hansen, 1981; Paris et al., 1984) early in the 1980s, strategy instruction expanded rapidly over the next 15 years, so rapidly indeed that it was the frequent object of review throughout the 1990s and into the early part of the 21st century (e.g., Dole, Duffy, Roehler, & Pearson, 1991; Duke & Pearson, 2002; National Institute of Child Health and Human Development, 2000; Pearson & Fielding, 1991; Pressley, 2000; Pressley et al., 1994; Rosenshine & Meister, 1994; Rosenshine, Meister, & Chapman, 1996).[20] Two basic findings, also present in the earlier iteration of strategy instruction research, were these: (1) when students are taught to apply strategies to text, their comprehension of those texts improves; and (2) often their comprehension of new texts (transfer tasks), in which they are required to apply the strategies, also improves. A major question in strategy instruction research is whether strategies should be taught as singletons, one by one, until many are acquired (this is the logic of the approach taken by Ellin Keene in her very popular book, *Mosaic*

of Thought [Keene & Zimmerman, 1997]) or as a "suite" of strategies from which readers select the strategy most appropriate to a problem confronting them, which is the underlying logic of two of the most
popular and well-studied approaches to strategy instruction—reciprocal
teaching (RT; see Rosenshine & Meister, 1994, for an extensive review
of studies on RT) and transactional strategies instruction (TSI; Pressley
et al., 1994).[21] Of all the approaches to strategy instruction that emerged
in the 1980s and 1990s, none has had more direct impact than RT,
mainly because it has been appropriated and adapted by a number of
instructional researchers for a variety of pedagogical contexts (virtually all subject areas) and ages (from kindergarten through community
college) (see Rosenshine & Meister, 1994; Rosenshine et al., 1996). The
line of work on TSI is noteworthy for two reasons. First, it was created
as a collaboration between university researchers (i.e., Michael Pressley
and his colleagues at the University of Maryland) and a host of teachers
from Montgomery County, Maryland; hence it embodied the connection between theories of metacognition and comprehension processes
and the problems of practice and implementation. Second, it surrounded
the four strategies of RT with a few more cognitive strategies (text and
story structure analysis) and a host of interpretive strategies that were
closely allied with literary analysis—character development, figurative
language, point of view, personal connections, thematic analysis, intertextual connections, and a range of literary elements. The inclusion of
the interpretive strategies was a brilliant stroke because its literary patina
softened what might otherwise have been construed as a highly cognitive
and routinized approach, and directly appealed to teachers who were
adopting literature-based reading approaches in the late 1980s and early
1990s.

The Achilles heel for strategy instruction, both in this period and
even today, is finding a way to make it a part of "daily life" in classrooms.
It is one thing to implement strategy instruction for a certain number of
minutes each day for the 10 weeks of a pedagogical experiment, but it is
quite another to sustain a strategy emphasis over an entire school year
(see Hacker & Tenent, 2002). In short, it is easy to teach strategies in
short spurts, but it is hard to curricularize them. Should a teacher have
students use the four strategies of RT every day? For every text segment
they read? Or should they encourage students to "select" the optimal
strategy for a particular situation or problem? And if a teacher encourages such flexible use, how will he or she make sure students select useful
strategies (i.e., strategies that actually solve their problems). Even so, the
consistent pattern of findings favoring the explicit teaching of strategies
over a period of 15 years virtually guaranteed them a place in the curriculum of the early to mid-1990s.

Literature-Based Reading

Even though selections from both classical and contemporary children's literature have always been a staple of basal selections dating back to the 19th century (especially after grade 2, when the need for strict vocabulary control diminished), literature virtually exploded into the curriculum in the late 1980s and early 1990s. Beyond basals, children's literature has played an important supplementary role in the classrooms of teachers who believed that they must engage their students in a strong parallel independent reading program. Often this has taken the form of each child selecting books to be read individually and later discussed with the teacher in a weekly one-on-one conference. And even as far back as the 1960s, there were a few programs that turned this individualized reading component into the main reading program.[22]

But in the late 1980s and early 1990s, literature was dramatically repositioned. Several factors converged to pave the way for a groundswell in the role of literature in elementary reading. Surely the resurgence of reader response theory as presented by Rosenblatt was important, as was the compatibility of reader response theory and its emphasis on interpretation with the constructivism that characterized both cognitive and sociolinguistic perspectives. Research also played a role; in 1985, for example, in the watershed publication of the Center for the Study of Reading, *Becoming a Nation of Readers*, Richard Anderson and his colleagues (Anderson, Hiebert, Scott, & Wilkinson, 1985) documented the importance of "just plain reading" as a critical component of any and all elementary reading programs.[23] But perhaps most influential were the perspectives of practitioners who championed literature. And no one was more influential than Nancie Atwell, who, with the publication of her influential book *In the Middle* (1987), brought many teachers into the world of literature in their classrooms. In her account she laid out her story, as a middle school teacher, of how she invited readers, some of whom were quite reluctant, into a world of books and reading. The credibility of her experience and the power of her prose were persuasive in convincing thousands of classroom teachers that they could use existing literature and "reading workshops" to accomplish anything that a basal program could accomplish in skill development while gaining remarkable advantages in students' literary experience.

In terms of policy and curriculum, the most significant event in promoting literature-based reading was the 1987 California Reading Framework. The framework called for reading materials that contained much more challenging texts at all levels. More important, it mandated the use of genuine literature, not the dumbed-down adaptations and excerpts from children's literature that had been the staple of basal programs for decades. Publishers responded to the call of California's framework and produced a remarkably different product in the late 1980s and early 1990s than had ever appeared before on the basal market.[24] Gone were excerpts and adaptations, and with them almost any traces of vocabulary control. Skills that had been front and center in the basals of the 1970s and 1980s were relegated to appendix-like status. Comprehension questions were replaced by more interpretive, impressionistic response to literature activities. All this was done in the name of providing children with authentic literature and authentic activities to accompany it. The logic was that if we could provide students with real literature and real motivations for reading it, much of what is arduous about skill teaching and learning will take care of itself.

Book clubs and literature circles are the most visible instantiations of the literature-based reading movement.[25] The underlying logic of book clubs is the need to engage children in the reading of literature in the same way as adults engage one another in voluntary reading circles. Such voluntary structures are likely to elicit greater participation, motivation, appreciation, and understanding on the part of students. Teachers are encouraged to establish a set of "cultural practices" (ways of interacting and supporting one another) in their classrooms to support students as they make their way into the world of children's literature. These cultural practices offer students both the opportunity to engage in literature and the skills to ensure that they can negotiate and avail themselves of that opportunity.

Integrated Instruction

Integrated instruction has been a much-discussed but seldom-enacted part of the thinking about elementary reading curriculum.[26] There was much talk of it during the early progressive period, but until the late 1980s, integration of the language arts curriculum assumed a minor role in American reading instruction. In basal manuals, for example, integration was portrayed almost as an afterthought until the late 1980s; it appeared in the part of the lesson that follows the guided reading and skills instruction sections, signaling that these are things that a teacher can get to "if time permits." Things changed in the late 1980s and early 1990s. For one, integrated curriculum fit the sociolinguistic emphasis on language in use—the idea that language, including reading, is best taught and learned when it is put to work in the service of other purposes, activities, and learning efforts. Similarly, with the increase in importance of writing, especially early writing of the sort discussed by Graves and his colleagues,[27] it was tempting to champion the idea of integrated language arts instruction; after all, reading and writing were both acts of construction (remember the builder metaphor). In fact, the constructivist metaphor is nowhere played out as vividly and transparently as in writing, leading many scholars to use writing as a model for the sort of constructive approach they wanted to promote in readers. The notion was that we needed to help students learn to "read like a writer."[28]

Whole Language

One might plausibly argue that whole language brought together all of the constructivist and progressive trends of the postrevolution period—comprehension, literature-based reading, integrated instruction and even process writing—by incorporating them into its fundamental set of principles and practices. It is also fair to argue that whole language owed its essential character and key principles to the insights that came from all of the linguistic, psycholinguistic, cognitive, sociolinguistic, and literary-theoretic research that was played out from the late 1960s through the early 1990s. That said, the whole-language movement has always had a strained and strange relationship with reading comprehension, particularly comprehension instruction. With the strong emphasis on authenticity of the texts and tasks we ask students to engage in and the equally strong disdain for skills instruction (see Pearson, 2004, for an extended analysis), comprehension that emerges from rich, authentic encounters from text in a meaning-making community of readers is preferred to explicit instruction in skills, strategies, or vocabulary, which have an excessive didactic emphasis that is inconsistent with the strong child-centered philosophy underlying whole language. So, to the degree that comprehension was emphasized in whole language, it was largely through classroom, preferably small-group, conversations about texts that students read together—with an occasional mini-lesson on a particular meaning-making (e.g., making predictions) or repair (e.g., clarifying unknown words through contextual analysis) strategy offered when the situation called for it. For these very reasons, the pedagogical premises of literature-based instruction were a very comfortable fit for whole language.

   This then was the set of instructional options available to teachers in the early to middle 1990s—elaborate strategy instruction, rich conversations about literature, a yearning for more integrated instruction, and an umbrella pedagogy in which to embed it all. No matter how different the approaches were in implementation, there were several underlying commonalities—a commitment to reading as the construction of meaning in response to text; a dynamic view of the teacher involving roles as one who moves from modeling and explicit teaching, to scaffolding and coaching, to facilitating and participating as students develop greater competence, confidence, and independence; and a general commitment to student- rather than teacher-centered practices.

THE CURRENT CONTEXT

For a host of reasons that go beyond the scope of this chapter, much of the momentum toward reading as a meaning-making process dissipated in the last few years of the 20th century and the first few years of the 21st. Suffice it to say that several forces conspired to create a movement that took us back to the basics—a kind of "first things first" reform movement that created fuel for its mission by arguing that the lack of attention given to fundamental skills in the constructivist pedagogies of the previous 20 years was responsible for what has often, and unfairly, been characterized as the awful performance of students on important outcome measures.[29] And while there has been nothing in these reforms to suggest that comprehension instruction should be suspended, there is a subtle repositioning. In the reforms ushered in with the critique of constructivist practices, comprehension has become the natural consequence of teaching the code well in the early stages of instruction instead of the primary goal and focus of attention from the very beginning of a child's instructional life in school. This is a return to the simple view of reading that formed the basis of pedagogy prior to the paradigm shift of the 1970s: reading comprehension is the product of listening comprehension and decoding (see Hoffman, 2009).

But some recent signs point in a more positive direction. First, there is the important work of the Rand Study Group (Snow, 2003), outlining an agenda for future work on reading comprehension, including the much-neglected topic of assessment (see Pearson & Hamm, 2005; Leslie & Caldwell, 2009). Second, the Carnegie Report *Reading Next* (Biancarosa & Snow, 2006) focuses our attention on older struggling readers, students for whom comprehension, especially of content-area materials, is an alarming problem. Third, we have relatively recent movements that hold promise for moving comprehension into different domains, domains that both challenge and excite students. The first is the domain of new literacies, including those emanating from technological advances (Kamil & Chou, 2009; Tierney, 2009) and those that reside in spaces outside of schools (Alvermann & Xu, 2003; Moje et al., 2004; Hull & Schultz, 2002). The second is a renewed interest in the role of conversations about text (see Almasi & Garas-York, 2009); more important, we seem to have much more intellectual and methodological muscle available to examine the issues than in previous eras. The third is a rejuvenation of content-area reading (Conley, 2009), particularly for secondary students. The trends within the field that seem particularly promising include (1) research in which reading and writing are put to work in the service of acquiring knowledge and skill in the disciplines (Guthrie et al., 2004; Cervetti et al., 2006; Sutherland et al., 2006), and (2) research that attempts to understand the discursive and social practices of disciplinary learning in school settings (Moje et al., 2004).

So, there are signs of both concern and hope in the current professional and policy context. With any luck, as these new ideas and perspectives play themselves out in classrooms, schools, and community contexts, they will alter the context in ways that will create more space for teachers and students to focus on what really matters in reading—understanding, insight, and learning—the very things that are both the cause and consequence of comprehension.

NOTES

1. It is somewhat ironic that the sort of thinking exhibited in this piece did not become dominant view in the teens and 20s. Unquestionably, Thorndike was the preeminent educational psychologist of his time. Further, his work in the psychology of learning (the law of effect and the law of contiguity) became the basis of the behaviorism that dominated educational psychology and pedagogy during this period, and his work in assessment led was highly influential in developing the components of classical measurement theory (reliability and validity). Somehow this more cognitively oriented side of his work was less influential, at least in the period in which it was written.
2. See Smith (1986, pp. 259–262) for an account of the emergence of child-centered reading pedagogy. Foundational thinkers for this movement were Pestalozzi (1898), Froebel (1887), and Herbart (1901).
3. Ironically, it was the field's most ambitious effort in readability by Bormurh in 1966 that provided the closing parenthesis on this 40-year enterprise.
4. The very latest iterations of readability take the form of tools to place students in books by purring student test scores and text readability on the same scale. Lexiles (Stenner & Burdick, 1997; Stenner, Smith, Horabin, & Smith, 1987) are the most common tool in the current educational marketplace. But the readability architecture underlying Lexile scaling is measuring average sentence length and average word length.
5. Smith (1986) documents the growth in size and changes in emphases of these two mainstays in each of the chapters detailing 20th-century reading instruction.
6. Smith (1986) suggests that, by the 1940s, teacher editions had expanded to more than 500 pages per student book.
7. See Smith (1986, pp. 208–229) and Gates and Humber (1930).
8. See Smith (1986, pp. 231–239).

9. This absence would prove prophetic some 30 years later, when Dolores Durkin (1978) conducted her infamous "where is the comprehension instruction?" study.

10. The term *reembrace* is used intentionally to capture the fact that intellectual ancestors from the early part of the 20th century, scholars such as Edmund Burke Huey, talked of these constructs freely in the days before behaviorism took hold in the field. Even the early Thorndike of the 1917 piece on reading as reasoning was a very different psychologist from the one who developed the laws of effect and contiguity.

11. During this period, great homage was paid to intellectual ancestors such as Huey, who as early as 1908 recognized the cognitive complexity of reading. Voices such as Huey's, unfortunately, were not heard during the period from 1915 to 1965, when behaviorism dominated psychology and education.

12. Smagorinsky (2001) uses the phrase "inscribed" in the text as a way of indicating that the author of the text has some specific intentions when he or she set pen to paper, thereby avoiding the thorny question of whether meaning exists "out there" outside of the minds of readers. We use the term here to avoid the very same question.

13. The most coherent model is the model that provides the best account of the "facts" of the text uncovered at a given point in time by the reader in relation to the schemata instantiated at that same point in time. This is very much akin to Kintsch's construct of situation model, which Kintsch defines as the reader's current best fit between the facts of the text (coming from the text base) and relevant concepts from prior knowledge. Both Kintsch and the schema theorists viewed this best fit as a dynamic phenomenon that gets updated as new information emerges from the text and triggers (*instantiates* is the operative word in schema theory) the activation of relevant schemas from memory.

14. See Baker and Beall (2009) for an extended treatment of metacognition, both its history and current instantiation.

15. The original version of the model actually emerged from many conversations between Pearson and Joe Campione and Ann Brown at the Center for the Study of Reading in the early 1980s, and was heavily influenced by the scaffolding metaphor from Wood, Bruner, and Ross (1976), the dynamic assessment work of Feuerstein, Rand, and Hoffman (1979), and the emerging zone of proximal development construct of Vygotsky (1978).

16. See Pearson and Stephens (1993) for an account of the forces that led to these shifts; see also McVee, Dunsmore, and Gavalek (2005) for a more analytic treatment of the shortcomings of schema theory and the tensions between it and more socioculturally grounded conceptions of comprehension.

17. By the mid-1990s, the transformation was complete, and NRC had the *Journal of Literacy Research*. No reading. Ironically, the organization kept its name, creating an emblematic disconnect between the name of the organization and the name of the journal.

18. It is most interesting that the ultimate psychometrician Frederick Davis (e.g., 1944) was fond of referencing the new criticism of Richards (1929) in his essays and investigations about comprehension.

19. Rosenblatt credited the idea of transaction to John Dewey, who discussed it in many texts, including *Experience and Education* (1938).

20. See Dole, Nokes, and Drits (2009) for a thorough treatment of the entire line of strategy instruction research, including work extending into the 21st century.

21. Even though it was conducted well after the end date (roughly 2002) for the original version of this chapter, it is worth noting that Reutzel, Smith, and Fawson (2005) found that the menu of TSI's suite was more effective in promoting understanding of science texts with young readers.

22. It is undoubtedly Jeanette Veatch (1959) who served as the most vocal spokesperson for individualized reading. She published professional textbooks describing how to implement the program in one's class in the middle 1960s.

23. Anderson and his colleagues (1985) reported several studies documenting the impact of book reading on children's achievement gains.

24. Hoffman and his colleagues (1994) painstakingly documented these sorts of changes in the early 1990s basals.

25. For a complete account of the book club movement, see McMahon and Raphael (1997).

26. Perhaps the most complete current reference on integrated curriculum is a chapter by Gavelek, Rafael, Biondo, and Wang in the 2000 *Handbook of Reading Research*. It is also interesting to note that in Chapter 10 of Huey's 1908 book on reading, two such programs, one at Columbia and one at the University of Chicago, were described in rich detail. It is Dewey's insistence that pedagogy be grounded in the individual and collective experiences of learners that is typically cited when scholars invoke his name to support integrated curriculum.

27. See Graves (1983) for an explication of his views on writing.

28. Tierney and Pearson (1983) carried this metaphor to the extreme, using the reading "like a writer" metaphor to emphasize the constructivist nature of reading.

29. Accusations of this sort are curious at best in light of 30 years of remarkably level performance on the National Assessment of Educational Progress (NAEP). A better argument for a crisis would be our inability to close the remarkably persistent achievement gap between rich and poor or majority and minority students. Some would argue (e.g., Pearson, 2004) that the use of achievement levels in NAEP (basic, proficient, and advanced) with rigid cut scores is the perfect policy tool for fomenting a crisis because it allows policymakers to make arguments of the ilk "Forty percent of America's fourth graders read below basic!" Such accusations fail to admit the obvious—that given the current standards and cut scores, 40% of America's fourth graders have read below basic for the last 30 years. In short, there is little compelling evidence to fix the blame for the achievement of America's students on any particular curricular movement or practice.

REFERENCES

Afflerbach, P., Pearson, P. D., & Paris, S. (2008). Clarifying differences between reading skill and reading strategies. *The Reading Teacher, 61,* 364–373.

Almasi, J. F., & Garas-York, K. (2009). Comprehension and discussion of text. In S. E. Israel & G. G. Duffy (Eds.), *Handbook of research on reading comprehension.* London: Routledge.

Alvermann, D. E., & Xu, S. H. (2003). Children's everyday literacies: Intersections of popular culture and language arts instruction across the curriculum. *Language Art, 81,* 145–154.

Anderson, R. C. (1977). The notion of schemata and the educational enterprise: General discussion of the conference. In R. Anderson, R. Spiro, & M. Montague (Eds.), *Schooling and the acquisitioning of knowledge.* Hillsdale, NJ: Erlbaum.

Anderson, R. C. (1984). Role of readers' schema in comprehension, learning and memory. In R. Anderson, J. Osbourne, & R. Tierney (Eds.), *Learning to read in American schools: Basal readers and content text.* Hillsdale, NJ: Erlbaum.

Anderson, R. C., Hiebert, E., Scott, J., & Wilkinson, I. (1985). *Becoming a nation of readers.* Champaign, IL: Center for the Study of Reading.

Anderson, R. C., & Pearson, P. D. (1984). A schema-theoretic view of basic processes in reading comprehension. In P. D. Pearson, R. Barr, M. L. Kamil, & P. Mosenthal (Eds.), *Handbook of reading research.* New York: Longman.

Anderson, T. H., Armbruster, B. B., & Kantor, R. N. (1980). *How clearly written are children's textbooks? Or,of bladderworts and alfa* (Reading Education Rep. No. 16). Urbana: University of Illinois, Center for the Study of Reading.

Armbruster, B. B., & Anderson, T. H. (1981). *Content area textbooks* (Reading Education Rep. No. 23). Urbana: University of Illinois, Center for the Study of Reading.

Armbruster, B. B., & Anderson, T. H. (1982). *Structures for explanations in history textbooks, or so what if Governor Stanford missed the spike and hit the rail?* (Tech. Rep. No. 252). Urbana: University of Illinois, Center for the Study of Reading.

Armbruster, B. B., & Anderson, T. H. (1984). *Producing considerate expository text: Or, easy reading is damned hard writing* (Reading Education Rep. No. 46). Urbana: University of Illinois, Center for the Study of Reading.

Atwell, N. (1987). *In the middle: Writing, reading, and learning with adolescents.* Portsmouth, NH: Heinemann.

Baker, L., & Beall, L. C. (2009). Megacognitive processes and reading comprehension. In S. E. Israel & G. G. Duffy (Eds.)., *Handbook of research on reading comprehension.* London: Routledge.

Bakhtin, M. M. (1981). *The dialogic imagination.* Austin, TX: University of Austin Press.

Beck, I. L., McKeown, M. G., McCaslin, E. S., & Burkes, A. M. (1979). *Instructional dimensions that may affect reading comprehension: Examples from two commercial reading programs.* Pittsburgh: University of Pittsburgh, Learning Research and Development Center.

Biancarosa, C, & Snow, C. E. (2006). *Reading next—A vision for action and research in middle and high school literacy: A report to Carnegie Corporation of New York* (2nd ed.), Washington, DC: Alliance for Excellent Education.

Bleich, D. (1988). *The double perspective: Language, literacy, and social relations.* New York: Oxford University Press.

Bloom, B. S. (1956). Taxonomy of educational objectives. *Handbook 1: Cognitive domain.* New York: McKay.

Bormuth, J. R. (1966). Reading: A new approach. *Reading Research Quarterly, 1,* 79–132.

Bormuth, J. R., Manning, J. C., Carr, J. W., & Pearson, P. D. (1971). Children's comprehension of between- and within-sentence syntactic structures. *Journal of Educational Psychology, 61* 349–357.

Brown, J., Collins, A., & Duguid, P. (1989). Situated cognition of learning. *Educational Researcher, 18,* 32–42.

Bruce, C. (1984). A new point of view on children's stories. In R. Anderson, J. Osbourne, & R. Tierney (Eds.), *Learning to read in American schools: Basal readers and content readers* (pp. 153–174). Hillsdale, NJ: Erlbaum.

California Department of Education (1987). *English-language arts framework for California public schools, K–12.* Sacramento: California Department of Education.

Cervetti, G., Pearson, P. D., Barber, J., Hiebert, E., & Bravo, M. (2006). Integrating literacy and science: The research we have, the research we need. In M. Pressley, A. K. Billman, K. Perry, K. Refitt, & J. Reynolds (Eds.), *Shaping literacy achievement* (pp. 157–174). New York: Guilford Press.

Chomsky, N. (1957). *Syntactic structures.* The Hague: Mouton.

Chomsky, N. (1959). A review of B. F. Skinner's *Verbal Behavior. Language, 35*(1), 26–58.

Collins, A., Brown, J. S., & Larkin, K. M. (1980). Inference in text understanding. In R. J. Spiro, B. C. Bruce, & W. F. Brewer (Eds.), *Theoretical issues in reading comprehension.* Hillsdale, NJ: Erlbaum.

Clymer, T. (1968). What is "reading"? Some current concepts. In H. Richie & H. Robinson (Eds.), *Innovation and change in reading instruction* (pp. 7–29). Chicago: National Society for the Study of Education.

Conley, M. W. (2009). Improving adolescent comprehension: Developing learning strategies in content areas. In S. E. Israel & G. G. Duffy (Eds.), *Handbook of research on reading comprehension.* London: Routledge.

Davis, F. B. (1944). Fundamental factors of comprehension of reading. *Psychometrika, 9,* 185–197.

Davison, A., & Kantor, R. N. (1982). On the failure of readability formulas to define readable texts: A case study from adaptations. *Reading Research Quarterly, 18,* 187–209.

Dewey, J. (1938). *Experience and education.* New York: Simon & Schuster.

Dole, J. A., Duffy, G. G., Roehler, L. R., & Pearson, P. D. (1991). Moving from the old to the new: Research on reading comprehension instruction. *Review of Educational Research, 61,* 239–264.

Dole, J. A., Nokes, J., & Drits, D. (2009). Cognitive strategy instruction: Past and future. In S. E. Israel & G. G. Duffy (Eds.), *Handbook of research on reading comprehension.* London: Routledge.

Duke, N., & Pearson, P. D. (2002). Effective practices for developing reading comprehension. In A. Farstrup & J. Samuels (Eds.), *What research has to say about reading instruction* (3rd ed., pp. 205–242). Newark, DE: International Reading Association.

Durkin, D. (1978–1979). What classroom observations reveal about reading comprehension instruction. *Reading Research Quarterly, 14,* 481–533.

Durkin, D. (1981). Reading comprehension instruction in five basal reader series. *Reading Research Quarterly, 16*(4) 515–544.

Durrell, D. D. (1949). The development of comprehension and interpretation. In N. B. Henry & A. I. Gates (Eds.), *Reading in the elementary school* (pp. 193–204). Chicago: National Society for Studies in Education.

Elson, W. H., & Gray, W. S. (1936). *Elson–Gray basic readers: Curriculum foundation series.* Chicago: Scott, Foresman.

Elson, W. H., & Keck, C. M. (1911). *The Elson readers, Book 5* Chicago: Scott, Foresman.

Fagan, W. T (1971). Transformations and comprehension. *The Reading Teacher,* 169–172.

Feuerstein, R., Rand, Y, & Hoffman, M. (1979). *Dynamic assessment of the retarded performer.* Baltimore: University Park Press.

Froebel, F. (1826). *The education of man.* New York: Appleton.

Gates, A. I., & Ayer, J. Y (1933). *Golden leaves.* New York: Macmillan.

Gates, A. I., & Huber, M. H. (1930). *The work–play books.* New York: Macmillan.

Gavelek, J., & Bresnahan, P. (2009). Ways of meaning making: Sociocultural perspectives on reading comprehension. In S. E. Israel & G. G. Duffy (Eds.), *Handbook of research on reading comprehension.* London: Routledge.

Gavelek, J., Rafael, T., Biondo, S., & Wang, D. (2000). Integrated literacy instruction. In P. D. Pearson, M. L. Kamil, R. Barr, & P. B. Mosenthal (Eds.), *Handbook of reading research* (Vol. 3). Mahwah, NJ: Erlbaum.

Gee, J. (1992). *The social mind.* Westport, CT: Bergin & Garvey.

Goodman, K. G. (1965). A linguistic study of cues and miscues in reading. *Elementary English, 42,* 639–643.

Graves, D. (1983). *Writing: Teachers and children at work.* Portsmouth, NH: Heinemann.

Gray, W. S. (1925) Essential objectives of instruction in reading. In G. M. Whipple (Ed.), *Twenty fourth yearbook of the National Society for Studies in Education: Report of the National Committee on Reading* (Vol. 24 (1), pp. 9–19). Chicago: National Society for Studies in Education.

Gray, W. S., Arbuthnot, M. H., et al. (1940–1948). *Basic readers: Curriculum foundation series.* Chicago: Scott, Foresman.

Gray, W. S., Arbuthnot, M. H., Artley, S. A., Monroe, M., et al. (1951–1957).

New basic readers: Curriculum foundation series. Chicago: Scott, Foresman.

Guthrie, J. T., Wigfield, A., Barbosa, P., Perencevich, K. C., Taboada, A., Davis, M. H., et al., (2004). Increasing reading comprehension and engagement through concept–oriented reading instruction. *Journal of Educational Psychology, 96,* 403–423.

Hacker, D. J., & Tenent, A. (2002). Implementing reciprocal teaching in the classroom: Overcoming obstacles and making modifications. *Journal of Educational Psychology, 94*(4), 699–718.

Hansen, J. (1981). The effects of inference training and practice on young children's reading comprehension. *Reading Research Quarterly, 17,* 391–417.

Hansen, J., & Pearson, P. D. (1983). An instructional study: Improving the inferential comprehension of fourth grade good and poor readers. *Journal of Educational Psychology, 71,* 821–829.

Harste, J., Burke, C., & Woodward, V. (1984). *Language stories and literacy lessons.* Portsmouth, NH: Heinemann.

Hartman, D. K. (1995). Eight readers reading: The intertextual links of proficient readers reading multiple passages. *Reading Research Quarterly, 30*(3), 520–561.

Herbart, J. F. (1901). *Outlines of educational doctrine.* New York: Macmillan.

Hoffman, J. (2009). In search of a "simple view" of reading comprehension. In S. E. Israel & G. G. Duffy (Eds.), *Handbook of research on reading comprehension.* London: Routledge.

Hoffman, J. V., McCarthey, S. J., Abbott, J., Christian, C., Corman, L., Dressman, M., et al. (1994). So what's new in the "new" basals. *Journal of Reading Behavior, 26,* 47–73.

Huey, E. B. (1908). *The psychology and pedagogy of reading.* New York: Macmillan.

Hull, G., & Schultz, K. (Eds.). (2002). *School's out! Bridging out-of-school literacies with classroom practice.* New York: Teachers College Press.

Israel, S. E., & Duffy, G. G. (Eds.). (2009). *Handbook of research on reading comprehension.* London: Routledge.

Johnston, P. H. (1984) Assessment in reading. In P. D. Pearson, R. Barr, M. Kamil, & P. Mosenthal (Eds.), *Handbook of reading research* (pp. 147–182). New York: Longman.

Johnston, P., & Pearson, P. D. (1982, June). *Prior knowledge, connectivity, and the assessment of reading comprehension* (Tech. Rep. No. 245). Urbana: University of Illinois, Center for the Study of Reading.

Kamil, M. L., & Chou, H. K. (2009). Comprehension and technology. In S. E. Israel & G. G. Duffy (Eds.), *Handbook of research on reading comprehension.* London: Routledge.

Keene, E., & Zimmerman, S. (1997). *Mosaic of thought: Teaching comprehension in a readers' workshop.* Portsmouth, NH: Heinemann.

Kintsch, W. (1974). *The representation of meaning in memory.* Hillsdale, NJ: Erlbaum.

Kintsch, W. (1998). *Comprehension: A paradigm for cognition.* New York: Cambridge University Press.

Langer, J. A. (1990) The process of understanding: Reading for literary and informative purposes. *Research in the Teaching of English, 24*(3), 229–260.

Leslie, L., & Caldwell, J. (2009). Formal and informal measures of reading comprehension. In S. E. Israel & G. G. Duffy (Eds.), *Handbook of research on reading comprehension.* London: Routledge.

Lively, B. A., & Pressey, S. L. (1923). A method for measuring the vocabulary burden of text books. *Educational Administration and Supervision, 9,* 389–398.

Matthews, M. (1966). *Teaching to read.* Chicago: University of Chicago Press.

McKee, P. (1949). Reading programs in grades IV through VIII. In N. B. Henry & A. I. Gates (Eds.), *Reading in the elementary school* (pp. 127–146). Chicago: National Society for Studies in Education.

McMahon, S. I., Raphael, T. E., with Goatley, V., & Pardo, L. (1997). *The book club connection.* New York: Teachers College Press.

McNamara, T. P., Miller, D. L., & Bransford, J. D. (1991). Mental models and reading comprehension. In R. Barr, M. Kamil, P. Mosenthal, & P. D. Pearson (Eds.), *Handbook of reading research* (Vol. 2, pp. 490–511). New York: Longman.

McVee, M. B., Dunsmore, K., & Gavelek, J. R. (2005). Schema theory revisited. *Review of Educational Research, 75*(4), 531–566.

Meyer, B. J. F. (1975). *The organization of prose and its effects on memory.* Amsterdam: North Holland.

Moje, E. B., Peek-Brown, D., Sutherland, L. M., Marx, R. W., Blumenfeld, P., & Krajcik, J. (2004). Explaining explanations: Developing scientific literacy in middle-school project-based science reforms. In D. Strickland & D. E. Alvermann (Eds.), *Bridging the gap: Improving literacy learning for preadolescent and adolescent learners in grades 4–12* (pp. 227–251). New York: Teachers College Press.

National Institute of Child Health and Human Development. (2000). *Report of the National Reading Panel. Teaching children to read: An evidence-based assessment of the scientific research literature on reading and its implications for reading instruction: Reports of the subgroups* (NIH Publication No. 00-4754). Washington, DC: U.S. Government Printing Office.

Nystrand, M., Gamoran, A. Kachur, R., & Prendergast, C. (1997). *Opening dialogue: Understanding the dynamics of language and learning in the English classroom.* New York: Teachers College Press.

Nystrand, M., Wu, L., Gamoran, A., Zeiser, S., & Long, D. (2003). Questions in time: Investigating the structure and dynamics of unfolding classroom discourse. *Discourse Processes, 35,* 135–196.

Palincsar, A. M., & Brown, A. L. (1984). Reciprocal teaching of comprehension-fostering and comprehension-monitoring activities. *Cognition and Instruction, 1*(2), 117–175.

Paris, S. G., Cross, D. R., & Lipson, M. Y. (1984). Informed strategies for learning: A program to improve children's reading awareness and comprehension. *Journal of Educational Psychology, 76*(6), 1239–1252.

Paris, S. G., Lipson, M. Y., & Wixson, K. (1983). Becoming a strategic reader. *Contemporary Educational Psychology, 8,* 293–316.

Paris, S. G., & Hamilton, E. E. (2009). The development of children's reading comprehension. In S. E. Israel & G. G. Duffy (Eds.), *Handbook of research on reading comprehension.* London: Routledge.

Pearson, P. D. (1974–1975). The effects of grammatical complexity on children's comprehension, recall, and conception of certain semantic relations. *Reading Research Quarterly, 10,* 155–192.

Pearson, P. D. (2000). Reading in the 20th century. In T. Good (Ed.), *American education: Yesterday, today, and tomorrow. Yearbook of the National Society for the Study of Education* (pp. 152–208). Chicago: University of Chicago Press.

Pearson, P. D. (2004). The reading wars: The politics of reading research and policy: 1988 through 2003. *Educational Policy, 18*(1), 215–252.

Pearson, P. D. (2007). An endangered species act for literacy education. *Journal of Literacy Research, 39,* 145–162.

Pearson, P. D., & Camparell, K. (1981). Comprehension of text structures. In J. Guthrie (Ed.), *Comprehension and teaching* (pp. 27–54). Newark, DE: International Reading Association.

Pearson, P. D., & Fielding, R. (1991). Comprehension instruction. In R. Barr, M. Kamil, P. Mosenthal, & P. D. Pearson (Eds.), *Handbook of reading research* (Vol. 2). New York: Longman.

Pearson, P. D., & Gallagher, M. C. (1983). The instruction of reading comprehension. *Contemporary Educational Psychology, 8,* 317–344.

Pearson, P. D., & Hamm, D. N. (2005). The assessment of reading comprehension: A review of practices: Past, present, and future. In S. G. Paris & S. A. Stahl (Eds.), *Children's reading comprehension and assessment* (pp. 13–69). Mahwah, NJ: Erlbaum.

Pearson, P. D., & Johnson, D. D. (1978). *Teaching reading comprehension.* New York: Holt, Rinehart & Winston.

Pearson, P. D., & Stephens, D. (1993). Learning about literacy: A 30-year journey. In C. J. Gordon, G. D. Labercane, & W. R. McEachern (Eds.), *Elementary reading: Process and practice* (pp. 4–18). Boston: Ginn Press.

Pestalozzi, J. (1898). *How Gertrude teaches her children.* Syracuse, NY: Barden.

Pressley, M. (2000). What should comprehension instruction be the instruction of? In M. Kamil, P. Mosenthal, P. D. Pearson, & R. Barr (Eds.), *Handbook of reading research* (Vol. 3). Hillsdale, NJ: Erlbaum.

Pressley, M., Almasi, J., Schuder, T., Bergman, J., Hite, S., El-Dinary, P. B., et al. (1994). Transactional instruction of comprehension strategies: The Montgomery County, Maryland, SAIL Program. *Reading and Writing Quarterly: Overcoming Learning Difficulties, 10,* 5–19.

Resnick, D. P. (1982). History of educational testing. In A. K. Wigdor & W. R. Garner (Eds.), *Ability testing: Uses, consequences, and controversies* (Part 2). Washington, DC: National Academy Press.

Reutzel, R. D., Smith, J. A., & Fawson, P. C. (2005). An evaluation of two approaches for teaching reading comprehension strategies in the primary years using science information texts. *Early Childhood Research Quarterly, 20*(3), 276–305.

Richards, I. A. (1929). *Practical criticism.* New York: Harcourt, Brace.

Rosenblatt, L. M. (1978). *The reader, the text, the poem: The transactional theory of the literary work.* Carbondale: Southern Illinois University Press.

Rosenshine, B., & Meister, C. (1994). Reciprocal teaching: A review of research. *Review of Educational Research, 64,* 479–530.

Rosenshine, B., Meister, C., & Chapman, S. (1996). Teaching students to generate questions: A review of the intervention studies. *Review of Educational Research, 66,* 181–221.

Rurnelhart, D. E. (1977). Understanding and summarizing brief stories. In D. LaBerge & J. Samuels (Eds.), *Basic processes in reading perception and comprehension.* Hillsdale, NJ: Erlbaum.

Rumelhart, D. E. (1981). Schemata: The building blocks of cognition. In J. T Guthrie (Ed.), *Comprehension in teaching* (pp. 3–26). Newark, DE: International Reading Association.

Smagorinsky, P. (2001). If meaning is constructed, what is it made from: Toward a cultural theory of reading. *Review of Educational Research, 71*(2), 133–169.

Smith, F. (1971). *Understanding reading: A psycholinguistic analysis of reading and learning to read.* New York: Holt, Rinehart & Winston.

Smith, F., & Miller, G. A. (Eds.) (1966). *The genesis of language: A psychology approach.* Cambridge, MA: MIT Press.

Smith, N. B. (1986). *American reading instruction.* Newark, DE: International Reading Association. (Original published 1966)

Snow, C. (2003). *Reading for understanding: Toward an R&D program in reading comprehension.* Santa Monica, CA: Rand.

Spiro, R. J., Vispoel, W., Schmitz, W., Samarapungavan, A., & Boerger, A. (1987). Knowledge acquisition for application: Cognitive flexibility and transfer in complex content domains. In B. C. Britton & S. Glynn (Eds.), *Executive control processes.* Hillsdale, NJ: Erlbaum.

Stein, N., & Glenn, C. G. (1977). An analysis of story comprehension in elementary school children. In R. Freedle (Ed.), *Discourse production and comprehension* (Vol. 1). Norwood, NJ: Ablex.

Stenner, A. J., & Burdick, H. (1997). *The objective measurement of reading comprehension.* Durham, NC: MetaMetrics, Inc.

Stenner, A. J., Smith, D. R., Horabin, I., & Smith, M. (1987). *Fit of the lexile theory to item difficulties on fourteen standardized reading comprehension tests.* Durham, NC: MetaMetrics, Inc.

Sutherland, L. M., Meriweather, A., Rucker, S., Sarratt, P., Hines-Hale, Y., Krajcik, J., & Moje, E. B. (2006). "More emphasis" on scientific explanation: Developing conceptual understanding while developing scientific literacy. In R. E. Yager (Ed.), *Exemplary science in grades 5–8: Standards-based success stories* (pp. 99–113). Washington, DC: National Science Teachers Press.

Thorndike, E. L. (1914). The measurement of ability in reading: Preliminary scales and tests: Introduction. *Teachers College Record, 15*(4), 1–2.

Thorndike, E. L. (1917). Reading as reasoning: A study of mistakes in paragraph reading. *Journal of Educational Psychology, 8,* 323–332.

Tierney, R. J. (2009). The agency and artistry of meaning making within and across digital spaces. In S. E. Israel & G. G. Duffy (Eds.), *Handbook of research on reading comprehension.* London: Routledge.

Tierney, R. J., & Cunningham, J. (1991). Research on teaching reading and comprehension. In R. Barr, M. Kamil, P. Mosenthal, & P. D. Pearson (Eds.), *Handbook of reading research* (Vol. 2, pp. 609–655). Mahwah, NJ: Erlbaum.

Tierney, R. J., & Pearson, P. D. (1983). Toward a composing model of reading. *Language Arts, 60,* 568–580.

Veatch, J. (1959). *Individualizing your reading program.* New York: Putnam's.

Vygotsky, L. S. (1978). *Mind in society.* Cambridge, MA: Harvard University Press.

Werrsch, J. (1993). *Voices of the mind: A sociocultural approach to mediated action.* Cambridge, MA: Harvard University Press.

Wittrock, M. (1992). Generative process of the brain. *Educational Psychologist, 27,* 531–541.

Wood, D., Bruner, J. S., & Ross, G. (1976). The role of tutoring in problem solving. *Journal of Psychology and Psychiatry, 17,* 89–100.

Index

"*f*" following a page number indicates a figure; "*t*" following a page number indicates a table.